psychological

 ASSESSMENT
OF HANDICAPPED INFANTS
AND YOUNG CHILDREN

GORDON ULREY, PH.D.
Director of Psychology
JFK Child Development Center
University of Colorado Health Sciences Center
Denver, Colorado

SALLY J. ROGERS, PH.D.
Psychologist
JFK Child Development Center
University of Colorado Health Sciences Center
Denver, Colorado

With Special Contributions

1982
Thieme-Stratton Inc.
New York

Georg Thieme Verlag
Stuttgart • New York

Publisher: Thieme-Stratton Inc.
381 Park Avenue South
New York, New York 10016

Ulrey and Rogers
Psychological Assessment of Handicapped Infants and Young Children

TSI ISBN 0-86577-046-8
GTV ISBN 3-13-628101-2

This work was developed under a grant with the Office of Special Education, Department of Education (#G007804222). The content, however, does not necessarily reflect the position or policy of OSE/ED and no official endorsement of these materials should be inferred.

Last digit is print number   4   3   2   1

To three very special young children:
Heather, Sara, and Amy

PREFACE

In recent years, nationwide recognition of the benefits of early intervention with young handicapped children has resulted in a well documented need for psychological assessment of these special children. Although federal and state mandates for free and appropriate education for all children have increased the demand for psychological services, there have unfortunately been few guidelines for how the professional should assess and treat children who are very young. Indeed, clinicians have found that many of the tests and assumptions that have been successfully applied to the psychological evaluation of school-age children are not applicable to those who are younger than six years.

The purpose of this book is to present the information that psychologists need to evaluate young, developmentally disabled children more accurately. The book describes important issues about assessment, factors that influence test performance, and special techniques for evaluating children with a variety of handicapping conditions. A conceptual framework is provided for: planning assessments; determining the tests and observation procedures that should be used; selecting techniques for assessing children with special handicaps (blindness or deafness); interpreting results; planning relevant interventions; and communicating findings to parents and teachers. Relevant research is reviewed to support assessment issues, and numerous specific techniques and protocols are presented to adapt and expand existing test procedures.

The chapters are organized into three sections. The first addresses general behavioral and developmental considerations needed to plan and conduct an evaluation. The focus is on normal child development and conceptual frameworks that are useful for organizing observations and interpreting test results. (For example, a Piagetian framework is used to describe cognitive development because it is useful both in interpreting test results and in planning interventions. The model allows an in-depth understanding of intellectual functioning without focusing on deficits such as mental retardation.)

The second section of the book describes specific handicaps and implications for adapting evaluation procedures for use with specific handicaps. Research findings relevant to the development and treatment of children with specific handicaps is also reviewed.

The third section emphasizes the relationship between handicapping conditions and the effect of the environment. Development of children with disabilities is seen as a series of complex interactions. The book does not contain a chapter focusing on mental retardation as a specific handicap, because mental retardation is seen as a form of developmental delay that must be understood in terms of the child's functioning in all areas of development.

This book was derived from a comprehensive training program for psychologists, developed through a Bureau for the Education of Handicapped grant (#G007804222), that consists of 20 videotaped lessons and related written materials designed to teach graduate students and practitioners who evaluate and treat handicapped young children. The program has been presented to and evaluated by more than 600 psychologists and educators in 16 different states as well as several European countries. The materials were developed primarily by the authors in conjunction with numerous national experts (see acknowledgments).

Development of the 20 half-hour videotapes and written lessons took more than two years, during this time the editors struggled with the problems inherent in assessing young children. As the vidotapes were developed, it became more and more clear that a clinical textbook describing the specialized techniques used to assess young handicapped children was needed. As a result, this book was developed.

Two major cautions appear necessary to those who would use this textbook to assess handicapped infants and young children. First, the evaluator must be an expert in early child development and behavior before existing standardized test procedures can be correctly administered and interpreted. Second, the clinician must make systematic observations of the child's behavior beyond simply observing the response to a test situation.

This book reflects the viewpoints of a number of different authors. The different opinions and areas of emphasis that result from their unique viewpoints reflect a reality in the world of psychology today—our knowledge of child development and educational psychology is new and constantly evolving.

Gordon Ulrey, Ph.D.
Sally Rogers, Ph.D.

FOREWORD

One of the main challenges facing professionals working with handicapped infants and preschool children today is the development of techniques and procedures that will insure that a handicapping condition does not become a disability. This aspect of secondary prevention, with which most of us working with young children are constantly faced, is very much dependent on appropriate early infant intervention programs. Here one of the major difficulties is the determination of which areas of growth and development should be approached first; that is, how to establish a priority system for working with the individual infant.

When dealing with children who demonstrate patterns of atypical growth and development, it is next to impossible to develop programs around the information produced from typical assessment procedures using currently available standardized instruments. All that such procedures are able to provide is information concerning the previous rate of learning with infants who have had a very limited experience with anything because of their age and who, because of their pattern of atypical growth and development, have not gained from those experiences the same types of information that normal youngsters would gain in the same period of time. Yet despite this difficulty, various levels of assessment information are absolutely necessary if we are to develop appropriate individual educational programs for these handicapped youngsters.

To be meaningful to an individual child, assessment information must be as nondiscriminatory as possible. It must be multifactorial, touching as many of the various aspects of intellectual and mental growth as possible. When dealing with young infants, it must certainly include information on sensory-motor development; cognitive development, including development of a receptive system, perceptive system, and apperceptive system; some information on the rate of learning (which is typically measured by IQ tests); information on the development of coping and adaptive strategies; and information

on social awareness. Such wide ranging assessment demands relate to the development of appropriate types of program organization, and they mitigate against the current over-emphasis on the use of the typical standardized instruments. Appropriate assessment must be based on observations and tests, which include the previous history of the child, field observations of the child's behaviors in a wide variety of open situations, observations and measurement of behaviors consistent for the age and cultural group of the child, and comparison of those data with normal developmental expectations.

Psychological Assessment of Handicapped Infants and Young Children provides much needed information concerning the latter two aspects of this assessment problem. This book describes a wide variety of processes and techniques related to the assessment of atypical children with a variety of diagnoses in the context of sensory-motor development, cognitive development (including the apperceptive aspects of emotional development), and the usual expectations centering around the rate of learning.

The book opens with general considerations relating to normal or typically developing children and gives the practitioner much needed information concerning what would be considered "baseline" essentials in looking at infant and preschool mental development. It then relates that information to the assessment of handicapped infants and preschool children, recognizing that there is an entirely different type of assessment requirement present in that situation. Because we are dealing with very young children, the book also enters into discussion of the handicapped child's milieu. This is a major addition for a book of this type, which often assumes that if the at-risk child or handicapped child can adapt in the school or training situation, then all requirements have been met, completely overlooking the fact that even normal children behave differently in different settings and that handicapped children have a greater problem with that type of adaptation. This discussion of the home situation as it relates to the emotional development of the child, the discussion of culturally different environments, and the overall discussion of the role and function of the family are obviously very highly related to all aspects of assessment information and, of course, provide the very necessary information relating to our first need, which is an appropriate history of the problem.

Psychological Assessment fills an important gap in the current literature. It provides the trained practitioner with information concerning the approach to handicapped infants and young children and helps all of us develop these very important aspects of prevention related, as we say, to making sure that the handicapping condition can be brought under the control of the infant and that it does not have to be a permanent impediment to appropriate community adjustment.

Henry Leland, Ph.D.
Ohio State University
Nisonger Center
1982

CONTRIBUTORS

The videotapes were developed by several national experts and consultants. All of the videotapes were field tested and evaluated by the developers. The project was developed and produced by Gordon Ulrey and Sally Rogers with the support and critiques of many consultants. The following is a list of the contributors to the production of the videotapes lessons:

Lani Bennett, Ph.D.
Psychologist
Denver University
Denver, Colorado

John Brown, Ph.D.
Psychologist
East Side Health
Denver, Colorado

Robin Hansen, M.D.
Acting Chief of Pediatrics
JFK Child Development Center
University of Colorado Health
    Sciences Center
Denver, Colorado

Karen Hosking, Ph.D.
Psychologist - D.E.C.
Children's Hospital Medical Center
Boston, Massachusetts.

Jan Young, M.D.
Pediatrician - Private Practice
Glenwood Springs, Colorado

Harold Martin, M.D.
Associate Director
JFK Child Development Center
University of Colorado Health
    Sciences Center
Denver, Colorado

Sally J. Rogers, Ph.D.
Psychologist
JFK Child Development Center
University of Colorado Health
    Sciences Center
Denver, Colorado

Richard Schnell, Ph.D.
Director of Psychology - D.E.C
Children's Hospital Medical Center
Boston, Massachusetts

Elizabeth Soper, M.A.
Audiologist - I.S.M.R.
University of Michigan
Ann Arbor, Michigan

Gordon Ulrey, Ph.D.
Director of Psychology
JFK Child Development Center
University of Colorado Health
    Sciences Center
Denver, Colorado

Jill Waterman, Ph.D.
Adjunct Associate Professor of Clinical
    Psychology
Department of Psychology
University of California
Los Angeles, California

ACKNOWLEDGMENTS

All the people who helped make this book possible are too numerous to mention. The feedback from the 600 school psychologists in the western states was invaluable for making this book more relevant to practitioners. The conceptualizing and production of the training program received valuable input from Bill Frankenburg, Stephen White, Marlin Cohrs, Nick Anastasiow and Kathy King. Much of the editing and reviewing of chapters was done by Susan Thornton. The production and typing of chapters was done by Diana Wustemann, Jolene Constance and Patti Schoenfeld. The artwork was done by Jay Lawson. There were also many other people who read the early drafts of the chapters and provided valuable input to the final versions; they know who they are and we thank them gratefully.

CONTENTS

Chapter 1

INTRODUCTION TO ASSESSING YOUNG CHILDREN

By

GORDON ULREY AND RICHARD R. SCHNELL

During the past decade, there has been a substantial increase in the demand for psychological services for children under 6 years of age. Public recognition of the advantages of early detection and treatment of handicapping disorders has led to federal legislation that mandates more services for children with developmental disabilities. The most significant mandate for change has been the Education for All Handicapped Children Act of 1975 (P.L. 94-142); this law specifically requires that nondiscriminatory evaluations and appropriate individualized education plans be provided for every handicapped child from the age of 3 years. In addition, many states have passed legislation that includes children from birth to 3 years of age in screening and assessment efforts.

THE NEED FOR TRAINING OF PSYCHOLOGISTS

The role of the psychologist in providing psychological services for young handicapped children under P.L. 94-142 is to ensure that appropriate assessments are conducted, and that the identified child's treatment plan meets his or her individual needs (Schaar, 1979). The mandate of P.L. 94-142 is specific about the full range of developmental disabilities, which includes emotional disorders, mental retardation, physical disabilities, and sensory impairments. However, several surveys have indicated that there is a dearth of qualified psychologists to meet the increased need

for assessment and treatment planning for young handicapped children (Bardon and Wenger, 1976; Mowder and DeMartino, 1979; Ulrey and White, 1980); few psychologists have sufficient training or experience with children under 6 years of age who have developmental disabilities. In addition, the survey by Bardon and Wenger indicated that only 12 percent of school psychology programs in the United States listed "needs for exceptional children" as a training emphasis.

Not only do few training programs provide an emphasis on assessment and treatment of young handicapped children, but there is widespread controversy within the profession of psychology about which clinical procedures are appropriate for young children. For example, recent reviews of infant testing continue to indicate poor prediction of later cognitive functioning and school performance for nonhandicapped infants (McCall, 1979). Yet there is evidence of positive predictive validity from developmental assessments of handicapped young children (DuBose, 1976). Vandeveer and Schweid (1974) reported that of twenty-three developmentally delayed infants, 73 percent continued to show retardation up to three years later. However, assessment of young handicapped children requires special training and experience if numerous pitfalls are to be avoided.

To avoid serious errors in conducting psychological evaluations, the clinician must recognize the limitations of existing test procedures used with young children.

This is important because the misunderstanding or misinterpretation of assessment outcomes may result in depriving a child of his or her right to an appropriate education, and/or may result in an inappropriate label that in itself may be a serious handicap. Psychologists who attempt to provide services for young handicapped children without sufficient skills and training risk harm to children and to the profession of psychology. Since the challenge of providing nondiscriminatory and appropriate services for young children is an important issue for all psychologists (Ulrey, 1981), this book will describe many of the factors that must be considered to obtain the valid and relevant assessment that is needed to plan interventions.

THE PURPOSE OF THIS TEXT

The purpose of this book is to describe issues and procedures for assessing children under the age of 6 with the full range of developmental disabilities. Psychological tests are viewed as important, but as only a part of the process of clinical assessment. This is not a book about how to administer tests to young handicapped children. Instead, emphasis is placed on the examiner as an expert in the assessment of behavior, and as one who understands early psychological development and learning in the context of the ecology of the child.

Assessment of the young child is viewed in this text from an interactive developmental framework (Piaget, 1952; Piaget and Inhelder, 1972). Development is assumed to progress from the complex interaction between the child's evolving cognitive skills and learning style and the changing environmental influences of parents and learning opportunities. An important part of assessing young developmentally disabled children is the clinician's attempt to understand how a child who is handicapped may experience interactions with the environment differently from a nonhandicapped child; in addition, the psychologist must be able to determine how the handicapped child's behavior and development are affected. It is also assumed in this book that the psychologist working with young children must know how and when to seek interdisciplinary assessment and treatment to assure appropriate services for the developmentally disabled child.

DIFFERENCES BETWEEN ASSESSING SCHOOL-AGE AND VERY YOUNG CHILDREN

There are several important differences between assessing school-age children (6 to 12 years) and children under the age of 6 years. Psychologists who are experienced in the assessment of school-age children must master additional skills to be able to evaluate accurately the younger child. Different skills are needed because many of the accepted assessment procedures used with school-age children do not work well with younger children. For example, developmental differences in language, motivation, and thinking skills, as well as differences in opportunities for previous learning, make it difficult both to obtain a reliable test performance and to predict later developmental disabilities or school problems. In addition, assessment of young severely handicapped children with disturbances of communication skills, motor skills, or emotional functioning often leads the examiner to conclude that the child is untestable (Alpern, 1976). The mandate and necessity of early intervention make it essential for assessment to be done, although adaptation of existing tests plus expanded testing procedures may be needed to obtain relevant and valid information.

One important difference between testing school-age children and children under 6 years is that the young child cannot simply be asked to perform; instead, cooperation must be elicited by the examiner. Obtaining the cooperation of infants, it should be noted, is particularly challenging. Obviously, the investment of school-age children in test procedures is important and may be difficult to achieve in some cases. However, because of differences in communication skills, emotional maturity, and thinking skills, there are specified approaches and precautions that are necessary to obtain a reliable test performance from all children under the age of 6. These will be described in subsequent chapters.

The young child's response to the examiner is critical. For example, Stevenson and Lamb (1979) found that an infant's response to a strange adult influenced test performance, and that "sociably friendly" infants scored higher on measures of cognitive competence. The preschool child, who often has not "learned the rules" of the test behavior, will have little regard for the "correct" answer and for obtaining feedback from adults which indicates the answer was understood. Indeed, Gelman (1978) has described the preschool child's relative lack of concern about how others perceive an answer as egocentric. The examiner must be aware of special procedures needed to engage the young child to obtain a reliable test performance.

While acceptable levels of reliability can be obtained by administering group tests to school-age children, tests for young children must always be administered individually, and they require that the examiner interact with the child. Such interaction is necessary for eliciting the performance of the child on standardized measurements. The model of simply presenting items and asking the child to complete a task is insufficient when applied to the assessment of younger children.

In all assessments of infants and young children, the examiner must make judgments about the degree to which an optimal performance was obtained from the child. This judgment is based on how the child interacted with the examiner, and the degree of involvement there was in test activities. The clinician must be aware of how he or she influences the test performance; because the psychologist is relating to the child, the understanding of how the child is responding is a crucial part of the assessment. Knowledge of how the child relates to a strange adult (examiner) and to the parents indicates emotional maturity, which is essential for assessing the child's performance on cognitive tasks. Chapters 2 and 3 discuss the behavioral characteristics of infants and preschoolers which influence assessment performance and interpretation of results.

THE ECOLOGY OF ASSESSMENT

The psychologist must carefully monitor how the child responds to the "ecology" of the assessment procedures. This concept of ecology is essential because of the importance of understanding the complex and changing interactions the child has with the environment as he or she matures. An understanding of young children must specifically include his or her impact on caregivers. The work of Bell (1968) and of Lewis and Rosenblum (1973) has emphasized how the child shapes and changes the caregivers. Sameroff and Chandler (1975) have described a means for examining the ecology of the child through a transactional model, with emphasis on the reciprocal effect of the child on the environment. These authors emphasize that specific characteristics of the child and of the parents interact or transact, producing a system that must be understood to determine how the child functions and to learn what is needed to plan relevant interventions.

The impact of a child's temperament as it interacts with various parenting styles has been described by Thomas and Chess (1977). They emphasize the need for understanding that temperament can only be understood in the context within which the behavior occurs. In other words, just knowing a child's temperament style is not useful unless information about the home environment and parental attitudes and expectations is also known. These authors emphasize the "goodness of fit" between the child's temperament and the child-rearing styles and attitudes of the parents. That is not to say that a bad "fit" between a child and parents always predicts problems. While the impact of a child's "difficult temperament" correlated significantly with behavior problems in mildly retarded children, a six-year follow-up showed less prediction of behavioral disorders. This suggests that parental and general environmental influences interact and prevail over time (Chess and Hassibi, 1970). The adaptation of parents and families over time suggests that early counseling may facilitate interaction to decrease the vulnerability of the child to later behavior disorders and family disruptions (Solnit and Provence, 1979).

Although there are no standardized psychological tests that assess the interaction of the child with either the examiner or the caretakers, an appropriate evaluation of a handicapped young child should include an analysis of the child's interaction with the environment. The present book emphasizes the need for systematically observing structured and unstructured interactions between the child and parents, siblings, teachers, or the clinician. For example, teaching the child a task or having a parent teach a task is not part of a standardized test, but provides invaluable information about the child's functioning in the context of environmental factors. Observing spontaneous play with the parents and/or siblings also provides information about the ecology of the child. Procedures for obtaining additional data about the child and his or her environment and suggested protocols for observing interactions will be described in later chapters.

DOWNWARD EXTENSION OF EXISTING TESTS

Another difference in testing younger children is that a simple downward extension of standardized tests used for assessing school children does not work well. This is true largely because many of the indicators of school performance and learning problems are not known for children under the age of 6 years. Although it is known that many infants who have experienced "risk factors," such as prematurity, perinatal complications, and/or chronic ear infections recover developmentally and do very well in school, several reviews of major longitudinal studies (Kessen and colleagues, 1970; Sameroff, 1976; Beckwith, 1979) have indicated that predictions of later learning and behavioral disorders are not possible based on the first two years of life. There are some children who do not recover, but psychologists currently cannot predict well which children will continue to be affected. One viewpoint is that extant tests for younger children generally do not reflect what is currently known about early development. The past two decades have

provided new information about the importance of visual fixations, smiling, and vocalizing (Zelazo, 1979), but that information has not been translated into a usable test instrument.

To do well on psychological tests, the school-age child must demonstrate verbal skills, conceptual skills, and emotional maturity which relate closely to the criteria for school success. The skills measured in the younger child often relate to less differentiated and changing competencies, such as sensorimotor adaptations and conceptual skills, that are qualitatively different (preoperational vs. concrete operations) from those required for school performance. The competencies that develop during infancy and the preschool years are not as clearly linked to later criteria of school performance, and in many cases show no observable relationship. Indeed, skills that are crucial during one phase of early development may be unimportant at a later phase. The downward extrapolation of tests used for children more than 6 years of age is based on an assumption of continuous development from birth until school age. However, the development of children from infancy to school age appears to be discontinuous, with many changes in emotional, cognitive, and sensorimotor functioning that result from complex interactions with the environment. Psychologists simply cannot rely on intelligence quotients and developmental indexes to predict what future learning or behavior problems will persist. Issues of validity and reliability are reviewed later in this chapter.

THE INTERDISCIPLINARY APPROACH TO ASSESSMENT

One other important factor in assessing younger children is the need for professionals from other disciplines (such as physical therapists or speech pathologists) to understand all the relevant factors contributing to an apparent developmental delay or learning disorder. The psychologist must know how and when to utilize the services of other professionals, and must be able to integrate the findings of a psychological assessment with the data of other disciplines. In addition, the psychologist must have the skills necessary to participate in the interdisciplinary evaluation, planning, and treatment of handicapped children under the age of 6 years. The use of interdisciplinary procedures and the interdisciplinary team process when working with developmentally disabled children has been discussed by Johnston and Magrab (1976) and by Meier (1976). Later chapters will emphasize when and how to utilize other professionals.

TESTS AND TEST PERFORMANCE

The psychologist should assume that the child's behavior is never "wrong," and should know that reliance only on behaviors that are elicited on standardized testing is insufficient. Instead, a systematic observation and study of how the child responds and copes with assessment procedures can be used to reveal information about how the child functions. When the primary question is to determine the child's optimal level of cognitive skills, reliable performance must be obtained. However, even the difficulty encountered when attempting to engage the child on standardized test items yields information; for example, use of test items may provide information about antecedents and consequences that are maintaining the child's behavior. Observations of the "untestable" child (Alpern, 1976) generally reveal indications of severe learning and/or behavior problems, as well as coping strategies that are potential strengths. The child who is difficult or impossible to engage is demonstrating a severe dysfunction that will also interfere with many opportunities for learning. The psychologist must use a wide range of approaches to obtain some control over the child's behavior.

As has been noted, dependence on tests with young children will not allow the clinician to obtain sufficient information; in fact, such dependence may obscure information needed for planning relevant educational programming. The psychologist's emphasis must be on observing and analyzing the behavior that is elicited by the assessment procedures. For example, the language disabled child may appear "hyperactive" when tasks requiring expressive speech are given, but may attend well on nonverbal performance items. The point is that observed behavior should be understood in the context in which it occurs. The psychologist who considers only behaviors that were intentionally elicited will never have sufficient information to understand the behavior of the young child.

From an assessment viewpoint, the problem is not so much what is wrong with tests for young children. Rather, the real problem is how tests are used and, more importantly, what is done with the results. That is not to deny the difficulty with reliability and validity of existing standardized measurements. However, the major problem for psychologists working with young children is the danger of the misuse of tests. The training of psychologists to assess young children must include much more than learning how to administer the tests reliably (this is a given requirement for assessing any age group). Because of various limitations of existing tests, there is a substantial need for psychologists to be trained to ensure appropriate and nondiscriminatory use of tests with young handicapped children. Not only are pitfalls of misusing tests with young children very real; the misuse of tests also threatens the future role of professional psychology in working with younger children (Ulrey, 1981).

The model of a consulting psychologist—who comes to a classroom to give a standardized test in a setting where the parents may not be present and who then has little control over how the results are used—is simply unacceptable for assessing young handicapped children. The psychologist must be more involved in the process of obtaining information, observing and analyzing the ecology of the child, and monitoring the treatment to make changes when needed. Evaluations must include observations from caregivers and educators to maximize the relevance of the data. The value of parents and educators as sources of clinical data will be discussed later.

Psychologists working with young handicapped children must be prepared to monitor and reassess the child's progress over time, since rapid and discontinuous changes in early development indicate that follow-up is essential. In short, the psychologist must assume the role of an advocate for the child to ensure that appropriate services are obtained, and that these services reflect the child's needs as growth and learning proceed.

Proficiency in assessment can be achieved only through supervised experience. Assessment techniques for children are deceptively simple in format, but the valid administration and interpretation of these techniques is more difficult. Thus the clinician who would assess young children should be "checked out" by other professionals who have extensive experience. While general experience with a wide variety of children can be very helpful, in-depth experience with the population of children who will be typically assessed is the most useful. One note of caution: It should not be assumed that even a well-trained psychologist can assess all children with developmental disabilities. Each psychologist must be acutely aware of the kind of children he or she is capable of assessing, and must know when to refer a child to another psychologist or other professional.

PLANNING THE ASSESSMENT

A few valid and reliable psychological tests for school-age children have emerged, and their accepted uses have been delineated in some depth (Sattler, 1974, new edition in press). In contrast, there is little agreement on the most acceptable scales for younger children, and the clinical uses of those scales have not been well defined. When assessing younger children the psychologist must be aware of the wide variety of available tests and the differences in appropriate uses with various handicaps and age groups. There are no standard batteries that yield the needed information on young children in the majority of situations.

This book emphasizes the importance of considering the specifics of the referral questions and the individual experiences and needs of the referred child. Therefore, a crucial step in assessment of a young child is determining what problem is being addressed. The assessment plan should be based first on the referral question, which unfortunately can be rather vague. An example would be, "Why is Johnny doing so poorly in preschool?" This question must be made specific by a more detailed description of Johnny's behavior. From the above question, the psychologist receives no clue as to whether Johnny is physically ill, mentally retarded, emotionally disturbed, learning disabled, has a sensory handicap, has a motor handicap, doesn't speak English, or comes from a different cultural background. (Another possibility may be that the standards of the preschool personnel are inappropriate.) Starting an assessment with such a vague question may lead to the psychologist simply giving tests and providing little if any useful information for teachers or parents.

To make the assessment most effective, a detailed description of the behaviors of concern and the circumstances in which they occur is essential for the clinician. This information can be gathered in several ways. For example, a parent questionnaire is very useful to provide pertinent background information as well as the parents' perceptions of the child's behavior and specific problems (see Appendix E for a sample parent questionnaire). In some settings, a teacher questionnaire (see Appendix F) may be useful to obtain data specific to preschool performance and/or behavior problems. Past information about the child as contained in appropriate records may also be sought. For obvious reasons, the reliability of each source of information should always be evaluated.

After clarification of the referral question, the next question—and one of critical importance—is what resources will be available in the school, community, and family to help the child after the assessment. For assessment to be of use, there must be a means to do something for the child and family. When few resources for young handicapped children are available, compiling documentation that a need exists for certain resources may help a number of handicapped children and their families and provide a basis for obtaining new resources.

The nature of resources potentially available helps determine the extent of the assessment. How much of the assessment information can be utilized to help the child and family? If the sophistication of the resource programs available is not equal to the depths of the assessment data, then some of the data might serve to confuse rather than lead to positive action. In addition, an assessment in such circumstances may waste the time and energy of the psychologist, child, family, and others involved. The point is that the assessment should not be an academic exercise—squeezing all possible data from the situation. Instead, the assessment data should focus on what will lead to practical help for the family, school, and child. Reliance on one standard assessment format is simply not sufficient with younger children.

With a clearly stated problem and knowledge about available resources on hand, the psychologist is prepared to hypothesize about the nature of the child's problem. This leads to a decision about whether information from other professionals should be gathered before the child is seen by the psychologist. For example, if it appears likely that a child has a hearing loss, an audiologic evaluation might be scheduled before the psychological assessment. When all this relevant information is obtained, the psychologist can best determine which assessment techniques can be most useful in investigating the problem and are most likely to increase the probability of obtaining relevant assessment data.

Assessment techniques that provide the information most needed should be chosen. A combination of standardized tests and informal procedures is always needed to ensure a nondiscriminatory assessment and to consider the child's performance in the proper context. The psychologist's most important strength in assessment is his or her understanding of young children's behavior, while test data are never relied on exclusively. Appendix A summarizes the uses of a wide variety of tests for infants and preschoolers. Some general guidelines based on psychometric properties of the tests and their clinical usefulness for different handicaps and age levels are provided to facilitate the selection of tests. Standardized tests are most often used to determine whether a child appears to be developing normally for his

or her age. An assessment with standardized techniques of current developmental status can be provided from birth onward. These can provide points of reference for comparison with other nonstandardized techniques, and can be used to evaluate future rates of development. The most controversial issues facing psychologists assessing young children are how accurate measurements of behavior are (reliability) and how well scores from standardized tests predict future behavior and learning problems (validity).

RELIABILITY AND VALIDITY

The psychologist must determine what clinical procedures will be both the most appropriate and nondiscriminatory. Despite limitations of existing psychological tests for young children, reliable and valid clinical assessments are possible with handicapped infants and preschoolers (DuBose, 1976). However, as emphasized above, such evaluations require specialized training and knowledge of factors that impact on test performance and interpretation of results. Later in this book, factors that influence reliability, validity of evaluation results, and implications for appropriate educational planning will be discussed in depth.

Several authors have emphasized that inconsistencies in the behavior of infants and preschool-age children often compromise test reliability, making it essential to interpret results cautiously (Flapan and Newbaner, 1970; Keogh, 1970). Murphy (1956) describes in cynical terms the young child as changing significantly from "hour to hour." Silverman (1971) found significant differences in preschoolers' dysfluency depending on whether they were seen in the home, at school, or in the clinical setting. Because of these maturational, experimental, and psychological differences, acceptable levels of reliability are most difficult to achieve with younger children. In spite of the special challenges in obtaining reliable assessments of younger children, acceptable test levels for clinical use are reported (Hatcher, 1976; Cattell, 1940; Bayley, 1969). It must be noted, however, that acceptable results come only when clinicians are trained to establish rapport through interactions with the child, to adjust procedures when needed, and to give careful consideration to the plethora of variables that influence test performance.

The validity of psychological tests used with young handicapped children must be carefully considered. For example, the clinician must know what infant and preschool tests purport to measure. Research shows, in general, that the younger the child is, the less predictive intelligence test scores will be of later school-age and adolescent test scores and academic performance (Bayley, 1969; McCall, Hogarty, and Hurlburt, 1972). It is also known that many of the indicators of later learning difficulties and behavior problems simply are not measurable (with current techniques) before the age of 6. Concern about test validity has led many investigators to caution psychologists who are using standardized assessments of younger children (Lidz, 1977). Many researchers, in fact, promote different types of tests (Kearsley and Sigel, 1979; Mercer, 1972).

There are inherent limitations to the validity of infant and preschool tests. Because a single index of development to predict later learning is of limited use (Keogh, 1970), dependence on an IQ level is inappropriate and less useful with young children than with school-age children. However, the global IQ combined with other data can be useful in identifying younger children who are developmentally handicapped. With normal children, scores on infant tests do not correlate highly with later measures before 18 to 24 months (McCall, 1979). The infant test is a good measure of present developmental status and has useful predictive validity with infants who are significantly developmentally delayed in the first year of life (Vandeveer and Schweid, 1974; DuBose, 1976; Honzik, 1976). However, even severely handicapped infants should be labeled cautiously and should always receive regular follow-up evaluation to monitor developmental progress and to ensure provision of appropriate treatment. As a child grows older, the correlation of his or her scores with later scores increases significantly, so that by 4 years of age there is a stabilization of the relationship between age and IQ scores (Bloom, 1964).

Although correlations become greater with age, there are IQ fluctuations for individual children. Some of these fluctuations reflect the fact that the age of acquiring various abilities sampled by the tests can be different for children; in fact, changes as great as 50 IQ points may be observed over time. The effects of extreme environment alone, it is now believed, may change the IQ by as much as 20 points. Bloom concluded that no decisions should be made about a child on the basis of a single test administered during the first years of life. Further, he stated that "a single early measure of general intelligence cannot be the basis for a long-term decision about an individual. When the results of several test administrations are combined, the reliability of these scores is enhanced, and their predictability increased" (p. 88).

At any age, intellectual handicaps are suggested when the IQ falls more than one standard deviation below the normal range (for example, below 84 for the Bayley Mental Scale and the Stanford-Binet). In addition, handicaps are assumed when scores are two or more standard deviations below normal; for example, when an IQ is below 68 (Hunt, 1976).

Changes in IQ have been demonstrated to be related to different personality patterns and environmental factors. Gains in IQ have been shown for children who are self-assured, competitive, and not easily frustrated, while losses in IQ scores have been associated with dependent, passive, and easily frustrated children. Environmental factors, such as prematurity, socioeconomic status, and constancy of emotional adjustment have also been linked to IQ changes (Broman, Nichols, and Kennedy, 1975). Suffice it to say that scores must be considered in the context of all the available information about the child and the family. Predictions of mental retardation should be made with caution, particularly for children under 2 years of age. Possibly such predictions should not be made at all, unless the data are irrefutable. This does not mean that children cannot be designated as "developmentally delayed" or "at developmental risk" so that they might get appropriate intervention. Yet the fact remains that developmental changes over time will provide much firmer data for conclusions about whether the child is retarded and about the significance of the retardation.

As a general rule, the more severe a child's handicaps, the more predictive tests are of later learning and behavior problems. For example, even infant tests have predictive validity of 70 to 90 percent when the child scores two or more standard deviations below the mean (DuBose, 1976; Honzik, 1976). Thus, children with severe motor, sensory, and cognitive deficits can be identified and appropriate intervention can be planned. While the tests are more predictive of future problems when the child is severely handicapped, assessment of such a child is difficult and requires specialized training. To determine how the handicap affects the assessment procedures and planning of intervention, the psychologist must make a "valid" and appropriate assessment without total dependence on the results of a standardized test and with the use of a variety of different tests (Simonson and colleagues, 1980).

ADAPTING TESTS

The psychologist planning to use standardized tests to assess the development of a young child is often confronted with the necessity of modifying procedures to fit the situation and the child. If the items are changed because of a different mode of presentation or response, then the norms of the test can no longer be used; however, the psychologist has observed the child's response to the task. Such observations may be more relevant to understanding the child than administering the test according to the directions and watching the child fail. Because the psychologist must attempt to understand how the child has adapted to the environment and what impact the handicap has on parents or teachers, observations made outside of standardized testing can provide information about a child's strengths and about important environmental resources available to him or her. Special adaptations of test procedures for various age levels and different handicaps will be described in subsequent chapters.

Some changes in standard test procedures are perhaps permissible. For example, it has been demonstrated that if the order of the presentation of items on the Stanford-Binet is changed, minority group children receive higher scores, while the scores of other children do not change. That is, if more difficult items are paired with easier items, the motivation of the minority child is increased, and his or her performance is improved (Zigler and Butterfield, 1968). Whenever there is a doubt about the reliability and validity of test results, the psychologist should interpret them in a very cautious manner in the context of the other behavioral and background data. Until different and better tests for handicapped young children are developed, the cautious and informed use of existing tests is the most appropriate way to provide nondiscriminatory and relevant assessments.

ORGANIZATION OF THIS TEXT

This book describes a wide range of issues that must be considered when assessing young handicapped children. Because there are no existing standard procedures for assessment and prescribing treatments, this book does not attempt to be a "cookbook" of what should be done when a child responds a certain way on a test. Indeed, there are no existing tests or batteries of tests for which this would be appropriate. The evaluator of young handicapped children must first be an expert in early development and child behavior before the standardized test procedures can be administered and interpreted appropriately. There is also a need for systematic observations of behavior beyond the response to the test situation. The current book presents the viewpoints of several different authorities in areas of behavior, specific handicaps, and the effects of the environment that must be understood when assessing young children. Relevant research is reviewed to support assessment issues and numerous specific techniques and protocols are presented to enable the clinician to adapt and expand existing test procedures.

The chapters are organized in three major areas (plus several appendices). These include:

Part I: Assessment of Infants and Preschool-Age Children's Behavior. Chapters

2 and 3 emphasize the impact of the child's behavioral and developmental changes on assessment outcomes. A Piagetian conceptual framework for cognitive assessment of infants and preschoolers is described in Chapters 4 and 5. Chapters 6 and 7 present special techniques for infant assessments and play interviews.

Part II: Assessment of Handicapped Infants and Preschool-Age Children. Chapters 8 through 14 emphasize issues and techniques for assessing children with different handicaps.

Part III: The Handicapped Child's Milieu. Chapters 15 through 17 discuss the important emotional, cultural, and familial factors that are important for understanding and assessing young handicapped children. The last chapter (18) discusses specific considerations for sharing feedback about an assessment with parents.

Part IV: Appendices. The appendices present suggested ways of selecting tests, reporting results, and designing protocols so as to obtain important assessment data.

SUMMARY

In conclusion, there are a variety of issues involved in assessing very young children which make such assessments different in purpose, scope, and content from other types of psychological assessments. The variables of environment and of handicapping conditions have a profound effect on the child's early development, and the psychologist needs experience with young handicapped children over time to have some knowledge of handicapped children's final developmental status. Early developmental assessments do not predict outcomes well. The effects of inappropriate or incorrect diagnostic labels are probably most destructive for very young children, because labels have a major influence on the kind of interventions the child will receive, and on the expectations teachers, therapists, and parents will have for the child. The challenge for the psychologist is two-fold: First, the clinician must gather accurate information about the child and the environment surrounding the child; second, the psychologist must compare that information to his or her own exten-sive knowledge about early development and about the effects of handicaps on development over time.

REFERENCES

Alpern GD: Measurement of "untestable" autistic children. Abnormal Psych 72(6): 478–486, 1976
Bardon JI, Wenger RD: School psychology training trends in the early 1970s. Prof Psych 7: 31–37, 1976
Bayley N: *Bayley Scales of Infant Development: Manual.* New York: The Psychological Corp, 1969
Beckwith L: Prediction of emotional and social behavior. In Osofsky J (ed): *Handbook of Infant Development.* New York: John Wiley & Sons, 1979
Bell RQ: A reinterpretation of the direction of affects in studies of socialization. Psych Rev 75: 81–95, 1968
Bloom BS: *Stability and Change in Human Characteristics.* New York: John Wiley & Sons, 1964
Broman D, Nichols L, Kennedy J: Precursors of low IQ in young children. Proc 80th Ann Convention Am Psych Assoc 77–78, 1975
Cattell P: *The Measurement of Intelligence of Infants and Young Children.* New York: The Psychological Corp, 1940
Chess S, Hassibi M: Behavior deviations in mentally retarded children. J Am Acad Child Psych 9: 282–297, 1970
DuBose RF: Predictive value of infant intelligence scales with multiply handicapped children. Am J Ment Defic 81(14): 388–390, 1976
Flapan D, Neubauer PB: Issues in assessing development. J Am Acad Child Psych 9: 669–687, 1970
Gelman R: Cognitive development. In Rosenwig MR, Porter LW (eds): Ann Rev Psych 29: 43–68, 1978
Hatcher R: The predictability of infant intelligence scales: A critical review and evaluation. Ment Retard 14: 16–20, 1976
Honzik M: Value and limitations of infant tests. In Lewis M (ed): *Origins of Intelligence.* New York: Plenum Publishing, 1976
Hunt S: Environmental risk in fetal and neonatal life and measured intelligence. In Lewis M (ed): *Origins of Intelligence: Infancy and Early Childhood.* New York: Plenum Publishing, 1976, pp 223–258
Johnston R, Magrab P (eds). *Developmental Disorders: Assessment, Treatment, Education.* Baltimore: University Park Press, 1976
Kearsley RB, Siegel IE (eds): *Infants at Risk: Assessment of Cognitive Functioning.* Hillsdale, NJ: Lawrence Erlbaum Assoc, 1979
Keogh BU: Early identification of children with potential learning problems. J Spec Educ 4: 307–363, 1970
Kessen W, Haith MM, Salapatek PH: Human infancy: A bibliography and guide. In Mussen P (ed): *Carmichael's Manual of Child Psychology,* vol 1, 3rd ed. New York: John Wiley & Sons, 1970
Lewis M, Rosenblum (eds): *The Effects of the Infant*

on its Caregiver. New York: John Wiley & Sons, 1974

Lidz C: Issues in psychological assessment of preschool children. J School Psych 15: 129–135, 1977

McCall RB: The development of intellectual functioning in infancy and the prediction of later IQ. In Osofsky J (ed): *Handbook of Infant Development.* New York: John Wiley & Sons, 1979

McCall RB, Hogarty PS, Hurlburt N: Transition in infant sensorimotor development and the prediction of childhood IQ. Am Psychol 27: 728–747, 1972

Meier J: *Developmental and Learning Disabilities: Evaluation, Management and Prevention in Children.* Baltimore: University Park Press, 1976

Mercer JR: *The Origins and Development of the Pluralistic Assessment Project.* Riverside, CA: University of California, 1972

Mowder BA, DeMartino RA; Continuing education needs in school psychology. Prof Psych 5: 681–686, 1979

Murphy LD: *Personality in Young Children.* New York: Basic Books, 1956

Piaget J: *The Origins of Intelligence in Children.* New York: International University Press, 1952

Piaget J, Inhelder B: *The Psychology of the Child.* New York: Basic Books, 1972

Public Law 94-142. Education for All Handicapped Children Act. 94th Congress, S.6, 1975

Sameroff AJ: Early influences on development: Fact or fancy? In Chess S, Thomas A (eds): *Annual Progress in Child Psychiatry and Child Development.* New York: Brunner Mazel, 1976

Sameroff AJ, Chandler MJ: Reproductive risk and the continuum of caretaking casualty. In Horowitz M, Heathenington S, Scarr-Salapatek S, Siegel G (eds): *Review of Child Development Research,* vol 4. Chicago: University of Chicago Press, 1975

Sattler J: *Assessment of Children's Intelligence.* Philadelphia: WB Saunders Co, 1974

Schaar K: Council adopts statement: Handicapped law beset with problems. APA Monitor, 10(3): 5, 1979

Silverman E: Situational variability of preschoolers' dysfluency: Preliminary study. Percep Motor Devel 33: 4021–4022, 1971

Simonson R, Huntington G, Basse S: Expanding the developmental assessment of young handicapped children. In Gallagher J (ed): *New Directions for Exceptional Children,* Vol 3. New York: Jossey-Bass, 1980, pp 84–108

Solnit A, Provence S: Vulnerability and risk in early childhood. In Osofsky O (ed): *Handbook of Infant Development.* New York: John Wiley & Sons, 1979

Stevenson MB, Lamb ME: Effects of infant sociability and the caretaking environment on infant cognitive performance. Child Develop 50: 340–349, 1979

Thomas T, Chess S: *Temperament and Development.* New York: Brunner Mazel, 1977

Ulrey GL: The challenge of providing psychological services for young handicapped children. Prof Psych, 12(4): 483–491, 1981

Ulrey GL, White S: *The need for training psychologists to assess handicapped infants and young children.* Unpublished manuscript, University of Colorado Health Sciences Center, 1980

Vandeveer B, Schweid E: Infant assessment: Stability of mental functioning in young retarded children. Am J Ment Defic 79: 1–4, 1974

Zelazo P: Reactivity to perceptual-cognitive events: Application for infant assessment. In Kearsley RB, Sigel I (eds): *Infants at Risk: The Assessment of Cognitive Functioning.* Hillsdale, NJ: Erlbaum, 1979, pp 49–83

Zigler E, Butterfield E: Motivational aspects of changes in IQ test performance and culturally deprived nursery school children. Child Develop 39: 1–14, 1968

ASSESSMENT OF INFANTS'AND PRESCHOOL-AGE CHILDREN'S BEHAVIOR

Chapters 2—7

Chapter 2

INFLUENCES OF INFANT BEHAVIOR ON ASSESSMENT

By

GORDON ULREY

The major concern and problem in evaluating infants who may be developmentally disabled is to obtain an accurate and meaningful assessment. Such an assessment depends on three things: (1) an examiner who is clinically trained and experienced with infants; (2) appropriate use of evaluation procedures with awareness of the reliability and validity of results; and (3) an appreciation of how the infant's behavior influences test performance and outcome. The limitations of traditional infant scales with normal infants are well documented (Bayley, 1969; McCall, Appelbaum, and Hogarty, 1973; Stott and Ball, 1965; Lewis and McGurk, 1972); they do not predict later levels of cognitive functioning at an acceptable or useful level. However, the situation is different for developmentally handicapped infants. Indeed, there is evidence that conventional infant tests adapted for use with handicapped infants can yield valid results and facilitate planning interventions when used by trained examiners (Honzik, 1976; DuBose, 1976; Vandeveer and Schweid, 1974) of exceptional young children. However, handicapped infants may receive artificially depressed scores on infant tests if procedures are not adapted (Hunt, 1976).

This chapter will cover the three criteria described above as necessary for a good assessment, with emphasis on observation and appreciation of the influence of the infant's behavior as a major factor in the assessment of handicapped infants. Some observation techniques and procedures for presenting items to minimize the variability of infant behavior on test results will be described.

THE NEED FOR ADEQUATE TRAINING

What training is necessary to assess handicapped infants? Most school and clinical psychologists have not received training in the assessment of very young children (Mowder, 1979; Ulrey, 1981), since such assessments require specialized training and supervision, as well as expertise in early childhood development. Infant evaluation is not simply a downward extrapolation of child assessment; instead, the examiner must obtain experience with an infant population and with infant tests. Nancy Bayley (1969) emphasized the importance of knowing test items well and obtaining supervised experience with a variety of infants before attempting an assessment of a child suspected of having learning or developmental problems.

Clinicians who wish to expand their diagnostic skills to include infant assessment must obtain training in the use of infant tests, early childhood development, and observations of infant behavior. Reliance on scores from infant tests is grossly inadequate for diagnosing handicapping conditions in infancy. It is known that scores of normal infants do not predict later cognitive functioning and that handicapped infants are often discriminated against because of the reliance on sensory and motor skills in test items. Therefore, examiners must know how to utilize infant scales in a nondiscriminatory and appropriate way to avoid serious misuse of the tests and harmful effects on the child and family.

The most practical means for training clinicians to evaluate young handicapped children appears to be through continuing education programs. The need for making more continuing education programs available to professional psychologists has been a growing concern (Jones, 1975). The fact that knowledge of infant development and behavior has expanded substantially in the past ten years (Stone, Smith, and Murphy, 1973; Lewis, 1976; Kagan, Kearsley, and Zelazo, 1978; Osofsky, 1979) strongly suggests this need for training to include current knowledge of infant development.

There are significant risks involved when unskilled examiners use infant tests. For example, Kearsley (1979) has described a potential danger referred to as the "iatrogenic" cause of mental retardation. In medicine, the term "iatrogenic" refers to an additional problem or disease caused inadvertently by a patient's treatment. The familiar pattern is of parents being told their child is developmentally delayed (based on a low infant test score), which leads to the parents having lowered expectations, the child therefore receiving less stimulation and fewer opportunities for learning, and the situation thus insuring delayed functioning. The "iatrogenic" problem may occur even though the infant's cognitive potential is normal; the child may score low because of a motor handicap. The examiner must be able to interpret the results of the infant's test performance based on knowledge of what the test measures and on observations of the child's behavior. Without adequate training for the examiner, there is danger of misdiagnosis, inappropriate placement, and/or labeling—with devastating effects on the child (Hobbs, 1975).

The psychological evaluation of an infant is based on the general assumption that maturation and learning proceed in a sequential and measurable manner. The clinician must understand, however, that there is a wide range in the rate of development, as well as individual difference in behavior (for example, temperament and movement). The rate of change in the infant's understanding of his or her surroundings and the manner of interacting with the environment is much faster and more dramatic than with older children. Qualitative changes occur in the behavior of a 6-month-old child compared with changes that occur in a 12- or 18-month-old child. Each of these levels requires different types of test items and different strategies for assessment. For example, at 5 or 6 months, reaching is beginning to emerge and is encouraged; in contrast, tasks for an 18-month-old require some voluntary inhibiting of reaching. There are also important differences in mobility, attending to various stimuli, relating to adults, and comprehension of directions.

A RELIABLE AND VALID ASSESSMENT

It is essential that the clinician have a thorough knowledge of the psychometric properties—reliability and validity—of infant tests. Reliability refers to the consistency of test measurement, while validity is how well a test measures what it was designed for. The examiner must be able to estimate the accuracy of the measurement of a child's test performance, based both on characteristics of the test instrument and on the child's relative cooperation with and investment in the activity. Obtaining a reliable assessment is difficult because of the variability in infant behavior and the need to elicit the child's optimal performance. The examiner's judgment, which is so important in this regard, must be based on knowledge of infant development and familiarity with a wide variety of behaviors. Psychologists learning to administer infant tests must have other experienced clinicians observe their efforts to be sure of achieving a satisfactory level of reliability. It is very difficult for inexperienced examiners of infants to administer test items, maintain the infant's attention to tasks, and observe the child's behavior. Yet in spite of these difficulties, traditional infant tests can be administered reliably by trained examiners at the .80 to .90 level as reported by Bayley (1969) and reviewed by Hatcher (1976).

Many psychologists assume that it may be more difficult to obtain a reliable measure when the child has a handicap. Unfortunately, no direct comparisons of reliability of assessments of handicapped and nonhandicapped infants have been reported in the literature. Since testing procedures may need modifications, and some items will be inappropriate for handicapped children, an acceptable level of reliability may be difficult or impossible to obtain. Flexibility is needed when assessing infants; for example, two different testing sessions (either at different times of the day or on two different days) may be needed. Similarly, the clinician must be able to judge when a child's performance is simply too unreliable to yield valid test results. To check the reliability of an assessment, the examiner must obtain data from a variety of sources to compare with the test performance. Observations of the child's spontaneous behavior outside the testing situation, and observations of the child's play, interaction with parents, teachers, and/or other strangers can all be helpful for determining if an optimal test performance was obtained. The use of adaptive behavior scales, such as the Vineland Social Maturity Scale or the AAMD Adaptive Behavior Scale (see Appendix A) provide additional data to compare with test performance. The examiner must then determine if significant discrepancies occur between test performance and other data; the judgment about performance discrepancies must be based on sound knowledge of child development and infant behavior.

There is major concern about the validity of infant tests, and the question of how to use infant tests appropriately is complex. While infant tests have greater predictive validity with handicapped infants, there are important pitfalls that must be avoided. The situation is not simply that infant tests are valid for handicapped infants but not for nonhandicapped infants. In fact, it can be argued that handicapped infants will produce a depressed score secondary to the handicap, a situation that leads to a low estimate of the child's ability which may lower expectations of caregivers (Hunt, 1976; Zelazo, 1979). Assessment procedures often must be adapted or altered for handicapped infants, but there are no clear guidelines available for interpretation of test results. Some areas of infant testing with handicapped infants will be described below.

The psychologist must first consider what the conventional infant tests (Bayley, Cattell, and Gesell) actually measure. The infant tests are norm-referenced scales that describe the expected behaviors of normal infants at different chronologic ages. The sample population used to determine the norms were children with no known handicaps and apparently intact neuromotor functioning. Infants with known sensory, motor, or behavioral disorders were excluded from the samples. Therefore, the norms are based on behaviors of nonhandicapped children. However, there is generally no reason to test nonhandicapped infants—so that, in practice, the majority of the children tested with infant tests are actually handicapped infants.

What does it mean to compare scores of developmentally disabled infants with norms for nonhandicapped infants? The results indicate how the skills of the handicapped infant compare with those of the general population. However, the test score does not indicate if a child's lower performance skills result from an actual cognitive deficiency, or if the score reflects difficulty with sensory or motor skills or other factors that may not relate to later intellectual ability.

Traditional infant tests are comprised of a mixture of items that are assumed to reflect neuromotor development and sensorimotor intelligence. Test items are included that measure skills in gross motor, fine motor, language, adaptive behaviors, and social-emotional functioning. Items appear on the scale because they have been found to select and discriminate maturity at various chronologic age levels. The items are not part of a unified theory of sensorimotor intelligence. Therefore, assessing a handicapped infant with a conventional test provides a profile of the child's relative strengths and weaknesses compared with normal infants in each of the areas. While the information is useful, it cannot be assumed that the component score reflects the level of intellectual skills, since most skills measured on infant tests do not relate directly to cognitive functioning.

Bayley (1970) has suggested that performance on an infant test should be seen as having contemporary validity. She argues that the assessment is a valid indication of a child's current developmental status, and that assessments can be used to monitor progress over time. Research shows that the traditional infant scales are valid indicators of grossly normal vs. abnormal functioning when an infant scores two standard deviations below the mean (Amer, 1967; Illingsworth, 1961; Simmon and Bass, 1956). One valid use of conventional infants tests is to establish the degree to which any infant is functioning within normal limits. Another may be to inform concerned parents that their child is demonstrating appropriate developmental status. However, estimates of intellectual functioning other than normal or abnormal are not possible.

Why do the norm-referenced infant scales fail to predict later cognitive functioning? There are two major reasons that are often cited for this poor predictive validity. One view is that discontinuity (Stott and Ball, 1965) and variability in development (Wilson, 1972) limit the usefulness of a linear prediction of later intelligence. Behaviors that indicate intelligence may differ from one chronologic age level to another, for one skill area may not lead directly to the next. A second view is that the items on traditional infant tests may be poor indicators of cognitive ability (McCall, 1971; Zelazo, 1979). In other words, the wrong behaviors for determining cognitive functioning are being measured. For example, the dependency on motor skills for performance on the Bayley Mental Scale will lead to to a low score for most children with cerebral palsy. However, according to Holman and Freedheim (1959), about one-third of all children with cerebral palsy have intellectual skills within the normal range by early adulthood. The fact is that a child may have a severe motor handicap and average intellectual capacity. It is also known that visually impaired and auditorily impaired children are quite capable of developing cognitive skills in the normal range. The fact that significant deficits in sensory and motor functioning can coexist with normal cognitive capacity makes it very difficult to obtain a valid score on infant tests that largely measure sensorimotor skills. It is difficult if not impossible at times to determine if an infant scored low on a test of sensorimotor skills because of a cognitive deficiency or a deficit in sensory and/or motor functioning. Hunt (1976) has reported that the traditional infant tests tend to underestimate the cognitive capacity of children suspected of having developmental delays.

Another problem with traditional infant tests which has already been touched upon is the problem of inaccurate labeling. Both Kearsley (1979) and Zelazo (1979) have reported some anecdotal data suggesting that infant tests may significantly lower parents' expectations and thus may inadvertently decrease the physically handicapped infant's performance. The possibility of lowering parents' expectations calls for cautious and conservative use of the conventional infant tests. The psychologist must realize that a handicapped infant's performance on a traditional test is more likely to underestimate than overestimate the infant's intellectual capacity.

Zelazo (in press) has recently described the possibilities of utilizing a perceptual-cognitive processing approach to infant assessment. Numerous studies in the past decade have demonstrated that infants' competence in processing visual and auditory information is related to later intellectual functioning (Fagan, 1978; Miranda and Fantz, 1974; Zelazo, 1976). There is compelling data suggesting the value of assessing auditory and visual processing of infants to avoid the pitfalls of dependence on motor skills. Although the laboratory procedures have not been converted to clinically useful instruments, perhaps they should be in the future (Kearsley, 1981).

Given the limitations of the traditional infant scales, what can be done to insure their appropriate use? In general, examiners should not rely on developmental quotients or component scores from infant tests. A child's performance may be significantly depressed because of a sensory deficit, a motor deficit, or because the child was not engaged behaviorally in the testing procedures. Any one or a combination of these factors may have attenuated the overall test performance and score, but they do not necessarily reflect a low level of intelligence. It is obvious that a child can be blind or deaf and yet have normal intelligence; but it may be less obvious that severe motor handicaps or behavioral withdrawal can coexist with normal intellectual skills.

When an infant's test score indicates a developmental delay (two standard deviations below the mean), the examiner must always determine the factors that have contributed to this level of performance. First, the test protocol should be scrutinized for scatter in performance that suggests relative strengths and weaknesses. For example, if all items that require verbal receptive skills are lower than items that do not require verbal instructions, then a language or auditory problem should be considered. If the infant passes some items up to his or her chronologic age level but scores significantly lower on others, it should be assumed that some problem exists but that a general developmental delay (in spite of a quotient two standard deviations below the norm) is not the problem. When a delayed performance is found, the child should have a more thorough evaluation of sensory (visual and auditory) and motor skills by other experts, such as an opthalmologist, pediatrician, or physical therapist. The existence of a sensory or motor deficit must be considered and the child's progress monitored to determine the degree of handicap. The psychologist must also make a judgment about the child's investment in the testing procedures. The infant whose performance indicates a significant delay, who has some type of handicap, and who is at risk for problems often needs further evaluation and monitoring of developmental progress to determine what specific handicap(s) may be. The major concern is that one type of problem—such as a motor deficit— should not be confused for a cognitive deficit. The clinician must determine what factors have contributed to the failure of a test item.

FACTORS THAT INFLUENCE TEST BEHAVIOR

Traditional test norms are based on children who (1) have had similar opportunities for learning, (2) were engaged in the testing procedures, and (3) do not have significant emotional or sensorimotor handicaps that could interfere with test behavior. The clinician must determine how appropriate a comparison is between a child being evaluated and the test norms. An awareness of the child's past opportunities for learning and a judgment about current physical and behavioral factors must be made to avoid misinterpretation of results. Engaging the child is difficult because of the many variables that compete for the child's attention.

One of the major challenges in assessing infants is simply to elicit the desired response for a given test item. This makes infant testing more difficult than testing older children—although it is often the most interesting and rewarding part of the evaluation for the examiner. While there are no standard procedures for engaging an uncooperative infant, there are suggested strategies that can be useful for eliciting the desired performance during testing. The following are variables that are important for interpreting the infant's test behavior, for determining what may be wrong, and for revealing implications for intervention.

TEMPERAMENT

The work of Thomas and Chess (1977) has been valuable for understanding the behavioral characteristics of infants which influence caretakers. These researchers use the concept of "temperament" to describe the child's individual behavioral characteristics that influence the child's development and persist throughout life. Thomas, Chess, and Birch (1968) have described nine behavioral variables that make up temperamental differences and are observable in early infancy (activity, rhythmicity, adaptability, approach, threshold, intensity, mood, distractibility, and persistence).

From these traits, three personality styles or three temperamental clusters have emerged which are useful clinical categories—although an individual may have traits in each area. The three temperament styles are as follows:

1. An "easy child" is characterized as mildly active, highly adaptive, positively

responsive, and predominantly cheerful of mood.

2. A "slow to warm up child" is initially inactive and aloof. The child avoids contact and shows little response to contact but is responsive once he or she is more familiar with the surroundings.

3. A "difficult child" is highly active, negatively responsive, and nonadaptive. The child's mood is expressed by a preponderance of crying.

Scales have been developed to measure temperament in infancy from 4 to 8 months (Carey, 1972) based on a sample of 101 infants. The examiner should note these behavioral characteristics to help form an understanding of the child's contribution to the environment, as well as to understand test behavior. For example, the "slow to warm up child" may require more time to assess, while the "difficult child" may require more structure. The inexperienced examiner—if unfamiliar with these temperamental styles—may move too quickly and assume erroneously that the child is unable to perform items.

Temperament has been found to be related to performance on the Bayley Scales. Sostek and Anders (1975) grouped infants as "worrisome" and "optimal" and found that the "optimal" temperament was positively correlated with higher test performance scores. Stevenson and Lamb (1979) have also reported higher test scores with children observed to be "sociable" as measured by the Bayley Observation Scale. Both studies suggest that a child who is more easily engaged in test procedures is more likely to perform better on infant tests. There is clearly a concern that children with a difficult temperament will score lower on tests and be identified as being developmentally delayed or less intelligent because of behavior rather than lower intelligence.

Another important consideration about temperament differences is how the child is perceived by the caregivers, which perhaps influences their reactions to the child. (The role of infant's temperament on caregivers is discussed in depth in Chapter 15.) The assessment of an infant should always include observations of the child's temperament and the parents' style of responding to the child. The psycholo-gist may get some clues by asking an important clinical question: "How did it feel to interact with the child?" Examiners should monitor how the child responds by asking themselves if the child was slow to warm up, difficult to engage, or oppositional when presented with tasks. The use of a temperament scale such as Carey's (1972) is valuable for a more objective assessment, although actual observed test behavior is important to consider.

Some structured activities for parent and child produce important evaluation data. For example, the clinician can first ask the parent simply to play with the child in the "usual manner." Second, the parent can be instructed to perform two tasks with the infant—one that will probably result in success, and another that is likely to be too difficult for the child; when the child fails the more difficult item, the parent can be asked to teach it. The success sequence provides information about how the parent reinforces the child and structures the environment. The failure sequence gives information about how the parent comforts the child and restructures a learning task. These observations are useful for explaining a child's deficits and how to work with the child to parents and teachers.

Although structured activities are useful, observing the child interact with the parents is the best method for determining how the child relates with caregivers. A child's temperamental style is always relative to how the parent's own style interacts with the child's (Thomas and Chess, 1977). Thus, systematic observation of how the child and caregiver interact is needed to assess the impact of the child's temperament.

THE STATE OF THE INFANT

Another important concern when testing infants is their state of alertness or arousal. The examiner must monitor the child's awareness, which varies according to how close it is to nap time or feeding time, or how fatigued the child is from test activities. For example, a child under 12 months of age is in an optimally alert state only about 20 to 30 percent of a 24-hour period (Parmelee, Werner, and Schulz,

1964). Since infant tests are based on optimal performance, items are reliable only when the child is in an alert state; thus, the evaluator should note the state of the infant and what is required to sustain an alert level.

Ashton (1973) has stressed the fact that there is widespread disagreement among investigators as to the definition of "state." Researchers and clinicians disagree as to what clusters of behaviors reflect different states and the number of different states. Berg and Berg (1979), in a comprehensive review of states, describe the dichotomy between "behavioral" states and "physiological" states. The reviewers suggest that there are no clear grounds for a distinction and that both are types of behavior that overlap. What is needed appears to be a clear description of clusters of behavior that can reliably be identified as different states of alertness or arousal ranging from sleep to an active, alert condition (Ander, 1978).

The most widely agreed-upon descriptions of "states" were developed by Prechtl (1974). The Brazelton (1973) neonatal behavior examination has incorporated the six levels of state described by Prechtl. The Brazelton Scale is administered by giving some items in various states, such as a rattle presented while the child is in State 1. The Scale takes into account behavioral differences in various states. Brazelton describes the range from sleep to active as follows:

1. Eyes closed, regular respirations, no movement;
2. Eyes closed, irregular respirations, no gross movements;
3. Eyes open, no gross movements;
4. Eyes open, gross movements, no crying;
5. Eyes open or closed, crying;
6. Other state—described.

Those who evaluate infants must be able to recognize states and observe changes in states during testing. Simeonson, Huntington, and Parse (1980) have suggested that identification of difference in states, such as the number of hours in an alert state, could be used to assess severely handicapped infants and older children. Examiners must always observe and record the state of a child during assessment to determine the reliability of testing.

PHYSICAL DISCOMFORT

Infants do not suppress physical discomfort during testing as an engaged child or adult may do. Although infants are obviously not able to tell the examiner about internal discomforts, observations of the child often reveal the difficulty. Generally, the parent who is present during the evaluation can help monitor the child's relative comfort level and can inform the examiner, who should ask the parent for help with interpretations of the child's responses. Indicators of discomforts—such as thirst, hunger, or gastrointestinal pressure—must be attended to.

Reactions of discomfort or fear may also result from aversive stimuli, such as a loud noise or sudden changes in test activities. Thus, sensitivity to the child's response to those stimuli is also essential for understanding the child's behavior. The best procedure for considering how the child may respond to discomfort is by history, using a parent questionnaire, and/or interviewing the parent prior to the evaluation. For example, when the infant has a history of colic, the evaluator must determine how frequently it occurs and the specific behaviors the parents are concerned about. An anxious parent may attempt to explain failures on test items as results of discomfort. The examiner should attend to the parents' descriptions and always compare them with the various behaviors that are elicited during an evaluation. When large discrepancies exist between parents' reports and clinical observations, having more than one specific time to observe the infant or requesting a three-month follow-up evaluation can be important. It should also be remembered that infants display a wide range of developmental levels when stressed or in different states of arousal.

MODALITY PREFERENCES

Another problem in infant assessment may be the child's preference for one type of activity (such as gross motor or visual attending) when a test item requires another type of activity. In addition, infants often persevere on newly learned tasks, may respond to moderately novel stimuli, or may be interested in an object totally for its visual display or its movement. The preference for one type of activity provides important information for the examiner; while it may contribute to a poor performance on a specific infant test item, it also indicates the child's learning preference and style. Another common example is when an infant is responding cautiously or curiously to the examiner and ignores the test items being presented. The challenge on infant tests is for psychologists to elicit particular responses; unfortunately, this often leads the inexperienced examiner to ignore incidental behaviors which can be so important.

As discussed earlier, an important criticism of conventional infant tests is dependence on motor skills. Early investigations (Richards and Nelson, 1939) described "all responses" measured on infant scales as "motor behavior." More recent critiques (Kearsley, 1981) have stressed that reliance on motor behaviors on infant tests often discriminates against motorically handicapped infants and suggests that models of sensorimotor intelligence are inadequate. Kearsley and his colleagues (Kearsley and Sigel, 1979) argue for consideration of other modalities, such as visual and auditory, from which attending and responding to selected stimuli without cooperative motor responses can be used for testing cognitive skills.

Kagan, Kearsley, and Zelazo (1978) have described several studies indicating an age-related change in response patterns to changes in visual and auditory stimuli in normal infants. The authors are attempting to develop a scale that will allow for systematic measurement of visual and auditory responses independent of motor skills. While the scale is not currently available, the data suggest the importance of observing the child's attending and reactions to stimuli that may not be part of the standard test but that may indicate awareness of environmental events. The infant who fails many motor-related items but appears to be utilizing other modalities (such as visual attending but not directed reaching) should be monitored carefully

with follow-up evaluations to decrease the chance of mislabeling a child.

NEED FOR STRUCTURE

How well is the infant able to attend to specific tasks and what antecedents are needed to elicit responses to items? The examiner should observe the activities the child appears to enjoy the most. How does the child cope with frustration or failure on tasks that are difficult? Is the child easily distracted by visual or auditory stimuli? Answers to these questions are essential for program planning. In addition, the test area should be free of unnecessary distractions to facilitate engaging the infant in testing procedures, and the examiner must determine how much structure the child needs to become engaged in a task.

While there is no formal test item that calls for teaching a task, such an effort often yields useful data. The examiner should choose an item in which the child shows some interest, but which appears to be too difficult developmentally. Observations can be made of the teaching techniques that work and the consequences that are reinforcing for the child. What antecedents are involved in eliciting a desired response from the child? A behavior analysis of the teaching task (Gagne, 1965) can be applied to determine the child's teaching needs. For example, does the child enjoy a success? Does the child enjoy interaction with the examiner or prefer playing alone?

One way to determine the child's need for structure is to describe what efforts were required to engage the child in testing and to establish rapport. The role of the examiner in establishing rapport with school-aged children has been reviewed by Sattler (1974), but the procedures are different with infants. For example, the infant under about 6 months of age is generally not expected to respond negatively to an examiner, because stranger anxiety has not developed. But handling of the very young infant in a way that is significantly different than the caretaker's style may cause some difficulties.

Infants functioning above the 6-month level begin to play "pat-a-cake" and other interacting games. Thus, the examiner should try to maintain this positive mode of doing things with the child and discourage or ignore negative behavior, and testing should begin with some type of exchange or cooperative play between the child and examiner, such as rolling a ball back and forth or playing "peek-a-boo." This will facilitate an interaction that tells the infant that you will do things together. In some cases, difficult children may grab items and throw them, or may simply hang onto them; if this happens, the examiner should stop that activity and attempt to get back a positive interaction set. At times, stopping the testing for several minutes or even an hour may be needed if the examiner is to retain control of the testing.

Another technique for providing the necessary structure to engage a difficult infant is using a familiar toy. When a child is particulary upset, is having difficulty accepting items, or is playing inappropriately with the toys presented (for example, throwing or refusing them), it is often helpful to use a familiar toy. This can be a toy in the office that is similar to one in the child's home, or it can be a toy that the parent has brought. Even the parent's key chain can be used. Such a familiar item is often useful for testing object permanence and pursuit of object tasks.

Another example of the use of structure is the use of a novel stimulus and/or reinforcers. It is always helpful to keep the items varied enough to maintain interest, and to use reinforcers to encourage a desired response. Toys that have a "novel" stimulus quality (such as a bell or a roly-poly toy) are useful to elicit responses when the child is distractible. In addition, distractibility can be minimized by keeping the test area free of other items or sounds. The examiner must constantly be aware of the potential for distraction and must monitor the test performance to determine whether or not an optimal response was elicited.

UNFAMILIAR ENVIRONMENT

The infant often requires considerably more time than the older child to adjust to the strangeness of a testing situation. Before beginning a test, the examiner must allow some time for the child to explore the strange new environment. Often the child will need some time very close to the parent while the examiner avoids being too intrusive. Observations of the child's awareness of a strange setting and the way the child eventually explores the room and/or approaches the examiner yield important information.

The most common mistake made by novices is to expect the child to become engaged in test activities too quickly. The examiner must avoid this pitfall and also be aware of the developmental differences in how infants of different ages and maturity are expected to respond to a novel setting and a stranger. When a child is experiencing stranger anxiety or difficulty with the newness of a situation, it may be helpful to have the parent administer items. Since infant testing is always done with a parent present, it is often helpful to involve the parent even when the child is not anxious, for such involvement makes possible the observation of interactions and the parent's style of managing the child.

Observe the child's spontaneous play with a toy and note what he or she does with it. This will generally indicate the child's level of interest and can be used to determine which items on the test are passed. For example, an infant who picks up things and drops them to the floor with delight may respond to tasks that involve putting things in a container. An appreciation of the developmental level of the child's play will greatly facilitate selection of appropriate items and interpretation of results.

SEPARATION AND ATTACHMENT BEHAVIORS

The child's interactions with the parents and response to a strange setting provide information about emotional maturity and emotional attachment (Ainsworth, 1969). Since there are no well-standardized tests of emotional development for infants, it is essential to make these observations. Difficulty with separation and attachment can make an assessment difficult and can depress the infant's test performance.

Children's responses to separation

from their parents occur on a developmental continuum, although the range of variability is considerable. A scale developed by Mosey, Foley, McCrae, and Thomas (1980) has recently been developed to assess a child's level of attachment and autonomy. There is evidence that even very young infants process and explore novel stimuli in the environment (reviewed by Kagan, Kearsley, and Zelazo, 1978); indeed, the normal infant shows evidence of discriminating a strange setting by about 4 months of age (4-month items on the Bayley Scales). Response to strangers and difficulties with separating emerge in the 6- to 8-month range. In general, the child should be able to use the parent for comforting. One also expects the child who is appropriately attached to explore the environment and show interest in strangers with the reassurance of the caretaker. A reliable cognitive assessment of a poorly attached child is often difficult or impossible, requiring multiple evaluations and observations. When emotional maturity appears to attenuate performance on a cognitive test, the scores should not be used, and there is also a need for a complete emotional assessment.

SUMMARY

This chapter has covered points the psychologist must know to conduct accurate infant assessments. The importance of three criteria has been emphasized: (1) the examiner must be an expert in child development, observation of infant behavior, and infant test administration; (2) the examiner must know the reliability and validity of the tests and procedures to avoid misuse and to make appropriate interpretations; and (3) the examiner must have an appreciation of how the infant's behavior influences test performance and what important behaviors must be observed in addition to test data. Some specific observations and testing procedures were discussed. An accurate and complete assessment should obtain information to answer specific referral questions and lead to relevant program planning.

REFERENCES

Ainsworth M: Object relations dependency and attachment: A theoretical review of the infant-mother relationship. Child Development 40: 969–1025, 1969

Amer L: Predictive value of infant behavior examinations. In Hellmuth J (ed): Exceptional Infant: The normal Infant, vol. 1. Seattle: Strant & Hellmuth, 1967

Ander TF: State and rhythm process. J Child Psych 17: 401–420, 1978

Ashton R: The state variable in neonatal research. Merrill-Palmer Quart 19: 3–20, 1973

Bayley N: The Bayley Scales of Infant Development. New York: Psychological Corporation, 1969

Berg W, Berg K: Psychophysiological development in infancy: State, sensory function and attention. In Osofsky J (ed): Handbook of Infant Development. New York: John Wiley & Sons, 1979

Brazelton T: Neonatal Behavioral Assessment Scale: Clinics in Developmental Medicine, No. 50. London: Heineman, 1973

Carey W: Measurement of infant temperament in pediatric practice. In Carey W (ed): Individual Differences in Children. New York: Westman, 1972

DuBose RF: Predictive value of infant intelligence scales with multiply handicapped children. Am J Ment Defic 81(4): 388–390, 1976

Fagan J: Infant recognition memory and later intelligence. Paper presented at the Society for Research in Child Development, San Francisco, March 1979

Gagne N (ed): Handbook of Research on Teaching. Chicago: Rand McNally, 1963

Hatcher R: The predictability of infant intelligence scales: A critical review and evaluation. Ment Retard 14: 16-20, 1976

Hobbs N: The Future of Children. San Francisco: Josey-Bass, 1975

Holman L, Freedheim D: A study of I.Q. retest evaluation of 370 cases of cerebral palsy. Am J Phys Med 38: 180–187, 1959

Honzik M: Value and limitations of infant tests: An overview. In Lewis M (ed): Origins of Intelligence: Infancy and Early Childhood. New York: Plenum Publishing, 1976, pp 59–97

Hunt S: Environmental risk in fetal and neonatal life and measured intelligence. In Lewis M (ed): Origins of Intelligence: Infancy and Early Childhood. New York: Plenum Publishing, 1976, pp 223–258

Illingsworth R: The predictive value of developmental tests in the first year with special reference to abnormality. J Child Psych Psychiat 2: 210–215, 1961

Jones N: Continuing education: A new challenge for psychology. Am Psychol 30: 842–847, 1975

Kagan J, Kearsley R, Zelazo P: Infancy: Its Place in Human Development. Cambridge: Harvard University Press, 1978

Kearlsey R: Iatrogenic retardation: A syndrome of learned incompetence. In Kearsley R: Sigel I (eds): Infants at Risk: Assessment of Cognitive

Functioning. Hillsdale, NJ: Lawrence Erlbaum, 1979

Kearsley R: Cognitive assessment of the handicapped infant: The need for an alternative approach. Am J Orthopsychiat 51(1): 43–53, 1981

Lewis M (ed): *Origins of Intelligence: Infancy and Early Childhood*. New York: Plenum Publishing, 1976

Lewis M, McGurk H: Evaluation of infant intelligence. Science 178: 1174–1177, 1972

McCall R: New directions in psychological assessment of infants. Proc Roy Soc Med 64: 465–467, 1971

McCall R, Appelbaum M, Hogarty P: Developmental changes in mental performance. Monographs Soc Res Child Devel 38(3): Serial No. 150, 1973

Miranda S, Fantz R: Recognition memory of Down's syndrome and normal infants. Child Devel 45: 651–660, 1974

Mosey A, Foley G, McCrae M, Thomas E: *Attachment-separation-individuation observation scale.* Unpublished manuscript, Pennsylvania Department of Education, 1980

Mowder B: Legislative mandates: Implications for changes in school psychology training programs. Prof Psychol 5: 681–686, 1979

Osofsky J (ed): *The Handbook of Infant Development*. New York: John Wiley & Sons, 1979

Parmelee A, Werner W, Schulz H: Infant sleep patterns from birth to 16 weeks of age. J Pediat 65: 576–582, 1964

Prechtl H: The behavioral states of the newborn infant (a review). Brain Res 76: 185–212, 1974

Richards T, Nelson V: Abilities of infants during the first eighteen months. J Gen Psychol 8: 20–25, 1939

Sattler J: *Assessment of Children's Intelligence*. Philadelphia: WB Saunders, 1974

Simeonson J, Huntington G, Parse S: Expanding the developmental assessment of young handicapped children. In Gallagher J (ed): *New Directions for Exceptional Children,* vol 3. New York: Josey-Bass, 1980

Simmon A, Bass L: Toward a validation of infant testing. Am J Orthopsychiat 26: 340–345, 1956

Sostek S, Anders: Effects of varying laboratory conditions on behavioral state organization in two- and eight-week-old infants. Child Devel 46: 871–878, 1975

Stevenson M, Lamb M: Effects of infant sociability and the caretaking environment on infant cognitive performance. Child Devel 50: 340–349, 1979

Stone L, Smith H, Murphy L (eds): *The Competent Infant*. New York: Basic Books, 1973

Stott L, Ball R: Infant and preschool mental tests: Review and evaluation. Monographs Soc. Res Child Devel 30: Serial No. 101, 1965

Thomas A, Chess S, Birch H: *Temperament and Behavior Disorders in Children*. New York: New York University Press, 1968

Thomas A, Chess S: *Temperament and Development*. New York: Brunner/Mazel, 1977

Ulrey G: The challenge of providing psychological services for young handicapped children. Prof Psychol, 12(4): 483–491, 1981

Vandeveer B, Schweid E: Infant assessment: Stability of mental functioning in young retarded children. Am J Ment Defic 79: 1–4, 1974

Wilson R: Early mental development. Science 175: 914–917, 1972

Zelazo P: From reflexive to instrumental behavior. In Lipstitt L (ed): *Developmental Psychobiology: The Significance of Infancy*. Hillsdale, NJ: Lawrence Erlbaum, 1976

Zelazo P: Reactivity to perceptual-cognitive events: Application for infant assessment. In Kearsley RB, Sigel I (eds): *Infants at Risk: The Assessment of Cognitive Functioning*. Hillsdale, NJ: Lawrence Erlbaum, 1979, pp 49–83

Zelazo P: An information processing approach to infant cognitive assessment. In Lewis M, Taft L (eds): *Developmental Disabilities: Theory, Assessment, and Intervention*. Jamaica, NY: SP Medical and Scientific Books, 1981

Chapter 3

INFLUENCES OF PRESCHOOLERS' BEHAVIOR ON ASSESSMENT

By

GORDON ULREY

The preschool child (2 to 6 years) is not just a little school-age child. The psychologic assessment of the preschooler must take into consideration the important psychological differences in thinking, motivation, and experiences between preschool children and those who are of school age. Testing procedures and knowledge of school-age children do not necessarily extrapolate downward when applied to preschoolers. Cognitive and emotional factors influence the behavior of the preschool child in important ways that affect testing and interpretations of results.

Many behaviors that occur during the preschool period would indicate a learning deficit or psychopathology if observed in a school-age child (6 to 12 years), but they are normal and expected for the younger child. A frequently observed example is the reversal of letters and numbers; while reversals correlate with specific learning disabilities in children over the age of 7 or so, such reversals are common with children under 6 years of age.

There is also a wide range of maturation of the neurologic functions and significant differences between the rate at which preschool-age boys and girls acquire early skills (Chall and Mirsky, 1978). There are a host of developmental changes occurring during the transition from infancy to school age that alter the child's behavior, such as emerging expressive language skills and increasing emotional autonomy from parents. Examiners' appreciation of the child's perception and understanding of events has been enhanced by Piaget's model of cognitive development. Piagetian

theory and recent studies of preschool cognition provide a framework for understanding the cognitive and behavioral differences between preschoolers and school-age children. This chapter will cover the impact of emerging developmental skills on test performance in the areas of cognitive functioning, behavioral controls, language skills, and transitional phases of growth. A model for assessing and interpreting the preschool child's behavior will be described, some specific strategies for eliciting optimal test performance will be discussed, and examples of test interpretations and related issues will be given.

PREOPERATIONAL THINKING

The preschool child's thinking and reasoning are in transition from the sensorimotor (nonverbal) level to the level at which there is use of mental symbols and language. During infancy, sensorimotor intelligence is expressed by adaptive actions in the form of interactions with objects. Between the ages of 2 and 6, the child learns to internalize this knowledge by way of symbolic representations. However, the preschool-age child's conceptual understanding of the world is incomplete, and the child's thinking is different than the school-age child's.

Piaget (1951) and Piaget and Inhelder (1969) have described the preschool child's thinking as "preoperational." The Piagetian model provides a conceptual framework for understanding the child's behavior relative to his or her current level of understanding events in the environment. The child's thinking is described as preoperational because of the child's restricted, one-dimensional point of view, which is limited in focus on a single action or direction of an operation. An action or operation is understood in terms of how it moves or changes without an appreciation of the reciprocal effect of the reverse of the action. For example, if the examiner shows a preschool child two identical pieces of clay and then elongates one, the child will often state that one is now "bigger" because it is longer; in other words, the child will focus on length, but will not account for width. The child is demonstrating preoperational thought.

There are numerous implications for how a preschooler's behavior might differ from that of the school-age child, who is often functioning at the concrete operational level (in which the actions or operations are understood as reversible or reciprocal). The difference can be seen in comparing the understanding of causality between preschoolers and school-age children. If both groups are asked a question such as, "Why do clouds move?" the preschoolers might say, "Because of the sun," while the school-age children might say, "Because of the wind." The preschooler's thinking is based on associations lacking an appreciation of causal relations that have reciprocal effects. The fact that the sun is seen when clouds are seen is a sufficient preoperational explanation of the event. In contrast, concrete operational thought shows appreciation of a relationship between wind and clouds. Several ways that the preschool child's behavior will differ during testing are discussed below.

In Piaget's theory, the preschooler's thinking is "egocentric" in that only one viewpoint is taken or expressed. This results in minimal regard for ensuring that a listener understands an explanation. The child is unable to assume the role of another person or to recognize other viewpoints. In contrast, the school-age child is generally more concerned about giving the "correct" answer and monitoring feedback that indicates the answer was understood. The preschool child generally has not developed a concern for the listener's understanding, feels no need to justify his or her reasons, and fails to see a contradiction in the logic used. As a result, a major problem during assessment is the young child's minimal concern for ensuring that the examiner understands an explanation or solution to a task. The child will respond to the approval or disapproval of the examiner, but may not perceive the examiner's concern about the incomplete or incorrect aspect of a test response.

Gelman (1978) suggests that young children may monitor test feedback poorly because they have not "learned the rules." However, very young children do appear to be capable of some appreciation of another's perspective when tasks are adequately structured. In addition, the child can appreciate adult responses of pleasure or displeasure but may not associate them with performance. An example of not having "learned the rules" is the lack of response by the preschool child to a social reinforcement (smiling or "good stacking"); the preschool-age child who does not continue an activity or work harder has not yet learned to be "reinforced" by pleasing an adult by the activity. One cannot assume that a social reinforcer was effective because of differences in a child's previous experiences. The involvement with a task at a level he or she can understand may be more reinforcing than a general social reinforcer. In contrast, the child may continue a task not understood simply because of the interaction with the examiner, with little regard for mastery of the task. In either case, this child may only be responding to one dimension of the test procedure.

Preoperational thought, when compared with the thinking of older children, can give the impression of loosely associated thinking and distorted logic. It is the lack of balance in the reasoning (only considering one aspect of an operation) that characterizes preoperational thinking. Because of this, the clinician must be aware of the age appropriateness of the child's reasoning. To be able to evaluate a deficit in the child's cognitive skills, the clinician must carefully observe the child's responses and inferred reasoning during problem-solving; the psychologist cannot simply focus on the right or wrong answers. Instead, the challenge for the examiner is to determine why the child failed the task and at what level it was understood.

Piaget has described in some detail the child's development of preoperational concepts of classification, numbers, and spatial and temporal relations. In addition, test items on the Stanford-Binet or other preschool cognitive measures can help reveal a child's levels of understanding and knowledge of how skills are developing. For example, during assessment of a child's counting skills and skills related to number concepts (such as those described by Gelman and Tucker, 1975), the clinician could follow-up a failure on a "number concept" item with other levels of tasks (see Chapter 5 for more detail).

BEHAVIORAL CONTROLS

The child's nonverbal behavior also indicates the limited dimension and egocentricism of preoperational thinking. Two- to 3-year-old children often seek to test behavioral limits and may refuse items or may be easily distracted by items of more intrinsic interest. In part, this is related to the child's emerging sense of self as an individual—to a struggle for autonomy. Indeed, the 2-year-old is infamous for resistance and independence during testing. The behavior reflects the child's unwillingness or "inability" to assume the perspective or point of view of the examiner: this limited viewpoint indicates preoperational thinking, the child's attempts to define boundaries between him- or herself and the environment, and appropriate development of behavioral controls. Although resistance and struggle make a reliable cognitive assessment difficult, they provide important information about the child's emotional development and should be noted as normal behavior reflecting the child's level of emotional functioning. For example, a 5- or 6-year old who requires frequent limit setting and is manipulative to avoid the test procedures may indicate the emotional maturity of a 2- to 3-year-old child. Techniques for eliciting a reliable assessment of an oppositional child will be discussed later in this chapter.

At the 3- to 6-year level, the child's behavior becomes less of a struggle with limits, and elaborate strategies evolve to obtain desired outcomes (reinforcement). With increased language and extensive imitative behaviors (identification with parent figures), the child uses "manipulation" or appeal to adults to gain some control. The coyness of the 3- to 6-year level is well known and appears to ensure adult attention and approval. The child's imitation skills allow for "adultlike" behaviors that lack the operational understanding of the adult. The child begins to model the parent's verbal and nonverbal behaviors with less appreciation of how it is perceived by others. During testing, this may be seen in the form of various social behaviors, such as more eye contact, smiling, physical closeness, or verbal responses. These behaviors are ways of getting attention but generally lack a concern about being correct or appropriate; in this sense they are cognitively egocentric.

The engaging and manipulative behavior of the 3- to 6-year-old is seen as emotionally appropriate. The major problem for the examiner is that these behaviors may not be contingent on task performance behaviors. The examiner will often have to structure and restructure tasks to elicit the optimal attending to a task from the child. For example, the child may not state an obvious verbal answer or complete a task because he or she is not attending to the cue that this is a valued response. This is again part of not having "learned the rules" for test and school behavior. More flexibility and creativity are required to sort out what the child knows. The clinician simply cannot assume that the child values answering specific test items correctly just because a correct answer was expected. The use of a conceptual framework is crucial for determining a child's level of understanding of the cognitive competency being assessed.

LANGUAGE DEVELOPMENT

Because most major language or communication skills emerge during the preschool period, knowledge of normal language development is important for the clinician who would evaluate young children. There are several language behaviors that may be mistaken for a language disability. One example of a general developmental consideration that should be kept in mind is the fact that some dysfluency (stuttering) is expected as the child learns new words or is constructing more complex sentences. While dysfluency is normal at 2 to 3 years of age, it may also occur normally when previously undeveloped speech is emerging at 4 or 5 years; this may be misinterpreted as a sign of a stuttering deficit. As a general rule, the dysfluency should be considered in the context of the child's developing language. A second developmental consideration is that there are frequently some expected omissions in articulation, such as leaving off the first syllable of a word such as "ut" for "but," or "uice" for "juice."

The psychologist should also be aware of differences between spontaneous speech and the child's conceptual understanding. A child may apparently have age-appropriate social speech (such as, "Hello, how are you today?" and so on), but can still have below age level conceptual understanding of words (such as defining words or explaining events). In short, the young child's verbal behaviors must be understood in terms of normal language and the child's own development to avoid misinterpretation of test observations and data. The use of a language sample from a spontaneous play situation is useful for comparing formal test responses with informal speech.

Another example, which is a less clear distinction, is that when eye contact is poor, the child may be seen as having an emotional problem. Instead, this method of interaction may be partly secondary to confusion with sounds (auditory processing) and/or poor social learning; it is not necessarily an indicator of serious emotional concerns. This is somewhat unique to the preschool period, because language and social skills are emerging for the first time and depend on interaction between experiences and maturation. The clinician who assesses a child with poor eye contact should always ascertain what opportunities for learning standard English the child has had.

In addition, the psychologist must appreciate the level of difficulty of verbal commands used during testing. Many items that attempt to measure concepts such as "alike" or "similar" may be failed because of complex verbal instructions. A number concept may be failed because of complex verbal instructions. A number concept may be failed because the child has to remember two or three steps in a sequence. Knowledge of language level acquisition is invaluable for interpretation of performance on tasks that require verbal receptive and/or expressive skills. The indications of language pathology that may influence testing are discussed in Chapter 12.

RAPID GROWTH AND TRANSITIONS

The preschool period is marked by many transitions and developmental changes. Behavior changes correspond to the transition from sensorimotor skills to preoperational skills to concrete operations. An early review by White (1965) stressed all the important behavior changes that occur in the 5- to 7-year age range. Transitions occur in many areas, including perception, language lateralization, and so on. The psychologist must be aware of the important differences in each individual child and must attempt to determine what stage or transition an individual child is demonstrating. One cannot assume a child is functioning at the preoperational level simply because she or he is between 2 and 6 years of age. A child may demonstrate some behaviors reflecting one level while other behaviors indicate a higher or lower level. The task for the clinician is to determine the child's profile of skills based on previous experiences and level of maturation.

The situational variability of the preschool child's behavior and the individual rate of rapid, uneven growth make it difficult to make an accurate appraisal of what the child "generally" does. Murphy (1956) describes the young child as changing significantly from "hour to hour." Preschool test performance is frequently criticized as being inconsistent and leading to poor test reliability (Flapan and Neubauer, 1970; Keogh, 1970), a factor that calls for cautious use of the scales. An important clinical example is Silverman's (1971) finding of significant differences in preschoolers' dysfluency depending on whether the children were seen in the home, school, or clinical setting. The psychologist must determine what impact the ecology of the assessment may have made on the child. Cross-checking observed behaviors against behaviors reported by teachers and parents is necessary to avoid errors. One problem is that the psychologist cannot simply ask the young child to perform; an examiner must instead establish rapport and elicit responses and cooperation to obtain an optimal performance from the child. In spite of those difficulties, trained clinicians using formal preschool tests can achieve reliability in the .80s and .90s on most frequently used preschool scales (Terman and Merrill, 1972; McCarthy, 1972).

The many psychological changes in preschool children are difficult to assess because of wide differences in the rate of maturation and/or experiences of the child. School-age children begin to have more comparable experiences after one or two years of school opportunities. The range of opportunities available to preschoolers who may or may not have attended programs is a signficant factor, because test items require various drawing, language, and perceptual motor skills that are greatly influenced by experiences. The psychologist should always consider what previous exposure a child has had to tasks presented on a test. How does the child respond to novel test items? A valuable way to assess the child's understanding of a new task is to teach the child the ones that have been failed. (The actual formal test items should not be used, since this would decrease the usefulness and validity of the item for testing in the near future.) Does the child learn the task quickly? How much structure is required? Does the child appear to be experiencing the materials for the first time? (While doing a block task, the examiner should ask the parents about use of blocks at home.)

A MODEL FOR ASSESSING PRESCHOOL-AGE CHILDREN

There are many factors that can contribute to a preschooler's test performance. The situations that have elicited behavior must be carefully observed and the examiner must remember that many deficits and developmental delays may be secondary to environmental and psychological factors other than the intelligence of the child. The psychologist must be able to determine a child's relative strengths and weaknesses in a developmental and environmental context to obtain a reliable and valid assessment of the child. A careful consideration of five general areas is necessary to interpret assessment results. These are: (1) behavioral controls, (2) level of cognitive skills, (3) integration of skills, (4) interpersonal skills, and (5) environmental supports.

The first step for assessment is to determine what the specific problem is as seen by the referring person. Information will be needed in each of the five areas to guide judgments about the child's problem and to plan treatment. For example, failure in a preschool child may result from a problem in any of the five areas or a combination of each. Each of the five areas will be described below.

1. BEHAVIORAL CONTROLS

These include the child's self-control and selective attending skills, as well as the child's need for structure in the environment and tolerance of frustration or failure. To make a judgment about controls, the examiner must observe or have information about the child in a variety of settings and must have the knowledge of age-appropriate expectations for young children. In other words, the psychologist must know what the child's behavioral controls are relative to his or her age level and experiences. Also, from teacher or parental reports, the examiner must know if the child is currently on any medications that may influence behavior (such as treatment for seizures or a cold).

2. LEVEL OF COGNITIVE SKILLS

A formal measurement of the child's current general cognitive skills based on appropriate norms for his or her age group may be needed. The child who functions with no learning problems will not need an intelligence test, although a screening test may be useful. When intelligence data are desired they can be obtained by using a general developmental assessment, such as the Wechsler Preschool and Primary Scale of Intelligence (WPPSI), McCarthy, or the Stanford-Binet Intelligence Test (see Appendix A). Test performance allows the psychologist to determine if the child shows a general developmental delay when considering a specific learning deficit.

3. INTEGRATION OF SKILLS

The various modalities that affect learning processes should be considered. The examiner must consider the child's capacity for sensory sensation (for example, visual or auditory acuity), perception, memory, and integration of modalities (for example, visual and motor skills used together). The relative skills in language and nonverbal skills should also be considered; for example, does the child have any specific learning deficits relative to his or her general cognitive skills? What are the child's strengths and weaknesses, and what learning style is evidenced?

4. INTERPERSONAL SKILLS

The child's relative level of adaptive behavior should be considered (for example, toilet training or spontaneous play). Observations of a child's play and interactions with the examiner are useful to assess emotional maturity. How well does the child relate to others? Does the child show age-appropriate emotional and adaptive behaviors? These data are obtained by observing the child's play and/or by using an adaptive behavior rating scale (see Appendix A). Parental and (when available) nursery or preschool reports are also essential to assess social maturity.

5. ENVIRONMENTAL SUPPORTS

Knowledge of the child's environment is essential for the psychologist making an assessment of a young child. Questions to be answered include how the child interacts with parents, and how stable the primary care providers are. Awareness of the relationship between cultural differences and opportunities for learning is an important part of interpreting a psychological assessment. What opportunities has this child had relative to the children he or she is compared with on the test norms and in the school situation (current or future)? How much structure and stimulation does the home provide? Information can be obtained by observing parent-child interactions and by parent interviews (in the home when possible).

APPLICATION OF THE MODEL

The five categories listed above must always be considered if the psychologist is to interpret psychological testing appropriately to determine the extent of developmental and learning deficits. Although the dangers of using test results without considering environmental, cultural, and physical differences are well known, the improper identification of young children can be even more damaging than the improper identification of older children. Thus, accurate and nondiscriminatory assessment is a primary concern to those working with young handicapped children.

To illustrate how knowledge of all the previous areas can be helpful, several examples will be briefly discussed. When a child has difficulty attending and monitoring his or her activity level, the child's emotional maturity and the amount of structure provided by the family will make a significant difference. Often a chaotic family situation will exacerbate children with poor control and delay emotional development. The child who shows general delays may have a home environment that artificially depresses performance because it offers little stimulation or is culturally different. A supportive middle-class family environment will affect the implications for assessment findings and treatment of a child who is developmentally delayed. In short, the child's environment must be considered for early intervention to have an optimal impact.

Cognitive and emotional factors are also important, for the child with generally high-level cognitive skills will have more resources to compensate for poor behavioral controls or specific learning deficits (such as poor visual-motor integration). A bright child with poor controls and emotional immaturity will need more structure and support than a child who is more emotionally mature. Each area must be carefully assessed and made part of the planning to ensure an appropriate educational intervention.

In cases of more severe handicaps, the psychologist should be aware of gross indications of deficits in a child's neurologic functioning. The implications for motor deficits and neurologic dysfunction are covered in Chapters 11 and 12. These delays should always be evaluated by a physician to ensure proper management of the disorder. Although the presence of known neuromotor problems does not mean a developmental or learning disability will exist, there is an increased probability that it will. Therefore, the child should always have psychological testing, and the psychologist must consider the limitations inherent in test items that depend on sensorimotor skills.

ELICITING TEST PERFORMANCE

The psychologist must always strive toward eliciting an optimal performance from the child. Because of differences in development and behavior, the preschool child presents some unique assessment challenges. The following are some suggested considerations and strategies for eliciting test performance.

REACTIONS TO FAILURE

Because preschoolers have not "learned the rules," they show a wide range of differences in attending and perseverance in the face of failure. For example, significant differences in test performances occur when comparing children from low socioeconomic and minority families to Anglo children from middle-class families. Children from low socioeconomic levels do better when failures and successes are alternated, compared with when there is a series of failures (Zigler and Butterfield, 1968). Presumably, middle-class families are more task- or achievement-oriented and reinforce the child for perseverance when failure occurs. To avoid obtaining a poor performance caused primarily by frustration resulting from failure, earlier test items (where success is more probable) should be frequently mixed with more difficult items. This can be done, for example, with Binet items at different age levels. Or if a child experiences several failures, it is helpful to have him or her demonstrate something successful, such as saying the alphabet or counting. The point is that completion of a task is often more reinforcing for the young child than social praise. Thus, observations and descriptions of reactions to failure are an important part of an assessment.

OVERACTIVITY AND DISTRACTIBILITY

A referral question commonly heard by psychologists evaluating young children is whether the child is "hyperactive." This often misused term is derived from a medical diagnosis of "hyperkinesis" or "selective attention disorder." This diagnosis suggests a disturbance of the neurologic arousal system, which is uncommon (Schmitt, 1975).

It is important to differentiate between children who can attend well on familiar structured tasks and those who are unable on almost all activities to attend adequately. The psychologist should be aware that preschoolers fail many tasks because they have not learned the set for answering test questions, or for performing tabletop tasks. In addition, the examiner must sort out the impact of normal stimulus overload (or task difficulty level) when observing distractible behaviors. A common example is for a child to attend well when faced with tasks he or she can successfully do, but for that same child to be highly distractible when presented with tasks that involve a deficit skill area or multiple stimuli. Another example is a child with delayed language skills who becomes visibly more fidgety and distractible when asked verbal comprehension questions but then attends well to completing a difficult puzzle. A diagnosis of hyperactivity should only be made in the context of a complete social and physical history (in conjunction with a medical examination), as well as after observation of behavior in settings with different degrees of structure. Visits to the home and classroom are very informative to determine the child's response to structure. For a more comprehensive discussion of hyperactivity see Ross (1974) or Saber and Allen (1976).

Testing a highly distractible child is most likely to be successful in a room that has minimal stimuli competing for the child's attention. The examiner should choose items that have some intrinsic interest for the child and should provide frequent reinforcement. Often, nonverbal items, such as peg boards, form boards, or puzzles are useful to elicit optimal attending behavior (for example, items from Merrill-Palmer Scales). Reducing the number of auditory or visual steps required in a task may also be helpful. The child's behavior in such a setting should then be compared with performances when more stimuli are present, such as classroom or background noise. Gelman (1978) has found differences in task performance based on reducing the number of stimuli. These differences are important for establishing educational programming.

NEGATIVISM AND OPPOSITIONAL BEHAVIOR

To elicit a cooperative response, the examiner must establish a positive set in which the child and the examiner do things together. This can be accomplished by starting with games, such as playing catch or building a tower together. When the child begins to avoid a difficult task, that task should be stopped. The examiner must then attempt various interactive strategies to get the positive set back. Changes from puzzles to drawings or from structured tasks to free play can be useful. In a Piagetian framework it can be said that the examiner is attempting to find the child's level of understanding, and that intrinsic reinforcers stem from the action with a task. Consideration of external (distractions, and so on) and internal (such as fatigue) factors should be carefully examined. At times, it may be necessary to stop the assessment and resume on a different day or at a different time.

While it may be difficult in school settings to test a child on more than one day, it is better to allow for more than one

testing session to obtain an optimal test performance from any young child. This is true because the young child is less willing or able to suppress other factors that may interfere with testing. Observation of the preschool child on two different days or in different settings improves the reliability of testing and facilitates interpretation of test results.

PERSEVERATION ON TASKS

When a child experiences a success or is enjoying a novel toy, it may become difficult to introduce a new item. This can be avoided by allowing the child to explore the toy, or by introducing different items until the child shows interest in the novel task. The examiner may also see repetition of a formerly successful behavior when the preschool child is presented a more difficult task. For example, if stacking blocks was praised as a correct response early in the test procedure, the child who is asked to build other things with blocks may instead continue stacking them. Such behaviors may indicate a regression resulting from the child's inability to do the task, or may be seen as a manipulation to avoid new tasks. These premises can be tested by setting firm limits, offering reinforcements for different responses, or by alternating more difficult activities with the one which is preferred.

PARENT-CHILD INTERACTION SEQUENCE

A structured interaction with a parent and the child reveals important information both diagnostically and for planning interventions. The examiner should observe an interaction sequence in which the parent presents a task that the child is likely to pass and another that the child is likely to fail.

PROCEDURES FOR PARENT-CHILD INTERACTION

Part 1. Spontaneous Play With a Variety of Options. The examiner provides the parent and child with toys that are appropriate for different developmental levels. The child or parent is instructed simply to select any activity and play in their "usual" manner.

Part 2. Parent Teaches a Task the Child is Able to Do. The examiner asks the parent to perform a task that earlier observations suggest will be easily completed by the child. Tasks that are analogous to test items using peg boards, form boards, or blocks provide tasks that can easily be demonstrated for the parent.

Part 3. Parent Teaches a Task the Child Has Been Unable to Do. The examiner instructs the parent to give the child a difficult task. The parent is to teach the child the task if the first attempt is failed. Activities should be used that are not part of the standardized tests.

Observations should be made of the interactions that occur betweeen the parent and child. When both parents are available it is important to have each parent go through all three parts of the interaction sequences. A standardized observation coding system has been developed for clinical assessment purposes by Ezberg, Robinson, Knickern, and O'Brian (1978). The system is called the Dyadic Parent-Child Interaction Coding System and has been found to have acceptable reliability and validity for children in the age range of 2 to 7 years (Robinson and Ezberg, 1981). The examiner attends to three questions when assessing the interactions: (1) How does the parent structure the activities? (2) How does the parent/child respond to the success of the child? and (3) How does the parent/child respond to the failure of the child?

The behaviors observed are very useful for explaining a child's handicap to a parent or teacher, using examples from the interaction sequence. The examiner must be sensitive to stresses on the parent caused by the expectation of performance and by being observed.

INTERPRETATION OF TEST DATA

Any time a child is being evaluated, the psychologist must consider the context in which the child's development and behavior have occurred. This means taking into account all physical and social history that relates to the child's current difficulties. For example, a child who relates poorly in preschool may be suffering from abuse or neglect rather than from an emotional disturbance. A child who has delayed speech may have a motor handicap that interferes with articulation. The culturally different or disadvantaged child who fails verbal items may not be comprehending the English usage of the words because little or no English is spoken in the home. The model for preschool assessment described above is useful for considering each area of influence on learning.

Preschool assessment must always account for differences in learning opportunities and experiences with test items. The distinction between functional and specific deficits must be considered, since a developmental delay may result from inexperience and should therefore be seen at least in part as functional rather than a specific deficit. In contrast, when two children have had similar experiences, the delayed developmental skills may result from different rates of growth and, in some cases, from specific deficits. This can only be determined by careful consideration of the child's history and by analysis of test behavior. For example, some deprived children will learn new tasks quickly and/or be overstimulated by the presence of multiple novel stimuli. It is often useful for the examiner to attempt to teach the preschool child the first few items that are failed, so that the child's learning skills can be observed.

The interpretation of test data must always take into consideration the similarities between the child tested and the population on which a test was standardized. The usefulness of the results is limited when large differences exist. For example, norms that did not include children from a minority group or lower socioeconomic level may not provide a valid score for a minority child. Since test scores derive their meaning by selecting and discriminating across a given population, the examiner must be familiar with the development of the test being used (see Appendix A). One major use of a Piagetian framework for clinical assessment is as a criterion-referenced measure that focuses on the child's level of functioning within a cognitive competency instead of emphasizing the age-level appropriateness of the task.

The potential for misuse of tests for preschool children is even greater than for older children for several reasons. The first, as has been mentioned, involves the variability in test performance, which may compromise the reliability and validity of the test results. Other reasons include the potential for long-term negative consequences of labeling (Hobbs, 1975), and overdiagnosing children with mild handicaps. While there is strong agreement that the instruments have serious inadequacies, rather than not using them, the author would appeal for their cautious and careful use. The advantages of and necessities for identification of a young child's handicaps are essential for obtaining services and ensuring his or her chances for optimal development.

SUMMARY

Some of the factors a psychologist should consider when evaluating a preschool-age child were discussed. It has been emphasized that behaviors that occur normally during the preschool period may suggest pathology when observed in older children. A Piagetian model was discussed for conceptualizing how the preschooler's behavior can influence test outcomes. The impact of preoperational thought, behavioral controls, and language skills were described. Because the preschool child has not learned many of the "rules" for testing, obtaining a reliable and valid assessment for this age group is more challenging. Some specific strategies for obtaining assessment data were described and some of the special issues involved in preschool assessments were discussed.

REFERENCES

Chall J, Mirsky A (eds): *Education and the Brain.* Chicago: University of Chicago Press, 1978

Ezberg S, Robinson E, Knickern J, O'Brian P: *Dyadic parent-child interaction coding system: A manual* (rev ed). Unpublished manuscript, 1978. (Available from S. Ezberg, Department of Medical Psychology, University of Oregon Health Sciences Center, Portland, OR 97201)

Flapan D, Neubauer P: Issues in assessing development. Acad Child Psychiat 9: 669–687, 1970

Gelman R: Cognitive development. In Rosenwig MR, Porter LW (eds): Ann Rev Psychol 29: 48–64, 1978

Gelman R, Tucker MF: Further investigation of the young child's conception of number. Child Devel 46: 167–175, 1975

Hobbs N: *The Futures of Children.* San Francisco: Josey-Bass, 1975

Keogh B (ed): Early identification of children with potential learning problems. Spec Ed 4: 307–363, 1970

McCarthy D: *Manual for the McCarthy Scales of Children's Abilities.* New York: The Psychological Corp, 1972

Murphy L: *Personality in Young Children.* New York: Basic Books, 1956

Piaget J: *Judgment and Reasoning in the Child.* London: Routledge & Kegan Park, 1951

Piaget J, Inhelder B: *The Psychology of the Child.* New York: Basic Books, 1969

Robinson E, Ezberg S: The dyadic parent-child interaction coding system: Standardization and validation. Clin Consult Psychol 49(2): 245–250, 1981

Ross A: *Psychological Disorders of Children.* New York: McGraw-Hill, 1974

Saber D, Allen R: *Hyperactive children: Diagnosis and Management.* Baltimore: University Park Press, 1976

Schmitt B: The minimal brain dysfunction myth. Am J Dis Child 129: 1313–1318, 1975

Silverman E: Situational variability of preschoolers dysfluency preliminary study. Percep Motor Devel 33: 4021–4022, 1971

Terman L, Merrill M: *Stanford-Binet Intelligence Scale.* Boston: Houghton-Mifflin, 1972

White SH: Evidence for hierarchical arrangement of learning processes. In Lipsitt L, Spiker C (eds): *Advances in Child Development and Behavior.* New York: Academic Press, 1965, pp 187–220

Zigler E, Butterfield E: Motivational aspects of changes in IQ test performance and culturally deprived nursery schoolchildren. Child Devel 39: 1–14, 1968

Chapter 4

ASSESSMENT OF COGNITIVE DEVELOPMENT DURING INFANCY

By

GORDON ULREY

Conventional psychological tests for infants (for example, Bayley, 1969; Cattell, 1940), measure the skills expected of children at various age levels. The tests are not based on a unifying theory of development that accounts for possible relationships among the items. For example, at about 9 months of age, infants are expected to "finger the holes in a pegboard" and "pick up a cup, secure cube" (Bayley Scales of Infant Development). What it means when a child passes one item but not the other is not made clear; they are both simply skills that emerge at about this time in a child's life and have been selected as test items based on norms of development. While it may be useful for the clinician to know when these skills emerge, it would be more useful for the examiner to know how the skills relate to the overall psychological development of the child.

Psychologists evaluating infants are often criticized for only confirming that a child is developmentally delayed, and for not helping the parents and/or teachers plan interventions. Evaluations that do not provide information about what action to take may only cause problems because of the hazards of labeling the child and stressing the parents. Frequent questions about infants are, "What toys or activities are appropriate?" and, "What new skills should be encouraged?" Traditional norm-referenced tests offer little specific information for treatment, because the items are not based on a conceptual model.

While these scales provide important diagnostic information and help determine strenghts and weaknesses in a child's cog-

nitive functioning, they do not provide an adequate framework for program planning. In contrast, sensorimotor scales based on Piagetian theory provide supplementary clinical procedures that facilitate both assessment and treatment plans.

This chapter focuses on the usefulness of a Piagetian conceptual framework for assessing the sensorimotor skills of infants. First, it will briefly compare different approaches to assessing cognitive skills in infants. Then it will cover the need to expand testing procedures for handicapped infants. To illustrate in some depth the application of a Piagetian scale to infant testing, specific examples from the Infant Psychological Development Scale (IPDS) developed by Uzgiris and Hunt (1975) will be presented. In addition, it will describe the six domains of cognitive competencies from the IPDS; several factors involved in measuring sensorimotor skills; the effects of cognitive competencies on item performance; and some clinical uses of sensorimotor assessment. A set of treatment activities based on test performance will be discussed, as will some of the advantages and disadvantages of sensorimotor scales.

COGNITIVE TESTS FOR INFANTS

There are three significantly different methodologic and theoretic approaches to cognitive assessment during infancy. Each procedure has advantages and disadvantages which clinicians should be aware of when planning an infant assessment. Why the assessment is being done will be the

35

major factor influencing which procedures are used. The three different approaches include the following: (1) "traditional" tests; (2) "Piagetian" criterion-referenced tests; and (3) perceptual-cognitive processing tests. The norm-referenced tests are by far the most widely used infant tests, while the second and third approaches are favored by researchers; all three types have important implications for assessing handicapped infants and planning interventions. The uses of each approach will be discussed, with emphasis on the applications to assessing infant intelligence. The clinical uses of traditional infant tests were covered in depth in Chapter 2.

NORM-REFERENCED TESTS

The traditional scales of infant assessment were developed by Gesell and Amatruda (1940), Cattell (1940), and Bayley (1969). Gesell and Amaruda were physicians and were primarily concerned about measuring the overall developmental status of the child. Cattell and Bayley were attempting to measure infant intelligence and demonstrate which infant behavior will predict later intelligence. Comprehensive discussions of the history and development of infant tests have been reported by Brookes and Weinraub (1976), and by Yang (1979). Norm-referenced testing is based on test items that have been found to select and discriminate behaviors at different age levels. Items appear on the conventional infant tests because they have been found to be related to specific age levels or age ranges. Behaviors measured on infant tests are assumed to reflect a normal and predictable sequence of neuromotor development. There is substantial evidence that traditional infant tests are useful for discriminating handicapped and nonhandicapped infants, but they do not predict later intelligence of nonhandicapped children. As such, the tests serve a valuable clinical purpose with handicapped infants when used by trained examiners who take certain precautions (described in Chapter 2 of this volume).

As has been mentioned earlier, norm-referenced tests are not based on a unified theory of intelligence. What do the tests measure? Factor analytic studies have identified several clusters of behavior measured by the Bayley Scales. A review by Yarrow and Pederson (1976) has examined data from earlier studies (Kohen-Ras, 1967; McCall, Hogarty, and Hurlburt, 1972). The authors have identified eight clusters of behavior measured on the Bayley mental and motor scales based on factor loading and assumptions about underlying skills required to perform a task. The eight factors are as follows: (1) goal directedness, (2) visually directed reaching and grasping, (3) secondary circular reactions, (4) object performanence, (5) gross motor, (6) fine motor, (7) social responsiveness, and (8) vocalization and language. Yarrow and Pederson found considerable overlap between motivation and skill components when tasks were analyzed. The high level of interdependence between cognitive and motivation functions requires the clinical judgments of trained examiners if errors on infant testing are to be avoided. These findings also point to the need for more tests items that can separate cognitive and motivation functions to obtain a more "pure" measure of cognitive skills.

The examiner must keep in mind that the traditional infant tests are not direct measurements of cognitive skills; in fact, a child's neuromotor status does not always correlate with later cognitive functioning. The clinician must be aware of what the tests measure to avoid serious misuse of infant tests results. The high level of dependence on both motor behaviors and cooperative behavior greatly increases the risk of invalid assessments of handicapped children (Hunt, 1976; McCall, 1971).

CRITERION-REFERENCED SCALES

The major criterion-referenced tests for infants were developed by Casati and Lezine (1968), Escalona and Corman (1969), and Uzgiris and Hunt (1975). All of these scales are based on a Piagetian conceptual model of sensorimotor intelligence. As such, they are based on sequences of sensorimotor skills that emerge, with more complex cognitive behaviors succeeding from simpler ones. The skills are not attached to an age level and no composite score is obtained. The behaviors measured are all part of some hierarchical sequence that describes the child's current sensorimotor skills within a competency (such as imitation skills). The usefulness of these measures derives from the relationship of items and the conceptual model of sensorimotor intelligence.

Piaget has described (Piaget, 1952; Piaget and Inhelder, 1969) a comprehensive model of the development of sensorimotor intelligence during infancy. It is useful because it provides a conceptual basis for understanding emerging sensorimotor skills. In this model, infants are seen as progressing through levels or stages of sensorimotor organizations; in other words, the child progresses from a simple reflexive level to a more coherent organization of sensorimotor actions. The child's basic motor and perceptual coordinations reflect an increasingly elaborate adaptation to the environment. Such adaptive behavior is assumed to indicate the child's understanding of his or her surroundings in various cognitive domains—such as causality, visual memory, and imitative skills. These sensorimotor behaviors are seen as systematically emerging vis-a-vis the interaction of maturation and experience. The child's behavior is viewed as motivated by the child's perception of discrepant events, which leads to explanation and advances learning.

Two important theoretic assumptions of the Piagetian assessment framework are the following:

1. The emergence of cognitive skills is orderly and unfolds as an invariant sequence (ordinal).

2. The sensorimotor behaviors are interrelated, with later skills building upon earlier skills as the basis for developing intellectual skills.

While both assumptions remain to be empirically demonstrated, they are part of a comprehensive theory of child development. An understanding of Piaget's model is essential not only for the interpretation of sensorimotor assessment, but also for the application of sensorimotor scales. Good descriptions and explanations of Piaget's theory can be found in Flavell (1963) and Phillips (1969).

What do the criterion-referenced scales measure? A factor analysis of the IPDS (Silverstein, McLain, Brownlee, and Humbbell, 1976) reveals three clusters of behaviors. These include: (1) causality, (2) object permanence, and (3) imitation. MCall, Eichorn, and Hogarty (1977), using data from the Bayley growth study and item analyses of the California First Year Mental Scales and the California Preschool Scale (precursors of the Bayley Infant Development Scales), found transition points on items at the 2-, 8-, 13-, and 21-month levels, which roughly approximates corresponding Piagetian stages of sensorimotor development. These findings suggest high similarity between what is actually measured on the conventional infant tests and the criterion scales. The measurement of neuromotor related skills seems inseparable from sensorimotor skills. Both approaches have the measurement problem of separating motivation and cognitive functioning; in addition, because of reliance on motor competence for most items, the problem is further complicated when an infant is handicapped. A description of the application of the IPDS will be presented in a later section of this chapter.

PERCEPTUAL-COGNITIVE PROCESSING MODEL

Central to the Piagetian view of sensorimotor intelligence is motivation resulting from the infant's perception of dissonant cognitive events. Dissatisfaction with the validity of infant tests—including the dependence on cooperative behavior and motor competence—has led several developmental psychology researchers to find alternative methods of evaluating cognitive skills of infants (Fagan, 1979; Kearsley, 1979; and Zelazo, 1981). These researchers have begun with the assumption that measuring a child's capacity to process visual and auditory information is a more direct way to measure cognitive skills during infancy. A research paradigm developed by Lewis and Goldberg (1969) has provided a means of systematically observing a child's response to familiar and unfamiliar visual and auditory stimuli without reliance on gross or fine motor skills. In a controlled environment the child's habituating and dishabituating to visual and auditory events can be reliably measured. The child's responses are seen as a function of his or her capacity for memory of events and perceptions of changes—which are assumed to relate to infant intelligence.

Zelazo (1981) argues that tests measuring sensorimotor skills, such as the Bayley, are inadequate and may discriminate against handicapped infants. He argues that the growing data for visual and auditory processing brings into question the appropriateness of extant infant tests, and also challenges the Piagetian view of sensorimotor and/or neuromotor approaches to infant assessment. Zelazo's major argument is that infant tests do not allow the differentiation between a failure on a test item based on a more central cognitive deficit. If, in fact, the perceptual-cognitive approach provides more "pure" cognitive measures, it should be developed further for clinical usage, for there is a clear need to incorporate a wider range of measurements to infant testing. More research is needed to demonstrate how the perceptual-cognitive data relates to later cognitive functioning. It is unlikely that this approach will replace existing tests, but the perceptual-cognitive approach could provide a valuable additional procedure for clinical assessment of infants. Unfortunately, there is no perceptual-cognitive test available for clinical use at this time.

APPLICATION OF A PIAGETIAN SCALE

The Infant Psychological Development Scale (IPDS) was developed to delineate the specific cognitive domains of sensorimotor development (based on Piaget's sensorimotor model). This test delineates the specific cognitive domains of sensorimotor development and is a very useful framework for assessing the progression of sensorimotor cognitive competencies. Uzgiris and Hunt (1975), in developing the IPDS, identified six domains of sensorimotor competency. These will be discussed independently in terms of the sequential progression of behaviors within each domain, and in terms of their interdependence in the larger context of overall sensorimotor development. These six areas

will also be described briefly in terms of their conceptual basis. The examiner's understanding of these concepts can facilitate observations of sensorimotor behavior and can be useful for discussing the child's development and recommending interventions to parents or teachers.

SCALE I—THE DEVELOPMENT OF VISUAL PURSUIT AND THE PERMANENCE OF OBJECTS

This scale describes the sequence (fifteen steps) of the development of visual memory. These include visually following an object, noticing the disappearance of a slowly moving object, finding the object when it is partially covered, finding the object when it is completely covered, and increasingly complex or delayed pursuit.

Conceptually, this first scale examines the child's emerging understanding of the permanence of objects. which has important developmental implications at several levels. It indicates the earliest visual memory and, perhaps, the beginnings of representational thought. The development of visual memory is seen in the child's concerns about separation and attachment, as reflected in his or her reaction to the disappearance of a parent or to the presence of a stranger. The child who is able to follow more complex displacements of an object is showing the important related development of attending skills and the ability to follow a sequence of events.

SCALE II—THE DEVELOPMENT OF MEANS FOR OBTAINING DESIRED ENVIRONMENTAL EVENTS

This scale describes the sequence (twelve steps) of the child's understanding of the physical basis of means-ends relationships. The behaviors include hand watching, visually directed grasping, use of locomotion as a means, the use of "tools," and problem-solving.

The child's level of understanding of means-end relationships is revealed by the extent to which he or she is able to control adaptively some events in the test environment. For example, Scale II measures whether the child is able to use the relationship between two things to achieve an end (that is, pulling a towel to reach a toy that is on it). Successful completion of these items reflects the child's early understanding of causality and indicates that the child knows that one action will elicit another. As more complex causality relationships are understood—such as the need to wind a toy to make it move—the child will begin to show "problem-solving" strategies.

SCALE III—THE DEVELOPMENT OF IMITATION (VOCAL AND GESTURAL)

This scale describes the sequence (ten steps) of the development of imitation. The steps range from simple vocalizing and responding to familiar sound patterns, to imitation of familiar sounds and gestures, to imitation of new words and gestures.

Scale III focuses on both verbal and nonverbal behaviors and provides a way of determining the child's use of imitative behaviors, which is crucial for the learning of many new skills, especially in the language area. An assessment of the child's imitation skills allows for the planning of appropriate methods for reinforcing or stimulating interest in imitative behaviors. This scale appears to be of most value for facilitating the development of communication skills.

SCALE IV—THE DEVELOPMENT OF OPERATIONAL CAUSALITY

This scale (seven steps) measures the child's emerging understanding of his or her effects on the environment. The child's understanding of operational causality is inferred from behaviors performed to affect the environment. A progression is observed around the child's attempts to have an event repeated (for example, ringing a bell again, seeing a colorful display again, or having a wind-up toy repeat an action). At the earliest level, children make "random" movements in their attempts to have actions repeated; they do not appreciate causality. Later, children seek to have an adult do things for them or attempt to discover how to do things for themselves. These behaviors reflect the child's understanding of causality in terms of having his or her own actions affect outcomes.

SCALE V—THE CONSTRUCTION OF OBJECT RELATIONS IN SPACE

This scale describes the sequence (eleven steps) of the child's understanding of spatial relationships. It includes observing two objects alternately, localizing sounds, recognizing the reverse side of objects, understanding the relationship of the container and the contained, using the concept of gravity in play, and so forth. The understanding of objects in relation to space appears to be the earliest developing of visual-spatial skills, which appear to be analogous to skills required later for discrimination and orientation of objects.

SCALE VI—THE DEVELOPMENT OF SCHEMES FOR RELATING TO OBJECTS

This scale (twenty-one steps) describes a hierarchy of ways in which a child manipulates and explores objects. These include such things as holding, dropping, waving, tearing, symbolically using toys, and naming objects.

To measure schemes for relating to objects, the examiner simply observes a number of qualitatively different things the child does with an object. The increase in complexity of sensorimotor behaviors can be observed and explained by noting their progression. When a child plays with a toy, the complexity level of the interaction provides important information about the child's motivation and apparent level of understanding. Scale VI is most useful when used to observe spontaneous play, and when used to indicate regression after higher levels of functioning have been noted.

CLINICAL USES OF A SENSORIMOTOR ASSESSMENT

There is no commercially available test kit for the IPDS; instead, Uzgiris and Hunt (1975) have described the materials and standardized instructions for administering the scales. The items used are generally toys for infants found in the home. It is important to realize that there are no scores based on norms of development with the IPDS, and there is no index of cognitive skills provided which would be analogous to an IQ or DQ. This is because the measurement is based on the child's progress in each sequence of cognitive skills. For example, one infant may be at the sixth step on the Construction of Object Relations in Space Scale, while another may be at the eighth step. While comparisons can be made between two infants' progress on the scale, there are no published norms that would tell the examiner how infants in general are likely to do at a given age level.

The clinician using the IPDS can assess the child's general level of sensorimotor functioning. Piaget identifies six stages of sensorimotor skills: Stage I, use of reflexes; Stage II, primary circular reactions; Stage III, secondary circular reactions, Stage IV, coordination of the secondary schemata; Stage V, tertiary circular reaction; and Stage VI, invention of new means (Piaget, 1952). The examiner must have a general conceptual understanding of each stage. Excellent descriptions are available in Phillips (1969) or Flavell (1963). Knowledge of Piaget's scales make it possible for the psychologist to estimate the child's level of sensorimotor functioning and current skills within each of the cognitive competencies.

The clinical usefulness of the IPDS is in measuring a child's specific sensorimotor skills. From the assessment, an examiner can decribe what the child is able to do within each area of cognitive competency, thus providing a positive focus on what the child can do, as well as an indication of what related skills are expected to emerge. In contrast, traditional infant tests are primarily used to measure a child's possible developmental delay with the focus on deficits; however, traditional scales provide little information about how achievements on current tests relate to the more advanced cognitive skills. While traditional scales serve an important clinical function, the psychologist is often asked for information that is not provided by such scales. In addition to wanting to know the child's developmental level of functioning, parents and educators also want to know what kinds of activities will be the most appropriate and helpful to the child. The IPDS can be useful for providing this information, since each cognitive domain involves skills that are related conceptually

(for example, object permanence or means-end relationships) and occur in predictable sequence. With an understanding of the Piagetian theory of sensorimotor skills and the concepts measured by the IPDS, the psychologist can explain the child's current level of understanding in one of the cognitive competencies and can advise the parents or teachers on the appropriate kinds of play and/or intervention activities for a particular child (Ulrey and Schnell, 1979).

Uzgiris and Hunt (1975) express concern over the ordinality of the IPDS and present evidence demonstrating some variability in the sequences of behavior in each scale. The instrument does, however, provide a useful criterion-referenced measure and acceptable test reliability for clinical use. Several other sensorimotor scales have been developed (Casati and Lezine, 1968; Mehrabian and Williams, 1971), but the IPDS is the most comprehensive and effective test of its kind available to date.

Activities developed from cognitive competencies on the IPDS (Ulrey, Schnell, and Hosking, 1979) are described below to illustrate an application of the model. The examiner can administer a scale from the IPDS to determine the child's level on sensorimotor skills from which conceptually similar activities for teachers or parents can be planned. The IPDS provides a sequential list of skills from which an "infant curriculum" can be planned. Some examples of related activities for the competencies that relate to object permanence (Scale I) and imitation skills (Scale III) are described below to illustrate the application. (See Uzgiris and Hunt, 1975, for a detailed protocol.)

SCALE I—THE DEVELOPMENT OF VISUAL PURSUIT AND THE PERMANENCE OF OBJECTS ACTIVITIES

Visual exploration and obtaining objects by reaching and grasping are important aspects of a child's early learning experience. Initially, young babies will not pursue an object when it is hidden, but eventually they will learn that it still exists even when they cannot see it. This is indicated when they continue to pursue and attempt to obtain a toy that has been totally hidden. While all children learn these behaviors, they vary in the amount of time it takes to master all of the activities; therefore, the suggested activities for this test area follow a general sequence of increasing complexity.

SITUATION 1: "NOTICING THE DISAPPEARANCE OF A SLOWLY MOVING OBJECT"

Activity. Use a colorful object to get the child's attention and then slowly move it behind a screen (a piece of upright cardboard, a pile of books, a towel, and so on) and make it reappear on the right side of the screen. Then reverse the direction of the object. Try to get the child to anticipate where the object will reappear.

Another related activity is to shake a container (cup, pan, or can) with objects in it (blocks, large beads, or a spoon) to interest the child in looking into the container for the noisemaker.

SITUATION 2: "FINDING AN OBJECT THAT IS COMPLETELY COVERED"

Activity. Attract the child's attention with an object and then let it fall noisily to the floor. Try to interest the child in looking for the disappearing object by reacting yourself to the noise and sight of it. Make sure the child sees the object reappear after the parent retrieves it.

Another related activity is to attract the child's attention to an object of interest and then partially cover it with a tissue or cloth (make sure the child is *not* more interested in the cover than the object). Allow the child to recover it; then continue to cover more of the object, working toward the recovery of a completely hidden object.

SITUATION 3: "FINDING AN OBJECT COMPLETELY COVERED IN TWO PLACES ALTERNATELY"

Activity. Attract the child's attention to a toy and then put it into one of two containers. Cover both containers with a cloth for increasing periods of time (that is, 2, 3, 4 seconds, and so on) and then ask the child to find the object.

Another related activity is to alternate hiding an interesting toy in one of three covers. (Make sure that the covers are distinctively different and all are visible at once.) Variations of repeating one cover and then switching to another should be included. Parents can create a variety of activities that involve multiple hidings, including displacing the object from one to another as the child watches.

SCALE III—GESTURAL AND VOCAL STIMULATION ACTIVITIES

An important part of an infant's early learning is the imitation and repetition of what he or she sees and hears the parents doing. Even before a child directly imitates another person, he or she will respond to familiar sounds or gestural movements in some identifiable way. The imitation behaviors progress from general responses to familiar sounds; and eventually to attempted imitation of new words. In general, parents should not wait for the child to make exact imitations but should instead encourage any apparent attempt, regardless of how incomplete it may seem.

Examples of activities the parent can use to encourage imitation are based on performances in situations described on the IPDS Scale III.

VOCAL IMITATION. SITUATION 1: "USE OF VOCALIZATIONS OTHER THAN CRYING"

Activity. Vocalizations other than crying can be encouraged by paying attention to the child when he or she makes them—smiling, talking, looking at the child, and picking the child up. These activities encourage the child to use noises to communicate. Vocalizations such as cooing and babbling can be reinforced by having the parents imitate the child's sounds as they occur or immediately afterward.

SITUATION 2: "RESPONSE TO FAMILIAR SOUND PATTERN"

Activity. Adult sounds and simple words can be encouraged by having the parent repeat sounds or words that are familiar to the child, such as "ma-ma" and "da-da." The reinforcement techniques discussed in Situation 1 should be used when the child imitates the sound.

USES OF SENSORIMOTOR SCALES IN CLINICAL ASSESSMENT

An important clinical use of the IPDS scales is to facilitate the interpretation of an infant's spontaneous play or performance on such traditional tests as the Bayley Scales. Performance on Bayley tasks can be understood in terms of some of the areas of cognitive competence, such as means-end relationship or schema for relating to objects. For example, a child pulling the string to obtain the red ring (Bayley item at the 7-month level) can be understood in terms of Scale II—"Development of Means for Obtaining Desired Environmental Events." While the Bayley item is scored differently depending on "adaptiveness" in obtaining the ring, Scale II of the IPDS could be used to explain what related skills preceded this level and to anticipate emerging skills. In addition, Scale VI: "Development of Scheme of Relating to Objects" can be used to systematize the observation of spontaneous activities (not activities that the examiner is attempting to elicit). For example, when hiding a cube under a cup (Bayley item at the 9-month level), the child may play with the cup and show sliding, dropping, or mouthing behavior that can be understood in terms of Scale VI.

An important skill for clinicians assessing infants is careful observation of the things that infants do spontaneously. Because it is often difficult to elicit an optimal performance from infants, the conceptual framework of the IPDS can be effectively used to enhance the understanding of observed behavior. When infants are given an item that is too difficult, they will tend to do something with it that they understand; in this sense, they "gravitate" to their level of understanding or functioning. The behaviors infants demonstrate in "failing" an item can be important indicators of perseverance, regression in the face of difficulty, application of early

skills, and other psychological phenomena. (There are always a multitude of extraneous variables that may interact and must be kept in mind, such as level of alertness, unfamiliar persons, or physical discomforts.)

A major question to be asked by the clinician testing an infant should be, "Why was this item failed?" This question is best answered by observing what the child actually does instead of the behavior that the examiner was attempting to elicit. Observations of the child's spontaneous play, parental reports, and multiple test sessions will improve the reliability and understanding of the child's behavior and level of skills. Some regression on the sequences of cognitive competences is expected as the child's attention varies or when he or she is stressed. There may also be perseverative activity after success with a novel task which will make it difficult to move the child from one task to another. It is often helpful to allow the child to simply enjoy the activity in order for some habituation to occur.

Another factor the clinician must consider is a child's relative inexperience with the type of task being presented. Teaching the child the items on an analogous activity will help clarify the extent to which the failure was due to unfamiliarity or to the emergence of a new skill. This kind of teaching can also be used to model for the parents the kinds of activities the child is able to do or learn.

The IPDS is not a test that can be used to replace traditional norm-referenced infant tests. It does not allow the clinician to make a judgment about a child's degree of developmental delay, for the range of behaviors measured is not comprehensive enough, in that no gross motor or personal-social items are included. Instead, the IPDS is best used as a supplement to norm-referenced scales, and for planning intervention or stimulation activities in a logical schematic manner.

There are several limitations of the IPDS that call for using the scale with caution. Uzgiris and Hunt (1975) emphasize that ordinality has not been firmly established for each cognitive competency and that more investigations of the scalability are needed. It is also unclear how the competencies interrelate or overlap. As mentioned earlier, a factor analysis of the IPDS has revealed that three similar factors were found (Silverstein, McLain, Brownlee, and Humbell, 1978) for the six subscales. These related to causality, object permanence, and imitation skills. The findings indicate the scales are not totally interrelated and that overlap occurs across the six scales.

Just as is true for conventional infant tests, the use of the PDS is limited by dependence on motor skills and on engaging the cooperation of the infant. What remains unclear clinically is how a child with known sensory or motor handicaps will progress through the competencies; that is, to what extent can a child progress without actual "motoric actions" or hands-on experience with the environment? The studies of perceptual-cognitive processing reviewed earlier suggest that children with motor handicaps may have normal intellectual capacity in spite of severe physical handicaps.

SUMMARY

The usefulness of a Piagetian framework to facilitate observation and interpretation of sensorimotor behavior has been discussed. The IPDS has been described, with some examples of how it can be used clinically. The observation of sensorimotor competencies can enhance the assessment of infants and complement the use of traditional norm-referenced measures. An application of the IPDS for determining a child's level of functioning and for planning activities to enhance the infant's learning has been described, and the clinical uses of a sensorimotor framework to enhance observation of infant behaviors and to facilitate the analysis of test performance has been discussed.

REFERENCES

Bayley N: *Manual for the Bayley Scales of Infant Development.* New York: The Psychological Corporation, 1969

Brookes J, Weinraub M: A history of infant intelligence testing. In Lewis M (ed): *Origins of Intelligence: Infancy and Early Childhood.* New York: Plenum Publishing Co, 1976, pp 19–58

Casati I, Lezine I: *Les Etapes de l'Intelligence Sensori-motrice.* Paris: Les Editions du Centre Psychologie Appliquee, 1968

Cattell P: *The Measurement of Intelligence of Infants and Young Children.* New York: The Psychological Corporation, 1940

Escalona S, Corman H: *Albert Einstein Scales of Sensorimotor Development.* Unpublished manuscript, Albert Einstein College of Medicine, 1969

Fagan S: Infant recognition, memory and later intelligence. Paper presented at the Society for Research in Child Development, San Francisco, March 1979

Flavell J: *The Developmental Psychology of Jean Piaget.* 2nd ed. New York: D. Van Nostrand, Inc., 1963

Gesell A, Amatruda C: *Developmental Diagnosis.* 2nd ed. New York: Hoeber, 1947

Hunt J: Environmental risk in fetal and neonatal life and measured intelligence. In Lewis M (ed): *Origins of Intelligence: Infancy and Early Childhood.* New York: Plenum Publishing Co, 1976, pp 223–258

Kearsley R: Iatrogenic retardation: A syndrome of learned incompetence. In Kearsley R, Sigel I (eds): *Infants at Risk: Assessment of Cognitive Functioning.* Hillsdale, NJ: Erlbaum, 1979, pp 153–180

Kohen-Raz R: Scalogram analysis of some developmental sequences of infant behavior as measured by the Bayley infant scales of mental development. Genet Psychol Monogra 76(3): 1967

Lewis M, Goldberg S: The acquisition and violation of expectancy: An experimental paradigm. Exper Child Psychol 7: 70–80, 1969

Mehrabian A, Williams M: Piagetian measures of cognitive development up to age two. Psycholing Res 1: 113, 1971

McCall R: New directions in the psychological assessment of infants. Roy Soc Med 64: 465–467, 1971

McCall R, Hogarty P, Hurlburt N: Transitions in infancy sensorimotor development and the prediction of childhood IQ. Am Psychol *1972*, 27: 728, 1972

McCall R, Eichorn D, Hogarty P: Transitions in early mental development. Monographs Soc Res Child Devel 42 (Serial No. 171): 1977

Phillips J: *The Origins of Intellect: Piaget's Theory.* New York: W N Freeman, 1969

Piaget J: *The Origins of Intelligence in Children.* New York: International University Press, 1952

Piaget J, Inhelder B: *The Psychology of the Child.* New York: Basic Books, 1969

Silverstein A, McLain R, Brownlee L, Humbell M: Structure of ordinal scales of psychological development in infancy. Educ Psychol Meas 6: 28–38, 1976

Ulrey G, Schnell R: Cognitive stimulation for handicapped infants based on Piagetian scales. In Lubin G, Poulson M, Magary J (eds): *Eighth Annual Piagetian Conference Proceedings.* Los Angeles: University of Southern California Press, 1978

Ulrey G, Schnell R, Hosking K: Cognitive assessment for handicapped infants based on Piagetian scales. In Lubin G, Poulson M, Magary J (eds): *Eighth Annual Piagetian Conference Proceed-*

ings. Los Angeles: University of Southern California Press, 1978

Uzgiris I, Hunt J: *Infant Assessment: Toward Ordinal Scales of Psychological Development.* Champaign, IL: University of Illinois Press, 1975

Yang R: Early infant assessment: An overview. In Osofsky J (ed): *Handbook of Infant Development.* New York: John Wiley & Sons, 1979

Yarrow L, Pederson F: The interplay between cognition and motivation in infancy. In Lewis M (ed): *Origins of Intelligence: Infancy and Early Childhood.* New York: Plenum Publishing Co, 1976, pp 379–401

Zelazo P: An information processing approach to infant cognitive assessment. In Lewis M, Taft L (eds): *Developmental Disabilities: Theory, Assessment and Intervention.* New York: S.P. Medical and Scientific Books, 1981

Chapter 5

ASSESSMENT OF COGNITIVE DEVELOPMENT IN THE PRESCHOOL YEARS

By

SALLY J. ROGERS

Two cognitive acquisitions of toddlers move them out of the sensorimotor stage and into preoperational thought: the ability to represent objects mentally and verbally. Before these abilities develop, there is no evidence of thought as we know it; there is no evidence of mental imagery. Instead, the infant uses the hands and body to "think" via sensorimotor actions on objects. With the advent of representational thought, the toddler is ready to begin thinking in a unique human way, using mental symbols—images, words, and eventually ideas—to understand the people, objects, and relationships in the physical world.

This chapter focuses on characteristics of cognitive processes and cognitive growth during the preoperational period, which includes approximately the years 2 to 6. It will begin with a description of the general cognitive style of preoperational thinkers, and then will look at the development of concepts related to classification, number, spatial relations, seriation, and time. The advantage of conceptualizing preschoolers' cognitive abilities in this mode—as opposed to the more typical, standardized intelligence test mode—is that this approach translates easily into intervention goals and strategies. By organizing the tasks, the psychologist samples a cognitive frame-work; and by looking at tasks in terms of classification, number, spatial relations, and seriation concepts, the psychologist is easily led to recommendations for educational curricula. The latter is es-

pecially important, since one of the major dilemmas for psychologists assessing preschoolers has always been translating the results of traditional intelligence tests into useful recommendations and curriculum suggestions for preschool educators. Now, as many psychologists are seeing more handicapped and delayed preschoolers as a result of Child Find activities, the need for psychological reports that assist with cognitive programming is even more pressing.

GENERAL CHARACTERISTICS OF PREOPERATIONAL THOUGHT

Early thought, as demonstrated by 2- and 3-year-olds, is concrete, involving familiar objects and people and single perceptual relationships in the immediate present. The concept of past, present, and future has not yet developed, and the child talks about present relationships without a sense of continuity (for example, a small child will say, "When I'm big and you are little, Mommy. . . ."). Because the child has not acquired the concept of continuity of relationships over time, the child's thinking is characterized by an emphasis on immediate perceptual relationships. Thus, the young child talks freely about things being bigger or smaller, more or less, round or square, and so on, without the sense that the relationship will always exist. This lack of constancy is easily discovered by the listener who hears a young child talk about being bigger than the parents when the child is grown, or the parents getting smaller as the child gets larger. It also accounts for the child's lack of conservation; the child does not know yet that because two amounts were the same before—and nothing was added or removed—they must still be the same. Because the child lacks a sense of continuity between past and present, when two stimuli appear perceptually different the young child has no rule to help him or her decide that there is any similarity still present. This cognitive bias makes the young child a keen observer of perceptual detail (Flavell, 1963).

In addition to preschoolers' attention to perceptual detail, Piaget has described several other characteristics of preschoolers' thought processes which are often responsible for the amusing things young children say (Piaget, 1929, 1930). One of these is *animism,* the child's tendency to attribute life to inanimate objects and to attribute human qualities to natural phenomena. An example of animism is a 4-year-old's comment when watching a pat of butter slide across a hot pan: "It's alive!" Another such characteristic is *finalism,* which is the child's belief that every object and every occurrence has a purpose or a reason. It's as though, having learned some cause-and-effect sequences, the child overgeneralizes and assumes that everything is part of a cause-and-effect sequence.

A third characteristic that Piaget (1929) discusses is *artificialism,* the idea that everything is man-made. Even young children who have been taught religious concepts and thus say that God made trees, and soon, conceive of God as a person (perhaps some type of super-person), and are still demonstrating their sense of artificialism in such answers.

A fourth quality of preoperational thought is *egocentrism,* the child's tendency to understand all situations only from his or her point of view. The classic Piagetian egocentrism experiment (Piaget and Inhelder, 1956) involved a plaster of paris model of three mountains clustered together. The center mountain was tall and snowcapped, the mountain on the right was rounded and had a cross on it, and the mountain on the left was the smallest and had a small cabin. Children in this experiment stood in front of the model. They watched a small doll "view" the scene from each of the four sides of the model, so that the doll's view of the mountain differed from the child's on three sides. Four photos of the mountains, one taken from each side, were given to the children, who were asked to choose the photo that represented the doll's perception of the scene from each side. The preoperational children were not able to decenter from their own perspectives to imagine what the doll would see. Because the preschooler's perceptual experience was too powerful to be ignored, the child consistently chose that photo that represented his or her own view of the mountains. Understanding this egocentric perspective can help professionals understand many of the social difficulties of young children. They have difficulty understanding the feelings, attitudes, and points of view of other people, and such social amenities as sharing and taking turns make no sense to preschoolers, who don't understand that others want a turn, too.

A final characteristic of preoperational thought is *irreversibility,* which is tied to the preschooler's lack of sense of continuity of past, present, and future. Although preschoolers understand some cause-and-effect sequences, they cannot mentally reverse a sequence to solve a problem, as seen in the difficulty that young children have with the Piagetian water glass experiment. In this experiment, children see two identical glasses with equal amounts of water, and they see water from one glass poured into a differently shaped glass. The question, "Does one glass have more or less water than another, or are they the same?" could be correctly answered if the child could mentally reverse the sequence and mentally pour the water back into the first glass to see that they are the same. But the preschooler has great difficulty reversing the sequence mentally (especially in the presence of powerful perceptual differences in the two), and so answers incorrectly (Piaget and Inhelder, 1941).

Thus far, this chapter has covered the basic characteristics of preschoolers' thoughts—their difficulty in applying past learning appropriately because of overgeneralization or lack of generalization from past to present and future, and their bias for relying on immediate perceptual judgments. As young children approach the concrete operations stage, their many more experiences, use of more abstract language, and repeated social experiences help them move beyond egocentric and perceptually bound thinking into the realm of true logical thought.

SPECIFIC COGNITIVE COMPETENCIES OF PRESCHOOLERS

Although preschoolers demonstrate the characteristics described above, those who work with young children are also aware of the tremendous cognitive growth that occurs in the preschool years. Preschoolers develop competencies in:

1. ability to group objects according to increasingly abstract classes (classification);

2. learning the concepts involved in number and counting skills;

3. increasing understanding of spatial relationships that involve both topologic and Euclidean features;

4. arranging items that vary in some systematic way into a logical series (seriation); and

5. increasing understanding of the temporal relationships involved in concepts of age, speed, clock time, and time as a way of sequencing events (first, next, and last).

Examining a preschooler's cognitive performance in terms of the above concepts can allow the psychologist to make helpful reommendations for cognitive programming to preschool teachers. Yet, this conceptual framework for describing a child's performance on cognitive tasks may be relatively new to many psychologists assessing preschool children. The rest of this chapter will review the growing body of literature on cognitive development in preschoolers, so that psychologists can begin to incorporate what the author believes to be a useful framework for assessing cognitive development and making educational recommendations in preschool assessments.

The research that has uncovered the cognitive abilities of young children is quite recent (occurring largely within the last ten years), and has been undertaken to document the cognitive growth that occurs during the preoperational period. As researchers have attempted to study cognition in young children, they have found that the typical Piagetian tasks and methods do not work very well (Gelman, 1978). Preschoolers react to experimental situations, tasks, and materials in ways that differ greatly from the school-aged child's reactions to the same stimuli; this, it has been found, occurs partly because of the preschooler's lack of experience with a structured, question-answer, or task-reward testing format. Because preschoolers don't "play by the rules," many of the discoveries of their abilities made in the last ten years are due to the creativity and flexibility of the experimenters, who have tried to explore what preschoolers know about the world through means that are relevant to the child's interests and abilities.

The level of task difficulty has been found to significantly alter the kinds of responses that children make. As Gelman (1978) points out, asking a child to explain something which he or she cannot possibly understand does not mean that the child is unable to explain something logically. Asking the child to hypothesize a cause for a simple effect that the child observes is a fair test of whether that child can logically explain a cause-and-effect sequence; asking the child how clouds move is not. Many researchers studying preoperational thought in recent years have come to believe that the Piagetian types of tasks were inherently too difficult for young children; these researchers believe that the children's failures were not due only to the lack of cognitive concepts, but rather were due to the many variables operating in such tasks (Gelman, 1978; Wohlwill, 1968).

Piaget felt that preschoolers' egocentrism was a key element in their many conceptual errors. Yet, recent research has uncovered evidence that preschoolers are able to appreciate another's perspective. This topic will be examined next.

STUDIES OF EGOCENTRISM

Traditional Piagetian assumptions suggest that preschoolers are extremely egocentric in their cognitive perspective. However, several kinds of studies support the idea that preschoolers are not totally egocentric and that the young child can indeed appreciate another's perspective. One question that has been studied is whether young children tailor their speech to the listener. Adults certainly speak differently to children than to other adults, demonstrating their grasp of the differences in listeners' comprehension. If young children were also found to alter their speech depending on the age of the listener, it would show that the child was not totally egocentric; it would tend to prove that the child did appreciate differences in various listeners' abilities. Gelman (1978) carried out three studies in this area. In the first, 4-year-olds were recorded having conversations with 2-year-olds and then with adults. Analysis of the recordings revealed that the 4-year-old speakers altered both the content of their conversations and the complexity of their sentences according to the listener's age. When they spoke with the 2-year-olds, sentences were short and simple, and served to direct, focus, or alter the younger children's attention. In contrast, comments to adults were syntactically and semantically more complex, and served to convey thoughts and feelings and to seek information.

Was this because of the feedback the 4-year-olds received from their listeners? Did the adults draw higher level language from them? Apparently not, for Gelman carried out a similar study that used dolls that were assigned different ages as the listeners (so that there would be no feedback to the speaker). Again the 4-year-old speakers ajusted their conversations according to the doll's assigned age. In a third related experiment, Gelman showed 4-year-olds pictures of children who were either 2 years or 4 years of age and asked the subjects to select toys for the pictured children. Again, the 4-year-olds chose simpler toys for the 2-year-olds, and more mature, complex toys for 4-year-olds. From Gelman's studies, it seems that 4-year-olds do understand age-related differences in other people involving cognitive capacities, linguistic level, and attention span, and are able to alter their behavior to fit their own mental representations of the listener's interests and abilities.

Other researchers have studied egocentrism from different perspectives. Because Piaget used a visual perspective in the mountain scene experiment, several studies have examined preschoolers' abilities to understand other people's visual perspectives. These studies have found that children as young as 2½ years have some understanding of others' visual perspectives. In one study (Flavell, Shipstead, and Croft, 1978), the experimenter used various types of screens and toys; the toys were arranged behind screens in such a way that sometimes the child could see the toy but the experimenter could not, sometimes both could see it, sometimes neither could see it, and sometimes the experimenter could see the toy but the child could not. In all situations, the child was asked if he or she could see the toy and if the experimenter could see it. Children aged 2½ to 4 years correctly answered such questions, indicating that they could distinguish the experimenter's perceptual experiences from their own. Another part of the same experiment required the child to arrange the toy and screens so that the experimenter could see it but the child could not, and then so that the child could see it but the experimenter could not. Again, children in the 2½- to 4-year age range were able to plan situations based on visual perspectives different from their own.

If young children are able to decenter from their own perspectives sufficiently to solve some problems, why are they unable to perform Piaget's mountain experiment? According to Gelman (1978), it is because the mountain task has too many variables. She reports one study that modifies the Piagetian mountain scene so that the child could rotate the platform to demonstrate the doll's perspective, rather than selecting pictures of it. The experimenter also altered the scene so that it contained only two stimuli rather than the three mountains with their different shapes, colors, and adornments. In general, the fewer the elements in the scene, the more successful preschoolers were at differentiating someone else's perspective from their own. Children as young as 3 years demonstrated their ability to decenter from their own perspective and to choose the visual perspective of an onlooker. Thus, these studies demonstrate preschoolers' nonegocentric ability to appreciate conceptual, perceptual, and communicative perspectives of others even when those perspectives differ from their own. But this is possible only as long as the tasks and responses required were appropriate to the skills of the age group.

STUDIES OF NUMBER CONCEPTS

Piaget studied number concepts and conservation of quantity with the following experiment. The experimenter places a row of evenly spaced pennies in front of the child. The child matches a second row to the first, so that he or she acknowledges the same number of pennies in both rows. Then the experimenter spreads the original row of pennies out so that it is longer but less dense than the first, and asks the child if the longer row has more pennies, less pennies, or the same number of pennies as in the child's row. Next, the experimenter masses the original row of pennies into a pile and repeats the question. Piaget found that preschoolers generally used length and density cues to judge which row had more pennies; he found that they could not even match the pennies 1:1 until age 4 or 5. Even after 1:1 correspondence was used, the child could not maintain the concept of equality of quantities in the test until age 6 or 7, when concrete operational thought begins to emerge.

From these studies, Piaget hypothesized four stages in the development of understanding of number:

Stage I. The child judges numeric relations in terms of the topologic relations of length and density.

Stage II. The child judges number via only one perceptual mode, typically length, but does not use 1:1 correspondence.

Stage III. The child can match objects using 1:1 correspondence but cannot hold onto the equivalence through perceptual transformations of the line of objects.

Stage IV. The child has invariance of

quantity concepts (Pufall & Shaw, 1974).

As in the case of research on egocentrism, research on preschoolers' number abilities has shed new light on their capabilities. Gelman's early work with the development of number skills has distinguished between children who are *estimators,* able to count, and *operators,* who are able to conserve invariance (Gelman and Tucker, 1975).

Let us first discuss counting abilities, which, according to Gelman and Tucker, are dependent on the following cognitive abilities:

1. counting, which in itself requires the coordinated application of several conceptual principles, and includes 1:1 correspondence of number to object, knowledge that anything (including imagined things) can be counted, knowledge that the order of counting is irrelevant as long as each object is tagged once only, and knowledge that the final tag represents the sum of the objects (Gelman, 1972);

2. subitizing, which is the perceptual recognition of the number of objects; and

3. judging quantity, which is possible from perceptual cues, such as length, density, or arrangement (Gelman and Tucker, 1975).

One important factor in studying both counting and operational skills in young children has been the size of the number array confronting the children. When numbers greater than five are used, young children have great difficulty with counting and invariance tasks, and perform as Piaget has described (Saxe, 1977; Henry, 1976). However, when set sizes of less than five are used, 3- and 4-year-old children accurately estimate the set sizes by subitizing rather than counting with a less than 60-second length of exposure. With an exposure time of 60 seconds, even 3-year-olds count small set sizes accurately and spontaneously (Gelman and Tucker, 1975), revealing accurate and useful number concepts.

The ability to conserve number concepts is considered much more advanced than the ability to use 1:1 correspondence and accurate counting. Some researchers exploring preschoolers' conservation of number concepts have found many discrepancies with Piagetian theory. One discrepancy concerns the use of length and density cues to estimate quantity. Although it appears that preschoolers do resort to length to estimate quantity when the size of the set is five or over, there is very little evidence that they use density in the same way (Smither, Smiley, and Rees, 1974). It seems instead that preschoolers treat transformations of density as an irrelevant number cue, much as they treat transformation in color as an irrelevant number cue (Gelman, 1972), and that density has little effect on a preschooler's judgment of quantity.

When the set size is small and the paradigm favors a nonverbal means of the child communicating knowledge, preschoolers have provided much evidence that they in fact conserve small quantities. Gelman has studied number skills using a "magic game" paradigm; in this paradigm the child is presented with two boxes, one containing a number of identical items (such as three plastic fish), and the other containing another number of the same objects. The child is taught to choose the "winner" based on a set number of objects, like always choosing the box that has three of something. After the child learns which array to choose, the "winner" is "magically" changed in one of several ways. Three fish may be changed to three flowers, so that the objects themselves are changed but the number remains constant; or a fish may be added or removed, changing the number; or the arrangement of the fish may be changed, as may the color of the fish. If the child chooses the box that has three objects, disregarding other types of transformations, then the child seems to be demonstrating the knowledge that physical transformations are irrelevant to number. If the boxes have been transformed so that there is no box with three objects, and the child refuses to choose a box with a different number of objects, then the child seems to be conserving the learned set of three, and rejecting others that do not represent it.

Gelman's research has demonstrated that, with number sets smaller than five, 3-, 4-, and 5-year-olds consistently treat addition and subtraction of an item as operations relevant to number; conversely,

they consistently treat substitution and displacement as operations irrelevant to number. Not only do they treat small numbers as invariant, they also demonstrate reversibility in their explanations of how the number transformation might have happened and how the first state could be regained. To test whether the children's performance was due to a perceptual grasp of the small numbers, the researchers then carried out the traditional Piagetian number conservation task using only three poker chips. With this paradigm, 95 percent of the 3-year-olds and 55 percent of the 4-year-olds were incorrect. Thus, it appears that the Piagetian paradigm itself seems to interfere with children's ability to demonstrate what they know about numbers (Gelman, 1972).

Others replicating Gelman's use of small numbers and invariance tasks that do not require verbal explanations of the reasons for the child's choice support her findings that young children can conserve small quantities (Winer, 1974; Calhoun, 1971). There seem to be several reasons why children have such difficulty performing the traditional Piagetian tasks, even when the numbers are small.

The first is that preschoolers have difficulty with the terms *less, more,* and *same* (Griffiths, Shantz, and Siegel, 1967; Kavanaugh, 1976; Holland and Palermo, 1975). Since these words are often used in test instructions, young children's judgments are not adequately conveyed by the terms they are asked to use. Also, the typical question to the child, "Are they the same, or is one more or less than the other?" is really two questions, which the young child may not be able to process at once (Pennington, 1977). Young children also have a consistent response preference for the most recent question asked them (Siegel, McCabe, Brand, and Matthews, 1978); for example, if asked, "Are these the same or different?" the child will tend to reply with "different," the most recent response given them. This interferes with their responses to verbally based tasks. The child's difficulty in estimating large number groups, and the shifts in attention which the traditional paradigm causes with its visual manipulations of objects, also make the Piagetian task extremely difficult for young children (Gelman, 1972). According to many researchers, the Piagetian paradigm tests more than the child's ability to conserve equality or inequality; they believe that while the older child may be able to handle extra and interfering variables, the younger child cannot.

In essence, the studies cited show that while young children lack a full understanding of number conservation as tested by traditional methods, they nevertheless possess counting and mathematical abilities. Mathematical abilities are not an all-or-nothing affair (Pennington, 1977). The young child, however, needs a specific representation of the number set and cannot use 1:1 correspondence rules to make judgments about equivalence (Gelman, 1978).

Research on the development of counting and subitizing skills reveals that children as young as 3 years of age can answer "how many" questions for one and two objects. Children as young as 3½ can count five objects correctly; children as young as 4 can answer "how many" questions for number sets through five; and 4½-year-olds can count up to ten objects and can do Piaget's traditional conservation of quantity experiment when no more than five stimulus items are used (Rogers and Lynch, 1980). A copy of a developmental test protocol that features these cognitive concepts as test items is presented in Appendix B.

CLASSIFICATION

The final area of cognitive abilities of preschoolers to be discussed is classification. This is the ability to group objects according to some dimension of similarity, and to assign objects to different classes based on other, differing dimensions. It also involves the understanding of subordinate and superordinate classes. A superordinate class is one that totally contains a subordinate class, like the superordinate class of animals that contains the subordinate class of dogs. A question asking a child to think of one way that two objects are different (placing them into separate classes), and another way in which they are the same (finding a larger superordinate class that contains both subordinate

classes) reveals the child's grasp of nesting superordinate and subordinate classes.

The classic Piagetian class-inclusion experiment (Piaget and Inhelder, 1956) involves giving the child five or six red wooden beads and two or three blue wooden beads, then asking the child, "Are there more red beads or more wooden beads?" According to Piagetian theory, the preoperational child cannot deal with two levels of classes—subordinate and superordinate—at the same time, and so answers that there are more red beads. In other words, the preoperational child is able only to compare the red beads with the other subordinate class of blue beads.

As was found in the study of preschoolers' number abilities, preschoolers' abilities to perform on the standard Piagetian class inclusion problems seems to be hampered by the methodology employed. However, several other factors seem to interfere as well.

First, Kalil, Youssef, and Lerner (1974) hypothesized that preschoolers—as a result of typical nursery school experiences—had built up a learning set that involved comparing two mutually exclusive, subordinate classes (Are there more cows or horses? Squares or circles?). This is a learning set which the traditional Piagetian task reinforces rather than attenuates. These researchers set up a study with 5- and 6-year-olds which sought to weaken the interfering learning set in three ways: (1) by making two subordinate groups equal in number, (2) by providing concrete physical references to the subgroups and altering the visual array, and (3) by altering the question to control for a recency preference. With these alterations, the 5- and 6-year-olds increased their percentage of correct responses from 6 percent on the traditional Piagetian tasks to 81 percent.

Wohlwill (1968) also believed that the visual stimuli of the traditional Piagetian class inclusion task biases the task against preschoolers, who tend to be strongly influenced by immediate perceptual experiences. When Wohlwill altered the task by removing the visual stimuli and making the task completely verbal, he found that preschoolers' performance improved significantly. Wohlwill tried two other alterations of the task; in the first, objects that were not part of the superordinate class were included; in the second, the children were trained in the qualities of the superordinate class. All of these manipulations resulted in significantly improved performances, and all could be interpreted as breaking up the interfering learning set and redirecting the children's attention to the most relevant aspects of the stimuli.

Another factor that seems quite important for success on this task is the salience, or meaningfulness, of the dimension that makes up the superordinate class. Tatarsky (1974) examined this question, exploring whether the dimension of woodenness is not as salient to preschoolers as another dimension—like color—might be.

In the belief that the color dimension is much more compelling to the child than the material dimension in the wooden bead task, he altered the task in several ways. One alteration involved using wooden blocks and exposing some of the wood by leaving part of the blocks unpainted. He also hypothesized that the two-dimensional comparison of color and woodenness was a source of real difficulty, and so designed blocks in which both the subordinate class and the superordinate class were based on the same dimension—color. He therefore used blocks that were all half yellow, but the other half of each block was painted either red or blue. Five- and 6-year-olds performed at better than 50 percent only on the one-dimensional task, revealing their ability to grasp the class relationships when they were not confounded by two different dimensions.

Another factor that might add to the task difficulty is the type of response required of the child. Many researchers have found that verbal responses lend themselves to more errors than nonverbal responses. Siegel and colleagues (1978) altered the task so that the stimuli were all candies (for example, M&Ms and jelly beans), and asked the children to use first pointing and then eating responses. They found that the children were correct significantly more often when using the eating response.

These same researchers hypothesized that the preschoolers' lack of attention to the relevant stimulus characteristics also hurt their performance. After a trial run with the candies task, they trained the children over six trials, using various kinds of objects and always giving the children the correct answers. This training period was followed by another test trial; after training, both 3- and 4-year-olds showed significant improvement, although they continued to show a recency preference. That is, they tended to answer with the part of the question stated last: "Are there more M&Ms or more candies? More candies or more jelly beans?" The children's peformance was interpreted as indicating that, while they understood class relationships, attentional factors and recency preferences seemed to interfere.

Research on the development of classification skills reveals the following progression: 3-year-olds are able to label pictures as same or different and to point to the one of three objects that does not belong with the other two. Three-and-one-half-year-olds can name objects by their use ("What do we ride in?"), revealing an understanding of the superordinate-subordinate relation. Four-year-olds, when given a group of pictures (animals, tools, or foods) and asked to put together those that go together in some way, can perform altered versions of the traditional Piagetian class-inclusion problem, revealing further superordinate-subordinate membership. And by 5½ years, children can describe the similarities and differences of a pair of objects (Rogers and Lynch, 1980). See Appendix B for items that tap these concepts.

APPLYING THE COGNITIVE APPROACH TO PSYCHOLOGICAL TESTING

The view of cognitive development being offered by recent research is that concrete operations abilities are not an integrated whole, interrelated and interdependent, which the child formulates as a totality. Rather, these studies support the view that cognitive abilities emerge slowly and asynchronously, and that only gradually do they come together to form a systematic, structured approach to problem-solving. The first emergence of such skills can be seen in preschoolers, but the cognitive processes of preschoolers are fragile, not a consolidatd part of the child's problem-solving repertoire yet, easily giving way when the stimuli are unfamiliar or when the task is too demanding or complex (Gelman, 1978).

There is one criterion-referenced developmental scale in which the cognitive section is constructed to reflect recent research about the child's development of cognition. This test is the Preschool Developmental Profile Scale (Brown and colleagues, 1980) and it is presented in Appendix B. However, one can interpret standardized test items in a more cognitive light, and thus use existing tests and items to describe cognitive functioning in more detail than has usually been the case. Table 5-1 presents items from familiar tests (grouped according to age and cognitive concepts of classification, number, spatial relations, and seriation) to help the psychologist interpret traditional test data in a more cognitive framework.

It is not suggested that this conceptual framework be used instead of the traditional, standardized tests, but rather as a complement to standardized tests. Norm-referenced tests are crucial tools for diagnosing the presence of cognitive handicaps, and are necessary and useful for preschool cognitive assessments. However, standardized tests are not as useful for recommending remedial programming as they are for diagnostic purposes. With the presence of PL 94-142 and the mandate for Individual Educational Plans (IEPs), psychologists are being asked to take a more active role in planning remedial programs; it is in making programming recommendations and developmental objectives that this cognitive framework and criterion-referenced cognitive tasks become quite useful

to the psychologist and to the educator. Thus, as was described in Chapter 4, the cognitive orientation is seen here as a most useful complement to standardized intelligence testing.

CONCLUSION

The cognitive processes of preoperational thinkers have certain global characteristics, such as bias toward immediate perceptual comparisons, egocentricity, problems with reversibility, and animistic thinking. Yet during the preoperational period, children are mastering the one-dimensional comparisons that later become coordinated into logical, operational thought. The development of these preoperational cognitive abilities can be seen in tasks involving classification, number, spatial relations, seriations, and time concepts. The tasks on many standard psychologic tests can be interpreted as reflecting cognitive abilities in these various dimensions, and this developmental approach translates into educational goals and objectives far more easily than a traditional approach to psychological test interpretation. Given the great increase in handicapped and delayed preschoolers being seen by psychologists, the developmental approach to cognitive performance interpretation leads to far greater usefulness of psychological reports and recommendations. The approach also allows the clinician to coordinate the approach taken in the psychologic assessment with the developmental approach generally taken by other professionals—motor therapists, speech and language pathologists, and educators—working with young children.

TABLE 5-1   Standardized Test Items Grouped by Cognitive Skill Area

Age	Classification Test*	Classification Item	Number Test*	Number Item	Spatial Relations Test*	Spatial Relations Item	Seriation Test*	Seriation Item
2–2½	S-B	a. Identify objects by use			S-B	a. 3-hole formboard	M-P	a. Nest of cubes
					Bayley	b. Pink formboard c. Train of cubes d. Blue formboard		
2½–3	Leiter	a. Match by color	Bayley	a. Concept of 1 b. Counts 2 blocks	M-P	a. Sequin formboard b. 3-cube pyramid	ITPA	a. Visual sequential memory
	ITPA	b. Match by form c. Auditory reception d. Visual association					M-P	b. Nest of cubes c. 3-cube pyramid
	M-P	e. Matching colors						
3–3½	ITPA	a. Auditory reception b. Visual association c. Various matching tasks	McCart	a. Number questions b. Counting and sorting	WPPSI	a. Block designs	WPPSI	Arith. items #1 and #2
	Leiter				M-P	b. Puzzles	ITPA	b. Visual sequential memory
	McCart	d. Verbal fluency e. Conceptual grouping			S-B	c. Block building—bridge	M-P	c. Little pink tower
					McCart	d. Puzzle solving e. Draw a design f. Draw a child		
3½–4	WPPSI	a. Similarities	Leiter	a. Item III-4	WPPSI	a. Clock design	ITPA	a. Visual sequential memory
	Leiter	b. Various tasks	WPPSI	b. Arithmetic subtest c. Inform. #2	M-P	b. Copying a cross c. Puzzles	WPPSI	b. Arithmetic items #1 and #2
	ITPA	c. Auditory reception d. Visual association	McCart	d. Number questions e. Counting and sorting	McCart	d. Puzzle solving e. Draw a design	S-B	c. Comparison of balls d. Comparison of sticks
	H-N	e. Picture association						

*Codes for test abbreviations are found at end of table

TABLE 5—1   Continued

Age	Classification Test*	Classification Item	Number Test*	Number Item	Spatial Relations Test*	Spatial Relations Item	Seriation Test*	Seriation Item
	S-B	f. Discrim. animal pictures g. Sorting buttons h. Verbal fluency i. Conceptual grouping				f. Draw a child		
	McCart							
4–4½	WPPSI	a. Inform. #4, #5, #7	WPPSI	a. Arith. subtest	WPPSI	a. Block designs	ITPA	a. Visual sequential memory
	McCart	b. Similarities	McCart	b. Number questions	VMI	b. Copying cross	M-P	b. 6-cube pyramid
	Leiter	c. Various tasks	M-P	c. Counting and sorting	M-P	c. 6-cube pyramid		
	ITPA	d. Auditory reception e. Visual association f. Picture association				d. Puzzles		
					H-N	e. Decroly matching game f. Block patterns		
	H-N McCart	g. Verbal fluency h. Verbal fluency i. Conceptual grouping			S-B McCart	g. Discrim. of forms h. Puzzle solving i. Draw a design j. Draw a child		
4½–5	WPPSI	a. Similarities	WPPSI	a. Information items b. Arithmetic items	VMI	a. Copying a square	ITPA	a. Visual sequential memory
	Leiter	b. Various tasks	Leiter	d. Task IV-3, IV-4	M-P	b. Decroly matching game		
	ITPA	c. Auditory reception d. Visual association	McCart	d. Number questions e. Counting and sorting	H-N	c. Block patterns		
	H-N	e. Picture association						
	S-B	f. Pictorial similarities and differences—I						

*Codes for test abbreviations are found at end of table

TABLE 5—1 Continued

Age	Classification Test*	Classification Item	Number Test*	Number Item	Spatial Relations Test*	Spatial Relations Item	Seriation Test*	Seriation Item
	McCart	g. Verbal fluency h. Conceptual grouping						
5–5½	WPPSI	a. Information items b. Similarities	WPPSI	a. Information items b. Arithmetic items	VMI	a. Copying oblique cross b. Copying triangle	ITPA	a. Visual sequential memory b. Copying bead patterns
	Leiter	c. Various tasks	McCart	c. Number questions d. Counting and sorting	M-P	c. Copying star	H-N	
	ITPA	d. Auditory reception e. Visual association			S-B	d. Picture completion—man e. Patience—rectangles f. Puzzle solving		
	H-N	f. Picture association			McCart	g. Draw a design		
	S-B	g. Pictorial similarities and differences—I						
	McCart	h. Verbal fluency i. Conceptual grouping	h. Draw a child					
5½–6	WPPSI	a. Information	WPPSI	a. Arithmetic	WPPSI	a. Block designs	H-N	a. Copying bead patterns
		b. Similarities	McCart	b. Number questions c. Counting and seriation	VMI	b. Square and circle c. 3-line cross	ITPA	b. Visual sequential memory
	Leiter	c. Various tasks			M-P	d. Manikin		
	H-N	d. Picture association			McCart	e. Puzzle solving f. Draw a design g. Draw a child		
	McCart	e. Verbal fluency f. Conceptual grouping						

TABLE 5—1 Continued

Age	Classification		Number		Spatial Relations		Seriation	
	Test*	Item	Test*	Item	Test*	Item	Test*	Item
6-6½	WPPSI	a. Information items	WPPSI	a. Block design				Leiter
b. Similarities	'	b. Arithmetic items	H-N	b. Block patterns				
c. Various items	H-N	c. Block patterns	VMI	c. Directional arrows	Leiter			
	ITPA	d. Auditory reception		d. Puzzle solving		c. Task VI-1		
		e. Visual association	McCart	e. Draw a design				
	H-N	f. Picture association		f. Draw a child				
	S-B	g. Differences						
		h. Opposite analogies						
	McCart	i. Verbal fluency						
		j. Conceptual grouping						

Code for Test Abbreviations

Bayley—Bayley Scales of Infant Development
H-N —Hiskey-Nebraska Test of Learning Aptitude
ITPA —Illinois Test of Psycholinguistic Abilities
Leiter —Leiter International Performance Scale—Arthur Adaptation
M-P —Merrill-Palmer Scale of Mental Tests
McCart—McCarthy Scales of Children's Abilities
S-B —Stanford-Binet Intelligence Scale
VMI —Test of Visual Motor Integration—Beery
WPPSI—Wechsler Preschool and Primary Scale of Intelligence

REFERENCES

Brown S, D'Eugenio D, Drews J, Haskin B, Lynch E, Moersch M, Rogers S: *Preschool Developmental Profile.* Ann Arbor: University of Michigan Press, 1980

Calhoun L.G: Number conservation in very young children: The effect of age and mode of responding. Child Devel 42: 561–572, 1971

Flavell J H: *The Developmental Psychology of Jean Piaget.* Princeton: Van Nostrand, 1963

Flavell J H, Shipstead S G, Croft K: Young children's knowledge about visual perception: Hiding objects from others. Child Devel 49: 1208–1211, 1978

Gelman R: Cognitive development. In Rosenzweig M R, Porter L W (eds): Ann Rev Psycho 29: 1978

Gelman R: Logical capacity of very young children: Number invariance rules. Child Devel 43: 75–90, 1972

Gelman R, Tucker M F: Further investigations of the young child's conception of number. Child Devel 46: 167–175, 1975

Griffiths J A, Shantz C A, Siegel I E: A methodological problem in conservation studies: The use of relational terms. Child Devel 38: 841–848, 1967

Henry D E: Interrelationships among attentional preferences, cardinal-ordinal ability, and conservation of number. Child Devel 47: 750-758, 1976

Holland V M, Palermo D S: On learning "less": Language and cognitive development. Child Devel 46: 437–443, 1975

Kalil K, Youssef Z, Lerner N M: Class-inclusion failures: Cognitive deficits or misleading references? Child Devel 45: 1122–1125, 1974

Kavanaugh R D: On the synonymity of more and less: Comments on a methodology. Child Devel 47: 885–887, 1976

Pennington B F: What Piaget's conservation of number task doesn't tell us about a child's understanding of numerical invariance and arithmetic. Unpublished doctoral dissertation, Duke University, 1977

Piaget J: *The Child's Conception of Physical Causality.* London: Kegan Paul, 1930

Piaget J: *The Child's Conception of the World.* New York: Harcourt Brace, 1929

Piaget J, Inhelder B. *Six developpements des quantités chez l'enfant.* Neuchatel: Delachaux et Niestle, 1941

Piaget J, Inhelder B: *The Child's Conception of Space.* London: Toutledge & Kegan Paul, 1956

Pufall P B, Shaw R E, Syrdal-Lasky A: Development of number conservation: An examination of some predictions from Piaget's stage analysis and equilibrium model. Child Devel 44: 21–27, 1973

Rogers S, Lynch E: *Cognitive Characteristics of Preschoolers.* Unpublished manuscript, 1980

Saxe G B: A developmental analysis of notational counting. Child Devel 48:1512–1520, 1977

Siegel L S, McCabe A E, Brand J, Matthews J: Evidence for the understanding of class inclusion in preschool children: Linguistic factors and training effects. Child Devel 49: 688–693, 1978

Smither S J, Smile S S, Rees R: The use of perceptual cues for number judgment by young children. Child Devel 45: 693–699, 1974

Tatarsky J H: The influence of dimensional manipulations on class performance. Child Devel 45: 1173–1175, 1974

Wohlwill J: Responses to class-inclusion question for verbally and pictorially presented items. Child Devel 39: 449–465, 1968

Winer G A: Conservation of different quantities among preschool children. Child Devel 45: 839–842, 1974

Chapter 6

TECHNIQUES OF INFANT ASSESSMENT

By

SALLY J. ROGERS

Psychologists who are newly faced with the challenge of assessing infants quickly discover that it is quite different from assessing older children. Infants, particularly after the age of 7 months or so, can be quite demanding individuals who require that the examiner have patience, energy, creativity, and a sense of humor if the assessment is to be successful. The differences between assessing infants and toddlers and older children are not due so much to the differences between the tests used as they are to the fact that a psychologic evaluation is an interactive process, and the infant's social and emotional immaturities do not allow him or her to participate the way an older child can.

The social and emotional climate of the assessment must be defined and set at an appropriate level for the infant before he or she will perform comfortably for the examiner. The key to a successful infant evaluation is the psychologist's ability to set a social atmosphere in which the infant is at ease and can show his or her range of behaviors with minimal inhibition. This chapter will cover techniques that can help the psychologist establish an atmosphere in which the infant feels comfortable.

CHARACTERISTICS OF THE EFFECTIVE EXAMINER

There are at least four characteristics that examiners who are effective with infants and toddlers share: experience with and enjoyment of infants and toddlers; an ability to fit one's behaviors to the infant's cues; understanding and respect for the infant's needs around physical distance and physical contact; and the ability to establish rapport with parents and put them at ease.

The first and most important characteristic of the good infant evaluation is experience with infants, comfort in handling them and talking to them, and genuine affection for and enjoyment of them. Infants are social creatures who learn early to judge the safeness of a situation from an adult's facial expressions and vocal qualities. Thus, eye contact with the infant, use of social smiles, and use of appropriate levels of communication (not necessarily baby talk, but friendly chatter directed to the baby) are extremely important in communicating friendly interest.

The second characteristic involves the examiner's ability to fit himself or herself to the infant's readiness for interaction, following the infant's cues, and working to establish an optimum level of rapport (which may be different for each infant). During the assessment, the examiner must move from the somewhat negative role of stranger to the role of an interesting person who offers enjoyable activities to the child. This transition goes through at least three stages in the 90-minute assessment: (1) the "unobtrusive stranger" stage in which the assessor stays on the sidelines of interactions while the child explores the room and grows used to the setting and the examiner's voice and presence; (2) the "offerer of interesting objects" stage in which the examiner begins to present interesting items, begins to make gentle requests for performance through modeling and praise, and liberally rewards performance; and (3) the "active examiner" stage, in which the examiner moves with the child to center stage, becomes more intensely involved in interactions with the child, uses much affect and praise to request performances or to control or inhibit some behaviors, and generally elicits the best performance possible from the child. While many infants and toddlers will eventually allow the examiner to become quite active (as described in the third stage), children who are extremely shy or frightened by strangers, and children who are in the midst of some strong control and autonomy issues may not allow the clinician to move past the much less active and less controlling interactions of the second stage described above. The psychologist's goal must always be maximum participation from the child, with the examiner fitting himself or herself to the child.

The third characteristic of the effective infant examiner is understanding and respect for physical distance and physical touch; these are closely related to the rapport issues above. Infants and toddlers from about 7 months to 18 months of age—especially in the presence of their parents—keep physically away from strangers, and a stranger's close approach is often enough to start up stranger distress responses. A stranger's touch may elicit a distress response even more quickly than a too-close approach. Thus, experienced examiners allow young children to set distance limits, and interact socially from a distance. As the toddler becomes more comfortable, he or she will begin to approach the examiner, especially to show or offer toys. The examiner responds to these approaches with smiling interest and attention, but usually does not approach the child. Because much infant testing requires the child to sit on the parent's lap with a table between the child and the examiner, this setting is usually not threatening to the child.

The same sensitivity applied to distance should also be applied to physical touch, since young children typically react negatively to being touched by a stranger. Maintaining appropriate physical distance does not allow the clinician to touch the child early in the assessment. As the child warms up to the examiner and approaches and talks to or gestures to the examiner, touching will generally not have such negative consequences. By the time the child is able to tolerate the physical nearness of the examiner and to give objects back and forth, patting the child on the back or shoulder will most likely be acceptable. In fact, such touches may even facilitate some rapport—but they are still fairly distant gestures. More intrusive holding, or hugging and kissing the child, are generally not facilitating when the parents are present.

A final characteristic of examiners who are able to put children at ease is that they put the parents at ease first. Because small children read their parents' gestures, expressions, and vocal tone to determine the safety of a situation, the parent must be at ease if the child is to be comfortable. Establishing rapport with the parents, giving the parents time to express their concerns, and treating the parents as important people in the evaluation will go far toward putting them at ease. Parents are always anxious about evaluations; recognizing that anxiety while at the same time trying to help build their self-esteem by commenting favorably about aspects of the family, their child, or observed interactions will help parents be more comfortable. Other steps in establishing rapport include using parents as important informants about their child, reading their expressions of concern, answering their questions, and explaining assessment procedures. It is also helpful for parents to receive clear instructions about how they should behave during the actual assessment. Telling them where they should sit, how much help they can give, and whether or not they should talk to their child during the testing will prevent indecision and conflict on their part as they try to ensure their child's maximum performance for the examiner.

STRUCTURING THE ASSESSMENT

Because young children generally react somewhat negatively to new situations and new people, the child will need some time at the start of the assessment to grow comfortable with the room and the examiner. In addition, it is clinically helpful to spend some time at the start of the assessment talking with the parents to help them become more comfortable and to explore their concerns about the child.

It is ideal to meet the needs of both parents and child at the same time. Thus, the clinician can begin the assessment by offering the child interesting toys that are not part of the test kit; the child can explore these toys and the room while the parents are being interviewed. Since the parents may not be sure that the toys are there for their child, the examiner should tell them: "I've set out some toys for your child to play with while we talk for a little while." If the child is reluctant to leave the parents, the toys should be placed near the parents. It is important for the psychologist to keep in mind that the overriding purpose of this first 20 minutes is to help the parents and child become more comfortable.

THE PARENT INTERVIEW

A good parent interview is a very important part of the overall assessment, for it not only gives the clinician a sound developmental history and an idea of what might be wrong in the child's development; it also provides important information about the characteristics and quality of the parent-child relationship, the parental relationship, and the child's role in the family.

The psychologist who uses an open-ended interview format with a warm and somewhat casual style can go a long way toward helping parents speak freely about their child and themselves—their fears, doubts, and frustrations about their child's developmental problems. It is important the the parents not feel rushed, since the best information will come from their expanded answers to questions. The interview should cover the following points:

1. The Parents' Concerns. These can often be revealed by simply asking the parents why they sought the evaluation. If

they answer that their pediatrician suggested it, ask what the pediatrician appeared to be worried about and whether the parents share that concern. This is probably the single most important piece of information that parents can provide. Their worries, fears, fantasies, or denial that there are any problems help the evaluator to know what assessment information is needed and what intervention strategies are most likely to be effective.

2. Developmental Milestones. These may be in the motor area, and may include when the child rolled over, sat, crawled, stood alone, or walked alone. In the social/emotional area, the clinician can explore when the child first smiled, discriminated parental faces from others, showed stranger and separation distress, used the word "no," spoonfed independently, and so on. In the language area, parents can report when the baby imitated some sounds, like "uh-oh" or smacking lips, when the first words were used with real meaning, and whether the child has put two separate words together (not "all done," but rather, "daddy shoe," "mama bye-bye"). Although the other areas of development are just as important as these, parents are most apt to remember when their child first sat, smiled, and spoke.

3. Health History. Information about past illnesses, hospitalizations, and medications are important for several reasons. Several illnesses, such as meningitis or prolonged high fever and seizures, may imply some residual central nervous system involvement that could be the causative factor in a child's delays. Hospitalizations, especially repeated or lengthy hospitalizations, often affect a child's emotional development by disrupting parent-child relationships and by forcing sometimes intrusive and painful medical procedures on the child. Medications frequently affect the child's behavior (see Chapter 11) and may result in increased or decreased activity levels, impaired attention, and ataxia. If a child takes medications that may affect behavior (consult the *Physician's Desk Reference)* and the child is showing such behaviors, the clinician may find it necessary to assess the child at another time when he or she is not medicated. The psychologist should by all means ask the parents if they think the medications make their child hyperactive, drowsy, or clumsy.

4. Feeding and Sleeping Habits. Parents should be asked whether their child has had feeding or sleeping problems, or whether the baby has had unusual habits or preferences in these areas, since emotional difficulties are often revealed quite early through disruptions in feeding and sleeping.

5. The Course of Attachment and Separation. Using a framework such as Margaret Mahler's (1975), the clinician can determine whether the child's periods of strong attachment, strong independence, and conflicts in these areas seem to follow a fairly normal developmental pattern. Significant deviations in this area may be diagnostic of early emotional problems.

6. Parental and Family Issues. The parents' emotional status (as individuals and as a couple), and how the family as a whole functions can be learned during the parent interview. This is important, because children with developmental problems put a great strain on the parents, both individually and as a couple, and also on the family system as a whole. In addition, it is common for grandparents and other extended family members to resist or deny the problem; it is also common for siblings to experience strong, conflicting feelings of resentment, anger, jealousy, and protectiveness for the handicapped child. These reactions all put stress on the parents, who themselves must cope with the emotional pain of having a handicapped child. Supportive counseling can make a great difference in the troubled family's ability to integrate a handicapped child into the family system. Thus, assessment of parental and family issues is important for the psychologist who must make decisions about intervention.

7. The Parents' Feelings About the Delayed Child. Feelings that surfaced when the child was born, when the child was a small baby, and when the child became a more demanding toddler can be revealing to the experienced examiner. For parents whose child has already been diagnosed as handicapped, the clinician may wish to explore how they have integrated that information into their feelings for the child, and how they felt differently about the child before he or she was diagnosed as handicapped.

8. Any Behavior or Management Problems. The clinican should explore any problems the parents are experiencing with the child or have experienced in the past. Areas that may reveal useful information include asking how the parents tried to handle the problem, what worked, what did not work, and whether they generally feel that they can handle problems as they arise, or whether they feel overwhelmed with managing the child.

TRANSITION TO THE ACTUAL TESTING

As the interview draws to a close, the evaluator should briefly explain the kinds of tasks that will be presented to the child and the kinds of information the evaluation is designed to gather. At this stage the evaluator will also begin to make more active overtures to the child, trying to engage the child and draw him or her into interactions. Bringing out the test kit and telling the child that it contains many toys is generally a strong enticement for the young child. Physical positioning of the toys, the child, and the adults should follow, so that a standardized presentation of items can begin.

The best items to begin with are small, easily manipulated items, such as blocks or pegs. Tasks that are inherently interesting are best presented first, while language tasks and more difficult tasks should be reserved until the child seems comfortable and ready to work. In presenting the early tasks, it is important for the psychologist to avoid being direct or demanding. Instead, the clinician should move nearer to the child, speak his or her name, and demonstrate the first block item in a playful manner. Then the blocks can be pushed into the child's reach while the child is gently encouraged to perform the task. Use of playful affect and praise for performance will help motivate the child.

Deciding when to move to another task is not always easy. Any item the child does not pass should be tried several times, though not necessarily in succession, since the psychologist who stays on one item too long risks losing the child's interest and building up negativism. On the other hand, switching items too soon risks frustrating the child. The clinician should give the child ample time with each stimulus item, then should introduce a new item *before* removing the old one. As the child reaches for the new item, the old one can be slid out of sight without frustrating the child. Since children will generally do more for the parent than for the examiner, the child's parent can be freely used to demonstrate items or to try to coax the child to perform. The parent should be encouraged to praise the child and in all ways to show approval and involvement with the child's activity throughout; indeed, the parent should hold the child or be quite close to the child much of the time.

It is difficult to watch a child struggle to perform a task, and the normal response is to assist. However, assisting the child or demonstrating a task when demonstration is not part of the administration of an item invalidates that item. It is much better for the psychologist to wait and see how the child tries to solve the problem. If the child still needs help to perform the item after several tries or presentations, the clinician can score the item as fail and then assist the struggling child (so that the child experiences some success). It should be emphasized that this should be done only rarely, and assisted items cannot be scored. This is another instance in which experience with many normal babies will help the psychologist understand what an appropriate response should be.

As the child's ceiling is sought, the examiner will have to introduce several items that the child will fail. At this point, the parent should be reassured that the failed items are too difficult, and that success was not expected. The psychologist should be sensitive to the child's frustration on these tasks as well. So that the end of the assessment is not abrupt or frustrating to the child, both the parent and child should be prepared for it approximately 10 minutes before its conclusion. The parent

can be expected to be anxious about the child's performance, and some way should be found to reassure him or her—even if findings cannot be shared at that time. Honest comments such as, "Your baby worked very hard," "I really enjoyed your child," or "Your child did just fine," are helpful to the parents. If feedback must be delayed, the clinician can thank the parent and remind him or her that answers will be prepared for the feedback session.

A final point for the psychologist to keep in mind is that there may be some items that cannot be scored because of the child's refusal, the examiner's own error, or too much parent help. The clinician's job is to keep these to a minimum. Occasionally a toddler will be so negative, tired, or upset that a valid assessment is not possible. In those situations, an intuitive guess as to what the child's performance could have been should not be made; instead, the assessment report should state what occurred, and no score or level should be recorded for the child at that time. Instead, another evaluation can be scheduled in two or three months. Situations that require such rescheduling are liable to be *very* hard on parents, and they will need considerable reassurance that the problem was not their fault, and that all children are sometimes negative. It should also be noted that these are trying and frustrating situations for the examiner, who must handle them with grace and good humor.

PREPARING FOR INFANT EVALUATIONS

A final point that will be made in this chapter is that although more and more psychologists are being asked to assess very young children, few are trained to do so. As a result, individual psychologists must find adequate training for themselves. It is important that this be approached in a somewhat formal manner.

Two aspects of preparation should be taken into account: classroom work and supervised experience. Classroom work should involve graduate-level courses that cover early child development in the areas of cognition, speech and language, fine and gross motor development, and social/emotional growth. These types of courses will provide the background knowledge and theoretical knowledge of early development that will be needed to interpret children's behavior during evaluations.

Supervision should involve work with a psychologist who is trained and experienced in infant assessment, and should first focus on learning administration and scoring techniques and becoming a reliable source with normal children. This is extremely important, for the clinician must have a solid understanding of what the normal response to tasks should be. Care should be taken to adhere to the manual exactly. The psychologist upgrading his or her skills should evaluate twelve or more normal children in the birth to 24-month age range, so that there is experience with administering items several times to children at different levels of maturity.

When the clinician moves to evaluating handicapped children, supervision should again be sought for the first evaluations—and as necessary after that for difficult cases. Because so much weight is placed on psychological findings, it is extremely important that psychologists be well prepared and that they understand the limitations of early childhood evaluations.

SUMMARY

In summary, infant evaluations are quite different from the evaluations of older children, primarily because infants are not motivated to cooperate or perform for unfamiliar adults; instead, they tend to react negatively to testing situations. To help the child demonstrate his or her abilities in that setting, the examiner should allow plenty of time for the child to accommodate, should hesitate to touch or correct the child, should refrain from placing demands on the child, should use playfulness and praise liberally, and should involve the parents in the assessment. The goal is to make both parents and child as comfortable as possible, so that the child can display the widest possible range of skills.

Reference

Mahler MS, Pine F, Bergman A: *The Psychological Birth of the Human Infant: Symbiosis and Individuation.* New York: Basic Books, 1975

Chapter 7

DEVELOPMENTAL CHARACTERISTICS OF YOUNG CHILDREN'S PLAY

By
SALLY J. ROGERS

Young children work at their play and grow and learn from play in the same way that older children grow and learn from schoolwork; hence, the familiar quotation, "Play is the child's work." Some believe play to be the most important source of development in the preschool years (Erikson, 1976; Vygotsky, 1976), affecting all areas of psychological development—cognitive development, emotional development, social development, and creativity.

Since so much psychological information about a young child can be revealed through play, many psychologists specializing in early childhood assessment include a play interview and/or play observations as part of their standard assessment procedure. They do this not only to assess emotional health, but also to get a more complete picture of the child. A psychologic assessment is generally controlled by the psychologist; the child is expected to cooperate and perform as directed, to submit to the adult's control. In a play interview, the roles are reversed and the child is given control of the situation. The way the child structures the situation, the amount of control the child tries to exert over the adult, the activities chosen, the level of symbolic play, and the play themes that arise help the psychologist considerably in fleshing out a picture of the whole child.

Because play is such an important and dominant developmental activity in young children, the author believes that an assessment of a child's play should be part of the psychological evaluation of young children. To aid psychologists in understanding the various developmental aspects of young children's play, this chapter will cover current theory and research on cognitive, social, and emotional aspects of play and will briefly discuss the effects of various handicaps on young children's play. Appendix F provides some guidelines for setting up and carrying out a play interview and for assessing emotional health via a play interview.

ORIGINS OF PLAY

Play appears to develop out of an interaction of three factors: the child's growing awareness of self; the child's growing cognitive understanding of objects in the world; and the child's growing attachment to and investment in the parents, and through them, to the outside world (Murphy, 1972). As Murphy states, "Narcissism, the cognitive experience, and Cathexis of the outside are all very closely interrelated in this first play" (p. 122). Thus, from the earliest examples of infant play—shaking a rattle, patting at the mother's face—Murphy sees the cognitive, social, and emotional aspects of play represented. And although infant play appears to be largely toy-centered rather than social, good parenting is still a necessary forerunner of object play, as seen in the lack of toy play in institutionalized infants (Provence and Lipton, 1962).

What is it that "good" parents provide? First, they reinforce the baby's early attempts to making something happen, thus assisting the baby to turn passive experiences into active ones. Second, they provide dependable life patterns, giving the baby a sense of orderliness and structure in the world. This is critical for play, because play involves the child's imposition of a structure on the outside world and, as Murphy states, one cannot externalize structure unless one has previously internalized it. Third, parents contribute to the baby's awareness of self through tactile and affective play, as well as through responsive caretaking, giving the baby a balance in experiences of doing and being done to. This provides the ground work for later turning passive experiences into active ones through play and fantasy, and through symbolic and constructive play. Fourth, Murphy feels that even creativity is dependent upon a capacity for play and upon good feelings about oneself which grow out of ". . . the joy, the delight, the fun of the earliest mother-baby duets" (Murphy, 1972, p. 126).

FUNCTIONS OF PLAY

According to Erikson, play provides "the restoration and creation of a leeway of mastery in a set of developments or circumstances" (Erikson, 1972, p. 133). Thus, the myriad forms of play can be seen to represent mastery of various skills, capacities, or experiences, determined by the child's current developmental status and personal life experiences.

This view of play as serving the function of active mastery (the child's assertion of some aspect of self on the environment) is a view taken by most authors, and it is seen as the *primary* function of play. As Murphy states, "With children, play is psychically active, if and when the child is free to enjoy and to impose something, some structure, some pattern, on the environment" (Murphy, 1972, p. 121).

Play involving the practice of motor skills, such as climbing, jumping, swinging, and so on, demonstrate the child's exercise and mastery of developing motor skills. Play involving creative or constructive activities—making paintings, working with clay or blocks, executing drawings, making up rhymes or songs—demonstrates the joy of self-expression. Play involving the acting out of unhappy incidents from the past demonstrates the child's active attempts to master traumatic experiences that were originally experienced passively. Social play involving role-taking with peers demonstrates the child's attempts to understand and master complex social life roles and situations (Erikson, 1972). Each of these aspects of play will be explored in this chapter.

COGNITIVE ASPECTS OF PLAY

Since Piaget has offered perhaps the most elaborate framework for understanding the various forms of play (Piaget, 1962), his interpretation of the various types and functions of play will be reviewed in some detail. Piaget believes that each new sensory motor or symbolic structure (schema) needs a continuous flow of functional activity in order to develop. Schemas develop via two processes—assimilation and accommodation. The infant assimilates new information into his or her existing level of understanding (or existing schemata); an example of this is an infant who has a schema for shaking and assimilates many new objects into this existing schema by shaking a bell, ball, rattle, hairbrush, necklace, and so on.

The infant also accommodates, or alters, existing schemata to adapt better to the environment. Thus, the infant with a well-developed shaking schema would, after many experiences with objects, realize that some objects are more shakable than others. This child might continue to shake the bell and rattle, but might accommodate the shaking schema for the other objects by trying new ways of manipulating the ball, hairbrush, and necklace. These new behaviors are new schemata, into which new objects can be assimilated. Learning has occurred.

Piaget differentiates play from the learning process in that while learning involves both assimilation and accommodation, there comes a point at which a schema is developed and requires no new accommodation. At this point the schema, or behavior, is reproduced purely for functional pleasure, and this is play. Assimilation is the primary process involved in play, and the child fits the outside world into existing schemata just for the pleasure of using the mastered schemata.

SENSORIMOTOR PLAY

Play is first observed in the second sensorimotor stage (1 to 4 months) after a primary circular reaction has been mastered; after such mastery, the infant reproduces the behavior for pleasure with a smile or laugh, without expecting any other results. In the third sensorimotor stage (4 to 8 months), schemata once learned unfailingly become games; once again the affects expressing *joy* and *power* (mastery) are the cues that let us know the child is playing. In the fourth stage (8 to 12 months) one can see strings of playful behaviors (a succession of schemata) one after the other, with no goal and no external aim or purpose except mastery and fun. In the fifth sensorimotor stage (12 to 18 months), one sees further development of these chains of unrelated actions; they now develop into rituals and are repeated again and again with playful affect and with the characteristics of a game.

So far, all of these levels of play fall into Piaget's category of practice games, which are exercises of various behaviors without modifying the behavior. Practice games occur throughout the preschool years as well as in infancy, and can involve motor or language games. The function, or purpose, of practice games is to exercise newly developed mental structures, mental or sensorimotor schemata, and various motor, mental, and linguistic skills motivated by the sheer pleasure of functioning. There are no symbols, no make-believe, and no rules. Practice games occur whenever a new skill is acquired.

In the sixth sensorimotor stage (18 to 24 months), a new kind of play emerges for the first time as the child demonstrates new capacities of representational, or symbolic, thought. Symbolic play, pretending, or make-believe, occurs when the child starts with a familiar schema—drinking from a cup, for instance—and then assimilates new objects into that schema. The new objects are in reality unrelated to the schema but are symbolically transformed to the schema by the child. An example would be a shell which the child holds to the lips so that it symbolizes a cup. Thus, in symbolic play, an absent object is represented. Objects are used as symbols of something unrelated to the actual object and are assimilated into the play theme. There is no accommodation to external reality. Rather, reality is transformed (assimilated) to fit the play theme.

The purpose of symbolic play is not skill mastery, as it is with practice games. Rather, the function is affective (here Piaget is quite close to psychodynamic theorists), and the child's emotional life, including emotional issues like compensation, wish fulfillment, and conflict resolution, form the content of the symbolic play. Mastery is focused on the child's emotional reality, and the symbol is a means for the child to assimilate, or transform, reality to the child's desires, interests, or feelings.

PREOPERATIONAL PERIOD
AGES 2 TO 4

During the preoperational period, the child's symbolic games become increasingly sophisticated. The first and most primitive form of symbolic play is seen in the final sensorimotor stage (stage six). Piaget labels this type of symbolic play the *symbolic schema,* which is the reproduction of a sensorimotor schema outside of its normal context and without the objects usually associated with it (like drinking from a shell). In this period the behavior is the symbol—drinking—and the child is pretending to carry out a familiar activity.

In the preoperational period, language becomes an important part of symbolic play and the child can describe or label symbols used in play. The first stage of preoperational symbolic play involves the *projection of symbolic schemata.* The child may project one of his or her own behaviors onto someone or something else, like pretending to give a doll a drink; alternatively, the child may project someone or something else's behavior onto him- or herself, and thus may imitate drinking out of a bowl like a kitten. Both of these involve an imitation of self or of other, and an assimilation of the prop into the child's play theme.

The second stage involves *identification of one thing with another,* rather than projection of a behavior onto another. Now the child says that an object *is* something else, holds up the shell and says, "This is my teacup." Or the child may identify his or her body with something else, and say, "I am a kitty." There are several crucial differences between this stage and the preceding one. First, the child makes the symbolic identification *before* beginning the imitative action and indicates the symbols' identification through speech. Second, the imitative action copies the symbolized object, not the child's own activities.

The third preoperational play stage involves *symbolic combinations.* After 2½ years of age, the first examples of simple symbolic combinations are seen. These combinations involve constructing and acting out whole symbolic scenes that may include role-played or imaginary characters. A striking feature of these symbolic combinations is the extent to which the child reproduces the real world in play, for the function of such play is to reconstruct and assimilate reality through make-believe.

In the next stage of symbolic combinations, *compensatory combinations,* the child changes or corrects reality rather than simply reproducing it for sheer pleasure. Thus, the child plays out make-believe scenarios, pretending to do something to change reality, like displacing an event onto another person or altering a characteristic or quality of a person or object. A related form of this type of play is catharsis, in which the child neutralizes a fear or painful event through acting out in play a wish or fantasy that could not be acted out in reality.

In the third type of symbolic combinations, *liquidating combinations,* the child relives a difficult or unpleasant situation by transposing it symbolically. In this type of play, Piaget feels, the psychologist sees most clearly the function of symbolic play. This function is to assimilate reality to the ego (allowing the ego to actively master reality) while freeing the ego from the real-life demands of accommodation. In these scenarios the ego runs the risk of failure but assimilates the risks and in so doing is the victor.

In the final type of symbolic combination, *anticipatory symbolic combinations,* the child symbolically anticipates the consequences of not obeying an instruction or warning that has been given in thematic play. The child's use of symbolic games in all of these cases involves assimilation of reality to the ego and intensification of assimilatory pleasure through fictitious control of the natural and social world.

INTUITIVE PERIOD—AGES 4 TO 7

Piaget believes that as the child's cognitive capacities develop, allowing the child to understand more about the natural and social world, symbolic games begin to lose their importance. The child continues to use play to present reality, but the symbols used in play become so close to reality that the play seems more a straight imitation than a playful representation of reality. This can be seen, for instance, in cooking sets that allow children to bake cakes packaged in miniature boxes and prepared with miniature cookware. This kind of play is more easily seen as a straight imitation of reality (accommodation) than as a fitting of reality to one's own needs or desires (assimilation).

The three distinguishing characteristics of symbolic games at this level are as follows:

1. The first characteristic is the relative orderliness of the playful construct, or theme. The flow of ideas is coherent and smooth.

2. The second is the increasing desire for exact imitation of reality.

3. The third is the appearance of collective symbolism. The child is far more able to adapt role-playing to other children's needs and desires, and so he or she both differentiates play roles and adapts them to coordinate the play with other children. In this instance, one can see the progress the child has made both in cognitive processes and in social growth, a real interaction of social and mental acquisitions. Play continues to change with increasing cognitive development, but further changes beyond the scope of this chapter will not be reviewed.

Given the depth and breadth of Piaget's handling of play, it is not surprising that there are other theories of play which actively compete with his viewpoints. Although there are, of course, criticisms of Piaget's theorizing about play (Sutton-Smith, 1966), most of the research on young children's play has focused on specific relationships of certain variables to children's play. These include play as it aids learning, thematic play, peer play, role play, and the relationship of play to creativity. Major research findings in these areas will be reviewed in the following pages.

THE RELATIONSHIP OF PRACTICE PLAY TO LEARNING

Several authors in addition to Piaget have hypothesized that young children's play with objects assists them in later learning of problem-solving tasks in two ways. First, play gives children practice with materials in a nonstressful situation. Second, play provides an opportunity to discover many new combinations of behaviors with objects (Smith and Sutton, 1979).

Two studies have examined this hypothesis using the problem-solving task that Kohler devised for his apes—a child's version of the stick and banana task. Sylva and colleagues (1976, 1977) examined the performance of white, middle class preschoolers on a task in which the children were to retrieve a piece of chalk from a small cage using sticks that had to be clamped together in order to reach the chalk. Children who manipulated the materials without adult interference performed as well as the children who had seen the adult demonstrate the task. The children who had manipulated the materials were also more eager and more flexible in their approaches. They exerted continuous effort to solve the problem and made better use of hints than the other groups. Sylva felt that the key element in this study was self-initiation, because the task required self-initiation as well as flexibility and low stress.

In a similar study, Smith and Sutton (1979) found that, while the play and demonstration groups performed fairly equally on the initial task, when the task was altered and made more difficult, the play group was clearly superior. Thus, practice play seems to aid problem-solving by providing self-initiated experiences with flexible combinations of behaviors.

FUNCTIONS OF SYMBOLIC PLAY

Given the stress that Piaget, Vygotsky, Erikson, and many others place on the importance of symbolic play for development, the various functions of symbolic play will be reviewed before the actual research findings are presented. Feitelson and Ross (1973) have focused on five functions of symbolic play. (The various authors cited in this section used different terms to describe this type of play: thematic play, fantasy play, imaginary play, sociodramatic play, and representational play. The term symbolic play will be used to signify all of these.)

First, symbolic play socializes; through it, children rehearse social roles and learn about social relationships. Second, symbolic play contributes to mental health by helping the child regain or maintain emotional equilibrium and by helping the child gain a sense of control (or mastery) over the world.

Third, symbolic play helps the child accumulate information about the objects being played with, about social relationships with peers in play, and about rules and routines of the real world. Fourth, symbolic play aids cognitive development and assists imagination and creativity. And finally, symbolic play helps the child develop positive personality traits or attitudinal styles involving perseverance, motivation, self-confidence, and social skills.

THE RELATIONSHIP OF SYMBOLIC PLAY TO ABSTRACT THOUGHT

The Russian cognitive theorist, Vygotsky, feels that symbolic play—creating imaginary situations and acting them out—is a primary source of cognitive development. There are two aspects of symbolic play which Vygotsky believes directly foster cognitive growth: the separation of thought from perception, and the development of self-control (Vygotsky, 1976). Regarding separation of thought from perception, Vygotsky believes that before the age of 3, children are compelled to act by their perception of the objects around them (observing any 2-year-old on a shopping trip should be immediate confirmation of this view). Thus, stairs are to be climbed, bells are to be rung, and so on. Vygotsky feels that imaginative play gives the child the first experiences in which the child's thoughts—not the nature of the objects—control the child's activity; and for the first time the child plans and controls his or her behavior with ideas. The preschooler can thus separate cognition from perception in play, a transitional step in logical problem-solving.

Regarding the second aspect, self-control, Vygotsky sees covert rules regarding role-appropriate behaviors appearing in preschoolers' play. The child must inhibit impulses and subordinate desires to these covert rules, requiring self-control. Note what a different orientation this is from Piaget, who sees the child subordinating reality to the self.

Both of these aspects assist in the development of logical or abstract thought by helping the child separate internal thoughts or impulses from external perceptions or rules. The child learns to differentiate subjective from objective, which is the basis for use of logic to solve problems, and thus is prepared for the transition to more abstract thought processes.

UNIVERSALITY OF SYMBOLIC PLAY

In the writings of Piaget, Vygotsky, Freud, and Erikson one is left with the impression that symbolic play is a universal phenomenon, an always occurring developmental phase of young children. Yet cross-cultural studies do not support this view. Instead, they suggest that symbolic play is a phenomenon of middle class Western cultures. In other cultures, play may be mainly rough and tumble play, or practice play, or there may be role play in which the children act out adult roles imitatively, but without symbolic transformation (Feitelson, 1977; Feitelson and Ross, 1973).

In addition, the play of Western children who are severely socioeconomically deprived has also been examined. It has been found to lack symbolic transformations; to lack higher level practice play involving language, materials, and concepts; and to lack advanced planning and goal-directedness. Instead, the play of poverty-level Western children continues to involve mainly sensorimotor practice play qualities (Murphy, 1972). Preschoolers in rural communities also demonstrate a paucity of symbolic play involving play themes (Feitelson and Ross, 1973).

If symbolic play is culturally mediated, what are the cultural variables that contribute to symbolic play? Feitelson and Ross (1973, 1977) mention several environmental factors suggested by various studies.

These include the following:

1. Play space seems necessary for formation of symbolic play. Children need a physical area for play, with adults allowing and encouraging play in that area and respecting the privacy of the area.

2. Play time is also necessary. This is time allotted for play by adults who support the play activity and recognize it as a legitimate activity.

3. Play objects help the child shift to representational play. They must be respected as such by the parents, and a place must be provided for the objects.

4. Play atmosphere is an important fourth variable. This is an atmosphere in which adults participate and model representational play. Soviet and Israeli researchers also emphasize this learned component of symbolic play.

DEVELOPMENTAL STUDIES OF SYMBOLIC PLAY

Several studies have examined the developmental course of symbolic play in preschoolers. Vygotsky suggests that children move from play with concrete objects to true use of symbols, either by substituting an object or by imagining it. Elder and Pederson (1978) asked 2- and 3-year-olds to perform realistic acts with appropriate objects, ambiguous objects, unrelated objects, and no object. The expected developmental trend was strongly supported, with the oldest children functioning truly symbolically without any props at all, and the youngest children performing the actions only with realistic props. The study demonstrated that children need progressively less environmental support for symbolic actions during years 2 and 3. (The reader may wish to refer to a related study by Fein, 1975.)

Overton and Jackson (1973) also studied young children's symbolic representation and had findings consistent with those of Elder and Pederson. As both Piaget and Vygotsky suggest and these researchers have found, with age the child's gradual internalization of symbols apparently grows increasingly distant from the represented object.

In examining symbolic transformations, Matthews (1977) found that the predominant modes 4-year-olds used to make the cognitive shift from reality to fantasy involved either *material transformations* or *ideational transformations*. In material transformations, an actual object in the playroom was assigned some property that it did not actually possess (a new identity, a new function, and so on); in ideational transformations, the children referred to objects, people, or situations that were not present and pretended that they were present. These findings are in line with the two studies cited above, which suggested that the symbolic play of older preschoolers would not be limited by having the objects present. In looking for cultural differences, McLoyd (1980) examined the fantasy play of black preschoolers living in low income families in urban settings. As in Matthew's study, almost half of the play for all age groups represented symbolic play.

In summary, these studies document the tremendous increase in symbolic thought that occurs between the ages of 2 and 3. They also indicate that while the young preschooler's symbolic play is greatly aided by the presence of realistic play objects, the older preschooler requires much less environmental support for symbolic play, because full symbolic thought was developed.

SYMBOLIC PLAY AND LANGUAGE SKILLS

In the studies mentioned above, the symbolic representations were language related. Either the child was verbally instructed in the desired symbolic activity ("Pretend to comb your hair") or the child's symbolic transformations in free play were rated according to what the child was saying. Piaget indicated that language and symbolic play come from the same cognitive well, which is the ability to represent things symbolically, whether through words, play themes, symbolic thought, or symbolic gestures.

Rosenblatt (1977) provides data from several studies which document that the child's development through the Piagetian play stages is accompanied by mental development (as seen on intelligence tests) and by increasing language development; thus it supports the notion that play reflects underlying cognitive development. Rosenblatt also notes the relationship between the appearance of representational play, the appearance of referential speech, and the appearance of object permanence concepts in the 12- to 18-month-old; all of these indicate the presence of internal representations in the child's mind of the external world.

Bates (1981) described studies in which aphasic youngsters (and adults) were found to lack the ability to use symbolic gestures on the kinds of tasks described in the Overton and Jackson (1973) studies. Bates discussed the relationship among use of symbolic gestures, use of unrelated objects in symbolic play, and use of language. She attributed these three abilities to underlying cognitive development in the use of mental symbolic representations.

Both Bates and Rosenblatt also discussed treatment of several language disordered children through play techniques. The autistic and aphasic children involved also showed very poor symbolic play skills. Through the use of play techniques, they were taught symbolic play, which resulted in an improvement in expressive language, in generalization, and in increased use of words as symbols rather than as rotely learned phrases. The use of one modality to improve another also points to a common underlying element between symbolic play and language. Thus, several studies as well as Piaget's work support the view that language and symbolic play both result from the young child's growing ability to generate and use mental symbols, and that the two behaviors are thus intimately related in cognition.

SYMBOLIC PLAY AND LEARNING

Various studies have demonstrated positive relationships between symbolic play and learning. Sylva and colleagues (1979) noted that children who played with test materials in a symbolic way were much better at solving tasks than were the children who played with materials in a nonsymbolic way.

Saltz, Dixon, and Johnson (1977) used Piaget's and Vygotsky's emphasis to study the relationship of symbolic play to cognition, impulse control, and empathy. They found that symbolic play—acting out of fantasy and engaging in sociodramatic play—aided the development of IQ, empathy, and impulse control for their black subjects. Thus, as was hypothesized, symbolic play seemed to help children develop symbolic thought, appreciation for others' roles, and self-control.

If symbolic play aids social, language, and cognitive development in so many ways, is it possible to enhance symbolic play skills? The study by Saltz and colleagues (1977) indicates that it is possible, as does Rosenblatt's (1977) work with language impaired children, whose symbolic play abilities improved, with resulting improvement in language. Rosen (1974) found that a long period of coaching significantly increased black urban preschoolers' spontaneous use of sociodramatic play during free play times; he also found an improvement in group productivity, and group effectiveness on role taking tasks and role taking skills. These studies, taken together, indicate that symbolic play skills can be taught to some extent and can be increased by training, with resulting improvement in cognitive, language, and social skills.

PLAY AND CREATIVITY

The final cognitive aspect of play to be considered in this chapter is the relationship between play and creativity. Bruner, a major American cognitive theorist, cites two qualities of play which enhance creativity. First, play is a means of minimizing the consequences of one's actions and of learning in a less risky situation. Second, play provides an opportunity to try combinations of behaviors which never would be tried under pressure. These descriptions of play and creativity seem to link practice play to creativity.

According to Dansky (1980) and Dansky and Silverman (1975), symbolic make-believe is also important in increasing associative fluency, a key characteristic of creativity. Dansky believes that the free combination and assimilation of ideas in symbolic play are analogous to the " . . . tendency toward broad attention deployment and non-evaluative ideational productivity which is considered central to creative thinking" (Dansky, 1980, p. 576). Dansky, examining the associative fluency of preschoolers, found a clear positive relationship between a high degree of symbolic play and a high level of associative fluency on specific tasks (Dansky, 1980). This relationship certainly supports Piaget's view of symbolic play as a source of creative imagination (Piaget, 1962).

Dansky and Silverman (1975) also studied the relationship of object play to associative fluency and found that children who experienced nondirected object play scored significantly higher than others in tests of associative fluency. Dansky and Silverman believe that free play created a set, or attitude, around generating associations to a variety of objects, whether or not the objects were encountered during the play. Thus, play facilitated imaginative adaptation.

Feitelson and Ross (1973) have found that tutoring in symbolic play appeared to increase the amount of symbolic play their 5-year-old subjects used when playing alone and to enhance performance on creativity measures of exploration, innovation, and originality.

In summary, play—particularly symbolic play—is considered to have an especially important role in the cognitive development of young children. Children's use of symbols in play provides much practice at functioning on an increasingly mental level, and the child's thoughts and ideas (rather than the physical surroundings) wield more and more control over the child's overt behavior. Thus, we see increasing self-control and decreasing impulsivity with age. The child's developing adeptness at using mental symbols in play parallels the child's ability to use verbal symbols rather than actions, to use goal-directed thought to solve problems, and to find creative approaches to problem-solving. Thus, in several ways, symbolic play appears to enhance cognitive functioning.

Many authors also focus on the social benefits of symbolic play, as children learn to assign and play out roles that require cooperation, leadership, and playing by the rules. Role play also provides children with information about social roles and thus aids their learning about adult roles. For these reasons, the focus of this chapter will now shift to theories and research involving social aspects of play.

SOCIAL ASPECTS OF PLAY

The seminal work in this area was Mildred Parten's (1932) observational study of the social behavior of nursery school children. Many of her observations are still forming the basis for present-day studies of young children's social behavior. Some of her most influential observations included the findings that the most typical play group size was two, and that even the youngest children played most often in same-sex dyads, with same-age partners (Fein, 1975). Parten's best known contribution, however, was her classification system for describing social participation: unoccupied behavior, onlooker behavior, solitary play, parallel play, associative play, and organized supplementary play, which is now usually referred to as cooperative play (Parten, 1932). Because of the limited sample Parten was examining and the number of years that have passed since her publication, many current researchers are re-examining the characteristics of modern-day preschoolers' social play.

One area of re-examination of Parten's work is in the area of parallel play. Several researchers have found the amount of parallel play that 3-, 4-, and 5-year-olds exhibited to be fairly constant, rather than diminishing with age (Barnes, 1971; Rubin, Watson, and Jambor, 1978), and to be more frequently seen in 3- and 4-year-olds than Parten's data indicated (Rubin, Maioni, and Hornung, 1976). These results lead the clinician to question whether parallel play is one of several sequential stages, as Parten's cross-sectional data suggested. In a longitudinal study of 2- and 3-year-olds' social behavior, Smith (1978) and the researchers cited above found no substantial decrease in parallel play with age. Rather, parallel play was found with various children from ages 2 through 4. Parallel play did not seem to be a sequential developmental stage; the majority of children in this study moved right from solitary to group (associative and cooperative) play. Rather, Smith suggests that parallel play is best understood as an immature social play form seen mainly in 2-year-olds. This view is supported by Rubin and colleagues (1976). Smith also suggests that social play does not follow a linear sequential model and that Parten's categories should be considered more as descriptive than as developmental categories.

A second area of Parten's work that has been recently examined and reformulated is her category of solitary play. Several researchers are currently looking at solitary play as a constructive, self-directed form of play, rather than as an immature play stage preceding more mature, social play forms. Part of this rethinking is due to the finding that solitary play occurs more frequently in preschoolers than Parten's data suggested (Barnes, 1971). Roper and Hinde (1978) also found that the amount of time preschool children spent playing alone was not related to the amount of time they spent playing with others. Instead of finding that this was a continuum, the researchers found solitary play and social play to be two separate factors; thus, solitary play does not indicate a lack of social maturity. Researchers have also found that children's solitary play is made up predominantly of constructive learning activities (Rubin and colleagues, 1976; Moore, Evertson, and Brophy, 1974). Moore and associates (1974) summarize what seems to be the current thought regarding solitary play: "Most solitary play appears to be independent, task-oriented behavior which is functional in school situations and indicative of maturity rather than immaturity" (p. 834). These authors also suggest that solitary play may have its own developmental continuum, beginning with passive watching, then moving to more active and expressive activities, then becoming involved in more challenging, educational activities.

To summarize the above, it appears that Parten's categories do not actually reflect a developmental continuum, but rather describe various types of social participation seen in young children. Parallel play appears to be the most immature level of social participation, though it is by no means a universal stage. Solitary play probably does not belong in the social participation continuum at all, but rather reflects a different form of play that is constructive and self-initiated. And, at least during the preschool years, group play (cooperative and associative) is seen from age 2 on but does not increase substantially thereafter (Roper and Hinde, 1978; Rubin and colleagues, 1976, 1978; Barnes, 1971).

ENVIRONMENTAL ASPECTS OF PLAY

Examination of social and environmental aspects of play has been increasingly influenced by social learning theory, which stresses the importance of the child's physical and social environment in shaping play skills and influencing many aspects of children's play. While cognitive and psychodynamic theories have provided great insight into the structural components of young children's play, these theories underplay the tremendous role of the environment in influencing play. Yet, even the symbolic structure of play is environmentally influenced, as seen in cross-cultural research which shows that certain cultures foster symbolic play, while such play does not occur in other cultures. As a result of social learning theory's influence on play research, the effects of many environmental variables on play have been uncovered, with some key findings noted below.

One variable that seems to affect preschoolers' social play is socioeconomic class. Children from lower socioeconomic status families have been found to demonstrate more parallel play and less group play than children from middle income families (Rubin and colleagues 1976). In examining a group of Canadian preschoolers, Barnes (1971) also found less associative and cooperative play than Parten did. In the earlier section on symbolic play, evidence was presented to suggest that the cognitive content of young children's play was negatively affected by socioeconomic deprivation; the present studies suggest that social maturity is also negatively affected.

Another environmental variable that has been examined is the physical setting in which play occurs. As was discussed earlier in this chapter, physical characteristics of space, time, and objects available for play are felt to influence symbolic play positively (Feitelson and Ross, 1973; Feitelson, 1977). The atmosphere determined by adults' attitudes toward and involvement in children's play also seems to effect play.

To explore this adult-mediated variable, Huston-Stein and colleagues (1977) compared the play of preschoolers in more adult-oriented, adult-structured classes with that of children in less adult-oriented, adult-structured classes. The researchers found that children in the less structured classes demonstrated more pro-social behavior toward peers, more imaginative play, and more role-taking fantasy play than the children in more structured classrooms. The results indicate both the social and cognitive effects on play.

In a similar study of a structured, formal learning classroom and a discovery learning classroom, Johnson and colleagues (1980) found no differences in social characteristics of play or in the amount of symbolic play in the two groups of children. However, they found that the formal classroom children spent more time in constructive play (purposeful building and drawing play which is almost identical to work), while the discovery classroom children spent more time in functional play. Thus, while Johnson's researcher confirmed that the learning approach stressed by adults during class time seemed to influence the play styles of children during free play, the earlier findings of social play and imaginative play differences were not supported.

Another characteristic of the play environment which has been found to affect play is familiarity. One study examined the effects on a child's behavior of being in a familiar setting. Both "shy" and "sociable" preschoolers were found to be more sociable (and more aggressive) in their own homes; they controlled the visiting playmate via positive verbal interactions and aggression (Jeffers and Love 1979). The familiarity of the playmate has been found to influence the maturity of the social play in a positive direction (Doyle, Connolly, and Rivest, 1980). Thus, it appears that many characteristics of the play environment—space, equipment, attitudes of surrounding adults, familiarity of the setting and the playmate, time allotted to play—affect the content of children's play.

ORIGINS OF PEER PLAY

Both Parten's work and social learning theory have stimulated detailed investigations of the origin and characteristics of peer play. One particularly interesting aspect of such research in the last ten years or so has been the work in infant peer relationships (Lewis and colleagues, 1975). Child development theories have been heavily influenced by Freud (who felt that the capacity for friendship in school-aged children developed out of earlier parent-child relationships) and Piaget (who felt that young children were too egocentric to have meaningful, mutual peer interactions). As a result, child developmentalists had been reluctant to attribute much importance or meaning to young children's friendships. Research on infant and toddler peer relations carried out in the 1930s reinforced this view (Bridges, 1933; Maudry and Nekula, 1939). However, these studies were carried out on institutionalized children who were placed in unfamiliar settings, and the observational techniques used were quite different from present-day studies.

Beginning in the 1970s, with better methodologies and better measurement

procedures, social learning theorists began to paint a different picture of infant peer relations. A picture emerged of the infant as nonaggressive, socially inquisitive being who prefers other infants to adults, who has some social competencies, and who has an ability to form differential relationships with familiar peers. Vandell and associates (1980) observed infants' use of socially directed behaviors to initiate and to respond to social contacts as early as 6 months of age. The study found that those 6-month-olds demonstrated coordinated, socially directed behaviors (several behaviors occurring at once) in a proportion equal to that of toddlers. The social interactions were overwhelmingly positive and vocal in nature and were more frequent and complex when no toys were present. These researchers did not find general developmental changes in social interest and interactions over the 6-month period, indicating that social behaviors were fairly stable in the first year of life and may be genetically programmed or may be the result of parent-child interactions in the first 6 months.

From year 1 to year 2, toddlers learn to sustain positive social interactions as a result of ongoing experiences with peers (Mueller and Brenner, 1977; Eckerman, Whatley, and Kutz, 1975; Lewis and colleagues, 1975). They increase their production of complex, coordinated, socially directed behaviors as a result of peer experiences. In addition, parallel play focused around toys is the most frequent kind of social play seen in the second year of life. Several researchers state that it is not that toys are necessary; indeed, toddlers in their study also interacted more when no toys were present. Rather, they believe that toys and the parallel play that toys elicit from toddlers help to provide a situation that triggers social interactions (Mueller and Brenner, 1977; Eckerman and Whatley, 1977). Thus, they see that parallel play is instrumental in producing social interactions because the toy play at the center of the parallel play situation is both the goal and the reward for interacting in a positive way.

Toys also seem to help toddlers play in groups, rather than dyads. In a study of five toddlers in a group play situation over a three-month period (Mueller and Rich,

1976), three or more children would cluster around one child playing with an object repeatedly. At the end of the three-month period, the children appeared to cluster in a group in order to be together; they gathered to play social and imitative games like follow the leader rather than just to play with toys. Thus, toys seem to serve as catalysts for many types of social growth in the first two years of life.

One-year-olds also demonstrate the capacity for friendships, in that they act differently with familiar than with unfamiliar peers. They stay closer to familiar peers, imitate them more, show more positive affect and more toy sharing and offering, less negative affect and less toy taking away (Lewis and colleagues, 1975). With a familiar peer, toddlers show higher level toy play than when alone, and much less reliance on mother (Rubinstein and Howes, 1976).

CHARACTERISTICS OF PRESCHOOLERS' PEER PLAY

Research on peer play with preschool-aged children has focused on such topics as sex role play, and effects of age, sex, and familiarity of the peer. As was true in the infant studies, 3-year-olds' play with a familiar peer evokes more social play than with an unfamiliar peer, and when toy play is involved, the cognitive level of social toy play is higher with a familiar peer (Doyle, Connolly, and Rivest, 1980; Scholtz and Ellis, 1975). Much more dramatic play also occurs with a familiar peer, the cognitive implications of which were discussed earlier in this chapter. As Doyle and colleagues (1980) state:

In summary, with a familiar peer, the child performs in a more socially active, socially competent, and cognitively mature fashion. These effects are possibly elicited and mediated by the previous learning of positive and successful social behaviors in the context of mutually shared and mutually understood interaction-response sequences (p. 222).

The age of the peer also affects preschoolers' play. As Lougee, Grueneich, and Hartup, (1977) point out, mixed-age play groups are the norm in most cultures, with same-age play groups a somewhat artificial creation of complex cultures. Lougee and associates' findings revealed young children's ability to vary their play according to the age of the peer. In general, children who were not age mates played like age mates, with the younger child generally showing more mature behavior and language when playing with an older child (Lougee and colleagues, 1977). Thus, there is evidence of positive effects of mixed age playmates.

Another area of peer research has grown out of social learning theory's view of social behavior as being instrumentally taught and maintained (reinforced) by peers themselves. These studies view peers as reinforcing or punishing agents who shape the behaviors of playmates. In an interesting study of reciprocity in preschoolers' interactions, Leiter (1977) examined the social interactions of 4-year-olds—leaders and followers, popular and unpopular children—to try to understand what kinds of interactions produce reciprocal relations in social behaviors. His findings were threefold: (1) friendly initiations elicit agreeable responses from peers and are thus reinforced, (2) demanding, aggressive initiations elicit aggressive, demanding responses, which could be experienced as either reinforcing (in that one receives attention from the peer) or punishing; and (3) whiny initiations are ignored, which would lead to extinction over time. Thus, Leiter states that the reciprocity of young children's interactions seems to be monitored at least partially by social reinforcers in the initiation/response dyads (Leiter, 1977).

In a study of peers as reinforcing agents, Charlesworth and Hartup (1967) observed 3- and 4-year-olds positively reinforcing each other, using such behaviors as approval, attention, submission, objects, and affection. As social learning theorists would predict, the older children used more reinforcers and distributed them to more children than did the younger children. They also found that giving and receiving was reciprocal. Children who gave the most received the most from others, and were thus more popular. Rubin and Maioni (1975) hypothesized that more popular preschoolers would have a better understanding of reciprocal relationships than their less popular peers, and that this understanding would be seen in their superiority in emphatic role taking, in dramatic play, in classification abilities, and in less egocentric thinking. They found much support for their hypothesis and the author assumes that experiences with social reciprocity and role taking underlie all these relationships.

Throughout these studies a picture is being drawn of young children as inherently social beings, reacting differentially and preferentially with peers from infancy on. Although some might argue that the earliest social behaviors are innate, these studies support young children's need for social experiences with peers in order to learn adaptive social behavior, and support theories that such learning occurs as early as the second year of life.

SEX ROLE PLAY AND GENDER PREFERENCES

The final topic to be covered in this section concerns children's preferences for same-sex playmates and for sex role play. The fact that young children prefer playmates of the same sex and the fact that they spend much of their dramatic play acting out sex-appropriate roles have been long established. Researchers in this area have been trying to find out why these preferences exist. Various theoretical explanations have been used in the past—an innatist, biologic explanation, for example, or the psychodynamic concept of identification, an internalization of the same sex parent and the desire to be as like that parent as possible; and there are social learning theory concepts that view such play as instrumentally learned via social reinforcement and punishment from peers and adults.

Bianchi and Bakeman (1978) found far more same-sex play in a traditional preschool that emphasized socialization than in an open school that stressed individual learning and growth. However, these researchers felt that this finding was probably not just a result of different reinforcement patterns between the schools, but also of the different value system of parents who choose one setting or the other for their child. To study the effects of social reinforcement in a classroom setting, Serbin, Tonick, and Sternglang (1977) sought to alter the same-sex preferences by having adults verbally reinforce mixed-sex play. Under reinforcement procedures, there was a large and significant increase in mixed-sex play; but when the reinforcement was stopped, mixed-sex play fell off. An interesting finding in this study was that as mixed-sex play increased, solitary play and same-sex play did not *decrease*. Increasing mixed-sex play thus seemed to expand the children's social contacts rather than just to substitute one sex for another. Both of these studies emphasize the environment's role in influencing same-sex and mixed-sex play and give support to social learning theory views.

Yet there are real differences in the play of same-sex pairs and mixed-sex pairs, even in children supposedly too young to have acquired a sex gender identity yet. In a very interesting study of play differences in same-sex and mixed dyads, Jacklin and Maccoby (1978) found that while 2½-year-old boys and girls did not actually behave differently when with a same-sex or opposite-sex playmate, the playmate reacted to them differently, *as if* they were behaving in different ways. Even in children this young, same-sex dyads played more compatibly than mixed-sex dyads. These findings can be explained in several ways: methodologic problems in the study itself; earlier cognitive awareness of gender identity and sex stereotypes than is generally accepted; or early child training from parents in a double standard for play (how one acts with girls and with boys). None of these explanations is definitive, but the findings are intriguing and emphasize the strength and consistency of same-sex play preference.

Now let us turn to sex-role play, the tendency of children to play out masculine and feminine roles in play. Again, much of the research has focused on environmental reinforcers and punishers for appropriate sex role play. In examining preschool teachers' reinforcement of sex-typed behaviors in preschoolers, Fagot (1978) found that while both sexes get equal amounts of teacher attention, both sexes were reinforced more for feminine behaviors, and that experienced teachers reinforced boys for feminine behaviors far more than inexperienced teachers. Rather than being critical of preschool teachers for this, Fagot points out that the behaviors expected of children in school—to work at a desk, to attend to the adult, to be interested in language activity, to favor table-type activities—are behaviors that girls prefer, and that in order to prepare children for school, boys need to learn these nonpreferred activities. Fagot raises the question of whether boys' greater difficulties and negativism in school may be related to this emphasis on nonpreferred activities.

Langlois and Downs (1980) examined parents' and peers' reactions to sex-role-appropriate and -inappropriate play with 3- and 5-year-olds, and found that girls were treated consistently by mother, father, and peers, all of whom rewarded girls for sex-appropriate play. Boys were treated quite inconsistently by mother and peers, and only the fathers consistently rewarded sex-appropriate play for boys. These findings support reciprocal role theory, which emphasizes the importance of the father in teaching appropriate sex-role behaviors to sons and daughters. In a related study, Fagot (1977) again found that boys received very inconsistent messages around sex-role behavior from peers. In observational studies of sex-role play and sex-typed toy play, both Grief (1976) and Schau and colleagues (1980) found that girls had more latitude around sex-inappropriate play and engaged in more of it than boys did, possibly because the male role is seen as more desirable by both sexes. Schau and colleagues (1980) also found less rigidity around sex roles in toy play than was expected, and found that parents expected more sex-typed play than was found, again supporting the view that parents shape their children's play to conform to sex-appropriate expectations.

In summary, social play in young children provides opportunities for learning new skills and practicing existing skills. The content of children's social play generally involves gross physical activity, object manipulation, and cognitive activities, language games, or dramatic role play. These activities exercise gross motor, fine motor, cognitive, language, and social skills. From infancy on, children demonstrate the capacity for social interactions with peers, and by age 3 children are adept at peer interactions. Preschoolers play mostly in same-sex dyads, although groups of three and four children are frequent. Children show individual differences in their play mainly around the level of social maturity (à la Parten), and major sex differences occur in gross motor versus fine motor play, and fantastic dramatic play (Superman or the Incredible Hulk) versus sex role dramatic play (house, dolls, or doctor) (Clark, Wyon, and Richards, 1969; Overton and Jackson, 1973).

AFFECTIVE ASPECTS OF PLAY

The emotional meanings of play have been most fully studied and described by psychoanalytically oriented writers. Peller (1954) has provided an excellent overview of the psychoanalytic understanding of play, the main points of which will be reviewed below.

In terms of personality structure, play is seen to be a function of the ego—the organizer of the personality, and the reality oriented part of the personality that mediates among the id, the superego, and the outside world. One function of the ego is to serve as a sort of balance mechanism to protect against painful thoughts and feelings. Play, like thought, comes from the ego. "Play is instigated by the ego in its attempts to deal with blows or deprivations exerted by reality as well as with pressures originating in the id or superego" (Peller, 1954, p. 179).

The real world may present an injury to the ego by making a child feel small, helpless, powerless, dependent, or unimportant. Or the world may deprive the child of positive ego feelings of independence, control, and mastery. Pressures on the ego may originate from the id in the form of instinctual drives, strong fantasies and needs, sexual feelings, anger and hate, or wishes for love and attention. Pressures on the ego also come from the superego (the conscience), producing feelings of guilt, shame, and self-hate. When any of these feelings are present, anxiety arises from the ego (owing to the perceived danger from the instinctual drives themselves, from a clash between the drives and the real world, or from a clash between drives and the superego). When this anxiety is of low intensity, the ego may turn to play as a way of assimilating the anxiety.

Play helps the child reduce anxiety in several ways. Play alleviates anxiety by gratifying wishes, needs, and fantasies through symbolic play that is compatible with reality and with the superego. Play may also repeat or confirm a gratifying experience. Play is a step toward sublimation, a defense mechanism that allows a more acceptable activity to substitute for a less acceptable one, thus attempting to obtain pleasure at minimum risk. And finally, play has a cathartic function and can serve as a safety valve for pent-up instinctual pressures. In these ways, the child uses play as adults use music, drama, art, and fantasies (Peller, 1954).

One emotional aspect of play which observers often find puzzling is the tendency of children to play out painful or frightening life events over and over again. This characteristic of play was first described by Freud, who felt that it was a demonstration of repetition compulsion. Analytic writers such as Wälder (1933) and Erikson (1976) see this as an extremely important emotional function of play. In playing out disturbing events, the child is re-enacting an experience that was too difficult emotionally to be assimilated immediately. The ego attempts to assimilate the event by reliving it again and again, attempting to master its meaning and the feelings that it elicited. The ego that was forced to experience the trauma passively now repeats it actively, hoping to direct and control the event (Wälder, 1933). Thus, in play, children project their own relevant personal themes—themes reflecting the child's generalized feelings—onto the microcosm of play. Through symbolic play, the child acts out the important emotional meanings in his or her life. The child also reconstructs personal experiences to learn what they mean, so that the child can master those events and move on to others (Vygotsky, 1976; Erikson, 1976).

PSYCHODYNAMIC TYPES OF PLAY

Peller (1954) describes several levels of play that appear progressively through the early childhood years. At the earliest level, symbolic play is related to one's own body. Objects used in play are versions of body parts, rather than tools, as the child works through this most basic level of sense of self—a body image and bodily identity.

At the second level (probably around 2 or 3 years of age), the child's symbolic play is related to relationships with the preoedipal mother, the infantile image of a good mother (the feeder and nurturer who cares for the child's body), and a bad mother (depriver, restrictor, punisher, or absent). The general theme of the child's play is, "I do to you what mother does to me," and in the play the child turns passive experiences into active ones that are inflicted on someone or something else.

At the third level, somewhere between 3½ to 5 years, symbolic play is most related to oedipal conflicts. During this period, the child works to master loving, possessive feelings toward the opposite-sex parent, and to master aggressive, competitive and fearful feelings about the same-sex parent. At this level, the clinician sees sociodramatic play, with well-developed, sex-appropriate roles and real social relationships played out. The child's oedipal anxiety ("I'm small; I can't have the pleasures of grown-up life") is compensated for in play with the fantasy ("I'm big, I'm a grown-up; I can do what grown-ups do").

At the fourth level, beginning somewhere around age 6, the oedipal conflicts have been put aside. Postoedipal play for the most part involves games—rather than symbolic play—with peers. New, important relationships are forming outside the family; this identification with peers helps the child extricate him- or herself from the past oedipal emotional entanglements inside the family. The rules of games mirror the rule system the child is building within the superego, and the competition with peers as equals replaces competition at home with parents.

The psychodynamic orientation regarding children's play is particularly useful when it is necessary to assess a child's emotional health through play. Child clinical psychologists and child psychiatrists are particularly well trained in this mode of child assessment, as are some psychiatric social workers. Because this type of an assessment requires special training, young children for whom there is a question of emotional disturbance are usually most appropriately referred to one of these professionals. (For more detailed information on how one assesses the emotional health of a young child through a play interview, please consult Appendix F, "The Play Interview.")

PLAY OF HANDICAPPED CHILDREN

Research on handicapped children's play is scarce, and much of the studies done before the 1970s that compared handicapped children's play with nonhandicapped children's play is confounded by the variable of institutionalization. Until the passage of Public Law 94-142, education for blind, deaf, and emotionally, mentally, and physically handicapped students was often available only in an institutional setting. Thus, studies of handicapped children most often used children in residential settings, where they were compared with nonhandicapped children living at home. Yet, as was discussed earlier in this chapter, play appears to originate and be nurtured by parental attentiveness. As Provence and Lipton (1962) discussed in their excellent book on the effects of institutionalization on children's psychological growth, physical space and play materials cannot by themselves support play. Without personal attention and interaction, children do not play. Thus, studies, like Horne's and Philleo's (1976), which compared the solitary play of lower class, institutionalized, mildly retarded children with nonhandicapped, middle class, home-reared children matched for mental age demonstrated differences in play; nonhandicapped children demonstrated more constructive, spontaneous, and creative play. But whether the differences are due to retardation, institutionalization, or socio-

economic class differences cannot be determined. Interpretation of Woodward's (1959) cognitive study of severely retarded, institutionalized children's play suffers from the same difficulties.

Li's (1981) survey of the literature on mentally retarded children's play indicates that such children have "a restricted play repertoire, both in the use of play material, verbal-language play, social child-to-child play, as well as pretend-symbolic play" (p. 122). However, it does not distinguish among studies controlling for the institutionalization or socioeconomic and other confounding variables. In an earlier article, Mogford (1977), who does discriminate between studies controlling for those variables and studies that do not, states that retarded children play at developmentally appropriate levels for their mental ages, *provided* that they have had the environmental supports that nonhandicapped, home-reared children have. This view certainly is in harmony with a developmental model of retardation (rather than a deficit model), and is also in keeping with the earlier reported negative effects of socioeconomic and environmental deprivation on children's play.

Li (1981) reviews several successful studies that improved the quality of mentally retarded children's social play, and she also points out how limited efforts have been to assist mentally retarded children to learn through play. Several writers have discussed the positive effects of play therapy techniques for mentally retarded, emotionally disturbed children (Leland and Smith, 1965; Newcomer and Morrison, 1974; Davidson, 1975), and Leland and Smith suggest an approach to play interviewing and play therapy specifically for mentally retarded children. Their approach systematically varies the amount of structure in the materials and the amount of structure the therapist uses to achieve various therapeutic goals. The emphasis falls on improving the child's adaptive behavior. Deutsch (1979) has developed a cognitive assessment strategy for "untestable" mentally retarded children from Leland and Smith's (1965) play interview approach. In this strategy, the child is placed in play situations in which structure from materials and evaluator is systematically varied, and indicators of cognitive, motor, language, social, and emotional development are gleaned from the child's play in the various situations.

Blindness is a handicap that clearly impedes play. Sandler and Wills (1965, as cited by Mogford, 1977) describe three effects of blindness which alter the normal developmental sequence of play. The first effect is the infant's inability to locate objects and attain them at will, and the second is distortion of parent/child interactions—which presumably is the core of play—owing to lack of facial expression and infant cues that the parents can easily interpret. The third effect is a delay in imaginative play and symbolic representation.

Selma Fraiberg (1978) describes in depth the deficit in self-representation and the inability to role play or to represent self symbolically in a blind child who had had excellent parenting and intervention. Fraiberg feels that blindness ". . . demonstrably impedes representational intelligence in the period 2½ to 4 years. . . ." (p. 281). She states that at every point in development in which representational thought is used by the nonhandicapped preschooler, the blind child is impeded in cognition, language, symbolic play, and human relationships, and thus in cognitive, emotional, and social development. From Fraiberg's and others' work with blind infants and children, it appears that some distortion of play (stereotypes, rituals, or lack of practice play with objects) is due to environmental and/or sensory deprivation, and that such distortions of practice play are not seen in well-stimulated, neurologically intact blind children. However, the difficulties in symbolic play and representational thought seem to be basic to the blind child's problem of constructing a lasting image of self and others without vision; it requires much longer for the image of self to develop in blind children than in sighted children.

As was mentioned earlier in this chapter, two groups of severely language handicapped children (autistic and aphasic) also demonstrate great difficulty with symbolic thought and symbolic play. Presumably this is because of an underlying cognitive symbolic disorder. Autistic children appear to be the most handicapped in all areas of play (toy play, social play, and symbolic play). A type of play therapy is often used with both autistic and aphasic children to try to develop some symbolic thought and thus to enhance language and social and cognitive development. Children with other types of language handicaps tend to show less social play than nonhandicapped preschoolers, presumably because they have difficulty communicating verbally with peers. The play of deaf children, who often develop a gestural system to aid communication in their early years before a formal language system is taught to them, is little affected by the handicap. Studies of young deaf children's play have shown that neither the quality of their play nor the developmental sequence or other aspects of their play are affected by the hearing loss (Mogford, 1977).

Thus, young children's play may or may not be affected by a particular handicap, depending on the type of handicap present. Autistic and blind children's play is particularly severely affected, in part because these children have problems with symbolic or representational thought. Because of the positive developmental contributions of play, therapies and intervention approaches to all the major handicaps tend to use play as a therapeutic medium. Whether one is trying to teach language, symbolic thought, reaching and grasping, locomotion, or use of toys, a playful environment is cited by writer after writer as an invaluable aid for stimulating development (Fraiberg, 1978; Leland and Smith, 1965; Li, 1981; Mogford, 1977).

SUMMARY

Play is such an all-encompassing activity for young children that virtually all areas of behavior and development—cognitive, motor, social, emotional, language—can be observed in a child's play. Similarly, children use play to master skills in all these areas, and thus all areas of a child's development are enhanced by the child's opportunities and experiences in play. Play thus appears to provide the major learning medium for young children's development.

Play does not unfold without the combination of positive, loving interactions with parents and more general environmental supports. Some types of play (especially symbolic play, sociodramatic play, and social play) are particularly dependent upon past experience and general environmental support (materials, space, adult encouragement) if they are to develop as richly and fully as possible. Attempts to help children develop more elaborate play have been successful for children who are economically deprived, mentally retarded, or autistic. Both symbolic play and social play skills have been enhanced by intervention. Given the central role of play in young children's development, there seems to be a clear indication that evaluators assessing young children should pay particular attention to various qualities of the children's play. Information about symbolic play, solitary play, and level of social play should be used to supplement psychologic test data in recommending various types of intervention approaches. In a similar manner, professionals who direct intervention programs for young children should assess the curricula, scheduling, and content of the programs to determine the support offered for children's play and the strategies that can be incorporated to help children develop their play skills.

REFERENCES

Barnes KA: Preschool play norms: A replication. Develop Psychol 5: 99–103, 1971

Bates E: Oral presentation at the Developmental Psychobiology Meeting, University of Colorado Health Sciences Center, April 1981

Bianchi BD, Bakeman R: Sex-typed affiliation preferences observed in preschoolers: Traditional and open school differences. Child Develop 49: 910–912, 1978

Bridges KM: A study of social development in early infancy. Child Develop 4: 36–49, 1933

Charlesworth R, Hartup WW: Positive social reinforcement in the nursery school peer group. Child Develop 38: 993–1002, 1967

Clark AH, Wyon SM, Richards MPM: Free-play in nursery school children. Child Psychol Psychiat 10: 205–216, 1969

Dansky JL: Make-believe: A mediator of the relationship between play and associative fluency. Child Develop 51: 576–579, 1980

Dansky JL, Silverman IW: Play: A general facilitator of associative fluency. Develop Psychol 11: 104, 1975

Davidson CD: Psychotherapy with mentally handicapped children in a day school. Psychother: Theory, Res Prac 12: 13–21, 1975

Deutsch M: The play diagnostic manual. Columbus, OH: Nisonger Center, Ohio State University, 1979

Doyle A, Connolly J, Rivest L: The effect of playmate familiarity on the social interactions of young children. Child Develop 51: 217–223, 1980

Eckerman CO, Whatley JL: Toys and social interaction between infant peers. Child Develop 48: 1645–1656, 1977

Eckerman CO, Whatley JL, Kutz SL: Growth of social play with peers during the second year of life. Develop Psychol 11: 42–49, 1975

Elder JL, Pederson DR: Preschool children's use of objects in symbolic play. Child Develop 49: 500–504, 1978

Erikson E: Play and actuality. In Piers MW (ed): *Play and Development.* New York: Norton, 1972

Erikson, E: Play and actuality. In Bruner JS, Jolly A, Sylva K (eds): *Play: Its role in Development and Evolution.* New York: Basic Books, 1976

Fagot BI: Consequences of moderate cross-gender behavior in preschool children. Child Develop 48: 902–907, 1977

Fagot, BI: Reinforcing contingencies for sex-role behaviors: Effect of experience with children. Child Develop 49: 30–36, 1978

Fein, GG: A transformational analysis of pretending. Develop Psychol 11: 291–296, 1975

Feitelson D: Cross-cultural studies of representational play. In Tizard B, Harvey D (eds): *Biology of Play.* Philadelphia: JB Lippincott, 1977

Feitelson D, Ross GS: The neglected factor-play. Human Develop 16: 202–223, 1973

Fraiberg, S: *Insights from the Blind.* New York: Basic Books, 1978

Grief EB: Sex role playing in pre-school children. In Bruner JS, Jolly A, Sylva K (eds): *Play: Its Role in Development and Evolution.* New York: Basic Books, 1976

Horne BM, Philleo LL: A comparative study of the spontaneous play activities of normal and mentally defective children. In Bruner JS, Jolly A, Sylva K (eds): *Play: Its Role in Development and Evolution.* New York: Basic Books, 1976

Huston-Stein A, Friedrich-Cofer L, Susman EJ: The relation of classroom structure to social behavior, imaginative play, and self-regulation of economically disadvantaged children. Child Develop 1977, 48: 908–916, 1977

Jacklin GG, Maccoby EE: Social behavior at thirty-three months in same-sex and mixed-sex dyads. Child Develop 49: 557–569, 1978

Jeffers VW, Love RK: Let's play at my house: Effects of the home environment on the social behavior of children. Child Develop 50: 837–841, 1979

Johnson JE, Ershler J, Bell C: Play behavior in a discovery-based and a formal education preschool program. Child Develop 51: 271–274, 1980

Langlois JH, Downs AC: Mothers, fathers, and peers as socialization agencies of sex-typed play behaviors in young children. Child Develop 51: 1237–1247, 1980

Leiter MP: A study of reciprocity in preschool play groups. Child Develop 48: 1288–1295, 1977

Leland H, Smith D: *Play Therapy with Mentally Subnormal Children.* New York: Grune & Stratton, 1965

Lewis M, Young G, Brooks J, Michalson L: The beginning of friendship. In Lewis M, Rosenblum LA (eds): *Friendship and Peer Relations.* New York: John Wiley & Sons, 1975

Li AK: Play and the mentally retarded child. Ment Retard 19: 121–127, 1981

Lougee, MD, Grueneich R, Hartup WW: Social interaction in same- and mixed-age dyads of preschool children. Child Develop 48: 1353–1361, 1977

McLoyd VC: Verbally expressed modes of transformation in the fantasy play of black preschool children. Child Develop 51: 1133–1139, 1980

Matthews WS: Modes of transformation in the initiation of fantasy play. Develop Psychol 13: 212–216, 1977

Maudry M, Nekula M: Social relations between children of the same age during the first two years of life. Genet Psychol 54: 193–215, 1939

Mogford K: The play of handicapped children. In Tizard B, Harvey D (eds): *Biology of play.* Philadelphia: JB Lippincott, 1977

Moore NV, Evertson CM, Brophy JE: Solitary play: Some functional reconsiderations. Develop Psychol 10: 830–834, 1974

Mueller E, Brenner J: The origins of social skills and interaction among playgroup toddlers. Child Develop 48: 854–861, 1977

Mueller E, Rich A: Clustering and socially directed behaviors in a playgroup of 1-year-old boys. Child Psychol Psychiat 17: 315–322, 1976

Murphy LB: Infants' play and cognitive development. In Piers MW (ed): *Play and Development.* New York: Norton, 1972

Newcomer BL, Morrison TL: Play therapy with institutionalized mentally retarded children. Am J Ment Defic 78: 727–733, 1974

Overton WF, Jackson JP: The representation of imagined objects in action sequences: A developmental study. Child Develop 44: 309–314, 1973

Parten MB: Social participation among preschool children. J Abnorm Soc Psychol 27: 243–269, 1932

Peller LE: Libidinal phases, ego development, and play. Psychoanaly Study Child 9: 178–198, 1954

Piaget J: Play, dreams, and imitation in childhood. New York: Norton, 1962

Provence S, Lipton R: *Infants in Institutions.* New York: International Universities Press, 1962

Roper R, Hinde RA: Social behavior in a play group: Consistency and complexity. Child Develop 49: 570–579, 1978

Rosen CE: The effects of sociodramatic play on problem-solving behaviors among culturally disadvantaged preschool children. Child Develop 45: 920–927, 1974

Rosenblatt D: Developmental trends in infant play. In Tizard B, Harvey D (eds): *Biology of Play.*
Philadelphia: JB Lippincott, 1977

Rubin KH, Maioni TL: Play preference and its relationship to egocentrism, popularity, and classification skills in preschoolers. Merrill-Palmer Quart 21: 171–179, 1975

Rubin KH, Maioni TL, Hornung M: Free play behaviors in middle- and lower-class preschoolers: Parten and Piaget revisited. Child Develop 47: 414–419, 1976

Rubin KH, Watson KS, Jambor TW: Free-play behaviors in preschool and kindergarten children. Child Develop 49: 534–536, 1978

Rubinstein J, Howes C: The effects of peers on toddler interactions with mother and toys. Child Develop 47: 597–605, 1976

Saltz E, Dixon D, Johnson J: Training disadvantaged preschoolers on various fantasy activities: Effects on cognitive functioning and impulse control. Child Develop 48: 367–380, 1977

Schau CG, Kahn L, Diepold JH, Chevy F: The relationships of parental expectations and preschool children's verbal sex typing to their sex-typed toy play behavior. Child Develop 51: 266–270, 1980

Scholtz GJL, Ellis MJ: Repeated exposure to objects and peers in a play setting. J Exper Child Psychol 19: 448–455, 1975

Serbin LA, Tonick IJ, Sternglang SH: Shaping cooperative cross-sex play. Child Develop 48: 924–929, 1977

Smith PK: A longitudinal study of social participation in preschool children: Solitary and parallel play reexamined. Develop Psychol 14: 517–523, 1978

Smith PK, Sutton S: Play and training in direct and innovative problem solving. Child Develop 50: 830–836, 1979

Sutton-Smith B: Piaget on play: A critique. Psychologic Rev 73: 104–110, 1966

Sylva K: Play and learning. In Tizard B, Harvey D (eds): *Biology of Play.* Philadelphia: JB Lippincott, 1977

Sylva K, Bruner JS, Genova P: The role of play in the problem solving of children 3-5 years old. In Bruner JS, Jolly A, Sylva K (eds): *Play: Its Role in Development and Evolution.* New York: Basic Books, 1976

Vandell DL, Wilson KS, Buchanan NR: Peer interaction in the first year of life: An examination of its structure, content, and sensitivity to toys. Child Develop 51: 481–488, 1980

Vygotsky S: Play and its role in the mental development of the child. In Bruner JS, Jolly A, Sylva K (eds): *Play: Its Role in Development and Evolution.* New York: Basic Books, 1976

Wälder R: The psychoanalytic theory of play. Psychoanalyt Quart 2: 208–224, 1933

Woodward WM: The behavior of idiots interpreted by Piaget's theory of sensori-motor development. Brit J Educ Psychol 29: 60–71, 1959

ASSESSMENT OF HANDICAPPED INFANTS AND PRESCHOOL-AGE CHILDREN

Chapters 8—14

Chapter 8

NEUROLOGIC AND MEDICAL FACTORS AFFECTING ASSESSMENT

By

HAROLD P. MARTIN

The developmental assessment of young children is difficult, albeit exciting, owing to the frequent and rich interplay between physiologic processes, environmental factors, and the child's psychoneurologic abilities. Biologic factors may interfere with development and may interfere with performance during testing; however, they may also provide clues as to the etiologic factors and pathogenesis of a young child's developmental delay. The younger the child, the more apparent biologic factors are during assessment. For example, the younger child's mental state is more variable and erratic, and thus more prominently affects test performance. In addition, the younger the child being assessed, the greater the chance that the clinician will note a previously undiagnosed neurologic dysfunction, seizure disorder, or sensory impairment.

As is discussed in other chapters, the task of the psychologist is to portray accurately a child's developmental status, to speak to the probable reliability of the results, and to raise hypotheses as to the etiologic factors and pathogenesis of any developmental delays. Attention to biologic factors will greatly aid in the last two of these three tasks. A conceptualization of these biologic factors will be clearer through categorizing them as follows.

SIGNS OF POSSIBLE BRAIN DAMAGE, DYSFUNCTION, OR IMMATURITY

Psychological assessment offers a unique opportunity to note, detect, and elicit signs of brain dysfunction. Indeed, the psychologist often has the chance to note signs of neurologic aberration that have been overlooked during previous medical examinations. Why might this be so? For one thing, a relatively complete assessment of the young child's neurologic status requires cooperation that is rarely obtained in a doctor's office. Children are typically too anxious and frightened when faced with a physician and the medical examining room to give the requisite cooperation. For another, the time required to obtain some trust and cooperation from a child is usually not budgeted during the typical physical examination. In addition, many behaviors that reflect neurologic status are best observed during play rather than during a physical examination. Because of these realities, the physician frequently must rely on history reported by parents, and on behaviors of the child that require little or no cooperation (for example, testing reflexes with a reflex hammer, palpating muscles, and observing face and body for signs of asymmetry when the child moves, cries, talks, and so on).

Psychological assessment of young children, on the other hand, provides the time needed to establish rapport with the child and leans heavily toward having the child interact with toys and test items that are of inherent interest. The blocks, puzzles, noisemakers, picture books, and so on that are found in almost any developmental test for young children are just the kinds of items with which children love to play. During psychological assessment, the clinician seeks to establish a milieu that will encourage the child's willingness and ability to speak, to cooperate, and to collaborate with the examiner.

There are a number of signs of possible brain damage or dysfunction which the psychologist assessing young children may note. The sensorimotor items, so common on developmental tests, are especially provocative in eliciting signs of impaired neuromotor dysfunction. Signs that might be seen during an assessment are listed in Table 8–1.

Table 8–2 lists some behaviors that may be associated with brain damage. Certainly the psychologist should try to understand and explain them.

It is important that the psychologist realize that none of the signs in Table 8–1 is diagnostic of brain damage. The more signs present and the more obvious those signs, the more likely is the hypothesis that the child has a significant neurologic problem. It is also true that the absence of any of these signs does not preclude the presence of brain damage, dysfunction, or immaturity.

The same is true of the behaviors noted in Table 8–2. These behaviors may be just as commonly based on psychological problems or social chaos; indeed, they may be a matter of individual temperamental difference in a normal child. (The signs and behaviors listed in Tables 8–1 and 8–2 will be covered later in this chapter.)

One must be cautious about relating cause and effect relationships between brain dysfunction and impaired developmental status. Certainly, if the brain has been damaged and that damage is being manifested by motor impairment, sensory loss, and so on, it is logical to presume that delayed development in the child is possibly due to this brain damage. Nonetheless, there are many studies that show that central nervous system insult does not predict later cognitive or academic performance well. Indeed, longitudinal studies of high-risk infants show that a child's socioeconomic status and the type of parenting he or she experiences are much better predictors of the child's later developmental course than early biologic risk factors.

TABLE 8–1   Signs of Possible Brain Damage that can be Noted During Developmental Assessment

1. Tremor of hands or arms when performing a task
2. Abnormal posturing of the limbs during rest or activity
3. Early hand preference (before 12 months of age)
4. Undue difference in skill between right or left arms or legs
5. Poor coordination—either in fine or gross motor tasks
6. Poor balance and equilibrium
7. Delay in acquisition of motor skills
8. Poor ability to plan and execute a motor task (dyspraxia)
9. Poor visual-motor integrative skills, often seen in tasks of drawing
10. Poor understanding and/or processing of what the child hears
11. Poor eye tracking
12. Poor motor control of tongue, lips, or mouth muscles
13. Impaired ability to inhibit movements as shown by associated movements, mirroring, or fidgeting

Table 8–2   Behaviors that may be Associated with Brain Damage

1. Short attention span
2. Distractibility
3. Hyperactivity
4. Emotional lability
5. Impulsiveness
6. Perseveration
7. Lack of interest in the environment

OTHER BIOLOGIC FACTORS THAT CAN IMPEDE DEVELOPMENT

The psychologist should be alert to factors other than brain damage which might be affecting the child's development. This is especially important because some of these factors lend themselves to specific treatment procedures. For example, even mild visual or hearing deficits may deleteriously affect development in infants and young children. Furthermore, it is common for these sensory impairments to go undiagnosed in early infancy. The standard tests to assess vision (for example, the Snellen chart or the illiterate E chart) are just not applicable for children under 3 to 4 years of age. However, during developmental assessment, the psychologist can note whether the child can see small objects close at hand, whether the child can see things at a distance, and whether there is visual attention to items in which the child is clearly interested. Similarly, by noting the child's attention to the examiner's voice, to noisemakers, and to surreptitious sounds in the examination room, the clinician may identify the child with a hearing loss.

Chronic disease, frequent hospitalization, and poor nutritional status can all affect developmental progress. A history of these factors should be elicited from the parents or caregivers.

A child's developmental progress may also be impeded by an untreated seizure disorder. One example is petit mal seizures, which are not uncommon in children after 3 years of age; these may go unnoticed, since they frequently are exhibited as brief staring spells. Frequent seizures, even when the altered state of consciousness only lasts a few seconds, can impede attending and mental processing. This is true even after the seizure episode itself is over.

BIOLOGIC FACTORS THAT CAN INFLUENCE TEST PERFORMANCE

There are a number of medical factors that interfere with test performance. If these conditions are chronic, they can also interfere with the child's developmental progress. An example of this would be seizure activity. If they are frequent and recurrent, seizures may interfere with development; and if the child has a seizure during an assessment, test performance will be artificially lowered.

If the child is acutely ill, or even recovering from a recent illness, mental alertness may be impaired and the evaluator may underestimate the child's ability. The examiner of young children knows the important effect on performance that a child's fatigue or hunger may have. Indeed, appointments should not be scheduled with a child during a time when the child typically naps.

Medication may also alter the child's state of consciousness and behavior. Young children are notoriously susceptible to behavioral and mental changes from the most innocuous and common of medications (for example, drugs used for colds, allergies, intestinal upsets, and so on). Sometimes the child reacts with mental overexcitement or physical hyperactivity. Just as often, the child responds with apathy and decreased alertness. The examiner should routinely determine by history the immediate and recent medical status of the child, medications being taken, and whether or not the parent feels that the child's behavior and performance are typical.

Another medical factor warranting special attention is motor coordination. Many developmental test items require sensorimotor responses, and these test items usually load onto some mental or cognitive score. It is obvious in the child with cerebral palsy that inability to place pegs, piece puzzles together, or draw with a pencil is due to motor impairment. However, when the motor incoordination is more subtle, it may be overlooked by the examiner who is not alert to biologic factors that can influence performance. Just as impaired vision or hearing can affect test performance, motor impairment or dyspraxia may lead the examiner to conclude that the child is less mentally competent than is truly the case.

ADVENTITIOUS MEDICAL FINDINGS

The psychologist who is assessing young children may note some physical findings or neurologic deviations that may be important to the child or family, but that may have no affect on development or test performance. An example of this would be the child with poor eye tracking, with nystagmus (a rapid, involuntary, repetitive eye movement), or with strabismus (crossed eyes). A mild strabismus is easy to overlook in a routine physical examination. In many children one or both eyes tend to drift inward at times of fatigue or stress. It is important to observe how well the child visually tracks, since strabismus can lead to serious problems and is usually fairly easy to treat if detected early.

Many other physical conditions may be noted or suspected during developmental assessment; these may or may not have any effect on test performance or on developmental status. The point is that the psychologist should be an astute observer of all the child's behaviors, rather than focusing only on test-related activities.

CORRECTION FOR PREMATURITY

Child developmentalists do not agree as to whether a child's chronologic age should be corrected for premature birth (or for what length of time this correction should be made). In the case of a child who is born two months prematurely, the question is whether she or he will attain developmental milestones two months later than would have been the case if she or he had remained in the uterus those last two months of pregnancy. While such data are not reliably available on most developmental tasks, there seems no question that the normal child who is born prematurely will be delayed in milestone acquisition if chronologic age is not corrected. Since neurologic maturation is required for most developmental tasks, the important age of the child would seem to be the post-conceptual age, not the post-delivery age. Additionally, it is clear that post-delivery experience also influences the attainment of developmental milestones. What is not known is how the experiences of the premature baby in a newborn nursery compare with the experiences the same baby would have had in the uterine environment during those last few weeks of pregnancy.

In a study of the onset of a baby's social smile, it was suggested that this milestone is delayed in premature children (if chronologic age is not corrected), but is at an age somewhere between chronologic and corrected age (Foley, 1977). This is what one would expect with a behavior determined both by neurologic maturation and also by visual and social contact with others. When a milestone, like walking, is more heavily weighted by neurologic maturation, one would expect it to be attained at the fully corrected age.

It is the opinion of this author that premature babies should have their ages corrected for the full number of weeks the child is premature. While some experts suggest that this should be done only for the first two years of the child's life, there is certainly no harm in correcting for prematurity until the child is 4 to 5 years of age, for the following reason: Take an example of a boy who is born three months prematurely. When his chronologic age is 12 months, the three months of prematurity that would be used for correction represent 25 percent of the chronologic age. This is really quite a significant correction. However, as a child grows older, the correction becomes less significant. By two years of age, for example, the significance of correction is only half as much. And by the time the child is 60 months old, his or her corrected age would be 57 months—a factor now only 5 percent of the chronologic age. The difference in neurologic maturation has not magically disappeared at 2 years of age, but the significance of correction decreases with age.

HIGH-RISK EVENTS

The presence of biologic high-risk events in the past history of the child are important to note. Common high-risk events include:

1. poor growth of the baby during pregnancy (that is, low birth weight for the length of pregnancy);

2. medical complications in the newborn period, such as hypoxia, infection, high serum bilirubin level, low blood sugar, respiratory distress, and so on;

3. medical complications during the pregnancy or during labor and delivery; and

4. illness or trauma. (Illnesses of special importance are those that might have affected the brain, such as meningitis or encephalitis. Head trauma, whether or not there is skull fracture or subdural hematoma, is of special importance.)

When a child is retarded in development, it may well be that some specific high-risk factor could be causally related (that is, it could be the basis of the retardation). However, the psychologist may not know the exact significance of the high-risk event; this may require talking with a physician, preferably with the physician most familiar with the child.

There is a risk of overestimating the importance of high-risk events in any child. Take as an example the phenomena of poor intrauterine growth. Most children who are undergrown at birth are completely developmentally and neurologically normal. Granted, it is a significant high-risk event, for the chances of the poorly grown newborn having developmental problems is considerably greater than in a normally grown newborn. However, one must keep in mind that most poorly grown newborns are completely normal; therefore, the clinician who sees a child who is developmentally delayed and who also grew poorly during intrauterine life must remember that the coexistence of these two factors may be quite coincidental. That is, poor intrauterine growth may not be responsible for the developmental delay.

Other high-risk factors are of minimal clinical significance. For example, cigarette smoking during pregnancy increases the chances of the child being of lower birth weight than if the mother did not smoke. However, it is extremely unlikely that cigarette smoking during pregnancy has any significant impact on the child's developmental progress. The psychologist should remember that the clinical significance of high-risk events must be determined before one can speak to the likelihood of any one event being the cause of a child's problems.

PHYSICAL ANOMALIES

It is not the role of the psychologist to do a physical examination. Nonetheless, the psychologist who sees many children gains skill in noting physical features that may stand out as different. The child may simply look different or unusual; the child may have specific minor physical differences (such as epicanthal folds of the eye, closely set eyes, floppy ears, unusually shaped fingers or hands, and so on). When a child is delayed, retarded, or brain damaged, the presence of a number of minor physical differences raises the possibility that the child's maldevelopment may be not only of parts of the body; there may also have been maldevelopment of the brain during the early pregnancy period. This is the case in obvious syndromes such as Down Syndrome. When the psychologist is considering possible etiologic factors in a child's developmental problems, the presence of minor physical anomalies would raise this hypothesis.

SEIZURE DISORDERS

A seizure occurs when there is an uncoordinated electric firing of cells in the brain. A seizure disorder may be present in a child or an adult with no other signs or symptoms of abnormality of brain function and with normal intellectual ability. However, in many children there is an association between seizure disorders and developmental delay. This is usually not a causal relationship, but rather the phenomena by which abnormal brain function manifests itself in several ways (that is, intelligence, motor performance, seizures, and so on). Usually, only a prolonged seizure, lasting more than 5 to 10 minutes, results in any brain damage. It may be important, however, to recognize a seizure disorder so that treatment can be established. This is especially pertinent, for many children have limited or distorted contact with their environment for some period of time before and after the seizure per se. The psychologist who spends time with a child during a developmental evaluation may suspect a seizure disorder. When this occurs, a careful medical history, physical examination, and often an EEG are indicated. The EEG is not diagnostic of a seizure disorder, for it can be normal in the presence of seizures; conversely, an EEG can be abnormal in completely normal children and adults.

Seizures are most often treated with a number of anticonvulsants, any one of which may impair a child's concentration and cognition. Nonetheless, these drugs may be necessary to eliminate the seizure activity. A brief discussion of the types of seizures follows. It is essential to note that there are several classification schemes of seizure activity, with no generally agreed upon unitary classification. The following is but one suggested description of the common types of seizures that the psychologist may read or hear about:

1. Grand mal (major motor) seizures need little description. The affected person generally loses consciousness, jerking movements are visible over all of the body, incontinence is frequent, and a post-seizure stage of confusion and drowsiness may be marked and prolonged. Immediate care requires keeping a clear airway by turning the child to his or her side. These seizures

may be quite frightening to the parents or to any person who has not previously witnessed them.

2. Petit mal seizures are more subtle. They consist of transient losses of consciousness that may appear as staring spells or lapses. The child rarely falls, but may drop things; there may be minor movements, such as rolling of the eyes, nodding of the head, or slight shaking of the trunk. These seizures are rare before three years of age and are uncommon after adolescence. They may be difficult to distinguish from willful inattentiveness.

3. Psychomotor seizures are the most difficult to recognize. There may be a motor component that is inappropriate, such as lip smacking, chewing movements, or a gradual loss of postural tone; older children may report dreamy or trancelike states. There may be emotional outbursts, disturbances of thought, and/or repetitive, complicated motor acts.

4. Focal seizures occur when a focal area of the brain has abnormal neuronal discharge. Depending upon the area of the brain involved, the corresponding motor area will show jerking movements; in older children there may be a sensory component. The muscles most often involved are those in the hands and face. Less often are the muscles of the feet and trunk involved.

5. Infantile myoclonic seizures are also known as infantile spasms, or "jackknife" epilepsy. These occur under 2 years of age. The most common type is a sudden dropping of the head with flexion of trunk and extremities, which is often accompanied by a typical EEG pattern called hypsarrhythmia. When infantile spasms occur before 6 months of age, the prognosis is quite poor, for usually there is gross brain malformation or damage as well. When the child has developed normally to 6 months and then these seizures occur, the outlook is only slightly better.

6. Myoclonic and akinetic seizures are described together. Myoclonic jerks (or involuntary muscular contractions) may occur alone or with some obtundation of consciousness, and a single group of muscles is usually affected. An akinetic seizure is a sudden loss of postural tone. Akinetic seizures and minor motor seizures can be similar to petit mal or infantile myoclonic seizures. They frequently are seen with central nervous system disorders and are often difficult to control.

7. Febrile seizures occur in 4 to 5 percent of all children (usually within the first 4 years of life). They are usually short, generalized seizures that are a response to an elevated body temperature. Some physicians put an affected child on prophylactic anticonvulsants, although this is usually not done unless there have been several febrile seizures. The amount of fever needed to spark such a seizure is quite variable from child to child. In the overwhelming majority of children, there are no sequellae.

Any seizure disorder that starts in the first year of life usually—but not universally—is associated with serious brain damage or dysfunction. Only about 75 percent of children have seizures that are completely controlled. In the difficult-to-control child, multiple medicines may be required. The price that may have to be paid is impairment of learning, although adjustment of dosages and types of medicine may minimize these side reactions without sacrificing seizure control.

MEDICATIONS

While medications often have side effects in children, this is not to say that medications should not be used. Medicines for seizures, allergies, infections, hyperactivity, or serious behavioral disturbance may be essential; nonetheless, the psychologist should be aware of potential side effects. Inquiry about medications being taken should be made routinely, and the parents should be asked how they perceive the effect of the medicine on their child's behavior.

One of the most common side effects of medications is some degree of tranquilization, or decrease of alertness. This reaction is frequent with antiseizure medications but may also be seen with behavioral medications and drugs taken for respiratory infections. When an apathetic child is seen, it is essential to determine whether the child's decreased alertness is due to medications, or whether it is one of the child's innate characteristics.

A second type of behavioral reaction involves increased activity, often with shortened attention span and distractibility. This reaction is frequently seen when phenobarbital is administered to brain damaged children. Children often react in unexpected ways to medication. For example, antihistamines that typically make people drowsy or sleepy may "hype-up" a child. Derivatives of epinephrine, which are found in most prescription and nonprescription drugs for colds, may increase a child's activity level and general metabolism.

A third common side effect of some medications is impaired coordination. Sometimes this may reach the point of true ataxia (poor balance, as is stereotypically seen in the state of drunkenness). Dilantin (which is used for seizures) is notorious for this, but a number of other medications can elicit this dyscoordination or impaired balance.

Some medications may alter personality, although this is not common. Nonetheless, drugs such as Clonopin (for seizures) or medications for behavioral control can result in any number of changes in personality—including behavioral problems.

When a child is receiving medication and a behavior is seen that might be a side effect of the drug, the psychologist should talk with the child's physician. Alternatively, the clinician can check the *Physician's Desk Reference,* which lists almost all prescription drugs used in this country. This is a valuable book for clinicians who work with children to have available. The first section of the book lists drugs by "company name" and then refers the reader to a section in the middle of the book which describes the medication in great detail.

Some of the most commonly used drugs are listed below, although this chapter cannot include a complete list. Commonly used anticonvulsants include phenobarbital, Tegretal, Dilantin, Clonopin, Zarontin, Valium, Celontin, Depekene, and Mysoline.

Commonly used antihistamines and decongestants come with many "company" names, most of which are found on neighborhood drug store shelves. Examples include Actifed, Benadryl, Chlor-Trimeton, Coricidin, Dimatane, Periactin, Phenergan, Rondec, Triaminic, and Ornade.

Medications are not frequently used to alter behavior in children under the age of 6. However, some of the most commonly used include Dexedrine, Ritalin, Benadryl, Tofranil, Librium, Valium, Atarax, and Vistaril.

COURSE OF ACTION WHEN MEDICAL, PHYSICAL, OR NEUROLOGIC FINDINGS ARE NOTED

At this point, the clinician must be wondering what good it is to note neurologic or medical conditions that might affect development or test performance. For that matter, the clinician must wonder what should be done when physical anomalies or high-risk events are suspected.

When such findings are noted, ideally a collaboration of psychologist and physician is called for, since both developmental and medical expertise are needed to piece together a full developmental picture of the child. The first course of action is for the psychologist to talk with the child's physician about the developmental assessment and about the medical or neurologic findings noted during that assessment.

When neurologic findings are seen or suspected by the psychologist, a discussion of these findings with the physician is essential. It may be that the physician has not noted the findings the psychologist suspects or it may be that the physician feels that these findings are not significant. More often, the presence of some neurologic findings during developmental assessment will call for the physician to examine the child again with a special emphasis on evaluating the nervous system. (This may include the need for special laboratory tests.)

When a child is retarded or delayed and also has signs of neurologic dysfunction, the question is raised as to whether the latter is etiologically related to the former. Brain damage may be the basis of a developmental delay—while just as often this may not be the case. The combined efforts and findings of the psychologist and the physician are required to establish the origin of a developmental delay.

It is even more problematic to know

what to make of the child who is completely normal developmentally, but in whom there are signs of possible brain damage or immaturity. Here again, collaboration with the physician can help determine if the findings are of significance, and what—if anything—to tell the parents about the findings or suspicions. The same is true of the normal child with a history of high-risk events or a few minor physical anomalies.

Physicians are not always the easiest professionals with which to collaborate. Like most professionals, they may resent the intrusion of other professionals into their presumed area of expertise. This territorial imperative can be diminished, however, through a tactful professional manner. The author suggests that the psychologist who feels that a child may have some neurologic or medical abnormality should immediately call the physician and try to establish a collegial collaboration. In such a call, the psychologist might indicate to the physician that he or she "would like to pass on some findings and concerns, and get some medical consultation" as to what to make of the physician's findings. The psychologist could then tell the physician what findings have been noted and what the concerns and suspicions are. There may be some specific questions, such as whether the physician has noted the findings before, what the physician has told the parents, whether or not he or she feels these findings are of medical or developmental significance, and so on.

There are some pitfalls to avoid in collaboration with physicians. First, the psychologist should not inform the parents of his or her findings until he or she has talked with the physician. It is especially important that the psychologist avoid making a diagnosis of brain damage, seizure disorder, or other medical condition before talking to the physician, who may or may not have already noted what the psychologist has seen. The physician may have become satisfied that the findings are not significant; on the other hand, if the physician has not noted the findings, the psychologist could place the physician in a potentially embarrassing position if the parents feel the physician has "missed" neurologic findings or medical conditions.

A second pitfall to avoid is calling the physician and asking him or her to perform specific tests or examinations. It may well be that—with experience—the psychologist will become quite skilled in knowing when a specific test (such as an EEG or CT scan) is indicated, but such specific medical advice to the physician will usually make professional collaboration impossible. However, one can raise the question of whether tests, examinations, or medical procedures might be helpful. How to raise these possibilities with professional graciousness and social adeptness will depend in large part upon a professional collaborative relationship that is usually built over months or years of contact with mutual patients.

SUMMARY

In conclusion, the child with neurologic abnormalities presents a very difficult diagnostic and prognostic problem to the psychologist. This is true because the clinician must attempt to discover what aspects of the child's behavior are attributable to the neurologic defect, what remedial steps may be taken to lessen any resulting learning or behavior problems, and what the future may hold for the child in terms of schooling, vocational expectations, and other such considerations. The more knowledgeable the psychologist is about the varying affects of brain damage, the better he or she can determine the effects of such damage on an individual child's behavior. However, the clinician must be extremely careful to separate the fact of brain damage from the concept of brain dysfunction, avoiding stereotyped views of "the typical brain damaged" child's behavior or outcome.

Finally, behavioral symptoms that may indicate neurologic abnormalities are extremely important; these should be noted and communicated to the child's primary care physician. Similarly, various medications can cause side effects that may appear to be symptoms of neurologic, learning, or attentional problems. The psychologist should know what medications a child is taking and how these may affect behavior before writing a psychological report about a child.

BIBLIOGRAPHY

Barclay A: The discrimination validity of psychological tests as indices of brain damage in the retarded child. In Khanna JL (ed): *Brain Damage and Mental Retardation: A Psychological Evaluation.* Springfield, IL: Charles C Thomas, 1968

Barlow CF: *Mental Retardation and Related Disorders.* Philadelphia: FA Davis Co, 1978

Birch HG: The problem of "brain damage" in children. In Birch HG (ed): *Brain Damage in Children: The Biological and Social Aspects.* Baltimore: Williams & Wilkins Co, 1964

Drillien CM, Drummond MB (eds): *Neurodevelopmental Problems in Early Childhood: Assessment and Mangement.* Philadelphia: JB Lippincott, 1977

Eisenberg L: Behavioral Manifestations of Cerebral Damage in Childhood. In Birch HG (ed): *Brain Damage in Children: The Biological and Social Aspects.* Baltimore: Williams & Wilkins Co, 1964

Foley H: When do pre-term and light-for-dates babies smile? Developmental Medicine & Child Neurology. 19:757-760. 1977

Honzik MP: Value and limitations of infant tests: An overview. In Oates J (ed): *Early Cognitive Development.* New York: John Wiley & Sons, 1979

Illingsworth RS: *The Development of the Infant and Young Child: Normal and Abnormal,* 7th ed. Baltimore: Williams & Wilkins Co, 1980

Johnston RB, Magrab PR (eds): *Developmental Disorders: Assessment, Treatment, Education.* Baltimore: University Park Press, 1976

Kennedy C, Ramirez LS: Brain damage as a cause of behavior disturbance in children. In Birch HG (ed): *Brain Damage in Children: The Biological and Social Aspects.* Baltimore: Williams & Wilkins Co, 1964

Knobloch H, Pasamanick B: *Gesell and Amatruda's Developmental Diagnosis,* 3rd ed. New York: Harper & Row, 1974

Paine RS, Oppe TE: *Neurological Examination of Children.* London: William Heinemann Medical Books, 1966

Richardson SA: The social environment and individual functioning. In Birch HG (ed): *Brain Damage in Children: The Biological and Social Aspects.* Baltimore: Williams & Wilkins Co, 1964

Ross AO: Conceptual issues in the evaluation of brain damage. In Khanna JL (ed): *Brain Damage and Mental Retardation: A Psychological Evaluation.* Springfield, IL: Charles C Thomas, 1968

Thompson RJ, O'Quinn AN: *Developmental Disabilities: Etiology, Management, Diagnosis, and Treatment.* New York: Oxford University Press, 1979

Vaughn VC, McKay FJ, Behrman RE (eds): *Nelson Textbook of Pediatrics,* 11th ed. Philadephia: WB Saunders Co, 1979

Wiener JM (ed): *Psychopharmacology in Childhood and Adolescence.* New York: Basic Books, 1977

Chapter 9

ASSESSMENT CONSIDERATIONS WITH THE MOTOR-HANDICAPPED CHILD

By
SALLY J. ROGERS

Young children with severe motor impairments of the upper extremities present some very difficult assessment problems to an evaluator. If the child is not verbal—either because of age or because of the severity of handicaps—the evaluator moves to performance tasks to assess the child's cognitive skills and receptive language abilities. The problem is that such tasks usually require much more fine motor ability than motorically impaired children are capable of. Because of this problem, many psychologists opt to use adaptive behavior measures to determine if the child is functionally retarded; many clinicians have considered the child untestable on standard batteries, with the hope that if the child has fairly normal intelligence, language or some sort of communication system will eventually develop so that intelligence can be demonstrated.

Yet there is a more rewarding way to approach the problem of cognitive assessment with severely handicapped children. This is an approach that requires the intermeshing of cognitive development theory and reflex development theory, a thorough understanding of the handicap and its effect on the child's motor abilities, and a strong dose of creativity and patience. This approach, which focuses on using whatever movement the child has and creating cognitive tasks the child can accomplish, will be the focus of this chapter.

REDEFINING THE EVALUATION QUESTIONS

The first step in creatively assessing motorically handicapped children is to redefine the evaluation questions. Since the behavioral repertoire of the young child who is cognitively normal but severely motorically impaired and nonverbal has not yet been documented, the norm-referenced evaluation approach is not particularly useful. Instead, the most helpful evaluation question seems to be, "What can the child demonstrate that he or she has learned about objects (cognition), communication, and people (social-emotional development)?" The goal of the evaluator then becomes to sample the child's full repertoire in these areas by whatever means are possible given the child's handicap.

The questions around which the psychological evaluation will be centered are as follows:

1. In the cognitive realm, what sensorimotor and preoperational concepts can the child demonstrate? What does the child know about object permanence, spatial relations, and causal relation? At what level are the child's verbal and motor imitation skills? Is there evidence of preschool-level classification, time, number, spatial, and comparative concepts?

2. In the language and communica-

tion realm, how does the child respond to various levels of verbal and nonverbal communication? How many ways does the child communicate needs and feelings?

3. In the social-emotional area, on what levels does the child discriminate human from nonhuman contacts? Who are the important people in the child's world, and what is the range of responses the child has to those people? Using an ego developmental model, where is the child along the attachment-separation-individuation continuum? What are the characteristics of the child's own coping and interactive style?

4. How are the child's handicaps limiting psychological growth? What steps can be taken to circumvent or limit the effects of the handicap on the child's growth?

These questions can form the basis of an assessment. However, to create tasks that the child can accomplish from these questions, the clinician must also understand the effects of the motor handicap on the child's ability to move, so that tasks which the child has the motor ability to perform can be created.

UNDERSTANDING THE EFFECTS OF CEREBRAL PALSY

Although this chapter will introduce some of the basic terms and concepts that apply to cerebral palsy, the psychologist who wishes to develop a real working knowledge of these concepts should work closely with an occupational or physical therapist, particularly in assessments of cerebral palsied children. These professionals understand the effects of the condition on movement and also know many techniques for reducing the negative effects of the condition, thus allowing the child to perform to his or her best advantage. The therapist can help the psychologist create tasks that the child has the motor ability to perform, and can also suggest various readings that will increase the psychologist's knowledge of the effects of cerebral palsy. The psychologist's goal must be to understand the disorder well enough so that the psychological evaluation is designed for an individual child's specific motor abilities and disabilities.

CLARIFICATION OF TERMINOLOGY

The term *cerebral palsy* is the commonly used name for many conditions that are characterized by motor dysfunction and are caused by nonprogressive brain damage early in life (Levitt, 1977). The term is used throughout this chapter to represent a wide range of motor disorders in which muscle tone and movement patterns are affected. This is a diagnostic category, rather than a descriptive one, and other terms are often used in medical and therapist reports to describe the motor effects of cerebral palsy. Some of the most common of these terms are:

1. Spastic quadriplegia, in which all four extremities are affected with spastic muscle tone. There is increased muscle tone of both extensor and flexor muscles in the limbs, so that movement is severely affected and the movements look stiff and jerky.

2. Spastic diplegia, in which the lower extremities are much more affected by spasticity than the upper extremities.

3. Rigidity, in which muscle tone is so severely increased that relaxation of muscle tone is virtually impossible.

4. Athetoid, or athetosis, in which muscle tone fluctuates from increased to decreased, and the result is excessive, repetitive, involuntary movements, especially in upper extremities and the face.

5. Ataxic cerebral palsy, or ataxia, in which there are motor problems involving balance.

6. Atonic cerebral palsy, in which there is severely decreased muscle tone.

See Table 9–1 for definitions of various terms used in this chapter.

MUSCLE TONE ABNORMALITIES

There are three major types of muscle tone abnormalities: hypotonia (decreased muscle tone), hypertonia (increased muscle tone), and fluctuating muscle tone (tone that fluctuates between hypertonia and hypotonia). These are described below.

The *hypotonic* child is generally called a "floppy" child. Hypotonic children have poor head and trunk control that can be

TABLE 9-1   Glossary of Terms Used to Describe Affects of Cerebral Palsy

Cerebral Palsy	A group of conditions caused by nonprogressive brain damage early in life and marked by motor dysfunction that affects posture, balance, muscle tone, and movement patterns. Marked by motor retardation and presence of certain abnormal reflexes.
Quadriplegia	Involvement of all four limbs. Often the arms are more severely affected than the legs.
Diplegia	Involvement of all four limbs, with legs more affected than arms.
Paraplegia	Involvement of both legs.
Triplegia	Involvement of three limbs.
Hemiplegia	Involvement of the leg and arm on one side of the body.
Monoplegia	One limb is affected.
Rigidity	Increased muscle tone in which the muscles offer continuous resistance to movement through the whole range of motion in that joint.
Spasticity	Increased muscle tone in which the muscles offer resistance at some point, or for a small part, of the full range of motion.
Hypotonus	Decreased muscle tone, which prevents maintaining a posture.
Hypertonus	Increased muscle tone.
Atonus	Extreme hypotonus.
Athetoid or Involuntary Movements	Bizarre, purposeless movements that are not under voluntary control. These may be slow or fast, writhing, jerky, tremor, swiping, or rotary patterns, or they may have no pattern. They may be present daily during attempts at voluntary activities or at rest.
Ataxia	Disturbance of balance mechanisms, often with resulting abnormal balance-saving movements.
Range of Motion	The normal full range of movement possible in one joint.
Neurodevelopmental Treatment Approach	Based on work by Karl and Berta Bobath, who view the fundamental difficulty in cerebral palsy as the lack of inhibition of reflex patterns of posture and movement. Treatment focuses on inhibition of abnormal tone and abnormal reflex patterns, and facilitation of more mature movement patterns and postural reflexes.
Extensors	Muscles that straighten a limb or body part.
Extension	Straightening of a body part or limb.
Flexor	Muscles that bend a limb or body part.
Flexion	Bending a limb or body part.
Supine	Lying on the back.
Prone	Lying on the stomach.
Abduct, Abduction	Movement of the limbs away from the midline of the body.
Adduct, Adduction	Movement of the limbs toward the midline of the body.
Abductors	The muscles that move the limbs away from the midline of the body.
Adductors	The muscles that move the limbs toward the midline of the body.
Associated Reactions	Increase in muscle tone in limbs, usually seen by stiffening, posturing, or fisting or clenching, resulting from effort.
Asymmetric	The two vertical halves of the body are different.
Clonus	Shaking or tremor of muscles after they have been suddenly stretched.
Floppy	Loose or poor posture and movements.
Head Control	Ability to control the position of the head.
Muscle Tone	The amount of tension in muscles, both at rest and during movement, regulated by the brain.
Primitive Relexes	Involuntary posture and movement patterns typical of extremely immature central nervous system development.

easily seen when the child is pulled up by the hands from a supine (lying on the back) to a sitting position. The head lags behind the body as the child is pulled upward, and the back is rounded in a sitting posture. When placed in a supine position, the child tends to assume a rather spread-eagle position. The child often has a protruding belly, and the arm and leg muscles feel flabby, giving the impression of chubbiness even though the child's weight is normal for age. In the supine position, the child's legs can be abducted (spread apart horizontally) much farther than normal. When the child is picked up under the arms and held vertically in the air, the shoulders "give" and may be pushed up almost to the ears. In a supine position, the child shows a "scarf sign"— that is, the upper arm can be laid flat, horizontally, across the chest, giving a clue to the abnormal flexibility of the shoulder joint.

All of these indicators are caused by the decreased tone of the muscles. The muscles do not exert their normal tension in the joints, so the joints are abnormally flexible, or "hypermobile." The child has an increased range of motion in the joints, which is especially obvious in shoulders, hips, and ankles (the foot can be pushed up toward the shin much farther than normal). The child with Down Syndrome is a good example of a floppy child, but a great many other children also exhibit hypotonia.

The hypotonic child typically does not show abnormal movements, although some abnormal postures, like sitting with the legs at 180°, may be seen. The hypotonic child is less active than normal because he or she has to work harder to maintain an upright posture and to move than normal children, and the child may be easily fatigued by motor activities or by maintaining an upright posture for an extended period of time.

In contrast to hypotonia, in *hypertonia* the muscles have too much tone. The flexor and extensor muscles in the limbs normally work in an alternating fashion. That is, one muscle contracts while the other flexes, allowing a limb to be flexed or extended. In hypertonia, both the extensors and the flexors have too much tone; they work against each other. This prevents move-

ment and results in stiff and rather rigid limbs.

When the severely hypertonic child is placed in a supine position, the hypertonia can be felt in the limbs in several ways. First, the hands are often fisted and elbows flexed, and the bicep muscles in the upper arms feel contracted. When one tries to extend the flexed arm, it feels "locked," and a slow, steady pressure at the elbow is necessary to extend the arm. The legs are straight and quite close together, often touching, because tone in the adductor muscles (muscles in the hips which pull the legs together) is so strong. When one leg is flexed—requiring slow, steady pressure—the same resistance is felt as was felt in the arm. When the knees are flexed and one tries to abduct the legs, again the resistance is felt, and slow, steady pressure is required to move the legs apart. Hypertonic children also generally lack head and trunk control, and if they are pulled from a supine to a sitting position, the head will lag behind the trunk and the trunk will be rounded in a sitting position.

Obviously, movements of the limbs are severely limited by hypertonia, so that the quantity of movements is severely reduced. The quality of the movements is also affected by the increased muscle tone. This often results in exaggerated movements, seen especially in the hands and face, or in facial grimacing or unusual posturing of hands and arms. The movements are often sudden, jerky, and inexact, since the competing muscle tone in the extensor and flexor muscles prevents them from being fluid and coordinated. Coordinated small movements, like individual finger and wrist movements, are very limited, and the child often must make do with more gross, general arm and shoulder movements.

Fluctuating muscle tone can be seen in children who are generally hypertonic or hypotonic. Typically in these cases, an attempt at voluntary movement sets off increased muscle tone, with resulting movement and posture abnormalities; however, when the child is resting, the muscles are somewhat hypotonic. During a movement, the muscle tone may fluctuate between the two extremes, resulting in "athetoid" movement patterns, which are repetitive, poorly coordinated voluntary movements. These are often accompanied by repetitive involuntary facial movements (the mouth opening and closing, the tongue moving in and out), which are caused by general muscle tone fluctuation throughout the body.

Fluctuating tone is most often seen when the child is attempting a task like trying to grasp a small object, or trying to release an object in a set place (for example, putting a peg in a pegboard). As the child tries to do something, not only are the fluctuating tone and abnormal movements seen in the arms, but also in abnormal movements in the rest of the body (face, mouth, and other limbs) as well.

As has been pointed out, fluctuating tone typically results in increased movements in all parts of the body when voluntary movement is attempted. Thus, the quantity of movements is increased. The quality of movement is also severely affected, for the child is again limited to gross, rather uncoordinated movements and often to abnormal postures owing to the increased tone. At the same time, the other uncontrolled body movements that accompany the child's goal-directed attempts further disrupt the child's movements.

PRIMITIVE REFLEXES THAT INTERFERE WITH MOVEMENT

From the above descriptions, it should be clear that the underlying muscle tone disorder may severely affect the child's ability to move his or her limbs. A critical factor in stimulating abnormal muscle tone is the presence of primitive reflexes (Table 9-2) which have not been normally integrated by continuing central nervous system development. These primitive reflexes increase muscle tone and thus interfere with movement. Because they especially limit head and arm movements, they are important for the psychologist to recognize. While these primitive reflexes can be seen in normal infants up to 6 months of age (after which they are inhibited by the developing nervous system), normal infants are never dominated by the reflexes in the way that cerebral palsied children are (Fiorentino, 1971). In addition, normal infants do not show the abnormalities of

TABLE 9-2   Reflexes & Reactions Commonly Seen in First Year of Life

Normal Age Range	Reflex or Reaction	How to Elicit Reflex	What to Look For
Birth to 2–3 mos.	Rooting	Move your finger from corner of child's mouth across cheek to earlobe once or twice. Test on both sides.	The child will turn head toward finger.
	Grasp	Place small object in child's hand, brushing it across fingers (not palm) as you do so.	Immediate, tight grasp of object.
	Stepping	Hold child in standing position with some weight on feet and tip the child's body slightly forward.	Child will take one or two high steps with each foot.
	Tonic labyrinthine prone (TLR)	Place child on stomach.	Some flexing of hips, legs, arms and neck.
	Tonic labyrinthine supine (TLR)	Place child on back with head in midline of body.	Flexing of arms and hand fisting that are resistant to straightening. Extended hips and legs that are somewhat resistant to flexing.
	Positive support	Hold child in standing position in the air, then lower onto feet.	Child will take weight on feet by extending hips, knees, and feet somewhat.

TABLE 9-2   Continued

Normal Age Range	Reflex or Reaction	How to Elicit Reflex	What to Look For
Birth to 5-6 mos.	Moro	Sit down with child's buttocks on your knees, head in your hands, facing you. Child should be at about a 45° angle. *Quickly* drop your hands down several inches, which will cause child's head to drop down into your hands.	The classic response has two phases. First, the arms straighten and extend out to sides, hands open. Second, the arms flex and come together at chest, hands fisted. You often only see the first part of this response.
	Asymmetrical tonic neck reflex (ATNR)	Place child on back on flat, rather hard surface. Encourage child to turn head to the side with your voice or toy. Test on both sides.	When child's head is fully turned to one side, the arm on the same side will straighten and extend out toward side. The opposite arm will flex along side of the head, hand fisted. This asymmetrical posture of the arms is also sometimes mirrored in the legs.
	Neck righting (log rolling)	Place child on back. Put yourself behind child's head. Put your hands on each side of head and turn it to the side.	The child's body will turn with the head.
	Negative support	Hold child in standing position in the air, then lower onto feet.	Child will not take weight on feet—hips and knees flex.
6 mos. & beyond	Landau	Hold child in the air in prone position, supporting only around hips.	Child will extend neck, arch back somewhat, and will extend hips and knees. Arms are raised.
	Segmental rolling	Stimulate as for neck righting, or watch child roll.	Body does not turn in one piece with head. Head may turn first, then body follows. Or child may roll by first turning shoulder, or hip, or head, with other part following.
	Propping	Only for children who sit independently. Place child in sitting position on floor. From behind child, push child forward from back.	Child will extend arms in front to support self.
		Push child sideways at the shoulder.	Child will extend arm to side and support self.
		Push child backwards.	Child will extend arms behind self to catch and support self.

muscle tone demonstrated in cerebral palsied infants. Two primitive reflexes that are especially obvious in hypertonic children and that significantly impair motor function are the asymmetric tonic neck reflex (ATNR) and the tonic labyrinthine reflex (TLR) (Figs. 9–1, 9–2, and 9–3).

The *ATNR* is elicited by placing the child in a supine position and having the child turn his or her head to one side. After a few seconds with the head to one side, the reflexive posture becomes apparent. The arm and leg on the "face" side of the body extend, while the arm and leg on the "skull" side of the body flex. The arm flexes up along the side of the head, and the leg flexes slightly; the posture is often more clearly seen in the arms than in the

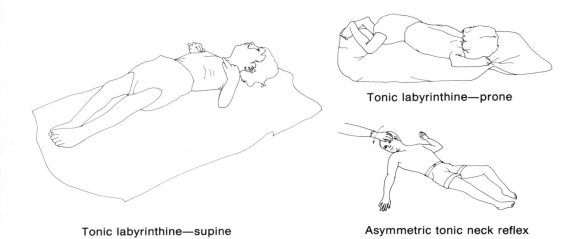

Tonic labyrinthine—prone

Tonic labyrinthine—supine

Asymmetric tonic neck reflex

Figure 9-1

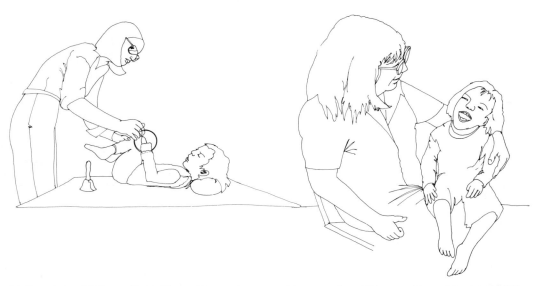

Hypertonic child—well positioned in supine

Hypertonic child—positioned in semi-sitting

Figure 9-2

legs. The posture is caused by the head position. Movement of the head to the side creates an asymmetric distribution of muscle tone, with the extensor muscles showing increased tone on one side of the body and the flexor muscles showing increased tone on the other side. The increased tone makes it very difficult for the child to move in this position, and the child may be fairly "locked in" to the position, unable to change head position and thus free his or her arm. Even eye movements are affected by the reflex in some children who are unable to track across the midline when in the ATNR posture.

The *TLR* is also stimulated by increases in muscle tone due to body position. When the child is placed in a supine position with the head in midline (turning the head to the side would stimulate the ATNR), extensor tone predominates in the trunk and lower extremities. Typically, the back and neck are extended, hips and knees are extended, and legs are close together; the hands, however, are fisted, flexed, and held close to the body at the shoulders.

When the child is prone, the flexor muscles predominate and there is flexion in the knees, shoulders, hips, arms, and neck. In this posture, the child is unable to lift his or her head or to extend the arms.

A growing body of literature is concerned with the neurologic dysfunction and related learning defects that can be diagnosed by the presence of immature reflex patterns. Much of this literature has grown out of the work by Bobath and Bobath (1974) with severely cerebral palsied children. According to the Bobaths (1972), the centers in the central nervous system which control movements do not stimulate each muscle movement individually. Rather, these centers organize muscle actions already integrated with each other into movement patterns. Thus, damage to these nervous system centers is most clearly seen in movement disorders.

The centers responsible for reflexive movements change as the central nervous system matures (Fiorentino, 1971). The first centers that control movements are located at the spinal level, which is the level of control seen in newborns. As the

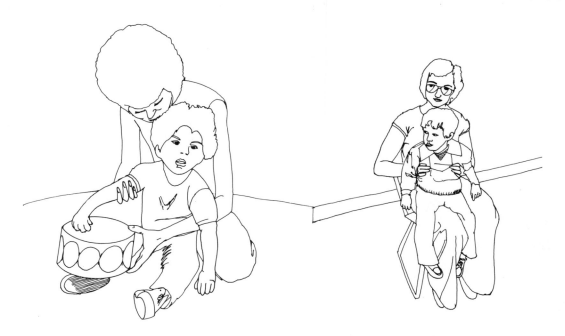

Hypotonic child-positioned in sitting   Hypertonic child—positioned in sitting

Figure 9-3

central nervous system matures, the brain stem takes over control of movements. The midbrain is the next higher level. Finally, the cortex controls the mature postural equilibrium reflexes, which are well developed by age 2 and continue throughout life.

As the higher brain centers take over control of automatic movements, the earlier movement patterns—reflexes—do not disappear. Rather, they are inhibited by the higher brain centers. According to Ayres (1972), the degree to which the higher centers suppress earlier reflexes reflects the degree of maturation and integration of these central nervous system sensory motor functions. Traces of earlier reflexes which appear in some handicapped preschoolers indicate incomplete integration and maturation of motor functions of the central nervous system. For instance, some preschoolers have difficulty assuming a prone position on a scooter board (belly on the board, legs and trunk extended in space), because residual effects of the TLR in the prone position cause some flexion in hips, knees, and trunk, making extension difficult.

In summary, then, the presence of primitive reflexes and the absence of higher level reflexes allow the motor therapist to hypothesize which level of the central nervous system is controlling movements, muscle tone, and posture. Knowledge of these developmental sequences also tells the therapist what level of motor patterns to be working toward.

POSITIONING TECHNIQUES TO COUNTERACT MOVEMENT PROBLEM

Positioning is important, since the primitive reflexes severely affect muscle tone. Thus, the professional should position the child so that the reflexes are not stimulated. The motor therapist has a number of ways of working to counteract movement problems. Some of these are listed below:

1. In the supine position—if the supine position must be used—the child's head must be maintained in the midline to avoid the ATNR, and the hips, knees, shoulders, and neck must be flexed to break up the TLR. Placing a pillow or bolster under the child's thighs and head and extending the child's arms may allow some tracking and reaching activities (Figs. 9-1, 9-2, and 9-3).

2. Side-lying is an excellent position for hypertonic children. If the child has more difficulty using one arm than the other, then the most functional arm should be free. The clinician should be positioned behind the child; a small pillow should be placed under the child's head, and the child should lie on his or her side with knees and hips flexed.

3. In the prone position, the child must be positioned to break up the TLR and to encourage extension of the back, neck, and hips. A small bolster placed at the child's chest with the child's arms over it may help the child reach, grasp, and track. One of the clinician's hands should be on the child's buttocks to help him or her maintain extended hips. The clinician's other hand can be used to present tasks.

4. Supported sitting is an excellent position for both hypertonic and hypotonic children. The child may sit in a lap, an infant seat, or a positioning chair. The child's hips and knees should be abducted and flexed, and the trunk and head should be supported. In this position the child can be helped to put all his or her energies into arm movements, without also having to control the head or trunk (Figs. 9–1, 9–2, and 9–3).

The effects of poor positioning on psychologic testing can be readily seen in administration of the Bayley Scales to cerebral palsied infants. For a hypertonic child with a TLR reflex, a supine position for the red ring item will cause the child's arms and hands to flex and fist, making reaching and grasping impossible. However, a side-lying position may allow the child to reach and grasp. For the hypotonic child, though, a supine position for the same item will also limit the child's ability to reach, not because of the reflex, but because of the effect of gravity on already weak muscles. The child may not be able to raise arms into the air against gravity. But for a child supported sitting on the mother's lap and presented with the ring in a plane closer to his or her hands, the effects of gravity are minimized and the child has a better chance of responding.

As can be seen from the above, working with a motor therapist (occupational or physical therapist) can be invaluable to the psychologist. The therapist is familiar with positioning techniques and can advise the psychologist of the position that will be best for given tasks. In addition, the therapist can position the child and maintain good positioning while the psychologist presents items. A final note: Try several positions for tasks that give the child trouble. The child may be able to reach well when lying on his or her side but may not be able to reach when sitting. Or the child may use the ATNR to reach to the side voluntarily, but may not be able to reach to the front.

TECHNIQUES TO NORMALIZE MUSCLE TONE

Therapists have many techniques for reducing muscle tone in hypertonic children and increasing muscle tone in hypotonic children; these can make a big difference in the child's ability to complete a task. For example, slow, gentle, repetitive movements, like gentle rocking, help to reduce muscle tone. Fast, abrupt movements, like bouncing a child on the knee, help to increase tone. The techniques are too numerous to discuss here, and their application depends on a child's specific motor problems, with other factors (like seizure disorders) taken into account. Thus, another reason for the psychologist to conduct an assessment with a therapist is that the therapist can closely monitor the child's tone during the evaluation and can normalize it as needed.

ADAPTATIONS OF TASKS

The most severely involved child, even after good positioning and normalization of tone, will still be unable to perform tasks that require an efficient reach, grasp, and use of fingers or body. Alternative methods of task presentation may allow the child to respond.

Some children who do not have voluntary grasp have a reflexive grasp, and may be able to use it to mark with a pen, move

a bell, swipe with a stick, or bang a spoon. Pressing the child's fisted hand downward toward the arm will release the fingers so that an object can be inserted. If the child has no grasp but has some arm movements, a universal cuff can be fashioned out of Velcro by an occupational therapist to simulate a grasp, and the goal-directedness of the child's arm movements can allow the assessment of imitation skills, of understanding of cause and effect, and of problem-solving abilities.

Children with motor impairments may also have difficulty with conventional pointing tasks; however, those who cannot point may be able to place a fist on a large picture, may be able to reach toward one of two pictures or objects, or may be able to swipe or bat at an object or picture. A child with no arm movements at all may be able to eye-point—to look at the item named. For example, if two choices are held fairly far apart and the child is instructed to look at one, the child may be able to respond.

The most common tasks in which a pointing response is needed are receptive language tasks, but many other tasks can be performed with pointing response in addition. Cognitive concepts like color, shapes, and size discriminations can be tapped in this way. Matching tasks can be presented by putting an object on the table and presenting two objects to be looked at—one like the first object, one that is different—to tap some varied concepts. Other types of classification activities that can be presented this way can involve things that go together (for example, spoon and fork, cup and plate, baby and bottle). Many preoperational tasks can be designed to be answered by some sort of pointing response.

Arm movement tasks can pose similar assessment problems with a motorically impaired child. For the child who has some arm movement, many sensorimotor tasks—object permanence, tool use, cause and effect, filling and dumping, making marks—can be designed. The larger the object and the grosser the movement, the more chance the child has to succeed. For that reason markers are better to write with than crayons, and cardboard may be better to write on than paper; in addition, large, fat pegs and holes, and large blocks and cans (instead of cubes and cups) will help. Often better materials will be found in toy stores than in test kits.

When a motorically impaired child is at the preoperational level, the psychologist must become more creative and use the child's movement to create grouping and matching tasks. Because the child can group objects by color, size, shape, class, or number by pushing an object in one of two directions, dichotomous groups can be set up to tap a number of concepts (see Chapter 5).

It is important for the psychologist to realize that many of the activities described may very likely be totally new to the child. For this reason, quite a bit of time may be required to teach the correct response before the child is able to link up the concept, the task, and the motor movement. Indeed, several teaching sessions may be needed in order for the psychologist, the therapist, and the child to know what is being asked of the child and what performance abilities the child has to which tasks can be fitted. If the child cannot immediately perform such tasks, it does not necessarily reflect poorly on the child's intelligence. The concepts may well be present, but learning to apply a motor movement may take some time. Or the concept may not be present because the child has not had any opportunity to learn it before. If learning occurs when the opportunity is provided, the child may be demonstrating only experiential deficits.

Another note of caution concerns the taxing nature of assessment procedures on a severely handicapped child. These children move only slowly and with great effort, and fatigue can occur extremely quickly because of the physical and mental demands placed on the child. Several sessions may be required to help the clinician assess the child's strengths. Because the child's psychological and physiological states can drastically affect muscle tone and movement abilities, the child's tone may differ considerably from one day to the next; thus, having several sessions will ensure that the child's real capabilities are reflected.

Techniques similar to the ones discussed above have occasionally been criticized as yielding "unscorable" results. If the purpose of the assessment is to compare the child's abilities with norms for his or her age, such criticisms may be well founded. Currently no norms exist which permit comparison of the cerebral palsied child's performance on adapted items with that of a normal child. This is because the cerebral palsied child's experiences with objects and with his or her body are vastly different from the normal child's. However, by adapting tests to allow the cerebral palsied child to respond, the psychologist permits the child to demonstrate the ability to use his or her body to communicate and to act, thus reflecting individual strengths and needs for which a treatment program can be evolved.

QUALITATIVE ASPECTS OF BEHAVIOR

The professional who examines the qualitative aspects of an infant's behavior watches for behavioral changes that typically accompany growing intelligence or awareness in normal infants. These include alertness, attention to changes in the environment, interest in objects, awareness of small details, growing responsiveness, a differentiation of various people, and general activity level. Some children—for example, deaf-blind infants or motorically impaired children—are so severely handicapped that the qualitative aspect of the assessment becomes the psychologist's major source of knowledge about the child. Videotaped records of the child's behavior and observing the child in a group setting can be extremely helpful in assessing the qualitative aspect of the child's performance. Noting what the child seems aware of can also be quite helpful. In this author's experience, children with greater intelligence will be aware of the clinician's activities no matter where he or she is in the room, and will also be aware of other children who are present. Lower functioning children will attend to the assessor when that professional is interacting with the child, but will not maintain this interest without such direct interaction. Higher functioning children also develop ways of gaining attention from a distance and maintaining it; these may be socially adaptive and positive behaviors (vocalizing, smiling, and moving about), or maladaptive behaviors (tantrums, regurgitating, or pouting). The author has found that the range of affect is also broader in higher functioning children, and professionals may see or hear reports of the child being jealous, having likes and dislikes among staff members, pouting or holding a grudge, laughing at a funny incident, refusing to perform for certain people or when angry, and so forth. The lower functioning child generally will not demonstrate such a wide range of affective behavior. Parents and therapists can be good sources of information about these qualitative aspects of children's behavior.

The psychologist who sees many severely impaired children learns that they vary considerably in social and affective characteristics. These levels of social awareness, which logically imply various levels of cognitive understanding of social situations, should be described in the psychologic report.

PARENT-CHILD INTERACTIONS

This chapter has focused on the infant's and evaluator's performance in the test situation. Yet it is the family system that will be the most important variable in determining the amount and quality of services the child receives. In addition, appropriate treatment for the very young disabled child requires that therapy be built into the family routine and be carried out by the whole family. Incorporating therapy into family routines is especially important in the areas of proper lifting and holding, positioning for sleep, play, feeding, and bathing. The family will also need to incorporate aspects of more traditional therapy involving range of motion and facilitation techniques.

Thus, information on the family's strengths and weaknesses around management of the handicapped infant is important. This information will affect decisions about the amount and type of professional intervention that is needed, the amount of responsibility the family can take for the child's treatment, and the family's needs for resolving such issues as the effect of the handicapped child on their home, their family, and their lives.

It is clear that a thorough, open-ended interview with both parents is necessary. Such an interview will provide an arena wherein the parents can discuss the impact of the child's handicaps on the family. While much important information can be gained by good interviewing, all areas of family-child interaction cannot be explored in this manner. Therefore, the psychologist must also observe interactions between the parents and the child. Three particularly important interactional situations that should be observed include feeding, interactions that are unstructured, and interactions in which the parents are asked to place some demands on the child. These interactional situations are described in more detail in Chapter 4.

The feeding interaction is important because so many children with motor impairments are difficult to feed, which frequently leads to a stressful interaction for both parents and child. The psychologist should note how each handles the stress, and the degree of positive interactions that becomes evident during feeding.

Unstructured interactions can be observed fairly easily during conversation with the parents. It is important for the clinician to observe whether the child demands attention from the parents during the conversation, and how the parents handle the conflict between their conversation and the child's demands.

After the interview with the parents, the clinician should look at the parents' ability to elicit responses from the child. This can be accomplished by asking the parents to get the child to do something that is within the child's range of abilities. The means that the parents use to elicit performance from the child, and how they respond to the child's success or failure, bring out another dimension of the parent-child relationship. Observation of both structured and unstructured interactions also provides important information about what the child understands and whether the child exhibits some signs of negativism and independence.

Qualitative differences in parent-child interactions may have many causes, including the child's age and handicaps, position in the family, parents' and siblings' needs, and so on. Whatever the basis for difficulties, corrective steps must be taken when someone in the family has needs that are not being met. Thus, the first step in the process of asessing the family is adequate conceptualization and diagnosis of the interactional problem.

SUMMARY

The motorically impaired young child presents a very specialized assessment challenge to the psychologist, who must know how to look at cognitive, communicative, social, and emotional development and potential without relying on the child's motor abilities to reflect those skills. Instead, the child's perceptual and affective responses must be relied upon more than is typical in most developmental assessments. Knowledge of the child's motor abilities and limitations is absolutely essential in planning the kinds of items to be presented and the kinds of behaviors to be sought; the aid of a motor therapist should be enlisted for the assessment. In addition, because the family's ability to work with the treatment program is essential, careful assessment of the family's abilities to be involved plays a large part in determining optimum intervention for the child.

The biggest concern for the psychologist who is assessing a cerebral palsied child is the degree to which the child's sensory, motor, and perceptual experiences are being limited by that child's lack of movement and/or locomotion. Bijou (1963) spoke from a behavioral theory of mental retardation when he said of motor experience: "... if body control, manual and locomotor skills are inadequately developed, the number and kind of physical and social stimuli available for contact are curtailed," (p. 102), limiting learning opportunities and cognitive growth. Charlesworth (1973) places tremendous emphasis on the importance of early skills that allow sensory input to be interpreted and integrated; he feels that perception is far more important to cognitive development than motor experiences.

Thus, the task of the psychologist is twofold: first, to help those providing therapeutic intervention to identify the ways in which the child's handicap is preventing normal sensory, motor, and perceptual experiences; and second, to help find ways to allow those experiences to occur despite the handicap.

REFERENCES

Ayres AJ: *Sensory Integration and Learning Disorders.* Los Angeles: Western Psychological Services, 1972

Bijou SW:Theory and research in mental (developmental) retardation. *Psycholog Rec* 12(1): 95–110, 1963

Bobath K, Bobath B: Cerebral palsy. In Pearson PH, Williams CW (eds): *Physical Therapy Services in the Developmental Disabilities.* Springfield, IL: Charles C Thomas, 1972

Bobath K, Bobath B: The facilitation of normal postural reactions and movements in the treatment of cerebral palsy. *Physiotherapy,* 50, 246–262, 1964

Charlesworth WR: Cognition in infancy: Where do we stand in the mid-sixties? In Stone LJ, Smith HT, Murphy LB (eds): *The Competent Infant.* New York: Basic Books, 1973

Fiorentino MR: *Reflex Testing Methods for Evaluating C.N.S. Development.* Springfield, IL: Charles C Thomas, 1971

Levitt S: *Treatment of Cerebral Palsy and Motor Delay.* Oxford, England: Blackwell Scientific Publications, 1977

BIBLIOGRAPHY

Capute AJ, Accardo PJ, Vining EPG, Rubenstein JE, Harryman S: *Primitive Reflex Profile. Monographs in Developmental Pediatrics,* vol 1. Baltimore: University Park Press, 1978

Finnie NR: *Handling the Young Cerebral Palsied Child at Home.* New York: EP Dutton, 1975

Chapter 10

ASSESSMENT CONSIDERATIONS WITH THE VISUALLY HANDICAPPED CHILD

By

ROBIN HANSEN, JAN YOUNG, AND GORDON ULREY

Vision has been described as the "co-ordinating sense," the organizer of sequential perceptions and sensory impressions into an understandable whole. Conducting an accurate assessment of the visually impaired child requires that the psychologist have an understanding of the variability of developmental sequences found in children with visual deficits, and that he or she also have good observational skills and the ability to be flexible in the test situation. The visually impaired population is highly heterogeneous with respect to etiologic factors, degree of impairment, and age at onset. In addition, the presence of associated defects is also highly variable; current estimates are that approximately 50 to 70% of visually impaired children have other handicaps (Fine, 1979; Jan, Freeman, and Scott, 1977).

Blindness must also be understood in the context of the organization of information received and processed through modalities other than vision. Because blindness carries an isolation from the environment that has been called "an assault on the function of the ego itself" (Klein, 1962), visually impaired children must discover alternate strategies to learn about themselves and their environments. Indeed, it is essential that the child learn to differentiate between self and others and self and the environment. Therefore, the psychologist who is assessing the child's abilities and adaptive skills must have an awareness of environmental factors that affect development in the visually impaired infant.

The world of the blind cannot be understood simply by closing one's eyes. To view the congenitally blind child as a normal child who is without vision is a misconception. In assessing a visually impaired child, it is important for the psychologist to understand how blind children develop and construct a sense of the world without sight.

DEVELOPMENT OF VISUALLY IMPAIRED INFANTS

Typically, visually impaired infants are very quiet; their limited range of activity and their muted facial expressiveness may impair the normal process of attachment to caretakers. Visual interchange plays a major role in a mother's relationship with her sighted baby. This is true because the mother can understand the child on the basis of her own sensory experience and can respond meaningfully. In contrast, the visually impaired infant responds to its mother's overtures in less obvious ways. For instance, the child may become silent when the mother enters the room in order to listen to her approach (Wills, 1979a, 1979b). Because visually impaired infants rarely initiate interactions—perhaps because they cannot see the results of their behavior—their parents must learn to use and interpret cues from other sensory systems.

Fraiberg (1968) has described blind infants who have a responsive smile to the mother's voice prior to 6 weeks of age. She notes that the smile itself becomes more and more selective in the second half of the first year and is used as an exclusive sign of affection. However, the smile is less frequent and more muted than in sighted infants. Other authors have noted social smiles in blind infants at 2 to 3 months of age; these tend to diminish with time, probably because of a lack of visual reinforcement or imitation of the mother's smile (Freedman, 1964).

Separation anxiety in children who are visually impaired emerges by 8 to 12 months of age, also the time when it appears in sighted infants. However, separation anxiety is prolonged through the second year in visually impaired children. This long period of resolution is thought to be caused by the difficulty a child has in developing an object concept (parent figure) without the aid of vision. For example, the child cannot track the mother's appearance and reappearance visually. In fact, it is not until 4 to 5 years of age that object constancy is established and that emotional separation and individuation from caregivers occurs. At that time, the visually impaired child realizes that caregivers do not cease to exist when they have left his or her perceptual field. The psychologist should realize that for much of the first year, the blind child lives in a world of accidental encounters with "things" (Fraiberg, 1974). There is little adaptive substitution of ear and hand coordination for eye and hand coordination until the last quarter of the first year, a time when most blind infants begin to reach on sound cues. The prolonged period of separation anxiety that visually impaired children typically experience often renders the child very passive, reluctant to explore the environment, and fearful of changes in daily routine.

The nervous system of the otherwise normal visually impaired infant matures at a normal rate, enabling the development of normal muscle tone and coordination, as well as postural and balance mechanisms. However, mobility items (such as crawling and walking) that normally follow postural achievements are delayed in visually impaired infants. In her work with blind infants, Fraiberg (1974) showed that the onset of self-initiated mobility was related to the ability to reach for and attain an object presented by sound cue alone. It is at this point—usually around 9 to 12 months—that the visually impaired child will begin to propel him- or herself forward into space by creeping or crawling. In Fraiberg and Adelson's 1974 study, the median age for creeping was 13.25 months. Independent walking is also delayed; the median age according to Fraiberg and Adelson was about 19.25 months. (The normally sighted child usually creeps by a median age of 7.0 months and begins walking at 11.7 month.)

Fine motor skills, most notably prehension, are especially important for the infant who is visually impaired. The infant's hands constantly search and locate things, as eyes do for the sighted. Fraiberg's 1968 research indicates that the critical period for the adaptive development of the visually impaired infant's hands occurs in the first 18 months. Vision acts as the "organizer" for midline hand activity; without help from caretakers, the visually impaired infant may not develop midline skills nor the required subsequent maturational refinements in coordination and reciprocity between the hands. Well-stimulated blind babies will grasp objects on contact by 5 months and will make fleeting pursuit movements when the object is removed. As previously mentioned, it is not until 10 to 12 months that the visually impaired infant begins to reach for objects based on sound alone. Until the child learns to do this, he or she is limited in learning about the environment.

The development of speech and language in visually impaired children has been seen by several authors to compare favorably with that of sighted children—at least in the first year. Norris, Spaulding, and Brodie (1957) compared the development of speech in their group of 66 children with norms from Gesell and Amatruda (1934); they found that more than 75 percent compared favorably at 9 months with Gesell's criteria of "talks and imitates sound." Reynell (1978) and Fraiberg (1968) also found that language in the first year was comparable in blind and sighted infants, diverged with the labeling of objects during the second year, and began to catch up again between 3 and 5 years of age. In contrast, a study by Graham (1968) of blind children with other handicaps revealed that nearly half of those children under 6 years of age had no speech. Haspiel (1965) contrasted the development of reflexive vocalizations into differentiated sound productions in normally sighted infants in whom normal babbling patterns never emerged. Sensory stimulation has been shown to play a major functional role in the development of vocal behavior, such as oral-motor development, integration of auditory and haptic sensory systems, and imitation of and reinforcement from caregivers.

Wills (1979) postulates that blind children may, in part, have language delays because it takes them longer to understand that they can act on the environment by the use of words alone. Fraiberg (1974) describes language delays in regard to difficulties that visually impaired children have in constructing an image of "self" and forming the concept of an objective self in a universe of other "selves." Associated with this is a delay in representative play, which is often not seen in visually impaired children until 3 to 4½ years of age (which corresponds to the emergence of self-reference pronouns).

The language of the sighted child is closely related to a world whose experience is largely based on vision. Parents use many words that have visual meaning and are difficult for the blind child to understand. He or she may learn to describe visual concepts well verbally; these are called "verbalisms." However, because of the lack of concrete experiences, the child may not have an accurate understanding of those concepts. In addition, the visually impaired child's language often seems rote and devoid of meaning, and blind children often talk excessively to maintain some control and contact with others. Echolalia is commonly observed, and when it is excessive, it indicates a disturbance in language development.

ASSESSING THE VISUALLY IMPAIRED CHILD

In assessing a child with a visual impairment, it is important for the psychologist to ascertain what is known regarding the degree of the child's visual handicap. This is true because there are very few children who are totally blind. Most children have some degree of functional vision, and a child with even a slight amount of sight can be taught to use it more effectively.

Accurate assessment of vision in a young child is difficult because when the child is too young to respond consistently to verbal instructions or gestures, reliance must be placed upon a medical examination. Unfortunately, such an examination can only detect tissue and structural abnormalities and gross sensitivities. When the child is old enough to respond appropriately to vision testing, visual activity can be more accurately determined. However, since evaluation of visual behavior is dependent on the child's ability to attend, follow directions, understand and use words, and cooperate in testing procedures, even this kind of assessment may be misleading.

Because of the difficulties of assessing vision in infants, and because visual acuity is so important to a child's development, any child with a suspected visual deficit should be referred to an ophthalmologist. Follow-up examinations should be encouraged if existing reports are more than a year old, or if the child was less than 1 year of age when the last examination was conducted.

In addition to referring the child to a physician, the psychologist can make pertinent observations about visual impairment during the assessment (Table 10-1). Since the human face is probably the most potent visual stimulus in the newborn period, the psychologist suspecting a mild

TABLE 10-1   Screening Assessment of Vision

1. Check response to face presentation (focusing, following movement)
2. Check response to light (blinking, squinting, pupil constriction)
3. Check ability to follow light by 1 month of age
4. Check ability to fix and follow object by 2 months of age
5. Check visually directed reach by 4 months of age
6. Look for misalignment of eyes (turning in or out), squint

vision loss should note whether an infant responds to such stimulus. If the child does not respond to a face, he or she might respond to bright light in a darkened room by blinking, squinting, or showing pupillary response. None of these responses indicates normal vision, however.

Knowledge of some normal milestones may be helpful in attempting to determine the degree of vision in an infant. The normal infant should follow a light by 1 month of age, should blink to a visual threat by 6 to 8 weeks, should fix on and follow an object by 2 months, and should begin reaching by 4 months. A mother's report that her child does not see is generally correct. Unfortunately, however, the mother may believe erroneously that her infant does see because the child turns to her in feeding. The developmental history obtained from parents should explore the child's apparent functional use of vision and milestones that are dependent on vision.

Another major problem to which the psychologist should be alert is the potential loss of vision in one eye. Any time that an eye is not adequately stimulated visually, there is the possibility for loss of vision in that eye. For example, when one eye is weaker than the other, or when one eye turns in or out, vision from that eye is suppressed by the brain; eventually, if treatment is not instituted, the connections between the weak or misaligned eye and brain will atrophy. Therefore, the child who has an eye that turns either in or out, or who appears not to see as well in one eye as the other, should immediately be referred to an ophthalmologist for evaluation.

Children who squint, rub their eyes often, or complain of headaches related to eye use may well have visual problems. They should be referred for evaluation of their vision, as should the child who works too closely to a piece of paper, or who does poorly in preschool. However, visual problems are rarely the reason that children frequently trip or bump into things. The same is true for children who sit very close to the television set, since this is something that many children seem to prefer.

Some children have normal visual acuity but have problems with visual perception or the interpretation of visual information. Visual perception problems and their importance in proper planning of educational programs will be discussed in another chapter.

PRINCIPLES OF ASSESSING BLIND CHILDREN

There are six general principles to be considered when conducting an assessment of a blind child. Table 10-2 summarizes the factors that are essential.

First, it may be appropriate to plan the assessment over a period of weeks rather than in one or two sessions. This will provide an observation over time of a wide range of behaviors.

Second, the child should be given ample time to become familiar with the surroundings. Visually impaired infants may take much longer than a sighted child to orient to new sounds, smells, temperature, excitement or anxiety in parents, and handling by a stranger. In the assessment setting, the visually impaired child may initially be very withdrawn and reserved, or may exhibit simple repetitive behavior because of increased anxiety. The older child will need time to explore the surroundings, usually tactilely.

Third, the child should also be given ample time to become familiar with each test object before a standardization response is expected. It generally takes longer for a visually impaired child to explore and become familiar with an object tactilely, orally, and so forth.

Fourth, familiarity with the normal and abnormal behaviors that can be antic-

TABLE 10-2   General Principles in Assessing Visually Impaired Children

1. Consider assessing over a period of time rather than in one session
2. Give child ample time to explore and become familiar with surroundings
3. Give ample time for child to become familiar with each test item
4. Be familiar with normal and abnormal behaviors in visually impaired children, such as automatisms or repetitive behaviors
5. Maintain flexibility in testing and observation
6. Use an observation protocol

ipated in visually impaired children is important. For example, "automatisms" have frequently been described in children wtih a visual impairment. These include hand flapping, moving hands repeatedly in front of the eyes, persistent mouthing in a nonexploratory pattern, repetitive banging of a hand or objects against the mouth, parts of the body, or other surfaces, poking fingers at the eyes, and rocking of the head and/or body. None of these behaviors is exclusive to blind children, but visual impairment should be considered when they are present.

All of the automation or stereotypic behaviors are abnormal and reflect understimulation and/or withdrawal from a frightening environment. The psychologist must carefully watch for such behaviors, and notation should be made as to how often and in what situations they occur, whether they interfere with testing, and whether they interfere with interactions with other people. These behaviors will frequently make an evaluation less reliable, so when they are present the clinician must be especially careful in interpretation of test results.

The fifth general principle is for the psychologist to recognize the particular importance of flexibility in testing and observation when assessing visually impaired children. It is important to focus on what the child can do and how adaptively he or she solves problems—not on whether the child can perform certain tasks designed to measure performance in sighted children. It is also important to attempt to determine what adaptations or compensatory strategies both the child and parents have developed.

Sixth, an observation protocol is essential. Barraga (1976) describes six important behaviors pertinent to the evaluation of a visually handicapped child:

1. Awareness of and attention to the surrounding environment and those within it. (For example, how does the child react to the surroundings or persons within it? Does the child withdraw and display self-stimulatory, repetitive behaviors, or does the child imitate intonations?)

2. Seeking and exploratory behaviors or patterns of movement. (How does the child explore new surroundings or a strange examiner? How does the child move about the room?)

3. Use of the senses in moving and acquiring information. (How does the child use his or her hands and mouth to explore ne objects? What cues does the child use to move and explore the surroundings? Has the child developed alternative strategies to compensate for inadequate visual feedback?)

4. Use of language to elicit contact or to respond to encounters. (What awareness and understanding of sound and language does the child show? Does the child show social awareness, including identification of and meaningful interaction with persons through language?)

5. Nature and variety of cues for self-directive and independent actions. (Observe the child during independent play and watch how he or she responds to cues from the environment by exploratory behavior or goal-directed activity.)

6. Extent to which the child originates behavior or adapts to materials or people. (Watch to see if the child relies on parents or others to provide stimulation rather than seeking it on his or her own.)

As previously noted, it is important to observe whether the child has any vision at all and how functional it is. In short, the observations should help to address the questions: How does the child solve problems? What adaptive solutions are available, and how effectively are they used?

Behavior checklists and adaptive behavior measurements provide some valuable information. The Vineland Social Maturity Scales has been standardized on a visually impaired group (Maxfield and Buchholtz, 1956). Many of the behavior measures are based on reported data, and it is important to check with direct observation whenever possible. When school personnel or parents report data that contradict observations made during testing, a further investigation of the child is needed to understand the test behavior and the child's functioning.

SELECTING TEST PROCEDURES

Selecting test procedures for use with the child with a visual handicap is difficult, because few standardized protocols are available. This is especially true for the visually impaired child who has additional handicaps. One of the early formally adapted tests is the Hayes-Binet (Hayes, 1943). This test includes verbal items but there are insufficient items for reliable assessment of visually impaired children under 5 years of age. As part of a resource project for early childhood education and intervention, O'Brien (1976) has devised a set of developmental scales for use in assessing visually impaired children. The scales are divided into five categories: motor, language, sensory-perceptual, self- and social awareness, and cognitive/creative.

Reynell and Zinkin (1975) have devised a set of developmental scales for use with infants and young children who are likely to have other handicaps in addition to lack of vision. Their motor scale covers the areas of manipulation, locomotion, and reflex function. The scales of mental development cover five main areas and progress from infancy to a level of approximately 5 years. The areas include social adaptation, sensorimotor understanding, exploration of environment, response to sound and verbal communication, and expressive language. Although there are no standardized scores, approximate age levels have been assigned for the mental scale; this is in order to facilitate assessment of relative strengths and weaknesses in different areas, and to enable an estimate of rates of progress. Table 10–3 summarizes the available scales for visually impaired children (see Appendix A for information about obtaining the tests).

What many clinicians do in practice is to pick items from existing tests (for example, Bayley, Binet, McCarthy, WPPSI) and administer them with the observation protocol already described. In selecting test items, it is important to consider which

TABLE 10–3   Tests for Assessing Visually Impaired Children

Hayes-Binet
Reynell and Zinkin Developmental Scales
O'Brien Developmental Scales
Maxfield-Buchholtz Revised Vineland Social Maturity Scale
Callier Azuza Scales (for deaf-blind children)

sensory skills and processes are involved in performing each task:

1. Certain items obviously require vision, and no adaptive solutions are possible (for example, reaching on sight alone).

2. Certain items are influenced by vision, but an infant can be expected to find an adaptive solution (for example, searching or reaching for an object through use of auditory cues).

3. Certain objects can be facilitated by vision, but adaptive solutions utilizing other sensory cues are readily available (for example, stranger discrimination).

4. Certain items are facilitated by vision but can be modified during presentation to eliminate the need for vision (for example, helping the child to clap his or her hands together in "patty-cake" so the child can learn what makes noise).

5. Certain items do not require vision, but accepted responses may need to be modified (for example, in response to the ringing of a bell, a visually impaired child may be alert and quiet, but may not turn his or her head toward the sound).

Many test items are not useful with the language-delayed child. Interpretation of results is often difficult because the items used have been separated from other items in the standardized tests, because their presentation and scoring must frequently be modified, and because all the items on a particular test do not have equal predictive validity.

SUMMARY

In assessing the child who is visually impaired, it is important for the psychologist to be aware of the sorts of behaviors that are normal or typical for blind children. The clinician must also understand the developmental progression of the otherwise normal visually impaired child, and how this parallels and differs from that of the normal sighted child. During testing, it is important for the examiner to give the visually impaired child ample time to orient to the testing situation and to each test object; the examiner must also be flexible in the administration of items and the interpretation of responses. Despite the dearth of standardized tests for assessing visually impaired children, a useful assessment can be accomplished by using appropriately selected test items, developmental scales, behavior checklists related to the child's environment, and careful observation. It is important for the psychologist to remember that the assessment should focus on learning what the child can do and how he or she adaptively solves problems— not how he or she responds to rigidly administered and scored test items designed for sighted children. Thorough knowledge of the special factors that affect the development of children with visual impairments is necessary if the psychologist is to obtain an accurate and useful evaluation.

REFERENCES

Barraga N: *Visual Handicaps and Learning: A Developmental Approach*. Belmont, CA: Wadsworth Publishing Co, 1976

Fine SR: Visual handicap in children. In Smith V, Keen J (eds): Clin Devel Med 73: 40, 1979

Freedman DG: Smiling blind infants and the issue of innate versus acquired. Child Psychol Psychiat 5: 171–184, 1964

Fraiberg S: Parallel and divergent patterns in blind and sighted infants. Psychoanalyt Study Child 23: 264–300, 1968

Fraiberg S, Adelson E: Gross motor development in infants blind from birth. Child Devel 45(1): 114–126, 1974

Gesell A, Amatruda C: *Infant Behavior: Its Genesis and Growth*. New York: McGraw-Hill, 1934

Graham MD: *Multiply Impaired Blind Children: A National Problem*. New York: American Foundation for the Blind, 1968

Haspiel GS: Communication breakdown in blind emotionally disturbed children. New Outlook 59: 98–99, 1965

Hayes SD: A second test scale for the mental measurement of the mentally handicapped. Outlook Blind 43: 37–41, 1943

Jan JE, Freeman RD, Scott EP: *Visual Impairment in Children and Young Adolescents*. New York: Grune & Stratton, 1977

Klein G: Blindness and isolation. Psychoanalyt Study Child 17: 260-272, 1962

Maxfield UB, Buchholtz S: *A Social Maturity Scale for Blind Preschool Children: A Guide to Its Use*. New York: American Federation for the Blind, 1956

Norris M, Spaulding P, Brodie F: *Blindness in Children*. Chicago: University of Chicago Press, 1957

O'Brien R: *Alive, Aware a Person*. Rockville, MD: Montgomery County Public Schools, 1976

Reynell J: Developmental patterns of visually handicapped children. Child Care Health Devel 4(5): 291–303, 1978

Reynell J, Zinkin P: New procedures for the developmental assessment of young children with severe visual handicaps. Child Care Health Devel 1(1): 61–69, 1975

Wills DM: The ordinary devoted mother and her blind baby. Psychoanalyt Study Child 31: 31–49, 1979a

Wills DM: Early speech development in blind children. Psychoanalyt Study Child 31: 85–117, 1979b

Chapter 11

ASSESSMENT CONSIDERATIONS WITH HEARING IMPAIRED PRESCHOOLERS

By

SALLY J. ROGERS AND ELIZABETH SOPER

Language is an integral part of human cognition. Because language helps to code information efficiently, it greatly aids in the formation of symbols and concepts that are basic to abstract thought. Although deafness may not seem to be as catastrophic a handicap as blindness or cerebral palsy, the cognitive abilities of deaf and hearing impaired children are seriously hindered by their lack of complex language.

This lack leads to lowered academic performance in all areas requiring language, reading, or writing skills; the result is that the performance skills of hearing impaired children drop further behind the performance skills of hearing children each year in school. For example, the mean reading level of 19-year-old students in schools for the deaf is fourth grade. In addition, the reading comprehension of deaf students who are in the 19th percentile (in comparison to other deaf children) is well below the performance of hearing students. In fact, when compared with hearing students, the previously mentioned deaf students scored only at the 50th percentile; this is true at all grade levels, including high school (Trybus and Karchmer, 1977). To compound the negative effects of deafness on academic performance, the child without useful reading or speech is limited in his or her ability to interact with others, and emotional growth can be seriously affected.

Because language problems can affect psychological development so profoundly, it is imperative that children with language delays—whether these are due to hearing problems or language processing problems—be diagnosed and treated as early as possible. This chapter covers the basic types of hearing loss, how these affect the child's development and performance in psychological assessments, and test batteries and techniques that are most appropriate for hearing and language impaired young children.

TYPES OF HEARING IMPAIRMENT

There are three types of hearing loss, of which the first is *conductive* hearing loss. In a conductive hearing loss, sounds received by the outer ear cannot be transmitted to the inner ear. A frequent cause of this type of loss in young children is recurrent ear infections—otitis media—in which build-up of fluid or scar tissue in the middle ear interferes with sound transmission. This type of hearing loss usually does not exceed 60 dB, and most such losses can be corrected medically. In addition, hearing aids can help greatly in overcoming a conductive loss.

The second type of hearing loss is sensorineural. In this condition, the damage may be in the sensory receptor of sound in the inner ear. Alternatively, the damage may involve the neural transmission of sound from the inner ear to the brain (damage to the auditory nerve). Although this kind of hearing loss is irreversible, hearing aids can be helpful.

The third category consists of a *mixed*

hearing loss. Children with a mixed hearing loss have both conductive and sensorineural losses (Northern and Downs, 1974).

SEVERITY OF HEARING IMPAIRMENTS

The severity of hearing loss is classified according to the decibel (or dB) level at which the child hears sounds. (The frequency of the sound—whether it is high or low in pitch—also plays a part in what the child can hear but will not be discussed here.) The four classifications of hearing loss are as follows:

1. A 15- to 30-dB loss is considered a *mild* hearing loss. This degree of loss may pass almost unnoticed, because the child uses vision to supplement understanding.

2. A 30- to 50-dB loss is a *moderate* hearing loss. With this degree of loss, the child will hear *most* speech sounds when near to and facing the speaker. However, the child may have articulation problems because not all sounds are heard well; in addition, he or she may have difficulty hearing speech if the speaker's voice is quiet or if the speaker is not facing the child.

3. A 50- to 80-dB loss represents a *severe* hearing loss. The child with a severe hearing loss will hear speech *only* if it is loud. The language development and vocabularies of children with a severe hearing loss are considerably hindered, and speech and voice quality are affected. Children with a severe hearing loss rely heavily on visual cues from the speaker to grasp the meaning of what is said.

4. Finally, an 81- to 100-dB loss is a *profound* hearing loss in which the child cannot hear speech (except perhaps for a few loud vowel sounds) and will hear few environmental noises without the help of hearing aids. Although hearing aids will provide some help to affected children, there will be considerable distortion of sound with the amplification required (Silverman, 1971).

EFFECTS OF HEARING LOSS ON LANGUAGE DEVELOPMENT

Because a child must hear a tremendous amount of well-structured language before he or she is able to speak, all degrees of hearing loss—including those that are mild—impair language development. Many experts in the field believe that the first few years of life are a critical period for language development. That is, they believe that after those years are past, the child actually loses some ability to discriminate sounds and to develop complex language. Northern and Downs (1974) state that "a baby who is deprived of appropriate language stimulation during his first three years of life can *never* fully attain his best potential language function, whether the deprivation is from lack of hearing or from lack of high quality language experience" (p. vi).

This critical period hypothesis has further implications. Because of the importance of language to reading, writing, and abstract thought, if the best potential language function cannot be attained, then neither can the best cognitive and academic function.

There are several research findings which Northern and Downs (1974) use to support the hypothesis of a critical period for language development. The first involves a follow-up study of severely hearing impaired teenagers, in which Downs found that these students had actually lost their ability to discriminate speech sounds despite months of high-quality auditory discrimination training. Presumably the lack of use for such a long period of time caused the loss of the discriminatory abilities.

A second research finding involves children who have had some period of normal hearing before becoming deaf. Even when the period of normal hearing has only been for the first year or two of life, such children develop language more easily then those who have never heard language. Presumably this is because of exposure to language during the critical period.

A third argument focuses on the language development of hearing impaired and deaf children who receive intensive therapy beginning as early as the age of 2. Despite the therapy, these children still show a language delay relative to children who have heard speech since birth. (It should be noted, however, that the delay in language is not as great when therapy begins at age 2 as when it begins even later—at age 3 or 4.)

Even for deaf children who receive intensive language therapy from an early age and develop language at a fairly normal rate, there comes a plateau in language development at about age 11. The language of hearing children becomes increasingly more abstract from ages 11 to 14, while the language of the hearing impaired does not—again, presumably owing to early language deprivation (Northern and Downs, 1974).

Remediation of a hearing loss with hearing aids or other means unfortunately *cannot* undo the effects of the loss, because the months and years the child has spent without hearing language cannot be made up. This is why many researchers are now trying to diagnose hearing loss in newborns and are putting hearing aids on tiny infants. They are trying to alleviate the loss of speech input during the critical years of birth through age 2.

One major and obvious symptom of hearing loss in young children is delayed language development. For children with mild hearing loss, this may be the *only* symptom. Thus, it becomes extremely important when assessing young children to note the presence of a language delay. This is not always as easy as it may seem, because slow language development may lead one to suspect cognitive delay or mental retardation rather than a hearing loss. Psychologists must be sure to see that young children with a language delay have an audiometric examination before diagnosing the cause as generalized cognitive or developmental delay. There are too many cases of residents in institutions for the retarded who are found, after years of institutionalization, to be deaf and of normal intelligence. For this reason, an important rule of thumb for the psychologist is: *When evaluating a young child who performs below age level on language tasks, always refer him or her for an audiologic and speech and language evaluation.* Furthermore, hearing impairments in young children may be progressive. Therefore, if a child with a known hearing loss has not had an audiologic examination in the preceding 12 months, such an examination should be repeated.

Children who are at particularly high risk for hearing impairments are those with a history of cleft palate, otitis media, viral diseases (like rubella and meningitis), Rh incompatibility, or parental hearing disorders (Northern and Downs, 1974). There is a strong genetic contribution to deafness, in that almost 53 percent of congenital deafness is from genetic causes; however, contrary to popular opinion, the probability of two deaf parents having a deaf child is only slightly higher than the probability for hearing parents, since the deaf parents' handicap usually does not result from the same genetic cause. Indeed, 90 percent of inherited deafness is due to recessive genetic defects (Northern and Downs, 1974).

A deaf child born to deaf parents is at an advantage in two ways. First, the child is surrounded by a language system from infancy. The positive effects of this are seen in the advanced (manual) language concepts and usage of deaf children with deaf parents, when compared with deaf children born to hearing parents. These advanced language concepts and uses lead to higher performances in reading and writing and are another example of the necessity for providing language input to the deaf child from infancy. The second advantage is that the deaf child can communicate with deaf parents using manual language. Fewer than 10 percent of hearing parents who have nonspeaking deaf children learn manual communication so that they can communicate with their child (Baker, 1980)—a situation that seems likely to interfere with the emotional development of the child.

ASSESSMENT PROCEDURES

We would next like to discuss assessment procedures that can be used with hearing impaired young children. The general assumption is that in order for an intelligence test to be valid for this population, the test must be a nonverbal performance instrument (Cantor and Spragins, 1977). While this view is generally accepted, Gerweck and Ysseldyke (1975) would add a further precaution: ". . . the mere fact that a test *can* be conveniently administered to hearing impaired individuals does not mean that it should be"

(p. 245). This leads into the heavily debated issue of the use with deaf subjects of performance tests of which the norms were determined on hearing subjects.

When performance items are taken from various tests standardized on hearing children, it is very difficult to interpret the deaf child's performance, because even young children use language to help them solve tasks. (This is easy to see in young hearing children on the Leiter test when they spontaneously name the colors or count the bunnies.) The only intelligence test for young children with norms based on a deaf sample is the Hiskey-Nebraska Test of Learning Aptitude; this is the test of choice for young children. (For older children the revised version of Wechsler's Intelligence Scale for Children can be used; it has recently been given norms for the deaf and thus is also useful.)

Some experts in the field hypothesize that deaf, preverbal children use different cognitive processes than hearing children to solve problems; this is presumably because they do not have readily accessible mental symbols, like words, to represent objects and experiences. In addition to these possible cognitive differences, young deaf children have social and emotional experiences very different from hearing children. It is increasingly recognized that developmental and intelligence tests generally reflect the cultural mainstream of white, middle-class America, and that children who are not exposed to that cultural mainstream will not have the same information available to them for problem-solving; this is as true for the deaf child as it is for the disadvantaged, black, urban preschooler.

The inability to understand what is being said, or to communicate one's needs, preferences, or feelings (except in the primitive, gestural way one sees with young children) greatly restricts social interactions with neighbors, peers, and extended family members. It will also, of course, greatly affect the child's relationship with nuclear family members. In a study that compared hearing mothers' interactions with hearing and with deaf toddlers, clear differences were found in the quality of the interactions. The deaf toddlers were more passive and less actively involved in inter-

actions with their mothers than were the hearing toddlers, and the mothers of deaf toddlers were more dominant, resulting in less reciprocity in those interactions (Wedell-Monnig and Lumley, 1980).

Teaching the child simple adaptive behaviors will be more challenging to the parents because of the hearing handicap, and limit-setting and behavior management are particularly difficult with a child who cannot understand speech. In addition, favorite activities of hearing toddlers and preschoolers—books, television, numbers, colors, records, trips to the zoo—are greatly dependent on language, and much of what is built into intelligence tests reflects these activities. The deaf child's cultural, social, and adaptive experiences are vastly different from the hearing child's; thus, even performance tests and adaptive behavior scales that appear not to rely on language still lean heavily on cultural experiences to which the deaf child will not have the same exposure.

Below the age of 2 years, deaf children appear to respond like hearing children on nonverbal developmental tests and on cognitive measurements (Best and Roberts, 1978; Levine, 1971). This is probably because both hearing and deaf children below 2 years of age are not yet using words as mental symbols and are still functioning in the sensory and motor modalities. Thus, it seems that norms from developmental tests standardized on hearing children can be used with hearing impaired children under age 2 as long as nonlanguage tasks are used.

In addition to the problem of test norms when using performance tests with young hearing impaired children, a second problem emerges. The resulting IQ scores do not represent the same types of abilities as the IQ score on a verbal test. The traditional verbal IQ tests predict school success well *because* they measure language abilities. Nonlanguage tests may not predict academic abilities as well, since academics are so dependent on reading, writing, understanding, and using speech. Skills that performance tests measure—spatial relations, visual-motor proficiency, perceptual discrimination, and reasoning—may correlate with some kinds of vocational abilities but cannot be used to predict school achievement in the same way as traditional IQ tests. Therefore, interpretation of test findings for deaf children differs from interpretation of the IQ scores of hearing children. In the Hiskey-Nebraska Test of Learning Aptitude manual, Hiskey discusses the problem of past performance tests used with deaf children, and states that his items were based on typical school tasks for children in schools for the deaf. When relationships between measurements of academic achievement and scores on the Hiskey-Nebraska Test are examined, respectable correlations for deaf children in grades two to four and grades six to twelve are found; the scores from this test may thus be helpful in predicting school achievement for deaf children (Hiskey, 1966).

A third problem is the selection of hearing and language tasks when the child has some hearing and/or speech. If mainstreaming is being considered, then language should be assessed, and the child's expressive and receptive language performance can be compared with that of hearing children by using standardized intelligence tests; however, it must be stressed that this is most useful if the purpose is assessing the feasibility of mainstreaming.

Even for children with some hearing and speech, it is best to begin the assessment with a nonverbal performance test. Then, if it seems appropriate, the nonverbal test can be followed with a verbal test. Each test should be scored separately; the psychologist should assume that the performance test is the best indicator of the child's abilities, while the verbal score shows the effects of the hearing impairment on the child's language development (Vernon and Brown, 1964).

Boone (1968) points out that the child with some hearing (such as a 45- to 65-dB loss) may appear to hear adequately, because such children learn how to *appear* to understand. However, that degree of hearing loss tends to affect the child in such a way that he or she responds to all sounds equally, leaving the child with spotty comprehension and resulting poor performance on tasks given with even partially verbal instructions. These children present a complicated picture to the psychologist, and the most accurate evaluation procedure probably should be to communicate instructions entirely with gesture, touch, and pantomime while speaking naturally.

CONDUCTING A PROPER ASSESSMENT

Conducting an assessment of a nonverbal hearing impaired child can be quite difficult for the inexperienced psychologist. Because examiners who lack experience with hearing impaired children make many more errors in interpreting the child's gestures and in understanding the child's responses than do experienced examiners, it makes sense for the novice in this area to work with a more experienced psychologist whenever possible.

Young hearing impaired children rely heavily on vision to understand; therefore, the examiner must be able to use gestures, pantomime, and facial expressions freely to communicate. To ensure that the child understands, it is necessary to demonstrate tasks and to test the child's understanding through imitation with samples. The psychologist should be sure to face the child and speak slowly and clearly, repeating key words. Gestures and facial expressions can provide further cues. A natural demeanor and normal voice quality will help the child be more comfortable with the examiner. Because of communication and concept difficulties, the young hearing impaired child has difficulty understanding speed and time, so timed tests are much less valid than untimed tests (Vernon and Brown, 1964; Gerweck and Ysseldyke, 1975). Thus, when choosing performance tasks from various developmental tests, it is wisest to choose untimed tasks. The validity of results will also be increased if the examiner tries to teach a task that the child has failed, and then administers the next level task to ensure that the child's failure was not due to misunderstanding of the task.

Many writers stress the importance of selecting more than one test, partially because young hearing impaired children—even more so than young hearing children—tend to be very unreliable test takers. It is suggested that subnormal scores should be questioned, and data from other tests, observations, interviews, and adaptive behavior be examined so that the examiner can refute or support initial low test scores. If there is wide discrepancy among scores, many experienced professionals in the field rely on the highest score as the best indicator of potential because of the many variables that can adversely affect the child's performance (Vernon and Brown, 1964). (Performance tasks that are frequently used with young hearing impaired children are discussed in Table 11–1.)

Psychologists knowlegeable in the field strongly recommend use of a battery of tests, including *two* intellectual tests, an assessment of fine motor and visual motor functioning, and an adaptive behavior assessment (Cantor and Spragins, 1977). Observing parent-child interactions in a play situation and interacting with the child in an unstructured situation will add greatly to knowledge about the child's social skills, communication abilities, and emotional development. This is relevant because these are important characteristics for making decisions about programs and curriculum, and they are characteristics that are not as easily tapped in the highly structured formal assessment format.

The kind of program to be recommended for young hearing impaired children depends in part on the severity of the hearing impairment. For profoundly deaf young children, the oral versus total communication debate continues, with compelling arguments put forward for both. If the psychologist is to help make the decision as to which program would be preferred for a child, he or she should review the arguments for both approaches carefully before making any recommendation. Moores, Weiss, and Goodwin (1978) compared performances of sixty preschool children with hearing losses of 70 dB or greater and of normal intelligence who had been placed in several types of preschool programs. Their findings, which are consistent with most research on the subject, were that in order for deaf children to be at an academic level equal to hearing children at age 6, the preschool program must provide both strong cognitive/academic training and use of total communication (oral training accompanied by manual language).

The approach that resulted in lowest academic abilities at age 6 was a socially oriented classroom with an aural/oral communication program. Contrary to the arguments of oralists (but again in agreement with the majority of research findings), there was no evidence that the use of the total communication approach interfered with the children's learning of speech reading or their use of residual hearing. These findings are certainly in line with the critical period hypothesis, in that maximum exposure to language and concepts in the preschool years will provide greater readiness for academic work—which depends on language skills—in school years.

SUMMARY

In summary, assessments of hearing impaired young children are difficult to carry out and to interpret. The absence of or deficits in language of these children which makes an assessment difficult can have severe repercussions on both cognitive and emotional development; *early* comprehensive treatment is crucial if the child is to develop language. For these reasons, it is imperative that the hearing loss be identified and the child's cognitive and emotional development be adequately assessed so a program of intervention can begin. The psychologist must understand the implication of a hearing loss on the child's behavior and development and must adapt the testing situation to gather maximum information about the child.

REFERENCES

Baker R: Personal communication, 1980

Best B., Roberts G: Early cognitive development in hearing impaired children. Am Ann Deaf 121: 560–564, 1976

Boone JN: Intellectual evaluation of children with major sensory deficits. In Khanna J (ed): *Brain Damage and Mental Retardation: A Psychological Evaluation.* Springfield, IL: Charles C Thomas, 1968

Cantor DW, Spragins A: Delivery of psychological services to the hearing impaired child in the elementary school. Am Ann Deaf 122: 330–336, 1977

Gerweck S, Ysseldyke JE: Limitations of current psychological practices for the intellectual assessment of the hearing impaired: A response to the Levine study. Volta Rev 77: 243–248, 1975

Hiskey MS: *Hiskey-Nebraska Test of Learning Aptitude.* Lincoln, NE: Union College Press, 1966

Levine ES: Mental assessment of the deaf child. Volta Rev 73: 80–105, 1971

Moores DF, Weiss KL, Goodwin MW: Early education programs for hearing impaired children: Major findings. Am Ann Deaf 123: 925–936, 1978

Northern J, Downs M: *Hearing in Children.* Baltimore: Williams & Wilkins, 1974

Silverman SR: Hard-of-hearing children. In Travis LE (ed): *Handbook of Speech Pathology and Audiology.* New York: Appleton-Century-Crofts, 1971

Trybus RJ, Karchmer MA: School achievement scores of hearing impaired children: National data on achievement status and growth patterns. Am Ann Deaf 122: 62–69, 1977

Ulrey G: *Selection and use of psychological tests for children.* Denver: John F. Kennedy Child Development Center, 1979

Vernon M, Brown DW: A guide to psychological tests and testing procedures in the evaluation of deaf and hard-of-hearing children. Speech Hear Dis 29: 414–423, 1964

Wedell-Monnig J, Lumley JM: Child deafness and mother-child interaction. Child Devel 51: 766–774, 1980

TABLE 11-1   Performance Tests Used with Hearing Impaired Preschoolers

Test	Purposes	Ages	Strengths	Weaknesses
Hiskey-Nebraska Test of Learning Aptitude Marshall S. Hiskey 5640 Baldwin Lincoln, NE 68507	General intellectual assessment	2½ & up	Normed for deaf and for hearing Based on school-type tasks	Somewhat complicated to administer
Leiter International Performance Scale & Arthur Adaptation C. H. Stoelting Co. 424 N. Horman Avenue Chicago, IL 60624	General intellectual assessment	2½ & up	Easy to administer	Not normed specifically for deaf Mean of 90 and SD of 20 vary from most tests
Merrill-Palmer Scale of Mental Tests C. H. Stoelting Co. 424 N. Horman Avenue Chicago, IL 60624	General intellectual assessment	1½ & up	Nice range of tasks Optional verbal items for children with some hearing and speech	Limited normative sample, none deaf Timed tests
Ontario School Ability Examination Ryerson Press 299 Queen St. West Toronto 2B Ontario, Canada	General intellectual assessment	3 & up	Normed for deaf	Not widely known or used in USA
Wechsler Preschool & Primary Scale of Intelligence Performance Psychological Corp. 304 E. 45th St. New York, NY 10017	General intellectual assessment	4 & up	Correlates well with verbal scales	Not normed for deaf Timed tests Some instructions are very hard to communicate nonverbally and require concepts deaf children may not have
Illinois Test of Psycholinguistic Abilities 5 nonverbal subjects U. of Illinois Press 54 E. Gregory Drive P.O. Box 5081, Sta. A Champaign, IL 61820	Visual memory and visual	4 & up	Researched with deaf and found to be fairly representative	Not normed for deaf

TABLE 11-1   Performance Tests Used with Hearing Impaired Preschoolers

Test	Purposes	Ages	Strengths	Weaknesses
Developmental Test of Visual Motor Integration (Beery) Follett Publishing Co. 1010 W. Washington Blvd. Chicago, IL 60607	Visual-motor skills	Best with 3 & up (can be used with younger)	Level of difficulty is suitable for preschoolers Fairly good standardization	Not normed for deaf
Bender Gestalt Test Koppitz Scoring System in The Bender Gestalt Test for Young Children by E. M. Koppitz Grune & Stratton, Inc. 111 Fifth Avenue New York, NY 10003	Visual-motor assessment	5 & up	Gives wealth of data for children over 5	Not applicable for preschool-aged children "Organic" and emotional scoring indicators have not shown adequate validity and reliability
Goodenough Intelligence Test (Draw a Man) Harcourt, Brace, Jovanovich, Inc. 757 Third Avenue New York, NY 10017	General intellectual assessment	3 & up	Simple to administer Provides some data on cognitive and visual-motor skills	Provides at best a *rough* indicator of cognitive level Motor problems may cause one to underrate cognitive abilities
Minnesota Preschool Scale Educational Test Bureau 720 Washington Ave., SE Minneapolis, MN 54414	General intellectual assessment	1½ & up	No information	No information

Compiled from Levine, 1971, Ulrey, 1979, and Cantor and Spragins, 1977.

Chapter 12

ASSESSMENT CONSIDERATIONS WITH LANGUAGE IMPAIRED CHILDREN

By

GORDON ULREY

The most frequent learning problem of young children involves a language disorder, for it is known that much of learning is affected by language, and that a child's thinking and language are highly interdependent. Difficulties with language also have important effects on psychological testing, for many items that appear to be nonverbal require communication and conceptualizing that depend on language skills. The psychologist evaluating young children must be aware of the extent to which performance on tests requires specific language skills and must be able to observe behaviors that reflect a language disorder.

Both Piaget (1926) and Vygotsky (1962) have written extensively about the theoretical relationship between language and thought. While it remains unclear which comes first, it is known that a disability in either area will have an impact on total learning and development in other domains. As language skills become more abstract, the thinking processes become more important. Indeed, the ability to comprehend abstract concepts appears to be related to the mastery of language. Studies show that severely hearing impaired children have difficulty developing higher level abstract skills. The result is lower average school performance and general level of intelligence (Trybus and Karchmer, 1977).

Learning may be limited both by language differences and deficiencies, as seen with low socioeconomic level inner-city children and severely hearing impaired children. The inner city child learns a "nonstandard" language that is generally not used by teachers in school systems (Carroll, 1973). This language form restricts the child's comprehension of concepts taught through "standard" English by middle-class teachers and children.

It is important to distinguish the concept of language from speech. The term language is used to describe a child's total communication system, including comprehension of verbal and nonverbal processes. Speech is used to describe the child's verbal output in talking and is seen as one part of the child's complex language system. Therefore, the total way a child communicates and interacts reflects that child's language competence.

When assessing a young child, the question the psychologist must ask is, "How does the child communicate?" rather than, "Does the child talk?" Most children communicate through some system—no matter how young or intellectually impaired the child may be. The various ways the child elicits responses from others and the ways the environment responds to the child reflect the communication and learning process. Recently, numerous studies of the reciprocity of children and caretaking interactions have increased our knowledge of how the child learns to communicate at an early age (reviewed by Nelson, 1981; Gratch, 1979). For example, Clarke-Stewart and Hevey (1981) have recently reviewed research that

123

indicates a decrease in physical contact between infants and mothers as a concomitant increase in words and sentences appear in the interactions.

The importance of nonverbal behavior has been reviewed by Bruner (1975); this includes such behaviors as gaze, eye contact, posture, interpersonal distance, touch, facial expression, and body movements. All of these behaviors enable a child to understand or to be understood when interacting with others. For example, a study by Yarrow, Rubinstein, and Peterson (1975) demonstrated that children as young as 4 weeks of age had differential responses to their parents compared with strangers. The infants in the study frowned more at strangers and smiled more at the parents. Other studies show that expressivity and receptivity are present in very young children.

Observations of nonverbal behaviors are important for determining how a child communicates his or her needs. A common example observed clinically is that a child is noticeably more distractible and shows increased activity levels when asked to perform a task that is difficult; conversely, that child will be more attentive and less active when asked to perform easier tasks. A child with a language disorder will often show this pattern on verbal versus nonverbal tasks. In fact, in a highly verbally oriented school or home setting, the child may be seen as hyperactive. The psychologist should note the situational antecedents of these behavior changes and should be aware that children often communicate that a certain task is difficult for them with nonverbal responses, such as overactivity or poor attending.

DEVELOPMENTAL MILESTONES

The psychologist must be aware of milestones of speech and language development in the context of the functional significance of the child's communication. Table 12–1 shows the norms for some of the major speech milestones. The examiner should observe different vocalizations and the situations in which they occur. For example, does the child show pleasure or displeasure by sounds and expressions? Does the child become alert and attend to human voices? The work of Lois Bloom (1973) indicates that as single words emerge, they are used both specifically and nonspecifically. The context of single word utterances often communicates a more elaborate request; for example, the simple word "Mom" may mean, "Mom, I want you to pick me up," or, "Mom, is it time for me to eat?" A sample of the child's spontaneous use of language should be compared with responses to verbal items on formal tests. Differences in the level of sophistication of spontaneous utterances compared with test responses (based on norms for milestones) should always be investigated further.

As children attach meaning to words, they learn to distinguish self from objects and to understand that sounds can symbolize or stand for objects. Prior to understanding this concept, the child sees the rest of the world as an extension of him- or herself. However, at 4 to 10 months, the child develops the concept of objects and begins naming of objects, which demonstrates the early symbolic functioning of language. Later, the preschooler's use of words reflects preoperational thinking and demonstrates a remarkable spurt of growth in the use of language. In this stage of development, the child can explain why things have occurred or will ask questions that reveal the level of understanding. A child who explains things verbally less well than what would be expected for his or her general level of intelligence may have a language disorder.

Difficulties with some aspects of speech and language can be normal at one age and abnormal at another. For example, the 2- to 3-year-old may stutter some normally, but 5- to 6-year-olds should rarely show any stuttering except when learning new words. Another example is that most children at about 4 years of age say "hisself" rather than "himself," because they have not internalized the rules of the English language. The mastery of irregularities also occurs later, with younger children commonly misusing such words as "seed" for "saw." Experience with young children and knowledge of early language development are essential to avoid pitfalls in misinterpretation of cognitive testing.

TABLE 12—1   Language Development of Preschool Child

Milestones of Language Acquisition*		
Receptive		Expressive
1 month—Reflex smile to Mother's voice		
2 months—Attends to speaking voice		Has a "hungry" cry; babbling begins
3 months—Localizes speakers with eyes and looks directly at speakers' faces	2 syllables (nonspeech)	Makes many vocal noises resembling speech sounds; vocalizes pleasure at social stimuli
4 months—Turns to noise and voice	Repeats 4 or 5 syllables in sound chain, ba-ba-ba, etc.	Vocalizes by self-initiated sound play
5 months—Responds to angry tone by crying, to pleasant speech by smiling		Imitates his/her own noises: oohs, ahs, bas, das
6 months—Seems to understand meaning of voice tones of friendliness and anger; appears to understand a few words, like Mama and Daddy		"Lalling" begins; uses intonational pattern with jargon speech; directs sound and gestures to objects; tries to repeat sound sequences
7 months—Pays attention to speech of family; responds appropriately to "bye-bye" and "up"		Vocalizes emotional satisfaction or dissatisfaction
8 months—Listens to greetings and other familiar phrases		Vocalizes syllable: da, ba, ka; vocalizes interjections and recognition
9 months—Action response to verbal request (open mouth when asked); understands no-no, hot, his/her name	3-4 syllables, but varies syllables in chain	Echolalia; tries variety of pitches; enjoys making lip noises; copies melody pattern of familiar phrases
10 months—Comprehends bye-bye, and waves; action response to verbal request: "Where's baby's shoe?"; shakes yes to some questions no to other questions	Says word-like syllable: ma-ma-ma	Tries to name familiar objects
11 months—Differentiates strangers from family; understands many action words	Median age of first word	Rudimentary language, proclaims biologic needs and psychological satisfactions; talks to self in mirror
12 months—Responds in action to commands; enjoys rhymes and simple songs; understands arrival and departure signals	5–6 words: mama, dada, baby, bye-bye, ball	Communicative speech begins; copies melody patterns more accurately but in jargon speech
14 months—Seems to understand emotional tone when spoken to; interested in looking at pictures while they are named up to 2 minutes	1-word sentences	Uses some true words with jargon
16 months—Will bring object from other room; recognizes names of body parts		More true words occurring in communication

TABLE 12–1   Continued

Milestones of Language Acquisition		
Receptive		*Expressive*
18 months—Carries out 2 consecutive commands; identifies correctly 2 out of 4 familiar objects; points to pictures of familiar objects		Repeats words spoken around him/her
20 months—Points to several body parts in pictures	10–20 words	Imitates motor and animal sounds while playing; imitates 2- and 3-word sentences
22 months—Identifies 8–10 pictures of common objects; can follow 2 related directions		Begins combining words into 2-word combinations; uses jargon and real words when telling about events
By 24 months—Understands most linguistic units, but not separate word units; recognizes names of many familiar objects, persons, pets	50–75 words; nouns 75% of vocabulary; most words by phonetic reduplication; 1.5- word-sentence length	Interjectional speech prevails; imitates speech segments, more bye-bye; uses prepositions off and communicates by pulling person and showing
27 months—Can point to a few smaller body parts; identifies words like baby, mother		Uses some personal pronouns; usually uses 2- or 3-word sentences
By 30 months—Action response to verbal request (close door); distinguishes *in* from *under;* listens to simple stories	272 words; nouns 38.6%; verbs 21.0%; adverbs 7.1%; pronouns 14.6%; other 18.7%; 1.8-word sentences	Egocentric speech; asks simple questions; names 1 color; names or describes objects in environment; uses pronoun this; adjectives and adverbs increasing
33 months—Identifies common verbs in pictures; understands common adjectives		Will tell if a boy or girl; will tell about drawing (scribbling), at least by naming
By 36 months—Understands yes-no, come-go, run-stop, give-take, grasp-release, push-pull; identifies action in pictures; understands 3 prepositions; listens to longer and more varied stories; understands semantic difference in subject-object relations; comprehends time words	446 words; 3.1-word sentences	Continues egocentric speech; gives full name; recites 1–2 nursery rhymes; names 5 pictures; begins to use me and I; uses this and that; uses 2–3 prepositions; pronunciation
3.0 years—Fairly intelligible speech; final consonants appear more frequently	Generative grammar develops; 2- word phrases more frequent form; 3.4-word sentences; 896 words	Egocentric speech prevails; asks questions; names 2 colors; tells sex and full name; verbalizes toilet needs
3.6 years—All English vowels used; medial consonants often omitted; some blocks on initial syllables; rate of speech increased	Makes questions out of declarative statements; uses auxiliaries, adverbs, adjectives; 4.3-word sentences; 1200 words	Communicative speech developing; commands, requests, threats; asks "why"; relates experiences; says nursery rhymes; names primary colors; counts one by one

TABLE 12–1   Continued

Milestones of Language Acquisition

Receptive		*Expressive*
4.0 years—98% speech intelligible; omissions and substitutions reduced; vocal pitch controlled; adult rhythm patterns; repetitions reduced, but still some blocking	Beginning to use complex and compound sentences; 4.2-word sentences; 1500-word vocabulary; uses some slang	Whole sentences, not isolated words; perception still first person, and realistic; ideation becoming less concrete; refers to events and persons not in immediate environment; tells tales, talks a lot, threatens; counts 3 objects
4.6 years—Reverses order of sounds within words; intonational pattern of mother; begins sentences with /um/, /uh/	Increasing use of compound and complex sentences; reverses syllables, word order at times; spontaneously corrects grammar; uses conjunctions; 4.7-word sentences; 1800 words; uses colloquial expressions	More adaptive social communication appears; links past and present events; defines simple words; tries to use new words, not always correctly

*From Berry MF: *Language Disorders of Children.* New York: Appleton-Century-Crofts, 1969; *Houston Test for Language Development, Part I;* Bzoch-League *Receptive-Expressive Emergent Language Scale;* Gainesville, FL: Anshinga Press, 1970

LANGUAGE DISORDERS

A problem with language development is always of major concern because of its potential impact on cognitive, emotional, and perceptual growth. The psychologist encountering a language dysfunction must assume that it is the primary or secondary aspect of a developmental disability; however, the diagnosis of a language disorder in young children is very difficult because of the complexities of evolving competencies. In addition, the absence of a validated test that allows for differentiation of a language disorder from low intelligence and inadequate environmental supports makes the diagnosis of a specific language disorder by a psychologist inappropriate. The task of the psychologist screening or assessing a young child is to:

1. Identify behaviors that suggest inadequacies of language skills.

2. Determine how language dysfunction influences test behavior, interpretation of assessment outcome, and planning for intervention.

3. Utilize appropriately the services of audiologists, speech and language pathologists, and ear, nose, and throat medical specialists.

Most language disorders of young children can best be conceptualized and categorized in four groups: (1) receptive language; (2) central processing; (3) expressive language; and (4) inadequate environmental supports. The first three are part of a functional model described by several language experts (Lerner, 1971; Johnson and Myklebust, 1967). The fourth category is emphasized because of the importance of appreciating how deficiencies and differences in opportunity to acquire language have many implications for psychologic assessment.

These four categories are described here to facilitate analysis of behaviors observed or reported during an evaluation. It is rare to find a child with a problem in only one discrete area of language functioning, since a problem in one area always affects functioning in the other areas. Consideration of how intact each of these functions is and how they interact with the child's environmental experiences is needed for test interpretation and for planning intervention. While psychologists should not attempt to diagnose specific language disorders, to ensure appropriate use of test data and to facilitate intervention planning, it is very important that psychologists observe behaviors that suggest language dysfunction. Behaviors that may suggest a difficulty in each area will be described below.

RECEPTIVE LANGUAGE

Most language pathologists define receptive language as the process of understanding or perceiving verbal symbols. A distinction is made between registering the sensation of sound (auditory acuity) and the interpretation or discrimination of sounds (auditory perception). Although the vast majority of children who have severe language disorders do not have deficits in hearing acuity (Friedlander, 1975), it is important that hearing disorders be ruled out when a child with a speech disorder is encountered. (Chapter 11 describes behaviors of hearing impaired children and special testing procedures that can be used with them.)

Problems with receptive language usually involve problems with the perception of verbal symbols. There are four categories of auditory perception, which include most receptive language problems (Northern and Downs, 1974): (1) auditory discrimination, (2) auditory blending, (3) auditory sequencing, and (4) auditory memory.

The psychologist can screen for some receptive language problems by being aware of the age-appropriateness of the child's verbal behavior, and by observing irregularities that suggest the need for further evaluations by an audiologist or speech pathologist. For example, a child who may be experiencing some difficulty with auditory discrimination and/or auditory blending may show reversed sounds in spontaneous speech. The child may consistently say "emeny" for "enemy," or "aminal" for "animal." Another example is the child who says words that are close phonetically but that are wrong because of letter sounds that are substituted (such as "kite" for "bike," or "boat" for "goat"). A referral should be made when a pattern of these behaviors is observed and/or reported by parents or teachers; referral is particularly important because Wiig and Semel (1975) have reported that children with learning disabilities show a higher frequency of auditory discrimination problems.

Problems with auditory sequencing may be present when a child is observed to repeat only the last word of a sentence; alternatively, the order of words may be mixed when the child attempts a sentence memory task. Children who remember all the digits presented to them but who reverse the order when repeating those digits back may have a sequencing deficit. Retaining a sequence of words is important if the child is to comprehend language and follow instructions. Problems with auditory sequencing may be subtle and may have an impact at several different language levels, so that in some cases the whole process may "break down," producing a reversal or confusion of order. The retention of sentences is complex and involves understanding of both syntax (structure of sentences) and semantics (meaning of words). The research of Savin, Perchonock, (1965) provides a hierarchy for the complexities of syntax and semantics in recall of sentence structure. The psychologist should not read too much into errors in memory of sentences without considering the various levels of language function. Instead, when irregular responses are observed, they should be analyzed further by a speech pathologist.

Difficulties with auditory memory are seen when a child is unable to reproduce digits or words from a sentence. Some children use a strategy of re-auditorizing to compensate for difficulty with auditory memory or sequencing (Johnson and Myklebust, 1967), suggesting a receptive language difficulty. The psychologist should observe how effectively the child can use these strategies in communicating, for strategies are often adaptive and reveal the child's way of mastering a mild deficit with little or no need for intervention.

CENTRAL PROCESSING

What happens to verbal symbols after they are perceived is a matter of longstanding theoretical debate. There are numerous theories of how language is perceived and organized (Piaget, 1926; Vygotsky, 1962). Because one can only infer what takes place, the distinction between receptive, central, and expressive language is somewhat arbitrary. Nevertheless, these concepts can be useful to the psychologist who suspects a language disorder. It is assumed that problems at the central level involve organizational and associative processes that are directly influenced by intellectual skills and emotional maturity. Wiig and Semel (1976) emphasize the role of both linguistics and cognitive semantic skills to interpret central processing difficulties at different levels of linguistic competence. Children seem to learn complex rules of language without formal instruction. Behaviors that reflect linguistic competence involve the specific forms of words used by the child and the order of words in sentences (the grammar). The rules for forming words are called morphology and the rules of sentences are called syntax. A child may have difficulty in one or both of these areas. Although it is known that the child's early language will progress systematically through levels of increasing sophistication reflecting linguistic competence, this develoment must be understood in the ecology of the child's developing communication system. There are language behaviors that suggest problems in either or both of these areas.

The work of Berko (1958) in development of morphology suggests that children first learn general rules and the progress to more specific ones. A common example is a child's use of the wrong tense of a verb, such as putting regular endings on irregular verbs. The child might say "sawed" instead of "seen," or "goed" for "went." The use of plurals at inappropriate times is also often seen. The psychologist should note the relative maturity level of the child's word forms, for when a child shows delayed word forms or uses abnormal patterns, he or she should be examined further by a speech pathologist. Some children will attempt to compensate for a word form problem and try to avoid making errors by echoing what others say. The speech pathologist can help sort out the pattern of deficits and the child's environmental experiences with language.

The form and functions of sentences also yield an assumed invariant order of increasing complexity in the use of grammar. The work of Menyuk (1969) has delineated the order of a child's rules of structuring sentences. He notes that most of the important regular rules are learned by age 3, although there is a wide range of variability in the consistent application of these rules. For example, Menyuk notes that simple nouns and regular verbs are combined first, and auxiliary verbs and irregular forms emerge later. Once again, a child who performs poorly on verbal tasks (compared to non-verbal tasks) and who shows poor grammar for his or her age level should be further evaluated by a speech pathologist. The psychologist should observe the parents' language behaviors to help determine the child's experiences with communication and models for grammar.

The area of cognitive-semantic processing involves how the child derives conceptual meaning from spoken language. At first the child simply makes concrete associations between a sound symbol (word) and an object or person. Examples are the word "chair" or "mama." The child's abilities to comprehend abstractions and reasoning and to use symbolic behavior (playing with one object and pretending that it's another) are a function of his or her cognitive-semantic processing skills. These skills reflect the child's general level of intelligence and should be compared with other language skills measured. Since a child's mental functioning may compromise language skills, it is often difficult or impossible to differentiate a child's intellectual deficits from a language disorder. The most common error of clinicians is to observe a low IQ score and assume that the child is generally dull, when the reason for the low score may be a function of a language disorder. Because of this potential error, children who score much lower on verbal comprehension questions than on nonverbal performance items should always have further speech and language assessments.

Conversely, when a child demonstrates delayed language skills, it may be a function of mental retardation with few if any specific language deficits. Neufield and Schlanger (1968) have found that most mildly retarded children progress through the same sequence of linguistic competence as higher-functioning children—but at a slower pace. It is also known that mentally retarded children show a higher percentage of language disorders than children functioning above the range of mental retardation. Therefore, children who are diagnosed as mentally retarded should always have a comprehensive speech and language evaluation because of their increased risk for language disabilities, as well as to determine how language skills may have depressed the general level of performance on an intelligence test.

A child with delayed speech is at risk for social-emotional problems. Brutten, Richardson, and Mangel (1973) have reviewed the various emotional disorders that are found more commonly with those who have language disorders. Since communication with parents and peers is crucial for the developing child, a language disorder can be a severe handicap for developing appropriate social skills and a good self-concept (see Chapter 8 for a discussion of emotional development). Children who are diagnosed as emotionally disturbed should always have a comprehensive speech and language evaluation to determine what part language problems may be contributing to the emotional pathology.

EXPRESSIVE DISORDERS

An expressive language disorder involves primarily a problem with the production of spoken language. Since the process of producing spoken language begins with the perception and understanding of verbal input and the central integration of the information, there are few if any pure expressive problems; thus the differentiation of expressive from receptive and central processing problems is difficult both conceptually and behaviorally. However, there are language behaviors and test performance outcomes that suggest problems primarily with the output of spoken language. For example, a child who scores higher on receptive verbal tasks than on expressive verbal tasks should be evaluated further to determine why the discrepancy occurred.

There are some disorders of the peripheral speech motor mechanism and paralysis of the oral mechanisms which result in expressive speech deficits. The designation of expressive disorders made here is to emphasize the language behavior observable by the clinician. These language behaviors are grouped in two general categories

of speech motor deficits: dyspraxia and dysarthria. There is frequently overlap between these disorders and a differential diagnosis is difficult with young children.

SPEECH MOTOR DIFFICULTIES: DYSPRAXIA

Language pathologists make a distinction between children who have difficulty producing speech because of oral motor problems (dysarthria) and children who have intact oral motor skills but have difficulty organizing and producing spoken language (dyspraxia). The term apraxia is more commonly used than the term dyspraxia; it literally means the inability to perform coordinated movements. The term dyspraxia is used here to indicate partial difficulty, since few children have totally incoordinate word production.

The clinical picture of a dyspraxic child is of a child who has difficulty producing speech, although there is no muscle paralysis. Speech in such cases is produced coherently and is usually articulated appropriately, but there is poor organization of output. Dyspraxic children may have a sophisticated gestural system and mouth "searching" behaviors. A good example is the child who has a problem finding words (dysnomia).

Behaviors that suggest a word-finding problem include latency in responses, frequent word substitution, and use of a number of words to express a relatively simple thought (Denckla, 1974). A common example is a child who is asked to name a picture of a rabbit, and who responds by saying, "a soft, fuzzy animal who eats carrots and runs quickly." In other words, the child with a word finding problem is unable to produce the word, a behavior called circumlocution. Another behavior is the use of stereotyped words (such as "like, you know . . ."). The younger child may simply show a delay in response or may avoid tasks requiring production of speech. A word of caution is necessary, however: As new words and skills emerge, and a child struggles to produce unfamiliar verbalizations, dysarthrialike behaviors may occur. These behaviors are analogous to those of an adult speaking a foreign language with long pauses or filler words while thinking of how to use a word or phrase.

Disorders of dysfluency—or stuttering—are often overdiagnosed in younger children because of inconsistencies in children's word production. Generally what the psychologist must do is observe the antecedent and consequences of current stuttering and take a detailed language history to determine the possible need for a referral to a speech and language pathologist. It is normal for young children to show a moderate degree of stuttering when first learning words, and as they make transitions to new complexity of word production. Dysfluency can also result from regression and anxiety under stress. The psychologist's and parents' descriptions of the behavior are essential for a diagnosis of a dysfluency disorder. Guitar and Peters (1980) have reviewed early development of stuttering behavior and provide a good review of current literature.

SPEECH MOTOR DIFFICULTIES: DYSARTHRIA

Children who have a paralytic condition that affects speech production and articulation may have a disorder called dysarthria. The major problem in this condition is with the motor skills needed to produce speech, and the most frequent behavior observed is poor articulation. The psychologist should observe articulation difficulties and note the frequency, as well as types of mistakes the child makes. The dysarthric child will often avoid using words and will rely more on gestures or other nonverbal behaviors to communicate (this is also true of disorders of oral periphery, such as cleft palate). The dysarthric child may also be dyspraxic, so that producing oral speech will be extremely difficult. Cases of "pure" dysarthria are rarely seen.

A child with severe articulation difficulties and limited production of words will often have concomitant behavioral and emotional difficulties. Because interactions with parents, siblings, and peers are affected by limited verbal interactions, the child is at great risk for problems with emotional development. For example, the 4- or 5-year-old child with average nonverbal intelligence and very low verbal skills will often develop behavior problems of acting out or withdrawing, secondary to the communication problems. The evaluation of a child with a speech delay should always include a comprehensive emotional assessment, which must include consideration of the environmental supports and family system. The importance of assessing the ecology of the language handicapped child is obvious with the child who has articulation deficits.

The origin of dysarthria is assumed to be some form of central nervous system or peripheral nerve damage. Children with dysarthria frequently have cerebral palsy and/or other motor handicaps. Severe articulation disorders can also be a function of birth defects that involve the physical structure of the oral periphery, such as cleft palate. While the palate can be repaired, the child may already have a history of misuse of the muscles and structures that were involved. Thus, the recovery from repaired cleft palate may be partial, and the disorder can be expected to have an impact on emotional development. In some cases, articulation disorders may be functional (no physical or organic basis) and may be accompanied by complex behavioral disorders. The psychologist and speech pathologist must work together when evaluating children with both language and emotional disorders.

INADEQUATE ENVIRONMENTAL SUPPORTS

Learning to talk appears to be an inherently reinforcing process for most children. As the child learns an appreciation of the function of language, that language becomes a powerful way to influence the environment. The most infamous example is the 2-year-old child's use of the word "no," which is important emotionally for the child who is developing autonomy from the parents. The child learns that he or she can have an influence on the environment through language; and the way in which the environment responds to the child's use of words and the language behavior models the child sees play a major role in appropriate acquisition of speech and language.

When assessing the child, the psychologist should note the language behavior of the parents. The use of nonstandard English or a bilingual environment will produce lower scores on verbal items measured on most standardized measures of cognitive skills. The research of Carroll (1973) on nonstandard English, and Mercer (1972) on cultural differences in children suggests the need to examine carefully differences in a child's opportunity for learning standard English. The psychologist must remember that comparing the verbal performance of children who have had experience with nonstandard English with children who have experience with standard English is often inappropriate.

In addition, the parent's response to a child's verbal behavior will often provide information about how much the child is encouraged to use language. The overprotective parent may anticipate the child's needs and may not provide support for the child's learning of the function of spoken words. The hostile and punitive parent may discourage or punish a child's verbal requests, and thus may reinforce withdrawal and limited use of language to express needs. A detailed language history and observations of parent-child interactions are always necessary when the adequacy of environmental supports for a young child's language development are being evaluated.

TEST INTERPRETATION

There is no psychological test that allows for reliable and valid discrimination between preschoolers who have low intellectual skills, a language disorder, and inadequate environmental supports. It is a serious error not to factor out the relative degree of problems in each of these areas, since a child's poor performance on an intelligence test may result from combinations of all three categories (or primarily from one). Overlooking a deficit in one of these areas can lead to inappropriate classification and an inadequate or unfair treatment program for a child.

The hallmark of a language impaired child is a large discrepancy between verbal and nonverbal performance on standardized testing. However, many nonverbal test items administered in the standardized manner require some comprehension of verbal commands. Thus, the psychologist should consider the degree of reliance on verbal instructions when interpreting outcomes. Initially all items should be administered while adhering closely to the standard procedures. When failures occur, the use of gestures and structuring of the child's attention should be attempted; if the child is still unable to perform a task, teaching an item similar to the task on the test will provide useful information.

A careful analysis of the procedures needed to obtain a success provides important information, for an item that has been modified cannot be scored using the test norms. When administering standardized test items, particular attention must be paid to the level of difficulty (that is, it may be easier for the child to imitate a task than to discover a solution). Information about the child's response to structure and procedures is valuable for treatment planning and often suggests strengths and weaknesses that are not evident when only standard test items are administered. Experience with a variety of young children and specialized training (which includes supervision) are needed to interpret the observations resulting from adapting the standard test administration.

The psychologist should always obtain a good measurement of the child's nonverbal intellectual skills. The Hiskey-Nebraska test and the Leiter International Performance Scale are often administered to hearing and languaged impaired children to avoid penalizing them for poor language skills. However, these scales are not as predictive of later school performance (Anastasi, 1968) as tests that include verbal skills, partially because many of the skills required for school performance are not included. (Chapter 11 reviews the uses of nonverbal tests and describes their strengths and weaknesses.)

The characteristics of the sample used to develop test norms are a major consideration to the clinician who is planning to use a nonverbal test since children with known language impairment are generally not included in the standardization of intelligence testing. A comparison of a language impaired child with a normal group is useful for determining the degree of deficit in language skills and in general intellectual functioning. Information about these deficits can be used in planning the amount of language intervention needed and the class placement that is most appropriate. The essential consideration is to identify the special language needs of a child to obtain adequate intervention that will facilitate language development and not discriminate against the child's optimal learning.

SUMMARY

This chapter has covered the importance of language development and the impact on thinking, as well as on emotional development; a framework that emphasizes milestones of language development; and methods of verbal and nonverbal communication. Observation of language behavior is facilitated by a model of receptive language, central processing, expressive language, and adequacy of environmental supports. Behaviors that suggest the need for referrals for language and audiologic evaluations were discussed. The impact of language deficits on psychological testing, interpreting results, and planning intervention were also described. When a child's performance on a cognitive assessment is interpreted, the examiner must consider the extent to which the general level of intelligence, a language disorder, or inadequate environmental supports for language development have influenced testing outcome.

REFERENCES

Anastasi A: *Psychological testing,* 3rd ed. New York: Macmillan Publishing Co., Inc. 1968

Berko J: The child's learning of English morphology. Word 14:150–177, 1958

Bloom L: *One Word at a Time: The Use of Single Word Utterances Before Syntax.* The Hague: Mouton, 1973

Bruner J: From communication to language: A psychological perspective. Cognition, 2:1–19, 1975

Brutten M, Richardson S, Mangel, C: *Something's Wrong with My Child.* New York: Harcourt, Brace, Jovanovich, 1973

Carroll J: Language and cognition: Current perspectives from linguistics and psychology. In Laffey J, Shury R (eds): *Language Difficulties: Do They Interfere?* Newark, Delaware: International Reading Association, 1973, pp 174–185

Clarke-Stewart V, Hevey C: Longitudinal relations in repeated observations of mother-child interactions from 1 to 2½ years. Develop Psychol 17-(2): 127–145, 1981

Denckla MB: Naming of pictured objects of dyslexic and non-dyslexic "MBD" children. Paper presented at the Academy of Aphasia, 1974

Friedlander B: Notes on language: Screening and assessment of young children. In Friedlander, B., Steritt G., Kirk G. (eds): *Exceptional Infant, vol 3. Assessment and Intervention.* New York: Brunner/Mazel, 1975

Gratch G: The development of thought and language in infancy. In Osofsky J (ed): *Handbook of Infant Development.* New York: John Wiley & Sons, 1979

Guitar B, Peters T: *Stuttering: An integration of contemporary therapies*: Memphis, TN: Speech Foundation of America, 1980

Johnson D, Myklebust H: *Learning Disabilities: Educational Principles and Practices.* New York: Grune & Stratton, 1967

Lerner JW: *Children with Learning Disabilities: Theories, Diagnosis and Teaching strategies.* Boston: Houghton-Mifflin, 1971

Menyuk P: *Sentences Children Use.* Cambridge, MA: MIT Press, 1969

Menyuk P, Looney P: Relationships between components of the grammar in language disorders. J Speech Hearing Res 15: 395–406, 1972

Mercer JR: *The Origins and Development of the Pluralistic Assessment Project.* Riverside, CA: University of California Press, 1972

Nelson K: Individual differences in language development: Implication for development of language. Devel Psychol 17(2): 170–186, 1981

Neufield M, Shlanger B: The acquisition of morphology by normal and educable mentally retarded children. J Speech Hear Res 4: 693–706, 1968

Northern J, Downs M: *Hearing in Children.* Baltimore: Williams & Wilkins, 1974

Osofsky J, Connors K: Mother-infant interaction: An integrative view of a complex system. In Osofsky J (ed): *Handbook of Infant Development.* New York: John Wiley & Sons, 1979

Piaget J: *The Language and Thought of the Child.* New York: Harcourt, Brace, 1926

Piaget J: *The Origins of Intelligence in Children.* M Cook, trans. New York: International University Press, 1952

Savin H. Perchonock E, Grammatical structure and the immediate recall of English sentences. J Verb Learn Verb Behav 4:348—353, 1965

Trybus RJ, Karchmer MA: School achievement scores of hearing impaired children: National data on achievement status and growth patterns. Am Ann Deaf 122:62-69, 1977

Vygotsky LS: *Thought and Language.* Cambridge, MA: MIT Press, 1962

Wiig E, Semel E: Production language ability in learning disabled adolescents. J Learn Dis 8:578–586, 1975

Wiig E, Semel E: *Language Disabilities in Children and Adolescents.* Columbus: Charles Merrill, 1976

Yarrow L, Rubinstein J, Peterson F: *Infant and Environment: Early Cognitive and Motivational Development.* New York: Halsted, 1975

Chapter 13

ASSESSMENT OF LEARNING DISABILITIES IN PRESCHOOL CHILDREN

By

BRUCE PENNINGTON

Consider the following dilemma: A clinician who works with preschool children was approached by a concerned mother, who wondered if her 4-year-old-son, Billy, has dyslexia. This is a particularly pressing question for the mother because her older son was diagnosed as dyslexic at the age of 9; the diagnosis was made only after several years of reading failure, confusing messages from teachers and other professionals, and increasing frustration for him and his parents. Watching her talented, confident son struggle so hard had reawakened painful memories from her own childhood, when she had been ridiculed for her awkward oral reading and spelling mistakes. She had finally made it through school and college, but not without hardship. She knew, too, that it was whispered in her family that her father, a successful banker, had had similar problems and could never spell. In talking with the clinician, the mother wondered aloud if dyslexia runs in families, and if there was a way of diagnosing and treating it in Billy before it caused him the problems it had caused his older brother and herself.

The clinician knew that some forms of dyslexia run in families, and that one familial form affects about half of the family members. The clinician also knew that Billy was one of the brighter boys in his preschool class and that his birth history and motor and language milestones were all normal. Yet the clinician was concerned, in part because the previous week Billy had refused to participate in an alphabet exercise. The teacher reported that Billy could copy the letters and could also write them when they were read out loud. So why, the teacher wondered, would he balk when asked to name them from alphabet cards held up in class? The clinician wondered whether this incident indicated a problem with letter naming or phonics that would later affect Billy's reading.

What should she say to Billy's mother? Certianly Billy's mother has a legitimate question, but just as certainly the clinician knows that her professional tools will not permit her to give a clear answer to the question until Billy is several years older. She tells Billy's mother that we can't definitely diagnose a learning disability until a child has experienced school failure in a particular subject or subjects. Therefore, it is hard for her to say at this point whether Billy needs intervention or not. Since his extended family shows a positive history for dyslexia, he is at increased risk and should be followed closely in first grade. If he has trouble with early reading skills then, he should receive extra help. Billy's mother accepts this answer but still wonders why there can't be a way to detect dyslexia "before it strikes" and treat it early.

Another clinician, in a related instance, discovered that a bright, verbal 4-year-old girl named Susie could not draw well. In addition, she regularly reversed some letters and occasionally wrote whole words backwards—much to her parents' dismay. Moreover, follow-up testing revealed that Susie had a specific delay in visuomotor abilities (or a "mild delay in sensorimotor integration," as the occupational therapist put it). Her parents wondered if this meant Susie would have a learning disability, especially in reading, since they had heard that letter reversals are symptomatic of reading problems.

The interdisciplinary team working with Susie was divided about the child's prognosis. Some team members maintained that she indeed had a learning disability; others said it was too early to tell. The clinician wondered if Susie should receive early intervention or if she would "grow out of it" if nothing were done. He also wondered if intervention now would prevent later learning disabilities and if drawing skill really is related to reading readiness.

The professional in this case knew that there are not yet clear answers to all these questions. However, because he knew that letter reversals are developmentally normal in Susie's age range and are not symptomatic of later reading problems, some reassurance could be given to her parents.

These two cases illustrate the more general problem of the early detection and treatment of learning disabilities. As is suggested above, clinically reliable means do not yet exist to predict which preschool children will develop specific learning disabilities. Even if such predictions could be made, there are no reliable, proven forms of early intervention to treat preschoolers who will later develop specific learning disabilities. As more screening and testing of preschool children is done, this lack of knowledge leads increasingly to clinical and ethical dilemmas. These are (1) what the clinician should say (if anything) to the parents of children who do not show a definite developmental delay but who have a mild delay in a specific area, and (2) what treatment (if any) should be initiated.

The remainder of this chapter will review what is and is not known about the early detection and treatment of specific learning disabilities. The implications of the current state of knowledge for clinicians who deal with preschool children will also be discussed.

DEFINITION, INCIDENCE, AND ETIOLOGIC FACTORS

For purposes of definition, it is important to distinguish between *learning disorders*, *learning disabilities*, and *specific learning disabilities*. *Learning disorder* is the most inclusive term and is applied to any child who is not making adequate academic progress, regardless of cause. *Learning disabilities* are a subset of learning disorders; the term refers to learning disorders that are caused by subtle brain dysfunction but excludes learning disorders primarily caused by mental retardation, documented brain damage, a peripheral sensory handicap, or sociocultural deprivation. However, there is no logical reason why a child might not have both a learning disability and one of these other conditions. In fact, in clinical practice, it is common to see children with multiple problems, even though the legal guidelines for remediation programs frequently imply that such children do not exist. Finally *specific learning disabilities* are a subset of learning disabilities; this term refers to children whose learning disability is specific to one academic skill (for example, handwriting or reading). There are many learning disabled children who have deficits in more than one academic skill area and thus do not have a specific learning disability.

Learning disorders are undoubtedly the most prevalent handicapping childhood condition, affecting as many as a third of all children (Silver, 1978). Despite such high prevalence, precise estimates of incidence are impossible because of disagreement and confusion around the definition and diagnosis of different kinds of learning disorders, especially learning disabilities. This disagreement and confusion reflect the relative ignorance regarding the causes of learning disabilities. While annoying, this state of affairs is not unique to learning disabilities. It is also true of infantile autism and schizophrenia and has been true in the past of Down Syndrome and other disorders. Once the pathogenesis of a disorder is understood, diagnosis and determination of incidence become much more precise. The diagnosis may now include individuals who were not previously diagnosed—false negatives—as well as exclude individuals who were previously diagnosed—false positives (Eisenberg, 1978; Benton, 1978). As researchers gain knowledge about the causes of learning disabilities, it may well be possible for professionals to make earlier and more accurate diagnoses. This possiblity is discussed in more detail later in this chapter.

Learning disabilities have only quite recently become a widespread concern, even though some forms of learning disabilities (that is, dyslexia) were first described at the end of the last century (Kerr, 1897; Morgan, 1896; Hinslewood, 1896). To a certain extent, learning disabilities are a cultural "luxury." That is, they only emerge as a major concern in cultures where good medical care has eliminated many of the more serious conditions affecting children and where there is an expectation of universal literacy. As both of these conditions have been met in the United States and other Western nations, concern about learning disabilities has grown.

Thus, in this sense, the incidence of learning disabilities is also relative to cultural expectations. For example, if a culture were to care little about reading but expected every child to learn to have perfect pitch, the incidence of "learning disabilities" would change and a different group of children would be labeled learning disabled. This analogy makes it clear that one cause of learning disabilities is not a pathologic process per se; instead, one "cause" is really a mismatch between the natural range of individual differences in various cognitive skills and a culture that strongly prefers one particular cognitive skill. There is no way of knowing at present what proportion of the total number of children with learning disabilities could be explained in this way, or what proportion definitely have a subtle abnormality of some sort.

It is also becoming increasingly clear that there are many kinds of learning disabilities, as well as many causes of learning disabilities. Thus, it is quite erroneous to think that *all* learning disabled children have a common set of characteristics or would benefit from the same therapy. Most authors agree for theoretical reasons that learning disabilities are due to various forms of subtle brain dysfunction, although at present hard neurologic evidence usually cannot be produced for these dysfunctions. The heterogeneity of learning disabilities is due to the complexity of academic skills and the complexity of the brain itself. An academic skill, such as reading, involves the coordination of many different information processing subroutines and thus may be disrupted in a variety of ways.

Thus, the nature of a given learning disability would depend on the particular etiologic factor acting on the brain, the portion of the brain acted upon, the developmental period in which this etiologic factor occurs, the specific genetic endowment of the individual involved, and the environment in which the individual develops. In other words, the nature of a learning disability involves a complex interaction of *what, where, when,* and *in whom.*

One can readily appreciate how many possible combinations there are and how erroneous it would be to assume that learning disabilities are always the same.

There are a few kinds of learning disabilities whose causes are known and which are beginning to be better understood at a neuropsychological level. Most of these learning disabilities have a genetic cause. For instance, recent research has shown that children with extra or missing sex chromosomes (that is, 47,XXX, 47,XXY, and 45,X) are at increased risk for developing learning disabilities relative to their siblings with normal chromosomes, and that the kind of learning disability the at-risk children develop is fairly specific to their particular sex chromosome anomaly (Pennington, Puck, and Robinson, 1980; Pennington and colleagues, in press). Although the actual mechanism involved is not yet known, it seems clear that each of these three variations in X-chromosome number has a somewhat different effect on brain development, which in turn leads to a somewhat different pattern of learning disabilities.

In the studies cited above, it was found

that speech and motor milestone delays in the preschool years were predictive of later learning problems in girls with a 47,XXX chromosome pattern. However, the same predictive validity was not found in the other karyotype groups. Thus, even in children who have a clearly documented genetic alteration, the prediction of school performance from preschool behavior is not perfect.

Another type of genetically based learning disability is familial dyslexia (specific reading disability). Investigators have recently identified a type of familial dyslexia that appears to be caused by a gene or group of genes on chromosome 15 and is inherited in an autosomal dominant fashion (Smith and colleagues, 1981). Dyslexia in general, and this form in particular, is a more subtle and specific learning disability than those found in individuals with sex chromosome anomalies (who frequently have difficulty in more than one academic skill area). Most of the dyslexics in this sample have above-average intelligence quotients and have shown normal performance on a detailed neuropsychologic battery that covers various language, visuospatial, and motor skills. Most of them eventually learn reasonably good silent reading skills but have a persistent spelling disorder (Smith and colleagues, 1981). Not surprisingly, a retrospective review of the development of both affected and unaffected family members yielded nothing that would have allowed the prediction during the preschool period of which family members would become dyslexic. It is possible that future research will yield a biological marker for this particular form of familial dyslexia, in which case early detection and treatment would be possible.

It is well known that perinatal complications cause a slightly increased risk for later learning problems. However, such an increased risk is slight and not reliably predictive, since many children who suffer perinatal complications do not develop learning disabilities. Thus, perinatal complications appear to cause learning disabilities in some children but not enough is known about other intervening variables to predict *which* children are at definite risk for later learning disabilities.

In a similar vein, it is known that maternal alcohol ingestion and environ-

mental exposure to lead (Needleman, 1980) can cause learning problems. However, later learning problems based on the presence of these risk factors cannot yet be reliably predicted.

In summary, learning disabilities are the most prevalent handicapping condition of childhood. The incidence of learning disabilities is to some extent relative to cultural expectations. These disabilities are reflective of different forms of subtle brain difference or dysfunction, are quite varied in both primary cause and clinical manifestation, and are difficult to predict even in children with genetic, prenatal, or perinatal risk factors. Very little is yet known about the etiologic factors and pathogenesis of most learning disabilities, and consequently there is confusion and controversy about the definition and incidence of learning disabilities. Understandably, reliable means of early detection or screening for learning disabilities are still remote.

In the next section the literature on early prediction of later learning problems will be reviewed.

PREDICTIVE STUDIES

There are a number of studies that have examined the usefulness of kindergarten screening batteries for predicting later reading failure. It is important to note at the outset that these studies were not exclusively concerned with identifying children who would develop a specific reading disability. Rather, they were concerned with identifying all children who would develop reading problems, only some of whom could justifiably be classified as having a specific learning disability.

Three of the best and most comprehensive studies are those of Satz and colleagues (Satz and Friel, 1974; Satz, Taylor, Friel, and Fletcher, 1978), Silver and colleagues (Silver and Hagin, 1976; Silver, Hagin, DeVito, Kresser, and Scully, 1976; Silver, 1978), and Jansky and De Hirsch (1972). Although the batteries used in these studies differed slightly in their theoretical orientation and significantly in their specific composition, they all shared an overall neuropsychological orientation and measured various neurologic "soft-signs" and visuomotor and linguistic skills which they felt were diagnostic of the brain's "readiness" for reading. Satz and colleagues (1978) found that the most predictive tests in his battery were Finger Localization, Alphabet Recitation, and Recognition-Discrimination (which taps visual perceptual skills). Silver's (1978) battery emphasized spatial orientation and temporal organization. Jansky and De Hirsch (1972) found that the five best tests (in order) were Letter Naming, Picture Naming, Gates Word Matching, Bender Gestalt, and Binet Sentence Memory.

Several general conclusions emerge from these studies:

1. The various batteries do detect with impressive accuracy (that is, around a 90 percent hit rate with few false positives) both the approximately 10 percent of children who will develop severe reading problems, as well as the approximately 15 percent who will become above-average readers. Thus, the batteries are good at identifying children who will fall at both extremes of the distribution of reading ability.

2. About one-third of elementary school children develop some degree of reading failure, a figure about twice as great as the generally accepted incidence (of around 15 percent) of children with special educational needs.

3. The batteries perform significantly less well in detecting children who will develop mild reading problems, so that the false-negative rate is unacceptably high in this group.

4. The overall correct classification rate for the various batteries is about 75 percent.

It is important to note that even though reading was the outcome measure of interest, the children identified in these studies were not necessarily specifically reading disabled (that is, dyslexic in the usual sense). In Satz's study (Satz and associates, 1978), the severely affected group also showed substantial lags in math, spelling, and handwriting skills. Thus, the children in this group generally had global learning disorders. Although the other studies cited did not report data on these other skills, it is likely that their severely affected groups were also globally learning disordered. Undoubtedly, some

portion of these children were either mentally retarded, brain damaged, or significantly language delayed. Since the predictive accuracy was best for children in the severely affected groups, but was unacceptable for those in the mildly affected groups, it becomes clear that these batteries were not very successful at the early detection of children who developed more subtle and specific reading problems. This is not to criticize the overall usefulness of these and other screening batteries, since they do reliably identify children whose problems are most severe. The point is that the batteries do not reliably identify children with *specific* learning disabilities, which is unfortunate, since educational intervention is probably most effective in this group. (Educational intervention is certainly important and effective in the severely affected group but is likely to be a long-term affair.)

It is also important to note that the studies cited all involved kindergarten children, rather than children who were truly preschoolers. It seems reasonable to argue that the correct classification rate would likely be lower in the younger population.

THE RELATION OF LEARNING DISABILITIES TO BRAIN DEVELOPMENT

As was discussed previously, the early detection of specific learning disabilities is difficult because of our relative ignorance of both etiologic factors and pathogenesis. Even if the etiologic factors and pathogenesis of a given specific learning disability (for example, familial dyslexia) were understood in detail, a behavioral marker that could be used for early detection or screening purposes in the preschool period might still not be available. In fact, some specific learning disabilities may simply not have behavioral precursors that appear before school age. Other developmental phenomena show significant discontinuities across the life span, and some specific learning disabilities may be yet another example (Brim and Kagan, 1980).

Various theories of development recognize the period from 4 to 6 years of age as being a very significant transition period in both the child's social and cognitive skills. White (1965) has catalogued the many competencies that emerge in this period and has argued that they reflect a biologically based qualitative shift in development. More recently, Epstein (1978) has identified several periods of rapid brain growth in humans that correspond fairly well with Piaget's stages of intellectual development, including a brain growth spurt at ages 4 to 6 years corresponding to the acquisition of concrete operations in Piaget's theory.

If the brain changes quantitatively and qualitatively in the 4- to 6-year-old period, some of the emerging capabilities are likely to be qualitatively different from earlier capabilities; this could be true even though the later capabilities may depend on the intactness of those earlier capabilities for their emergence. At a neural level, the new capabilities would reflect the myelination of new brain regions (Yakovlev and Lecours, 1967) and the integration of these new regions with previously developed regions. Although there is no direct evidence for this theory at present, it seems likely that academic skills, such as reading, depend on the newly emerging capabilities. Thus, at the neural level, different sorts of difficulties could interfere with the development of reading. These are:

1. Damage or dysfunction in those brain regions that had developed earlier and that mediate some of the precursor skills necessary for reading.

2. Damage or dysfunction in the newly myelinating areas.

3. Damage or dysfunction of the fiber tracts responsible for the integration of the new and old areas.

It can be readily appreciated that only difficulties of the first sort would be amenable to early detection, whereas the other two would be "silent" at the time that early detection was attempted. This obviously oversimplified model of brain-behavior development would explain the results of the prediction studies discussed above. Specifically, it would explain why the early detection (using behavioral tests) of children who develop mild or specific learning disabilities would be difficult, if not impossible (since their problems would more likely be reflective of points 2 or 3

above). Conversely, this model would also explain the substantially successful detection of children with more severe or pervasive learning disabilities; they would more likely have deficits in the early developing language and visuomotor skills necessary (but not sufficient) for reading.

CLINICAL IMPLICATIONS

What implications do the issues discussed in this chapter have for the clinician working with preschool children? First, the early detection of children who will have more global and serious learning disorders is both possible and desirable. Second, the early detection of children who will have more subtle and specific learning disorders (that is, children with specific learning disabilities) is not possible at present. Thus, it is clinically inappropriate to diagnose a child as having a "specific learning disability" in the preschool period.

Third, a child who is found on screening tests to have a mild delay in a specific skill area may be at risk for developing a learning disability and thus should be followed closely and should receive an in-depth developmental evaluation if school difficulties develop. In other words, some children with normal or above-average developmental quotients will show more than the usual amount of "scatter" across specific subtests or items. This increased variability in specific abilities may persist until school age and may cause the child to have difficulty with a specific academic skill. On the other hand, the "scatter" may be a temporary phenomenon, which can be explained by the fact that the skills in question are undergoing a developmental transition or just have not been "practiced" very much. The overall point is that, like the other risk factors discussed here, abnormal "scatter" is not necessarily predictive of later learning disabilities.

Fourth, children whose histories contain high-risk factors, such as significant perinatal complications, family histories of learning problems, abuse, neglect, or significant sociocultural deprivation should be followed closely and should be referred for an in-depth developmental evaluation should school difficulties develop.

What tests are useful for assessing the preschooler who, for the reasons discussed above, appears to be at risk for developing a learning disability? The Wechsler Preschool and Primary Scale of Intelligence (WPPSI) and the McCarthy Scales of Children's Abilities (see Kaufman and Kaufman, 1977) are two of the most useful instruments. Because these tests cover a fairly broad range of abilities and have specific subtest scores, it is considerably easier to evaluate "scatter" with them than with the Stanford-Binet. (These tests are all discussed in greater detail in Chapter 2.)

If a particular skill area is found to be significantly low relative to other skill areas, a follow-up evaluation by a specialist in that area (for example, a speech and language therapist if the child is selectively low in verbal areas, or an occupational therapist if the child is low in performance or motor areas) may be advisable. Throughout this process, the clinician must maintain a balance of providing appropriate evaluation and treatment while not prematurely labeling the child as having a learning disability.

CONCLUSION

In conclusion, it is clear that much more research is needed into the etiological factors, diagnosis, and treatment of learning disabilities. Such research may eventually permit early detection and intervention for what is by far the most widespread handicapping condition of childhood.

REFERENCES

Benton AL, Pearl D: (eds): *Dyslexia.* New York: Oxford University Press, 1978

Brim OG, Kagan J (eds): *Constancy and Change in Human Development.* Cambridge: Harvard University Press, 1980

Eisenberg L: Definitions of dyslexia: Their consequences for research and policy. In Benton AL, Pearl D (eds): *Dyslexia.* New York: Oxford University Press, 1978, pp 28–43

Epstein HT: Growth spurts during brain development: Implications for educational policy and practice. In Chall JS, Mirsky AF (eds): *Education and the Brain.* Chicago: University of Chicago Press, 1978

Hinslewood J: A case of dyslexia: A peculiar form of word blindness. Lancet 2:1451–1454, 1896

Jansky J, de Hirsch K: *Preventing Reading Failure—Prediction, Diagnosis, Intervention.* New York: Harper & Row, 1972

Kaufman AS, Kaufman NL: *Clinical Evaluation of Young Children with the McCarthy Scales.* New York: Grune & Stratton, 1977

Kerr J: School hygiene in its mental, moral, and physical aspects. J Roy Stat Soc 60:613–680, 1897

Morgan WP: A case of congenital word-blindness. Brit Med J 2:1543–1544, 1896

Needleman HL: Human lead exposure: Difficulties and strategies in the assessment of neuropsychological impact. In Singhal RL, Thomas JA (eds): *Lead toxicity.* Baltimore-Munich: Urban & Schwarzenburg, 1980, pp 1–17

Pennington B, Bender B, Puck M, Salbenblatt J, Robinson A: *Karotype-Specific Patterns of Learning Disabilities in Children with Sex Chromosome Abnormalities.* Manuscript submitted for publication, 1981

Pennington B, Puck M, Robinson A: Language and cognitive development in 47,XXX females followed since birth. Behav Gen 10(1):31–41, 1980

Satz P, Friel J: The predictive validity of an abbreviated screening battery: A preliminary two-year follow-up. J Learn Dis 7:437–444, 1974

Satz PT, Taylor HC, Friel J, Fletcher JM: Some developmental and predictive precursors of reading disabilities: A six-year follow-up. In Benton AL, Pearl D (eds): *Dyslexia.* New York: Oxford University Press, 1978, pp 313–349

Silver AA: Prevention. In Benton AL, Pearl D (eds): *Dyslexia.* New York: Oxford University Press, 1978, pp 349–377

Silver AA, Hagin RA: *Search.* New York: Walker Educational Book Corporation, 1976

Silver AA, Hagin RA, DeVito E, Kresser H, Scully E: A search battery for scanning kindergarten children for potential learning disabilities. J Am Acad Child Psychiat 15:224–239, 1976

Smith SD, Pennington BF, Kimberling WJ, Lubs HA: *An Investigation of Familial Dyslexia Using Both Genetic and Cognitive Analyses.* Presented to the Society for Research in Child Development, Boston, April, 1981

White SH: Evidence for a hierarchical arrangement of learning processes. In Lipsett L, Spiker C (eds): *Advances in Child Development and Behavior.* New York: Academic Press, 1965, pp 187–220

Yakovlev PI, Lecours AR: The myelogenetic cycles of regional maturation of the brain. In Minkowski A (ed): *Regional Development of the Brain in Early Life: A Symposium.* Philadelphia: FA Davis Co, 1967, pp 3–69

Chapter 14

ASSESSMENT CONSIDERATIONS WITH THE EMOTIONALLY DISTURBED CHILD

By

JILL WATERMAN

The most severe and disabling forms of childhood psychopathology are evident in the first few years of life and affect many areas of a child's development. It has become increasingly clear that the earlier the emotional difficulty manifests itself in a child's development, the more developmental lines will be disrupted and the more profound the resulting disturbance will be (Freud, 1965). The major exception to this pattern occurs with emotional problems caused by situational trauma, such as prolonged hospitalization or loss of a parent. While the outcome of such trauma may be severe emotional disturbance, the extent of damage to a child's developing personality from such events depends heavily on factors such as the quality of substitute caretaking and the child's developmental stage at the time of the trauma (Bowlby, 1973; Furman, 1974). Psychoses in childhood are generally categorized into four types: (1) early infantile autism, (2) symbiotic or interactional psychosis, (3) atypical ego development, and (4) schizophreniform psychosis (Group for the Advancement of Psychiatry [GAP], 1974). One diagnostic criterion is age of onset, since severity is inversely proportional to age of onset.

AUTISM

Early infantile autism (Kanner, 1943) is thought to be noticeable during infancy, through disturbances in development of social relationships. The child does not

form strong attachment bonds, tends not to be responsive to stimulation from people, and does not enjoy being held or cuddled. The symptoms are almost always evident before the child is 2½ years old. While early researchers in autism felt that problems in parenting styles caused the disturbance (Kanner, 1943; Bettelheim, 1967), there is increasing evidence that an organic dysfunction underlies the disorder. Current investigations of possible etiologic agents include biochemical and hematological studies (Ritvo and colleagues, 1978; Rodnight, 1978); neuropsychological investigations (De Long, 1978; De Myer, 1975) and neurophysiological studies (Ornitz, 1976). Extensive research has shown that autism is not usually associated with parental psychopathology, unlike other forms of childhood psychosis (Cox, Rutter, Newman, and Bartak, 1975; Lennox, Callias, and Rutter, 1977).

While many different symptoms have been reported in autistic children, there seem to be three major characteristics shared by most autistic children (Rutter, 1978). These are as follows:

1. *Greatly impaired social relationships.* An attachment bond with the parents generally does not develop appropriately in the first years of the autistic child's life, and a relative failure of bonding results. Eye contact with people is minimal, is often actively avoided by the child, and does not occur in social situations. The child typically does not seek out people for interaction or comfort and does not seem to place a positive value on what can be

gained from human contact. During the school years, the social relationships of autistic children are characterized by a lack of cooperative play with peers, failure to develop personal friendships, an inability to perceive the feelings of others, and an inability to respond empathetically.

2. *Deficits in language and pre-language skills.* As infants and toddlers, autistic children engage in very little social imitation and lack imaginative play skills. Their language comprehension tends to be poor, and they also rarely use gestures or mime to demonstrate wants and desires. Approximately one-half of all autistic children never develop useful speech that allows social communication. Those who do develop speech tend to be echolalic and repeat in rote fashion words or phrases they have heard (frequently in the form of television commercial jingles). Other common language deviations include reversal of pronouns (such as you, me, and I), a lack of social chatter, and overuse of social lines memorized by rote, such as good morning, good night, and bye-bye.

3. *Insistence on sameness.* Autistic children tend to exhibit rigid, repetitive play patterns, such as spinning objects. They may become intensely attached to such unusual objects as, for example, vacuum cleaners or bleach bottles. Some children develop rather elaborate routines that must be carried out in a very compulsive manner. Even minor changes in the environment may be very upsetting and may precipitate withdrawal, violent tantrums, or self-stimulatory behaviors. Table 14–1 summarizes major characteristics of autistic children.

SYMBIOTIC OR INTERACTIONAL PSYCHOSIS

In contrast to the onset in infancy of autism, symbiotic or interactional psy-

choses usually develop between 2½ and 4½ years of age. These psychoses often develop in response to a perceived threat to the relationship with the mother (Mahler, Pine, and Bergman, 1975; GAP, 1974). The psychosis appears to be the result of the child's and mother's inability to allow the child to individuate and become a separate person; the result is that the child remains fused psychologically with the parent long past the appropriate developmental stage. While autistic children do not form strong attachments, children with a symbiotic psychosis have very strong, clingy attachments to the mother. Indeed, the child with a symbiotic psychosis cannot tolerate separation. Often a regression occurs and previously acquired abilities are lost; language is especially vulnerable to regression. Some symptoms, such as self-stimulatory behaviors and language problems, may be similar to those in autism. Children with symbiotic psychosis may or may not have a noticeable thought disorder, including hallucinations, delusions, and unrealistic fears. While autism involves a *failure* of development of certain types of thinking, symbiotic psychoses and other forms of childhood schizophrenia involve a *confusion* in certain types of thinking (Wolman, 1966). Table 14-2 summarizes characteristics generally found in symbiotic or interactional psychosis.

ATYPICAL EGO DEVELOPMENT

Atypical ego development is a term used for children with early-onset psychoses who do not clearly fit pictures of autism or symbiotic psychoses (GAP, 1974). Generally, these children exhibit some autistic behavior, emotional aloofness, or symbiotic clinging; however, un-

Table 14–1   Symptoms of Autism

Onset prior to age 2½
Greatly impaired social relationships
Deficits in language and pre-language skills
Insistence on sameness
Lack of association with parental psychopathology

Table 14–2   Symptoms of Symbiotic Psychosis

Onset between ages 2½ and 4½
Strong, clingy overattachment to mother
Inability to separate and individuate
Frequently, regression of previously acquired abilities
Noticeable thought disorder may or may not be present
Association with parental psychopathology

like autistic children, they usually demonstrate some beginning capacity for relating to others and playing appropriately with toys. They generally also have some strengths in adaptive behavior.

SCHIZOPHRENIFORM PSYCHOSIS

Unlike the above three types of psychoses with early onset, schizophreniform psychosis has an age of onset from 6 to 12 years (Jordan and Prugh, 1971). Many of the symptoms are similar to those of adult schizophrenia, but not all children with schizophreniform psychoses will later develop adult schizophrenia. Symptoms may include regression, somatic delusions, bizarre behavior, suicidal ideation, loose thinking, and so on. This psychosis appears qualitatively different from the early-onset psychoses that are the main focus of this chapter.

THE CLINICAL PICTURE

The clinical picture of the emotionally disturbed preschool child is complex and often confusing. An individual child may present symptoms from all the criteria described above, or may have just one or two symptoms of a simple disorder. For example, a 6-year-old child with a severe language disability may show symptoms of poor communication, poor eye contact, and concern about sameness. The child would therefore fit all three categories for autism. However, at least two aspects of the child's behavior should be considered. One observation is that the child's poor communication and eye contact may result from the language disability, although gestures and other cues may be used to make needs known. Also, the concern about sameness may be the child's way of coping with the stress of a strange situation in which expectations for language may occur. In other words, these symptoms may be a function of the language disorder rather than emotional disturbance. The second factor to consider is whether the child shows interest in relating and has developed some relating skills without using very much spoken language. The child will still have problems

relating socially with peers because of the language handicap, and emotional development will be affected by the handicap—but the child will not be autistic or severely emotionally disturbed. Third, the diagnosis of emotional disturbance must be made by a clinician who has special training and experience with disturbed young children.

The clinical picture of an emotionally disturbed infant is also complicated. The behaviors of a severely retarded infant, a severely visually and auditorily impaired infant, and an autistic infant are very similar during the first year of life. All three disorders will substantially alter or delay the attachment to a primary caretaker. The child with any of these problems often must be followed over a period of several months (or even a year) to determine what developmental deficits are contributing to the disturbed behaviors. The diagnosis of emotional disturbance during infancy must be made with great caution, and obviously only by an experienced clinician. Because of the high incidence of physical disorders that occur with emotionally disturbed infants, and so that sensory or motor handicaps can be sought, a psychologist should always seek assistance from a physician when an infant appears to be disturbed.

RELATIONSHIPS BETWEEN COGNITIVE AND EMOTIONAL DEVELOPMENT

Because the onset of these psychoses occurs relatively early in life, they disrupt many developmental functions. Cognitive skills may fail to develop in autistic children, while children with interactional psychoses may regress and lose previously acquired functions. In both cases, the disruptions in cognitive functioning are real and must be considered seriously in terms of planning for remediation. The treatment must be designed to respond to the appropriate cognitive level of the child.

Accurate evaluation of cognitive functioning is very important in autistic and psychotic children; this is because intellectual level is of great prognostic significance, and in addition is needed for planning treatment. A child's developmental status at the age of 5 seems to be a critical prognostic factor. The prognosis is very poor if, at this age, the child has no communicative speech, no appropriate play strategies with toys, and severe developmental delays. In fact, several investigators (for example, De Myer, 1979) have asserted that IQ is the most accurate predictor of later functioning level. Rutter (1970) found that very few severely retarded autistic children gained a useful level of spoken language, while the majority of those with a nonverbal IQ in the normal range did. De Myer (1979) reported that in children with preschool IQs less than 40, outcome was universally poor, regardless of type of treatment or intensity of special education. In large samples of autistic children, tests during the school years revealed that only about 11 percent had a general IQ in the normal range, 11 percent fell in the borderline normal range, and the remainder suffered some degree of mental retardation (De Myer and colleagues, 1974; Rutter and Lockyer, 1967). Less retardation is evident in children with other types of childhood psychoses. Rutter (1978) feels that the type of cognitive deficit is specific in autism as compared with mental retardation and involves language and central coding processes.

COGNITIVE ASSESSMENT OF SEVERELY EMOTIONALLY DISTURBED CHILDREN

Because of the prognostic significance of intellectual level—especially in the preschool years—gaining an accurate assessment of a psychotic child's cognitive functioning is essential. Of course, it is also extremely difficult to achieve, given the specific problem behaviors involved. Several factors must be taken into account when trying to evaluate the cognitive development of severely emotionally disturbed young children.

First, the child has seriously impaired interpersonal relationships that will be evident with the examiner in the testing room. It is likely to be difficult to gain and maintain the child's attention, eye contact will be avoided, and the social demand characteristics that work to enhance cooperation in less disturbed children are not effective. Social praise and encouragement are likely to be ineffective in motivating performance in psychotic children.

Second, such children may be more attuned to their inner demands than to outside demands imposed by the testing situation. For example, one 5-year-old girl with symbiotic psychosis appeared to hallucinate a hugh black hole in the ceiling of the examination room; she became very frightened, fearing she would be swept up into the hole. As a result, she could not concentrate on the tasks at hand. Other children may almost totally withdraw into themselves and shut the examiner out, as if he or she were not present.

Third, unusual behavior is the rule rather than the exception. Such behaviors include a wide range of self-stimulatory behaviors; eating odd things; engaging in bizarre and/or repetitive rituals; demonstrating sudden outbursts of rage or tears; or having either lack of speech or unusual verbalizations. The examination situation tends to elicit anxiety, and the mechanisms that psychotic and autistic children utilize for dealing with anxiety tend to be primitive and sometimes overwhelming. The examiner may find that his or her own emotions—including rage, frustration, disgust, disappointment, and despair—are strongly aroused by the child's behavior. Because of this, the clinician must not only cope with odd behaviors from the child, but must also deal with his or her own strong feelings.

Fourth, the examiner must be flexible and creative in planning and carrying out the assessment. Alternative methods and plans for evaluation must be considered and must be available for immediate use if formal assessment techniques prove to be inappropriate. Because of the great prognostic significance of intellectual potential in young autistic and psychotic children, it is vital that the examiner take all possible steps to facilitate an accurate assessment.

Two basic strategies are commonly used in performing cognitive assessments with seriously emotionally disturbed children. The first involves some modifications of standard formal testing procedures, and the second involves alternative methods of assessment if modification of procedures for standardized tests is not successful in eliciting accurate assessment of the child's functioning. However, a prerequisite for success with either of these methods is the building of sufficient rapport during the initial approach to the child.

This basic consideration becomes even more important when dealing with a severely emotionally disturbed child. The examiner must meet and begin relating to the child in a cautious and sensitive manner that will facilitate cooperation. An autistic child will often have a tantrum or completely withdraw if subjected to quick changes in environment. Therefore, it is imperative that the child be approached slowly and that his or her nonverbal cues be closely observed. Often contact can be made through a toy or object that the child might enjoy, since direct social approaches are apt to be scorned.

In working with a symbiotic psychotic child, special care must be given to the issue of separating the child from the parent. This must be done gradually, after the child has become comfortable with the examiner; unfortunately, it is sometimes impossible to accomplish this separation. Frequently, the cognitive assessment must be carried out with the parent present to ensure that the child does not become overwhelmed by separation anxiety that would significantly diminish test performance. When a symbiotically psychotic child cannot be separated from the parent for a cognitive assessment, a separation should be attempted later to assess the relationship between the child and parent. Occasionally, several exposures to the examiner and to the assessment situation are needed before formal cognitive assessment can be successfully attempted.

MODIFYING STANDARD ASSESSMENT PROCEDURES

One issue when considering formal cognitive assessment with severely emotionally disturbed children involves the choice of test instruments. Many psychotic children have no language skills or may only use language that is echolalic or bizarre. Therefore, standard assessment instruments that require a great deal of understanding of language or that require a verbal response are inappropriate measures of intellectual potential for such children. Utilization of instruments that measure cognitive abilities in most nonverbal ways is generally more productive.

Examples of such tests include the Leiter International Performance Scale and the Merrill-Palmer Scale. Both of these instruments measure conceptual abilities through nonverbal means—not simply through perceptual motor skills. Frequently, infant tests such as the Bayley Scales of Infant Development may be utilized despite the fact that the child is over the age norms; these tests, often in combination with adaptive behavior measures, can provide an assessment of the wide scatter often found in the performance of severely emotionally disturbed preschool children. Additionally, such tests rarely require more than a minimum of verbal understanding or responsiveness and include stimulus objects that are generally of great interest to infants and young children. While standardization and rules of administration elaborated in test manuals should be followed whenever possible, creative use of test instruments to gain increased responsiveness from a severely disturbed child frequently necessitates deviating from described procedures.

Other modifications of standard testing procedures involve the interpersonal process between the child and the examiner. Since gaining and keeping the attention of severely disturbed young children is a major task, the examination room should be bare of extraneous objects and other sources of stimulation that might be distracting, and the child must be firmly in his or her chair. The clinician may repeatedly have to say, "Look at me," or may have to turn the child's head physically in order to gain eye contact. The child may be able to tolerate the intensity of the relationship for only brief periods of time, necessitating frequent breaks or the use of several short testing sessions.

A third area of modification of standard assessment procedures involves the use of reinforcement. Often, tangible reinforcers such as cereal or candy may be used to gain the child's attention or stimulate task performance. For autistic children who are generally not interested in relating to people, the praise and encouragement that motivate other children have little meaning. As a consequence, tangible reinforcers represent an alternative means of motivating such children. In general, the child is rewarded for attending and responding appropriately to the task, whether the specific responses to stimuli are right or wrong.

NONSTANDARD ASSESSMENT PROCEDURES

Play observations are one type of nonstandard assessment procedure. If the child remains unmanageable or unresponsive in the assessment situation after modifications of standardized procedures have been attempted, informal observations of development can be made. The examiner can allow the child to manipulate the test materials in his or her own fashion and observe the level of conceptual ability shown in the child's use of the materials. Alternatively, the child and the clinician may play together with developmentally oriented materials that are not related to tests; or the examiner may watch the child in solitary play. In such an observation, the clinician should watch for level of object exploration; development of concepts such as size, form, color, and number; level of object permanence; adaptability and creativity; and development of language concepts (if present). The child's skills and styles of approaching and solving problems can be compared with standard developmental norms, such as those elaborated in the Gesell Developmental Schedules (Knoblock and Pasamanick, 1974) or Piagetian scales (see Chapters 4 and 5). Thus, a rough estimate of developmental level and cognitive status can be attained even if formal testing is not possible.

If the child refuses to play with any of the materials offered, there are two options that allow the examiner to gather more data about the child's functioning. One involves observing the child and possibly attempting formal assessment in the child's home environment. Because severely disturbed children are not comfortable with change and may be much more relaxed in the home setting, more accurate observations can probably be made in the home. For more formal types of assessment, the advantage of the increased com-

fort the child experiences at home may be offset by the difficulty in finding a nondistracting space for testing where the examiner feels able to control the child's behavior if necessary. A second means for gathering information about development when a child continues to be unmanageable or unresponsive involves gathering data from the parents. The examiner may wish to use his or her own questions about the child's development, or may prefer to utilize instruments such as the Vineland Social Maturity Scale or the Alpern-Boll Developmental Profile (see Appendix A). While such information is subject to all the biases inherent in parental report measures, some ideas about the child's development can be gleaned in this manner. Table 14–3 summarizes both formal and informal procedures that can be used to assess children who are seriously emotionally disturbed.

SUMMARY

Most forms of psychopathology that develop early in a child's life are quite severe. They tend to affect dramatically the child's ability to relate to others and

---

Table 14–3 Procedures for Assessing Cognitive Development in Severely Emotionally Disturbed Children

I. Make a careful approach to child and build rapport

II. Attempt formal assessment
  A. Select appropriate instrument
    1. Nonverbal conceptual tests
    2. Infant tests
  B. Ensure maximal attentiveness
    1. Provide distraction-free environment
    2. Encourage eye contact through verbal and physical means
    3. Allow for short sessions and frequent breaks
  C. Use tangible reinforcers
    IF UNSUCCESSFUL:

III. Attempt play observations
  A. Allow spontaneous exploration of test materials
  B. Play together with child with developmentally oriented materials
  C. Observe child's spontaneous play
    IF UNSUCCESSFUL:

IV. Gather information from parents *or*

V. Observe the child in home environment

generally involve disturbances in attachment, unusual affect, and problems with communication skills. These factors tend to make formal cognitive assessment very difficult; however, since intellectual capacity is an important prognostic indicator, it is vital to make as accurate an assessment as possible. Methods of improving the adequacy of cognitive assessment of severely emotionally disturbed children include (1) modifying standard assessment procedures, including using different instruments, structuring the situation for maximal responsiveness of the child, and using tangible reinforcers; (2) using play observations to estimate developmental levels; and (3) obtaining parental reports of current functioning or observing behavior in the home. Severely emotionally disturbed children are often upsetting to assess because their raw primitive emotions and atypical patterns of relating to people arouse strong emotions in the examiner.

REFERENCES

Bettelheim B: *The Empty Fortress—Infantile Autism and the Birth of the Self.* New York: The Free Press, 1967

Bowlby J: *Separation: Anxiety and Anger.* New York: Basic Books, 1973

Cox A, Rutter M, Newman S, Bartak L: A comparative study of infantile autism and specific developmental receptive language disorder: II. Parental characteristics. *Brit J Psychiat 126: 146–159, 1975*

De Long GR: *A neuropsychologic interpretation of infantile autism.* In Rutter M, Schopler E (eds): *Autism: A Reappraisal of Concepts and Treatment.* New York: Plenum Press, 1978

De Myer M: The nature of the neuropsychological disability in autistic children. J Autism Child Schizo 5: 109–128, 1975

De Myer M: *Parents and Children in Autism.* Washington DC: VH Winston & Sons, 1979

De Myer M, Barton S, Alpern G, Kimberlin C, Allen J, Yang E, Steele R: The measured intelligence of autistic children. J Autism Child Schizo 4: 42–60, 1974

Freud A: *Normality and Pathology in Childhood: Assessments of Development.* New York: International Universities Press, 1965

Furman E: *A Child's Parent Dies.* New Haven: Yale University Press, 1974

Group for the Advancement of Psychiatry (GAP): *Psychopathological Disorders in Childhood.* New York: Jason Aronson, 1974

Jordan K, Prugh D: Schizophreniform psychosis of childhood. Am J Psychiat 128: 323–331, 1971

Kanner L: Autistic disturbances of affective contact. Nervous Child 2: 217–250, 1943

Knoblock H, Pasamanick B: *Gesell and Amatruda's Developmental Diagnosis,* 3rd ed. Hagerstown, MD: Harper & Row, 1974

Lennox C, Callias M, Rutter M: Cognitive characteristics of parents of autistic children. J Autism Child Schizo 7: 243–261, 1977

Mahler M, Pine F, Bergman A: *The Psychological Birth of the Human Infant.* New York: Basic Books, 1975

Ornitz E: The modulation of sensory input and motor output in autistic children. In Schopler E, Reichler R (eds): *Psychopathology and Child Development.* New York: Plenum Press, 1976

Ritvo E, Rabin K, Yuwiler A, Freeman B, Geller E: Biochemical and hematologic studies: A critical review. In Rutter M, Schopler E (eds): *Autism: A Reappraisal of Concepts and Treatment.* New York: Plenum Press, 1978

Rodnight R: Biochemical strategies and concepts. In Rutter M, Schopler E (eds): *Autism: A Reappraisal of Concepts and Treatment.* New York: Plenum Press, 1978

Rutter M: Autistic children: Infancy to adulthood. Sem Psychiat 2: 435–450, 1970

Rutter M: Diagnosis and definition. In Rutter M, Schopler E (eds): *Autism: A Reappraisal of Concepts and Treatment.* New York: Plenum Press, 1978

Rutter M, Lockyer L: A five to fifteen year follow-up study of infantile psychosis: II. Social and behavioral outcome. Brit J Psychiat 113: 1183–1199, 1967

Wolman BB: Classification of mental disorders. *Acta Psychotheraputica.* 14:50-56, 1966

THE HANDCAPPED CHILD'S MILIEU

part three

Chapters 15—18

Chapter 15

EMOTIONAL DEVELOPMENT OF THE YOUNG HANDICAPPED CHILD

By

GORDON ULREY

Earlier version of this chapter appeared in: Anastasiow, N. J. (ed.) *New Directions for Exceptional Children: Socioemotional Development,* San Francisco: Jossey-Bass, 1981, No. 5, pp. 33-52.

Traditional psychological assessments of school-age children delineate the child's deficits and may or may not describe specific competencies or capacities. For young handicapped children, this deficit model is often inadequate for diagnosing behavior disorders and for planning relevant intervention or educational programs. In the past decade research in early development has outlined some important changes in emphasis and the need for new applications of findings to existing models of assessment and intervention.

Four relevant issues have emerged in recent research with very young children (Yarrow, 1979):

1. The young child has a multitude of competencies that influence the behavior of the primary caregivers.

2. Early development is a function of a complex reciprocal interaction between the child and caregivers. The role of the child in eliciting responses from the caregiver and the attitudes and expectations of parents interact and change as the child matures.

3. The interdependence of cognitive and emotional development is important

for understanding behavior and personality growth.

4. Understanding behavior in the context of the ecology of the child is necessary to determine the impact of existing handicaps. The application of current child development research and analysis of the ecology of the child help professionals appreciate two major points. One is how the young handicapped child may experience the world differently from nonhandicapped children; the second is how the handicapped child may experience additional stress, which can increase vulnerability for emotional deviance.

IMPACT OF HANDICAPS ON INTERACTIONS

Consideration of these two issues is an important step toward more relevant and valid assessments, and toward more effective planning for interventions. The clinician and educator must attempt to understand the ecology of the handicapped child, since a valid assessment or appropriate treatment plan simply cannot be obtained without considering how the child's handicap influences his or her interactions with the environment and caregivers.

Insights from the Blind, Fraiberg's 1971 account of ten otherwise normal blind children, is a model of what can be learned by considering how differently a handicapped child may experience the world,

150

and the impact this may have on the primary caregiver. The blind child is less able to produce important behaviors, such as eye contact, often has a muted or delayed smile response, and exhibits delayed discrimination and recognition of the caregiver—thus greatly increasing the risk of altering or delaying the formation of an attachment with the primary caregiver. A poor early attachment may compromise all later emotional development and the capacity to relate to others (Bowlby, 1969). Fraiberg's findings have resulted from her careful study of how interactions with the environment are altered or disrupted because of a child's handicap, demonstrating that there is much that can be learned from the study of the effect of abnormalities on the emotional development of children.

Several longitudinal studies have attempted to determine which factor or factors in early development predict later emotional and behavior disorders. Reviews of the major longitudinal studies have concluded that there simply are no known consistent single indicators of later handicaps present in the first two years of life (Sameroff, 1976; Beckwith, 1979). The limited prediction of single factors is seen most dramatically in the fact that some children with multiple risk factors develop later normal emotional functioning. Sameroff (1976) has suggested that the problem is that most longitudinal studies have assumed that single variables or events in a child's life have a linear causality to later disabilities. One longitudinal study by Werner (1971) of children in Kaui reported and compared both child factors (biologic and psychological data) and environmental factors (socioeconomic levels, family stability, and so on). The consideration of both types of risk factors as well as interactions between the child and caregivers increased prediction of later behavior and learning problems.

Impressed with the Kaui study, Sameroff (1976) argues for the importance of considering the interactions or "transactions" that occur between the child and environment. Study of human interactions requires a more complex model of development, which not only sees the child responding to the environment but also stresses the reciprocal effect of the child on the environment. A linear model focused on single variables is seen as too simplistic to explain the complexity of emotional development. Sameroff argues that "only when development is appreciated as a complex interplay between the child's changing competencies and temperament and the changing attitude and behavior of the important socializing agents in the environment can the prediction problem be squarely faced" (p. 147). Not only is this transactive model needed for accurate prediction, but it is also needed for understanding the dynamics of emotional development of the handicapped child. Thus the professional must examine how a given handicap may affect the risks for emotional and behavior disorders.

Children with a wide range of handicaps are found to have a higher incidence of emotional and behavior problems than their nonaffected peers. Recent findings indicate an increased incidence of behavioral disorders among children with such handicaps as minimal brain dysfunction (Graham, Chir, and Rutter, 1968), mild mental retardation (Chess and Hassibi, 1970), a hearing impairment (Schlesinger, 1972), or a visual impairment (Fraiberg, 1969). Thomas and Chess (1977) conclude from several longitudinal studies of handicapped children that the presence of a disability increases the stress of accomplishing normal tasks of emotional development.

What insights can the professional gain by examining the ecology of the early emotional development of the handicapped child? The vulnerability of and risk factors for developmentally handicapped children will be discussed. The theoretical framework of attachment-separation-individuation will be described as the developmental process for the formation of human relationships so that the clinician can better understand the impact of a disorder on emotional development. Since establishment of a primary relationship is seen as the foundation for future human relations throughout life, the impact of specific disorders on early emotional development will be described and implications for prevention, assessment, and educational planning will be discussed.

CONCEPTS OF VULNERABILITY AND COPING

The handicapped young child is generally more vulnerable to developing behavior problems and to experiencing stress when attempting to cope with the problem of daily living. Studies of "wellness" (the successful process of coping and adapting) offer a positive orientation to helping children at increased risk for problems. For example, Murphy and Moriarty (1976) have reported the results of a longitudinal study of middle-class children in Kansas and have reviewed general characteristics of the children and families who are successfully coping and adapting to stress. Anthony (1974) has introduced the concept of an "Invulnerability Syndrome," which is associated with the coexistence of high-risk factors and low vulnerability. The study of children who survive substantial risk, such as a psychotic parent, provides insights for what makes children more or less vulnerable (Anthony, 1974; Garmezy, 1972; Pines, 1979). The resiliency of children who survive multiple risk factors has been described by Sameroff and Chandler (1975) as a "self-righting tendency." In this view, the child is seen as able to elicit support and resources in the face of stress and to stay on course toward healthy emotional development. Supporting this view is Goldberg's (1977) finding that a critical factor appears to be the infant's competence in eliciting attention and care from the environment.

Werner and Smith (in press) have reviewed current studies of vulnerability and invulnerability and have reported data on a longitudinal study of a subgroup of 72 children in Kaui (selected from 693). Their study compared children categorized as at high risk for behavior disorders who did not show problems at 18 years of age (invulnerable) with a matched group of high-risk children who did develop problems (vulnerable). They found the following

characteristics of young children who were described as invulnerable:

1. More were firstborn males.
2. Few of the children had congenital deficits or central nervous system damage.
3. They were socially responsive and energetic (temperament).
4. They were able to elicit attention from caregivers.
5. They had a "good" genetic background (that is, their family histories showed few mental health problems).
6. They had autonomous personality patterns.

Werner and Smith also noted the characteristics of families in which high-risk children were found to be invulnerable. They were:

1. At least one caregiver in the environment was stable.
2. Other caregivers (such as a father, older sibling, or grandparents) were available.
3. There were few chronic illnesses and low total stress factors.
4. A primary caretaker was available.

The studies reviewed by Werner and Smith indicated in general that the invulnerable child was seen as developing a strong early attachment and autonomy during the preschool years, as mastering competencies in childhood, and as having a sense of some control over life events during adolescence. The home environment was seen as having at least one stable caregiver (a parent, sibling, or grandparent) who was supportive but not overprotective and who fostered the child's growing autonomy. These appear to be necessary factors that contribute to healthy emotional development when the risks for vulnerability are high. More research is needed to learn about how behavior characteristics of high-risk children interact with specific risk factors. For example, sex differences, birth rank, cultural difference, and socioeconomic status are all factors related to vulnerability, but they are interrelated in ways that are not yet fully understood. The study of vulnerability and invulnerability provides useful information for the clinician about factors that may help individual children survive increased stress and other risk factors, and that help professionals plan anticipatory guidance. Vulnerability and coping relate directly to early emotional development. One thing that is clear from the research is that basic autonomy and competence are formed in the infancy period through the child-caregiver attachment system. We will next examine how attachment is accomplished.

THE ATTACHMENT PROCESS

The role of attachment in early emotional development has been emphasized as a critical phenomenon by several investigators (Bowlby, 1969; Ainsworth, 1973; Yarrow and colleagues, 1972). It is assumed that the infant must form an attachment with a primary caretaker to devlop ego functions and master later tasks of emotional development (Spitz, 1965). That is, the child must first attach before psychological birth or the process of separation and individuation can occur (Mahler, 1972). Sroufe and Waters (1976) conceptualize attachment as a "developmental/organizing construct" that must be understood as a constellation of enduring behaviors rather than as a static trait. However, some investigators (Weintraub, Brooks, and Lewis, 1977) disagree and argue that the attachment construct as a qualitatively different relationship between the child and caregiver is of limited value; they describe attachment as a behavioral trait. Considering attachment from a developmental, interactive model (Sroufe, 1979), the emphasis is on seeing attachment as a persistent affective bond between the young child and the caregiver. In this model, attachment is seen as a function of cognitive and affective devlopment and can only be understood as a complex interaction of the maturation of these factors and environmental events.

One important implication of the belief that attachment is an affective bond is that differences in the quality of attachment will occur. Yarrow (1972) reports that differences in the quality of attachment have been linked to the quality of later attachments and relationships. Since formation of the affective bond results from

the complex and subtle process of interactions between the child and caretaker, insights may emerge into why handicapped children may be more vulnerable than normal children for later emotional disorders. While there are few—if any—factors in early development that predict later emotional problems (Beckwith, 1979), there are numerous implications for helping parents cope and for facilitating the emotional adaptation of the child and caregivers (Solnit and Provence, 1979).

Investigators of the attachment process have been impressed with the degree of interdependence of cognitive, affective, and motivational aspects of infant behavior. For example, the formation of a "good attachment" is dependent on the infant eliciting behaviors from the caregiver and receiving reciprocal responses from the environment. Attachment studies reveal that the infant's visual discrimination (recognition of the caregiver), activity level (degree of responsiveness), and smiling behavior are essential for obtaining optimal responses from the caregiver. Conversely, the consistency and quality of response from the caregiver also influence the endurance of these attachment-producing behaviors. The child who has abnormalities that result in decreased potential for eliciting these behaviors from the caregiver may be more vulnerable to later behavior problems, depending on the attitudes, expectations, and stability of the family. For example, the visually handicapped child may not show the expected recognition and smiling behaviors (Fraiberg, 1969), and the motor handicapped child may be more or less active (Prechtel, 1963); parents' understanding of their own needs and their abilities to adapt to the special circumstances are critical if a quality affection bond is to be formed.

Ainsworth (1973) describes the attachment process for normal children as progressing through four phases and requiring from ten to twelve months. During the first phase, the child indicates a discrimination of a primary caregiver, usually by smiling. The second phase consists of a differential response to the caregiver during a time of stress, usually crying followed by the child being comforted by the caregiver. In the third phase, the child initiates contact with the caregiver by crawling or reaching specifically to her or him. During the fourth phase, stranger anxiety emerges; the child shows strong preference for the primary caregiver and demonstrates a fear of strangers and of separation from the caregiver.

As the child forms an affective bond, he or she begins what Mahler (1972) has described as psychological birth, in which the child separates from the caregiver and begins to function with increased autonomy. The separation process overlaps with attachment and takes from three months to about three years. Mahler describes this phase of emotional development as separation and individuation and sees it as the basis for all future emotional health (Mahler and Pine, 1975).

THE SEPARATION AND INDIVIDUATION PROCESS

During the first three or four months of life, the primary caretaker (usually the mother) meets the child's basic needs. The child begins to associate the mother with the pleasure of having needs met, which strengthens the attachment bond. The affective bond must occur if the child is to begin slowly to grow psychologically and physically away from dependence on the caretaker. As the child learns to differentiate the caretaker from others and responds accordingly, he or she begins the slow process of moving away from total dependence. The child's specific smile response to the caretaker (2 to 3 months) and fear reaction to strangers (8 to 10 months) are not only milestones of the attachment process; they are also signs of the discrimination that is needed for separation and individuation from the primary caretaker.

As has been noted, the separation process begins when the child differentiates himself or herself from the primary caretaker. Later, the child's cognitive, emotional, and motoric maturation makes possible increased movement away from the caretaker. Having developed the capacity for walking, the child can then periodically return to the caregiver for what Mahler calls "emotional refueling" (1972). The

successful mastering of separation results in the child's autonomous functioning, although he or she continues to need some closeness to the caregiver.

The individuation process requires that the child internalize both a cognitive and affective sense of the caregiver. The child who successfully individuates has a mental image of the parent and only occasionally needs to actually see the caregiver. Mahler describes the image as "object constancy," which implies that the child is satisfied both that the caregiver exists when not seen, and that emotional support will be provided if necessary.

Mahler (1972) describes four subphases of the separation-individuation process:

1. *Differentiation (5 to 10 months).* The child begins to discriminate differences in people and the environment and explores the world by sight and reaching. Cognitive maturity and increased motor skills for exploration and movement (crawling) allow the child to move from close physical contact with the caregivers.

2. *Practice (10 to 15 months).* The child normally learns to walk; greatly expanded exploration is done with excitement and enthusiasm. The child now returns periodically to the caregiver for emotional refueling and needs reassurance that the caregiver is there and dependable.

3. *Rapprochement (15 to 25 months).* The child now expands exploration and movement away from the caregiver but at the same time becomes more aware of his or her helplessness and dependence. This results in ambivalence, with more extremes of alternate closeness to and rejection of the caregiver (for example, saying "no," and the temper tantrums of the 2-year-old). The child's ambivalence and what appears to be regression is seen as communication; although words are used in this phase, the frustrated use of gestures when the child is not understood is also seen.

4. *Partial Object Constancy (24 to 36 months).* The image of the caregiver is now internalized, and the child can function independently. Because the child is struggling for autonomy, there is some conflict when parents make demands. While the child is working through the conflict of

limits placed by parents and his or her own striving for independence, the child also is aware of his or her helplessness and dependence on the parent.

The separation and individuation phase of early emotional development overlaps with and is seen as an extension of the attachment process. The overall attachment-separation-individuation (A-S-I) process provides a conceptual framework and observable developmental milestones. The factors that influence A-S-I can only be understood as a complex system of interactions between the child's growth and maturation with the environment. The clinician should be aware that abnormalities in any part of the process, such as parental attitudes or behavior of the child, will change the system.

THE IMPACT OF HANDICAPS ON A-S-I

While attachment occurs in almost all cases—with the exception of early infantile autism (Kanner, 1943)—there are important differences in the quality of attachments that occur (Sroufe, 1976). When a poor attachment occurs, the subsequent development of human relationships may be compromised. The presence of a developmental handicap represents a significant stress on the process of A-S-I; it increases the vulnerability of both the child and caregivers.

There has been little research on the impact of specific handicaps on A-S-I behaviors and later emotional development. However, there is an increase in information about the impact of various characteristics of infants, caregivers, and interactions that influence early child-caretaker interactions; these have recently been reviewed by Osofsky and Connors (1979). In a recent study, Stone and Chesney (1979) observed that fifteen infants with a variety of handicaps in an intervention program all showed disturbances in one or more attachment behaviors. They hypothesized that impairments in the infants' expression of affective states makes it more difficult for caregivers to receive and understand the child's signals. The authors stress the need for research to determine the impact of various handicaps on the attachment

process and to facilitate anticipating guidance and intervention.

When the A-S-I process is viewed as a system, the implication is that any significant change or event will produce disequilibrium; some assimilation, accommodation, and adaptation will be required to restore equilibrium. The presence of a handicap is just such a significant event, and it will alter the system in some way. The process is complex, because changes in one area will influence other areas. For example, in the case of a handicapped infant, the mother may feel rejected by her child's passivity (temperament) or actual deficit (decreased muscle tone). She may subsequently be unable to respond with the extra patience and sacrifice needed to form a strong affective bond with the child. Based on what is currently known about factors influencing the A-S-I process and relationships between young children and caregivers, some implications for various handicaps will be discussed below.

THE IMPACT OF MOTOR DEFICITS ON A-S-I

The importance of early physical contact between neonates and mothers has been emphasized by several authors (Klaus and Kennell, 1976; Wolff, 1959). Kennell and colleagues (1974) reported that mothers who were allowed physical contact with their nude baby for 1 hour in the first 2 hours after delivery and an extra 5 hours for each of the next 3 days showed increased later contact. When compared with a matched control group (routine neonatal care involving less physical contact) two years later, early physical contact mothers showed significantly more later physical contact, more vocalization, and more eye contact during a stressful physical examination. The authors concluded that physical contact is important to facilitate the development of a child's attachment with the primary caregiver. Recognition of the importance of early physical contact has resulted in a number of changes in neonatal care (Wolff, 1959), and the Brazelton Neonatal Behavioral Scale (Brazelton, 1973) is now frequently used to help parents develop individualized approaches to facilitate reciprocal interactions (Erickson, 1976).

Clinicians may question how differently a newborn with a motor deficit experiences early interactions with caregivers. Prechtel (1963) reported on a group of infants with "minimal brain dysfunction" who had abnormal muscle tone (hypertonia). These babies were not able to relax when handled by their mothers and were also observed to have difficulty molding to their mothers. In a study of motor disorders of infants and young children, Molnar (1978) reported that a significant number of mentally retarded young children show delays in postural adjustments to caregivers. Children with motor deficits (such as abnormal muscle tone or persistent primitive reflexes) may be at increased risk because the early physical responses of these infants may result in parents feeling rejected or inadequate. If the child is not able to adjust to the physical comforting offered by the parent, there is an increased risk of the parent avoiding the use of physical contact.

There is also evidence that subtle but important communications, which are dependent on motor movements and response, take place between the infant and caregiver. Condon and Sanders (1974) reported that normal infants develop complex synchronized motor movements in response to parental voice and physical contact. They postulate that achieving such a synchronous interaction is important for future child and caretaker interactions and communication. Infants with abnormal motor skills may take longer to respond in a synchronous manner, or may not be able to respond in such a manner at all.

Abnormal muscle tone may also influence a child's activity level and facial movements; these are important because they provide clues to the mother, which determine her emotional responses (Bennett, 1971). Children with cerebral palsy often have delayed expressive language, which will also decrease the child's potential for interacting with or eliciting positive responses from the parent (De Hirsch, 1973). The subtle decreases in a child's emotional expressions caused by a motor deficit require special adaptations by parents if quality attachment is to occur. When parents are unable to help the child compensate, or when parents feel rejected and withdraw, the child becomes more vulnerable to the stresses of emotional development.

Motor deficits or delays may also disrupt the A-S-I process if they limit a child's actual movements away from the caregiver. Behavior such as reaching, crawling, and walking enables the child to separate from the caregiver and thus to develop autonomy. The prolonged dependence of the child may stress the parent as well.

Many parents are able to make the sacrifices and adjustment needed to form a healthy relationship with a child who has a motor handicap. When the child and/or parents are vulnerable, there are several things professionals can do to help. Accurate assessment of the child's motor skills and of the parent-child relationship can be used to plan intervention or anticipatory guidance. For example, physical therapy techniques (Bobath, 1977) can be used to alter the child's muscle tone and encourage mutual cuddling. However, the clinician should be aware that programs that provide intensive motor therapy without involving parents may further delay the development of A-S-I.

THE EFFECT OF VISUAL HANDICAPS ON A-S-I

Since many of the signals of communication and indication of emotion between infants and caregivers are visual, the importance of vision in the A-S-I process is obvious. Within several hours after birth, normally sighted infants prefer a familiar face to a nonfamiliar stimulus (Goren, 1975). The normal child's recognition of the caregiver and discrimination of strangers are also primarily mediated by vision. In contrast, the early development of psychotic children indicates relative lack of eye contact and increased aversion to gazing at the human face. Blind children may not successfully complete these tasks and all future tasks of emotional development unless alternative modalities can be used to process external cues for interactions.

There is an increased risk that the affective bond of attachment will be disrupted or will not occur for blind children (Fraiberg, 1971). In her longitudinal study of ten otherwise normal blind children, Fraiberg emphasized that the blind child's major task during early infancy was to form a quality attachment with the caregiver (1969). There are several reasons why the blind child is less able to elicit positive responses from the caregiver during early infancy. Smiling and recognition of the caregiver do develop in blind children, but they are altered by the lack of visual feedback; the smile is often muted and delayed (Fraiberg, 1968). The recognition of caregivers and discrimination of strangers is also delayed for blind children (Adelson and Fraiberg, 1973), occurring between 10 and 18 months of age, while sighted children show stranger anxiety between 8 and 14 months of age. Other modalities, such as tactile and auditory, can be substituted for visual skills so that the blind children form early relationships. However, development of these modalities requires adaptation by parents and still will be delayed.

The fact that blind children show a 25 percent higher incidence of emotional and behavior disorders than sighted children suggests the increased stress they experience in their emotional development. These stresses can be reduced if parents are helped to form an appropriate relationship with the blind child, and if they are taught the ways their child can learn to use other senses to mediate recognition of caregivers and discrimination of strangers. The parents must be informed that later separation and individuation may also be delayed because of the child's dependence on close proximity to caregivers.

THE EFFECT OF HEARING LOSS ON A-S-I

The A-S-I process is mediated in important ways by vocalization of the child and caregiver (Ainsworth, 1973). There is evidence of early discrimination of sounds that influence interactions. For example, mothers are able to differentiate crying responses indicating pleasure, recognition,

hunger, or fear within the first month of their child's life (Wolff, 1971). Conversely, an infant demonstrates differential responses to the mother's voice and the voice of a stranger as early as 2 weeks of age (Hammond, 1970). Condon and Sanders (1974) have observed synchronized motor movement responses to vocalization. Clearly, the recognition and discriminating of vocalization interact in a complex and important way to influence the early relationship between the child and caregiver.

The child with impaired hearing or intermittent hearing loss secondary to infection (otitis media) may be at increased risk for disruption of the attachment process. Early screening of hearing deficits and careful following of children with an intermittent hearing loss are needed so that counseling can be provided to parents and potential disruptions can be avoided.

Because a hearing impairment will delay verbal skills, the deaf child's limited verbal language may also delay separation and individuation. The development of autonomy normally begins with the word "no" and the child's testing of limits; when the process occurs without spoken words, it is difficult for the child to express needs and for the parent to understand them. Toddlers with delayed verbal skills may become locked into a behavior struggle with parents because the child is only able to get attention to his or her needs by being behaviorally disruptive.

THE IMPACT OF OTHER DEVELOPMENTAL DELAYS

The special problems in the emotional development of mentally retarded children (Zigler and Harter, 1969) and children with physical disabilities (Richardson, 1969) have been described by other authors. While developmental handicaps affect the entire socialization process, there may be specific adverse influences on early emotional development. For example, the authors mentioned above stress the need to focus on the feelings and behaviors of parents of very young handicapped children, for how they feel about having a disabled child and what they believe other people think about their child will influence early parent-child interactions.

In general, delayed milestones of development decrease an infant's potential for eliciting responses from caregivers (Stone and Chesney, 1979). When the appearance of smile response, recognition, and discrimination of caregivers and strangers is delayed, the parents must make an extra effort to maintain the interactions necessary for achieving a strong attachment. Counseling parents of children born prematurely or identified early as developmentally delayed (for example, children with Down Syndrome) can be used to facilitate the interactions between the child and caregiver. Having children remain in families instead of placing them in institutional settings has resulted in a significantly higher functioning of the child both intellectually and emotionally (Koch and de la Cruz, 1975).

One other point should be clear to the clinician: The early identification of infants who have experienced high-risk events (for example, prematurity or anoxia at birth) may have inadvertent effects on parents. Kearsley (1979) has argued for possible iatrogenic causes of mental retardation in which focus on the "sick" child may cause parents to withdraw and to lower their expectations for and investment in a child. When an infant is identified as handicapped, the psychologist must consider the vulnerability of parents and families and must plan interventions that include the feelings and behaviors of caregivers.

ATTITUDES AND EXPECTATIONS OF CAREGIVERS

The impact of a handicap on an infant can only be understood in terms of the expectations and the changing attitudes of the parents. Anthony and Benedek (1970) have described the process by which parents prepare themselves for parenthood and the adjustments that must occur subsequent to the birth. The psychological preparation for the birth of a child involves fantasizing about the idealized child (preferred sex, temperament, size, and so on) and the feared child (defective, weak, pas-

sive, or tyrannical and difficult to control). The parents must work through discrepancies between the imagined child and the reality of the actual child. When a child is perceived as defective or as having a difficult temperament, the working through feelings elicited by the child and feelings of loss of the idealized child make parents more vulnerable. This, in turn, increases the risk that they may form a poor attachment with the child.

The birth of a handicapped child introduces a significant stress to a family system; indeed, some researchers have reported an increase of marital discord and divorce (Bloom, Asher, and White, 1978) when a handicapped child is born. The vulnerability of the mother may escalate because of postpartum depression or marital discord, making it even more difficult for her to respond to the child's extraordinary needs. When the child is limited in capacity to elicit responses from caregivers, the risk increases. The combination of factors may lead to the vicious circle of feelings of rejection and avoidance, which contribute to a poor attachment.

The importance of numerous parental characteristics, attitudes, and expectations to the early relationships between infants and caregivers have been reviewed by Osofsky and Connors (1979), and by Parke (1979). Some differences that relate to socioeconomic status have been noted. For example, Messer and Lewis (1972) reported that middle class mothers observed when their child was 2 years old verbalized with their toddlers seven times more frequently than comparable lower class mothers. Cultural differences have also been found; for example, American mothers use more face-to-face or visual contact and less physical contact compared with Oriental mothers (Goldberg, 1977). When a child is handicapped, the parents may need special intervention to change patterns inadequate to meet their child's needs.

For parents, adjusting to having a handicapped child may be analogous to the grieving process (Solnit and Stark, 1961). The parents may psychologically experience the awareness of a child's deficit or the discrepancy between the idealized child and the actual child as a loss. For example, when the parent expects a warm cuddling child and the child is over-active and aloof, the parent must resolve the loss of the expected responses of the child. The clinician must therefore study the compatibility between parents and infants to plan interventions and help parents adapt.

"GOODNESS OF FIT"

Studies of differences in the temperaments of children have led to insights into how behavioral characteristics of children affect interaction with caregivers. Chess and Thomas (1968) investigated nine different behavior categories that relate to temperament (activity level, rhythmicity, approach-withdrawal, adaptability, intensity of reactions, threshold responsiveness, quality of mood, distractibility, attention span, and persistence). Temperament behaviors are found to cluster in three different groups described as (1) easy, (2) difficult, and (3) slow-to-warm-up. A scale developed by Carey (1977) makes it possible to assess the temperament of infants and young children; such a measurement of temperament has made it possible to examine the impact of different styles of parenting on children with different temperaments. Thomas and Chess (1977) stress the fact that measurements of temperament are meaningful only when considered in the context of the child's environment and (specifically) each parent's own temperament and parenting style.

"Goodness of fit" is defined as the degree of consonance and/or dissonance between the child and parent. A fit is consonant when the properties of the environment and the parent's expectations and demands are in accord with the child's capacities, characteristics, and styles of behaving. Dissonance occurs when environmental opportunity and parental demands are discrepant with the capacities and characteristics of the child. The "goodness of fit" is always relative to attitudes, expectations of parents, and the demands of a given culture (or socioeconomic pressures). In theory, a consonant fit leads to optimal development of the child.

The "goodness of fit" provides a model for intervention with the vulnerable or at-risk family with a handicapped child. The patterns of parent-child interaction can be identified, along with the temperamental style of the child and parental behaviors that contribute to dissonance in the family system. Specific parental attitudes and practices that may interfere with the child's optimal development may be identified and modified. This helps the clinician plan intervention strategies to minimize the dissonance. It is important that the parent not be viewed as a "bad" or "good" parent—but merely as a parent who needs help to find a more adaptive way of responding to the child's constellation of behaviors. At times work is needed to help the parent appreciate and accept deficits in the child (for example, working through the grief of the "lost child").

CONCLUSION

A conceptual framework of early emotional development through the A-S-I process has been described. There has been discussion of a complex model for understanding the reciprocity and changes that result in the interaction between a child and his or her caregivers. The fact that an increased incidence of later emotional and behavior problems occurs in handicapped children suggests that a handicap increases the stress for mastering tasks of emotional development. Several specific (although complex and overlapping) effects of handicaps on the A-S-I process have been discussed. An appreciation of how specific deficits may influence the ecology of an individual child's family environment is necessary for the clinician who would understand the emotional development of young handicapped children. The interactive model provides a framework from which the psychologist can plan relevant and reliable assessment, anticipatory guidance, and intervention programs.

Several important implications for prevention, assessment, and intervention are based on clinical practices and research findings reviewed above. For prevention, risk or vulnerability factors in the child and environment must be determined. Parent counseling and specific techniques can be used to minimize the stress on the family and handicapped child but are most effective during early infancy. A cautionary note is that parents must not be made to feel guilty if they have difficulty attaching to a severely handicapped child, or in effecting significant changes. The clinician should not imply that if parents can only be "good," the child will be alright. Instead, the child's impact on the caregivers must be considered, as must the "goodness of fit" between caregivers and the child.

When assessing young children, the clinician must observe parent-child interactions, as well as characteristics of the child and/or parents that may make forming relationships more difficult. In addition to traditional psychological scales, scales for measuring attachment (Ainsworth, 1973), temperament (Carey, 1977), separation and individuation (Mosey and colleagues, 1980), and self-help skills (Doll, 1965) should be used. The need for psychologists to expand procedures for assessing young handicapped children has been stressed by Simenson, Huntington, and Barse (1980). Expanded scales and observations of interactions provide valuable information about the ecology of the child and the child's level of emotional development.

When the child's level of A-S-I is considered, some traditional techniques for treatment may appear inappropriate. For example, when a child has temper tantrums, the use of ignoring and "time out" procedures may not always be appropriate. If the child is emotionally immature, he or she may need emotional refueling from a caretaker, and physical contact and reassurance may be most appropriate; isolating a child during separation and individuation may actually increase the stress of emotional development. The caretakers must be involved in early intervention, since delayed children may need to learn how to interact better with parents. Placing very young handicapped children in programs without caretakers for a full day may actually prolong emotional development (Mordock, 1979); the young child may benefit more from interactions with caregivers for completion of A-SI.

There is a need for research to determine the effectiveness of helping caretakers interact with a handicapped child and to learn which intervention procedures are most appropriate. As psychologists come to understand better how handicapped children develop emotionally and how they experience the world differently, they will be better prepared to decrease vulnerability and risk factors. Segal and Yahraes (1978) have described helping children to cope as producing "children who will not break." As has been seen, it may be much more difficult to achieve this state with sensory impaired children, but it is possible once parents are aware of the process of development and are helped to compensate for deficits.

REFERENCES

Adelson E, Freiberg S: Gross Motor development in infants blind from birth. Child Devel 45: 114–126, 1973

Ainsworth M: The development of infant-mother attachment. In Caldwell B, Ricciuti H, (eds): *Review of Child Development Research*, vol 3. Chicago: University of Chicago Press, 1973

Anthony EJ: Introduction: The syndrome of the psychologically vulnerable child. In Anthony EJ, Koupernick L (eds): *The Child in His Family and Children at Psychiatric Risk*. New York: John Wiley & Sons, 1974

Anthony EJ, Benedek T (eds): *Parenthood and Psychology and Psychopathology*. Boston: Little, Brown and Company, 1970

Beckwith L: Prediction of emotional and social behavior. In Osofsky J (ed): *Handbook of Infant Development*. New York: John Wiley & Sons, 1979

Bennett S: Infant-caretaker interactions. J Am Acad Child Psychiat 10: 321–335, 1971

Bloom BL, Asher SJ, White SW: Marital disruption as a stressor: A review and analysis. Psycholog Bull 85: 867–894, 1978

Bobath B: *Abnormal Postural Reflex Activity Caused by Brain Lesions*. London: Heineman, 1977

Bowlby J: *Attachment and Loss*. New York: Basic Books, 1969

Brazelton TB: Neonatal behavioral assessment scale. *Clinics in Developmental Medicine*, No. 50. Philadelphia: JB Lippincott, 1973

Carey WB: Clinical application of infant temperament measurement. J Pediat 81: 823–828, 1977

Chess S, Hassibi M: Behavior deviations in mentally retarded children. J Am Acad Child Psychiat 9: 282–297, 1970

Condon WS, Sanders L: Neonatal movement is synchronized with adult speech: Interactional participation in language acquisition. Science 183: 99–101, 1974

De Hirsch K: Early language development and minimal brain dysfunction. In de la Cruz F, Fox B, Roberts H (eds): Minimal brain dysfunction. An NY Acad Sci 205: 158–163, 1973

Doll E: *Vineland Social Maturity Scale.* Circle Pines, MN: American Guidance Service, 1965

Erickson ML: *Assessment and Management of Developmental Changes in Children.* St. Louis: CV Mosby, 1976

Fraiberg S: Parallel and divergent patterns in blind and sighted infants. Psychoanal Study Child 23: 264–199, 1968

Fraiberg S: *Insights from the Blind.* New York: Basic Books, 1971

Fraiberg S: Interaction in infancy: A program for blind infants. J Am Acad Child Psychiat 10(3): 1971

Fraiberg S: The development of human attachment in infants blind from birth. Merrill-Palmer Quart 21: 315–334, 1975

Fraiberg S, Smith M, Adelson E: An education program for blind infants. Spec Educ 3(2): 121–139, 1969

Garmezy N, Nuechterlein K: Vulnerability and invulnerable children: The fact and fiction of competence and disadvantage. Am J Orthopsychiat 77(abstract): 1972

Goldberg S: Social competence in infancy: A model of parent-infant interaction. Merrill-Palmer Quart 23: 163–177, 1977

Goren C: Form perception, innate form preferences and visually mediated head turning in human newborns. Paper presented at the Society for Research in Child Development Conference, Denver, 1975

Graham PU, Chir B, Rutter M: Organic brain dysfunction and child psychiatric disorder. Brit Med J 3: 695–700, 1968

Hammond J: Hearing and response in the newborn. Develop Med Child Neurol 12: 3–5, 1970

Kanner L: Autistic disturbances of affective contact. Nerv Child 2: 217–240, 1943

Kearsley R: Iatrogenic retardation: A syndrome of learned incompetence. In Kearsley R, Sigel I (eds): *Infants at Risk: Assessment of Cognitive Functioning.* Hillsdale, NJ: Erlbaum, 1979

Kearsley R, Sigel I (eds): *Infants at Risk: Assessment and Intervention.* New York: John Wiley & Sons, 1979

Kennell JH, Jerald R, Wolfe A, Chester D, Kreger N, McAlpine W, Steffa N, Klaus M: Maternal behavior one year after early and extended postpartum contact. Develop Med Child Neurol 16: 172–179, 1974

Klaus M, Kennell J: *Maternal-infant bonding: The Impact of Early Separation on Loss on Family Development.* St. Louis: Mosby CV, 1976

Koch R, de la Cruz F (eds): *Down's Syndrome (Mongolism): Research, Prevention and Management.* New York: Brunner/Mazel, 1975

Mahler M: On the first three subphases of the separation-individuation process. Internat J Psychoanal 53: 333–338, 1972

Mahler M, Pine F: *The psychological birth of the human infant.* New York: Basic Books, 1975

Messer SB, Lewis M: Social class and sex differences in the attachment and play behavior of the year-old infant. Merrill-Palmer Quart 18: 295–306, 1972

Molnar GF: Analysis of motor disorder in retarded infants and young children. Am J Ment Defic 83(3): 213–222, 1978

Mordock J: The separation-individuation process and developmental disabilities. Exception Child 20: 176–184, 1979

Mosey A, Foley G, McCrae M, Thomas E: *Attachment-Separation-Individuation Observation Scale.* Pennsylvania Department of Education (unpublished), 1980

Murphy LB, Moriarty M: *Vulnerability, Coping and Growth from Infancy to Adolescence.* New Haven: Yale University Press, 1976

Osofsky J, Connors K: Mother-infant interactions: An integrative view of a complex system. In Osofsky J, (ed): *Handbook of Infant Development.* New York: John Wiley & Sons, 1979

Parke R: Perspectives on father-infant interactions. In Osofsky J (ed): *Handbook of Infant Development.* New York: John Wiley and Sons, 1979

Pines M: Superkids. Psychol Today 53-63, January 1979

Prechtel H: The mother-child interaction in babies with minimal brain damage. In Foss BM (ed): *Determinants of Infant Behavior,* vol 2. New York: John Wiley & Sons, 1963

Richardson SA: The socialization of the blind child. In Goslin A. (ed): *Handbook of Socialization: Theory and Research.* Chicago: Rand McNally, 1969

Sameroff AJ: Early influences on development: Fact or fancy? In Chess S, Thomas A (eds): *Annual Progress in Child Psychiatry and Child Development.* New York: Brunner/Mazel, 1976

Sameroff A, Chandler M: Reproductive risk and the continuum of caretaking casualty. In Horowitz FD, Hetherington M., Siget SG (eds): *Review of Child Development Research.* Chicago: University of Chicago Press, 1975

Schlesinger H: The hearing impaired preschooler. In Enger N and Gain K (eds): *Social and Emotional Development: The Preschooler.* New York: Walker, 1978

Schlesinger H, Meadow K: Development of maturity in deaf children. Exception Child 38: 461–467, 1972

Segal J, Yahraes H: *A child's journey.* New York: McGraw-Hill, 1978

Simenson R, Huntington G, Barse S: Expanding the developmental assessment of young handicapped children. In Gallagher J (ed): *New Directions for Exceptional Children,* No. 3. New York: Josey-Bass, 1980

Solnit A, Provence S: Vulnerability and risk in early childhood. In Osofsky J, (ed): *Handbook of Infant Development.* New York: John Wiley & Sons, 1979

Solnit A, Stark M: Mourning and the birth of a defective child. Psychoanalyt Study Child 16: 523–537, 1961

Spitz RA: *The First Year of Life.* New York: International Press, 1965

Sroufe L: Socioemotional development. In Osofsky J, (ed): *Handbook of Infant Development.* New York: John Wiley & Sons, 1979

Sroufe L, Waters E: The ontogenesis of smiling and laughter: A perspective on the organization of development in infancy. Psycholog Rev 83: 173–189, 1976

Stone NW, Chesney B: Attachment behaviors in handicapped infants. *Ment Retard 16: 8–12, 1979*

Thomas A, Chess S: *Temperament and Development.* New York: Brunner/Mazel, 1977

Weinraub M, Brooks J, Lewis M: The social network: A reconsideration of the concept of attachment. Human Develop 20: 31–47, 1977

Werner E, Bierman J, French F: *The Children of Kaui.* Honolulu: University of Hawaii Press, 1971

Werner E, Smith R: *Vulnerable, but Invincible: A Longitudinal Study of Resilient Children and Youth.* New York: McGraw-Hill, 1981

Wolff PH: Mother-infant relations at birth. In Howels JG (ed): *Modern Perspectives in International Child Psychiatry.* New York: Brunner/Mazel, 1971

Wolff PH: Observations on newborn infants. Psychosomat Med 21: 110–118, 1959

Yarrow L: Historical perspectives and future directions in infant development. In Osofsky J (ed): *Handbook of Infant Development.* New York: John Wiley & Sons 1979

Yarrow L, Rubenstein J, Peterson F, Jankowski J: Dimensions of early stimulation and their differential effects on infant development. Merrill-Palmer Quart 18: 205–218, 1972

Zigler E, Harter S: The socialization of the mentally retarded. In Goslin A (ed): *Handbook of Socialization: Theory and Research.* Chicago: Rand McNally, 1969

Chapter 16

ASSESSMENT OF THE CULTURALLY DIFFERENT AND DISADVANTAGED CHILD

By

JOHN R. BROWN

The adequacy with which psychological services are provided to culturally different and disadvantaged populations continues to be of great concern. Although strides have been made in approaching this problem, one of the basic elements in the process—testing—remains a source of multifaceted controversies that manifest themselves at many levels. Bryen (1976) indicated the breadth of the problem by asserting that the placement of a disproportionate number of black and Spanish-speaking children into lower tracts, special classes, and compensatory education programs may be partially due to linguistic and/or cultural biases in tests; he further argued that the biases result in the destruction and waste of these children's potential. The Association of Black Psychologists (1969), reflecting the sentiments and concern expressed in Bryen's comments, called for a moratorium on the testing of black people. In addition, the California State Supreme Court ruled in recent years that standardized tests, such as the Stanford-Binet, could not be used to make education decisions when those decisions involved black children (Opton, 1979). Both of these actions reflect the seriousness of the problem. The focus of the criticism goes beyond the characteristics of tests. Concern is also often expressed about how and by whom tests are administered and the manner in which they are used. This focuses on the social consequences of testing which Cleary, Humphreys, Kendrick, and Wesman (1975) see as the source of much of the difficulty.

This chapter will examine characteristics of tests to determine sources of potential bias against disadvantaged and culturally different children. It will also discuss some alternatives that have been suggested to avoid some of these difficulties and will provide suggestions about how the test performance of young disadvantaged and culturally different children might be facilitated.

Before proceeding, a clarification of terms used is in order. The terms "disadvantaged" and "culturally different" are often used synonymously in research and theoretical discussions. Because virtually all research has used subjects who were both culturally different and disadvantaged, confounding the two variables, most of the data presented in this chapter refer to young minority children from lower socioeconomic status groups.

THE RELATION BETWEEN TEST DESIGN AND CONSTRUCTION AND TEST DISCRIMINATION

The term "test" encompasses a wide range of instruments, from individual and group tests of intelligence and/or ability to tests of aptitude, interests, and achievement. Because most of the controversy focuses on tests of intelligence or ability, the present discussion will be restricted to these tests; however, it must be recognized that some of the points made will be relevant to other tests as well.

The intelligence tests that will be discussed include individual and group measures of ability (for example, the Stanford-Binet, the Wechsler Scales, the California Test of Mental Maturity, and so on). They are designed to measure the child's repertoire of skills developed through interaction with the environment. In addition, these intelligence tests assume that: (1) the tasks included reflect those experiences to which children have equal access, (2) the tests measure innate ability, and (3) ability—as measured by these tests—does not change over time. Although these assumptions were considered appropriate in the past, they are currently regarded as incorrect.

Cleary and colleagues (1975) reflect the changes in perspective regarding these assumptions. They point out that there is simply not equal opportunity for every child to learn the tests' tasks, because opportunity is mediated by characteristics of the father, mother, siblings, neighborhood, schools, and so forth; obviously these factors are not equal for all children. Furthermore, Cleary notes that intelligence, as measured, is not a capacity. Rather, it is a behavioral trait that reflects past learning as seen in the changes in an individual's IQ score over time. Bennett (1970) reiterates these points by noting that there is much less assurance in defining the natural endowment of a person than in describing the person's present repertoire of skills. As has been indicated, views regarding the validity and appropriateness of these test assumptions continue to change. However, they still remain a source of conflict—as are many other variables. One such variable is the test itself, characteristics of which are discussed below.

Tests traditionally have been standardized on white, English-speaking, middle class children and contain many culturally loaded questions (Sabatino, Kelling, and Hayden, 1973). Recent restandardizations of the Stanford-Binet (Terman and Merrill, 1972) and Wechsler Scales have involved more minority children in the standardization group. However, critics such as Williams (1970) do not consider this sufficient, because the content of these tests has not been modified sufficiently.

Messick and Anderson (1970) cite several specific ways in which tests may discriminate against disadvantaged and culturally different children.

1. The tests use formats and items that are more germane to one group than another. For example, the tests may include restrictive time limits, vocabulary tasks that require the child to read the word, items that require a child to read in a task designed to measure listening comprehension ability, and so on.

2. Children have differing amounts of "test wiseness," which is likely to be a more significant problem with the preschool-aged child than with the school-aged child. For example, white, middle class preschool-aged children tend to be familiar with question-and-answer formats, with puzzles, and with pointing and naming tasks often included on tests. The same degree of familiarity cannot be assumed when evaluating a disadvantaged child.

3. The skills reflected by the test items may not be relevant to the skills demanded by the disadvantaged and culturally different child's environment. This, in part, is what is referred to by Williams (1970), Bryen (1976), and Mercer (1972); they state that the tests, rather than assessing the disadvantaged child's ability, measure the extent to which such children have assimilated aspects of the dominant culture. As a result, there is a lack of understanding about the abilities of children from different cultural backgrounds (Bryen, 1976). This deficit of information led Williams to recommend the development of tests that explore the unique resources and strengths of different cultural groups and that assess the extent of the individual's coping within that group.

These factors—test formats, "test wiseness," and irrelevant cultural loading—while not related to the test content per se, increase the difficulty level of the test for disadvantaged children. By so doing, the face (content) validity and predictive validity of the test may no longer hold for some individuals (Messick and Anderson, 1970). More careful test construction and better preparation of test manuals and test administrators are seen as means of ameliorating some of the difficulties cited. However, Bennett (1970) notes that it is unlikely that some new type of test will soon emerge which will be able to predict socially useful criteria while remaining uninfluenced by the degree to which the individual has acquired the skills valued in the prevailing culture.

Can test items reflecting the prevailing culture's values predict criterion performance for members of different cultural and socioeconomic groups equally well? Critics of current tests think not. They express the view that current tests tap a limited repertoire of skills, many of which are irrelevant to the experiences of minority children and hence are not predictive of their future learning potential. In contrast, measurement specialists, such as Cleary and colleagues (1975) and Thorndike (1971), see cultural bias as a minor issue; they suggest that the most important issue is fair use of tests, which can be determined empirically. In this regard, Clemans (1970) states that if the concern is for ascertaining immediate capability to perform some function in a certain way, one can justify using a particular test which is predictive of that performance. However, if decisions are being made about the disadvantaged child's long-term potential for performance of a certain skill, there would be no justification for using the same test. This is an important distinction. Unfortunately, it does not appear to be practiced in any systematic way; indeed, there is little research concerning the bias of specific items in favor of certain groups, despite long-standing recognition of this source of potential difficulty.

INFLUENCE OF THE EXAMINER ON TESTING

One area that has received a great deal of attention has been the effect of the examiner on the performance of the child. The professionals who most frequently administer tests are usually white, middle class adults who may know little about cultural differences. Consequently, a number of writers have suggested that when tested by white examiners, black or other minority children evidence fears, suspicions, or apprehension which adversely affect their performance (Oakland and Matuszek, 1977). However, much of the research does not support this assumption. The majority of research examining the effect of the examiner's race on the performance of black children reveals no general tendency for them to score higher or lower when tested by a white or black examiner (Sattler, 1973; Shuey, 1966). Little and Ramirez (1976) observed the same findings when white and Chicano examiners evaluated Chicano elementary school children. In contrast, the race of the examiner *did* have an effect on the performance of Chicano junior high students used in the study. This corresponds with the observation by Sattler (1974) that research indicates that black adolescents and adults tend to prefer black counselors and psychologists.

Solkoff (1974), and Bucky and Banta (1972) reported findings that may account for exceptions to the findings previously cited. Each study reported differences in performance related to the race of the examiner; black children were found to perform better with white examiners, and each study indicated that the white examiners provided a more positive social atmosphere during the testing. These findings correspond with Oakland and Matuszek's (1977) conclusion that, when working with young children, the examiner's ability to evidence a warm, responsive, receptive, but firm style appears to be more directly related to motivating the children to do their best than ethnic or racial characteristics of the examiner. This does not preclude the possibility that ethnic or racial variables can influence performance, but it does suggest that to study race alone—without considering other interactional and attitudinal variables—is likely to be futile (Solkoff, 1972). The variables that psychologists should be aware of include the social climate and milieu in terms of racial and ethnic relationships as well as the individual's perceptions regarding these relationships.

INFLUENCE OF TEST LANGUAGE

Language is an additional variable that has received substantial attention in the literature. Language has been investigated as a source of interference in the performance of black and Spanish-speaking children and those from bilingual backgrounds. Quay (1972) points out that non-standard English patterns used by disadvantaged black children are sufficiently different to cause problems in communication between them and black or white middle class teachers, psychologists, and researchers. The potential for this type of problem is similar for the bilingual or Spanish-speaking child. It has been this type of thinking, coupled with the obvious disparity between the language characteristics of these children and the language on tests, which has led to so much attention being devoted to this variable.

Quay (1972) translated the Stanford-Binet into a dialect style similar to that used by the four-year-old children in her study; she sought to determine if the use of dialect would contribute to or detract from the children's performance. Quay's results indicated that there were no significant differences in the performance of the children; that is, the two groups of black children performed at the same level whether the traditional test or the dialect form of the test was administered. The children's use of dialect did not interfere with their ability to comprehend and respond to tasks that were presented in standard English, and the examiners had no difficulty comprehending and translating the children's dialect into standard English. These results suggest that—at least with black disadvantaged children—the language in which the test is presented is not a crucial variable affecting performance. They also suggest that psychologists should not be led to expect less from the child merely because he or she expresses a pattern of speech that is "different." It is possible that focusing negative attention on the child's use of a dialect may affect motivation and depress performance, but there is no research indicating this at the present time.

Although the previous study suggested that the pattern of language used by some black disadvantaged children does not necessarily indicate cognitive deficits, there is a great deal of concern about the amount of language these children produce in testing situations and its subsequent impact on their overall performance. In some cases, verbal behavior is difficult to elicit, and in others it is monosyllabic in nature. The author is not aware of research that has investigated this specifically, but some research does suggest factors to consider.

For example, Labov (1972) illustrated how a child's performance can be manipulated by variables within the testing situation. In the study, a friendly white interviewer asked a young black child to describe an object placed in front of him; but in spite of much coaching, the child only uttered a few monosyllabic remarks. Even when the adult-child interaction was considered favorable—a black male adult familiar with child—the responses were similar. However, when the child's best friend was brought into the interview and the adult knelt to reduce the height imbalance, the responses were dramatically changed in both volume and style. Labov's description of interaction with this child clearly demonstrates how variables not directly related to the demands of the task can influence verbal behavior and hence the performance of the child.

One such variable includes social conventions concerning appropriate adult-child interaction. Hess and Shipman (1965) provide one way of explaining how such conventions develop, and there are probably other explanations as well. Hess and Shipman state that language systems interact with social systems (such as child-rearing orientation) to influence how a child interacts with the environment. Specifically, they point out that when a tendency to use restricted language codes is combined with a status-oriented child-rearing approach, the child is much more likely to be passive and compliant, and negative interactions are likely to be characterized by silent coercion and defiance. Hess and Shipman point out that both restricted and elaborated language codes and both status- and person-oriented child-rearing practices can be observed in disadvantaged families; however, there tends to be greater use of restricted language codes and status-oriented child-rearing practices in disadvantaged families. These findings suggest that some disadvantaged children learn that a child is to be seen and not heard when in the presence of adults, and some children may have difficulty going beyond this convention even after being given explicit directions to do so. However, the psychologist should not expect this to be characteristic of the adult-child interaction of *all* black disadvantaged children.

Research involving Spanish-speaking and/or bilingual children has investigated the effect of administering tests in English and in the child's first language. Results have been mixed. For example, in a study of bilingual children, Swanson (1971) reported that administration of the verbal section of the WISC-R in English enhanced performance, while administration of the performance section in Spanish enhanced scores. On the other hand, Palmer and Godfrey (1972) found that administration of the WISC in Spanish did not improve the performance of a group of bilingual children. They suggested that with impoverished bilingual children, the level of deprivation may be more crucial than language in influencing performance on tests.

The two studies, while presenting somewhat disparate results, actually provide further insight into the complexity of the variables. First, these studies suggest that although language may influence performance, it does not affect all tasks equally. Second, they suggest that even though language may affect performance, its influence may not override the pervasive impact of an impoverished background.

METHODS OF MINIMIZING TEST BIASES

One of the initial attempts to remove the sources of bias in tests was the development of culture-fair tests (for example, the Davis-Ells Games, Cattell's Culture Fair Intelligence Tests, and Raven's Progressive Matrices). However, these attempts have not been very successful, and interest in developing culture-fair tests has been declining (Oakland and Matuszek, 1977). This is in part because research has indicated that some disadvantaged children perform more poorly on culture-fair tests than on traditional tests of intelligence (Jensen, 1973). Furthermore, some researchers believe that culturally biased tests are useful *because* they predict socially relevant behavior; therefore, removal of all cultural loading from tests would make them useless.

More recent efforts have been directed at exploring ways of using current tests fairly. Several different models have been designed to accomplish this (for example, Cleary, 1968; Thorndike, 1971; Darlington, 1971). These models involve statistical procedures designed to improve the accuracy with which tests predict certain criteria, but they do not modify characteristics of the tests. One notable exception is the evaluation system developed by Mercer and Lewis (1977), known as the System of Multi-Cultural Pluralistic Assessment (SOMPA). An in-depth discussion of this system is not possible within the scope of this chapter. However, because the SOMPA system emphasizes an assessment procedure that utilizes sociocultural characteristics of the child as a basis for administering and interpreting test performance, it is of importance to all who are concerned with the evaluation of disadvantaged and culturally different children.

Performance tests, such as the Leiter International Performance Scale and the Columbia Mental Maturity Scale, are often used to circumvent some of the problems associated with culturally biased tests. However, cultural bias continues to be reflected in tasks included in the tests, although these tests avoid some of the linguistic problems of verbal tests. Another shortcoming associated with using performance tests is that they do not provide information about language skills (which is an important source of information about cognitive abilities.)

Test makers have not been oblivious to the problems being discussed, and they generally provide standardization information to assist one in determining if a particular test is appropriate in a specific situation. However, in many cases there is no test that is entirely appropriate. For example, how does one assess a child who has spoken only Spanish in the home? A Spanish language test is better than a nonlanguage performance scale in such a situation, whereas the intellectual repertoire of a bilingual child can only be sampled by testing in both languages. Tests to accomplish this have not been developed, and testers should assume that either language score alone is undoubtedly an underestimate of the bilingual child's current repertoire (Cleary and associates, 1975).

Numerous other variables have been investigated in an attempt to isolate factors that may enable examiners to optimize the performance of disadvantaged children during testing. Quay (1971), for example, notes that research has generally indicated that disadvantaged children are more responsive to material reinforcement than they are to social praise. However, in a situation in which candy was used with four-year-old black children who were enrolled in a Head Start program, Quay did not observe any effects of the material reinforcers. Therefore, Quay posited that, in situations in which children are already receiving high levels of reinforcement, material reinforcers may not contribute to performance. In general, the liberal use of praise and attention is considered very useful when evaluating young disadvantaged children. Zigler and Butterfield (1968) reported findings indicating that performance was greater when difficult and easy items were alternated, rather than presented in their usual format (which progresses from easy to difficult). Warner and Kauffman (1972) showed that younger children displayed higher performance on tests when they had been previously informed about the test (as opposed to those children who were not previously informed). The studies mentioned above generally emphasize the motivation aspects, which can affect test performance significantly.

Piersel, Brody, and Kratochwill (1977) examined the impact of different feedback procedures and observed the following. Utilizing a self-monitoring procedure during testing increases anxiety and lowers performance, as does providing specific feedback after each response; in contrast, a situation in which children are exposed to an affectively warm and rewarding experience with the examiner prior to the evaluation seems to enhance performance. A related study of Johnson (1974) indicates that performance in natural settings tends to be higher than that observed in standard situations. This was especially true of those children who had not been exposed to a preschool experience.

These findings correspond with the observations of Messick and Anderson (1970), who suggested that much irrelevant difficulty can be avoided by utilizing familiar and congenial settings, by reducing the adversarial quality of the testing situation, and by emphasizing the positive values associated with the testing. For preschool children who have little experience with the materials and tasks on the test, Messick and Anderson suggest that the child be allowed to practice on a few pretrial tasks, preferably with feedback. It is also suggested that the examiner teach the child the strategy necessary to solve the tasks. This concept may be difficult for some examiners to accept, because much of the training associated with testing emphasized that examiners should not provide extra help beyond that specified in the test manual. The point here, though, is that in some cases young children simply do not know how to approach a task, and that without some initiative on the part of the examiner to determine the reason for their lack of performance, very distorted and inaccurate results will be obtained.

A final way of reducing test bias is to broaden assessments to include the child's ability to learn from and function in his or her environment. The unique resources and strengths of different groups should be explored, and the individual's coping within that group should be assessed. Mercer (1972) suggested that the concept of adaptive behavior be used to supplement intelligence test data whenever a disadvantaged or culturally different child is evaluated. (Adaptive behavior refers to children's ability to learn the rules and skills of their particular cultural group.) Not only is information about a child's adaptive skills necessary for a complete evaluation of the child's cognitive abilities, but information concerning the adaptive skills required by different cultural groups could serve two additional functions. First, this information could provide input into future modifications of tests—modifications that may avoid some of the current biases of the tests. Second, this information could provide the basis for individual examiners to adjust procedures so as to evaluate children from culturally different groups more effectively.

Obviously, much of what has been discussed concerning the many ways in which tests inadvertently discriminate against disadvantaged and culturally different children falls beyond the power of individual psychologists to redress. However, the author believes that an understanding of the larger issues involved will enhance appreciation of the magnitude and complexity of the problem. Generally speaking, a much more active and affective style—instead of a somewhat neutral and reserved style—of interacting with the young child, coupled with sensitivity to and steps to avoid some of the irrelevant difficulties discussed, will contribute to the maximum performance of the child. Finally, a number of suggestions can be gleaned from the research to assist psychologists in minimizing the negative effects of cultural bias when assessing a culturally different or disadvantaged preschooler.

First, the child's ethnic and cultural background should be determined, at least in terms of race and ethnic origin, urban or rural location, and socioeconomic level. Tests should be selected which included representative children of the same age, race and ethnic background, locale, and socioeconomic level in the standardization sample. Parents and others familiar with the social expectations of the child's culture should be interviewed to get a sense of whether the child is fulfilling his or her culture's expectations for adaptive behaviors, such as self-care, responsibility, independence, language, and age-appropriate behavior in social situations. People who might have a good sense of how a particular child compares with others of the same cultural and socioeconomic group—in addition to parents and other family members—would include local Head Start or day care staff members, babysitters, ministers and Sunday school teachers, and public health nurses.

Second, before the evaluation the psychologist should determine whether the child has had many experiences with puzzles, books, picture naming, and block play. If the child attends preschool or a day care center, a visit to the center to interview the staff and observe the sur-

roundings will provide clues as to whether the child has had such experiences. If the child does not attend any group programs, then a home visit is in order; this is for the combined purpose of interviewing the child's parent, observing the child at home, and determining what types of toys and activities the child has experienced. If the child has not been exposed to typical preschool tasks that appear on tests (puzzles, naming pictures, pencil paper tasks, blocks, and so on), the evaluator can plan several play sessions, either at home or in the testing room. At these sessions the psychologist can use play materials to teach the child the general behaviors needed to string beads, draw circles and lines, point to and name pictures, complete puzzles, build with blocks, and so forth.

Preparing the child beforehand for the assessment and familiarizing the child with the test setting and the evaluator can be accomplished by scheduling a short play session in the testing room a few days before the actual assessment. The purpose is to build rapport and to make the child as comfortable and relaxed as possible. Use of warmth, praise, positive affect, and clear structure and expectations in all interactions with the child should aid rapport.

During the actual assessment, alternating difficult items with easier items may help the child's motivation, as will the use of praise and warmth. If the child is unable to perform a task when it is administered in a standardized way, one might wish to vary the administration—adding instructions or demonstrations, or breaking the task down to easier steps—to find out with what amount of teaching or structure the child can perform the task. The child's ability to learn the strategy and generalize it to other tasks, and the child's ability to learn when certain kinds of teaching styles are used are important pieces of information in their own right and should be a part of the report.

Finally, when the child's language background is not standard English, it is recommended that two intelligence tests be used. One test should be in standard English, so that the child's ability to use the language of the dominant culture can be assessed. A second test should be either a test in the child's other language (if the child is bilingual), or it should be a nonverbal test, like the Hiskey-Nebraska, Leiter, or performance sections of the McCarthy, Wechsler Scales, and so on. (The nonverbal test should be chosen partially on the basis of the match between test sample and child's cultural background, as discussed above.)

Another important point that must be made about language functioning is that the clinician should not equate restricted language with restricted intellectual abilities. Some culturally different children are virtually silent in the testing situation, and the examiner may need to listen to the child in play with other children to hear a representative sample of the child's language. Use of the SOMPA assessment procedures with culturally different and disadvantaged children is strongly recommended.

SUMMARY

When discussing terms such as cultural skills, values, biases, and diversities, psychologists and other professionals must realize that they are dealing with potential and very real conflicts in values. These are conflicts that all who assess minority children face, with social values and social issues weighed on one hand, and educational and psychological theories, practices, and decisions weighed on the other. It is at this point that each individual psychologist has to make an ethical decision about whether a particular test (or testing itself) is appropriate (Messick and Anderson, 1970). The deciding factor always has to be whether the positive consequences associated with testing will outweigh the negative consequences.

REFERENCES

Association of Black Psychologists: Position paper adopted at a meeting of the Association. Washington, DC, September 1970

Bennett GK: Response to Robert Williams. *Counseling Psychologist.* 2(2) 88-89. 1970

Bryen DN: Speech-sound discrimination ability on linguistically unbiased tests. Except Child 42: 195-201, 1976

Bucky SF, Banta TJ: Racial factors in test performance. Develop Psych 6: 7-13, 1972

Cleary TA: Test bias: Prediction of grades of Negro and white students in integrated colleges. J Educ Meas 5: 115-124, 1968

Cleary TA, Humphreys L, Kendrick S, Wesman A: Educational uses of tests with disadvantaged students. Am Psychol 30: 15-41, 1975

Clemans WV: A note in response to a request by the editor to comment on R. L. Williams article entitled, Black pride, academic relevance, and individual achievement. Counsel Psychol 2(2): 90-92, 1979

Darlington RB: Another look at "Culture fairness." Journal of Educational Measurement. 8: 71-82. 1971

Hess R, Shipman V: Early experience and the socialization of cognitive modes in children. Child Devel 12: 869-886, 1965

Jensen AR: *Educability and Group Differences.* New York: Harper & Row, 1973

Johnson DL: The influences of social class and race on language test performance and spontaneous speech of preschool children. Child Devel 45: 517-521, 1974

Labov W: Academic ignorance and black intelligence. The Atlantic 229: 59-67, 1972

Little J, Ramirez A: Ethnicity of subject and test administrator: their effect on self-esteem. Journal of Social Psychology. 99: 149-150. 1976

Mercer JR: IQ: The lethal label. Psychology Today, September 1972, 44-47, 95-97

Mercer J, Lewis J: *SOMPA: System of Multi-cultural Pluralistic Assessment.* New York: Psychological Corp, 1977

Messick S, Anderson S: Educational testing, individual development, and social responsiveness. Counsel Psychol 2(2): 80-88, 1970

Oakland T, Matuszek P: Using tests in nondiscriminatory assessment. In Oakland T (ed): *Psychological and Educational Assessment of Minority Children.* New York: Brunner/Mazel, 1977

Opton EJ: A psychologist takes a closer look at the recent landmark Larry P. Opinion. APA Monitor 10(12): 1, 4, 1979

Palmer M, Godfrey P: Effects of administration of the WISC in Spanish and English and relation of social class to performance. Psychol Schools, 9: 61-64, 1972

Piersel W, Brody G, Kratochwill T: A further examination of motivational influences on disadvantaged minority group children's intelligence test performance. Child Devel 48: 1142-1145, 1977

Quay L: Language, dialect, reinforcement, and the intelligence: Test performance of Negro children. Child Devel 42: 5-15, 1971

Quay L: Negro dialect and Binet performance in severely disadvantaged black four-year-olds. Child Devel 43, 245-250, 1972

Sabatino D, Kelling D, Hayden D: Special education and the culturally different child: Implications for assessment and intervention. Except Child 39: 563-567, 1973

Sattler J: Racial experimenter effects. In Miller KS, Dreger RM (eds): *Comparative Studies of Blacks and Whites in the United States.* New York: Seminar Press, 1973

Sattler J: *Assessment of Children's Intelligence.* Philadelphia: WB Saunders Co, 1974

Shuey A: *The Testing of Negro Intelligence.* New York: Social Science Press, 1966

Solkoff N: Race as a variable in research with children. Develop Psychol 7(1): 70–75, 1972

Solkoff N: Race of examiner and performance on the Wechsler intelligence scale for children: A replication. Percep Motor Skills 39: 1063–1066, 1974

Swanson E, Deblassie R: Interpreter effects on the WISC performance of first grade Mexican-American children. Measur Eval Guidance 4: 172–175, 1971

Terman L, Merrill M: *Stanford Binet intelligence scale manual*, 4th ed. Boston: Houghton Mifflin, 1972

Thorndike R: Concepts of cultural fairness. J Educ Measur 8: 63–70, 1971

Warner R, Kauffman J: Effect of prearrangement of testing on anxiety on performance of second and sixth grade boys. *Psychol Schools* 9: 75–78, 1972

Williams R: Black pride, academic relevance, and individual achievement. *Counsel Psychol* 2: 18–21, 1970

Zigler R, Butterfield E; Motivational aspects of changes in IQ test performance of culturally deprived nursery school children. *Child Devel* 39: 1–14, 1968

Chapter 17

ASSESSMENT OF THE FAMILY SYSTEM

By

JILL WATERMAN

When a handicapped child is born or when a child's significant handicap is discovered, severe stresses are experienced by family members (Dalton and Epstein, 1963; Solnit and Stark, 1961). How a family copes with these stresses affects the handicapped child's development as well as the satisfaction and functioning of the family unit as a whole. Therefore, when a psychologist is evaluating a handicapped child or a child suspected of having developmental problems, it is important for the professional to remember that the child is both the product of and an active participant in the family system. Indeed, family dynamics will also affect how the clinician should present the results of an evaluation to parents, and how treatment should be planned.

The first major stress that a family must cope with is recognition that the child is handicapped. Although the general stages involved in adjusting tend to be similar, parental reactions to the emerging awareness of a child's problem vary.

FACTORS THAT AFFECT PARENTS' ACCEPTANCE OF A HANDICAPPED CHILD

Parents' ability to accept realistically their child's handicap is affected by four major factors.

The first factor is the type of handicap the child has. Parents generally find it easier to accept the reality of handicaps that are physically noticeable, such as

birth defects, spina bifida, or certain types of mental retardation in which a child exhibits characteristic facial features. Parents tend to have more difficulty accepting handicaps that are not physically evident, such as deafness, autism, or forms of retardation with no physical manifestations. There appear to be two reasons for this discrepancy. First, it is more difficult to believe that a child who does not look "different" from other children has a major handicap. Second, often the disability in normal-appearing children is not evident until later in infancy or in the preschool years, so that parents have developed attachments to and expectations for a non-handicapped child (which they are then forced to reexamine). The meaning of the particular handicap to different parents also varies, and parental reactions will be partially based on their previous experience with other children or adults who were afflicted with similar handicaps (Martin, 1975). For example, if parents know a severely retarded child and are told that their child is retarded, they will tend to imagine that their child will resemble the severely retarded child. This will be true even though their own child may be only mildly retarded.

A second factor affecting parents' ability to accept their child's handicap is the personalities of the parents. How parents have dealt with stressful events in the past tends to be predictive of their reactions to having a handicapped child. The defense and coping mechanisms they have used to deal with past losses, such as death of a parent, divorce, loss of a job, and so forth, will probably be reactivated (Martin, 1975). Similarly, a parent's level of self-esteem may relate to how much responsibility the parent feels for causing the child's handicap. Understanding the social support structure that parents utilize is also very important for the psychologist who would help the family cope. For families with good support from the extended family, friends, church, community, and so on, adjustments to having a handicapped child may be easier than for families who are socially isolated.

A third major factor is the birth order of the delayed child. Having a handicapped child may have a different meaning to parents, depending on whether the child is the firstborn, the only child, or a later-born child. When the child is the parents' first-born, a major handicap is often more difficult for them to accept. New parents are generally less familiar with developmental norms and milestones than more experienced parents who may recognize a developmental problem by comparing the behavior of the child with what a sibling could do at a similar age. As a consequence, new parents are less likely to notice slowness of development in their child. In addition to having less knowledge of child development, first-time parents frequently have a greater emotional need to have a normal child. Having already reassured themselves of their ability to produce a normal child, experienced parents can sometimes accept a handicapped child better than new parents who would wonder if there is something that prevents them from bearing normal children. Parents sometimes experience great fear when contemplating more children, worrying that their second-born would be afflicted also. If parents have successfully borne and raised other children, there generally is less threat to their self-esteem than if the handicapped child is the parents' first and only offspring.

A fourth factor involves the etiologic factors of a delay in development. Whether the cause of the handicap is known or unknown contributes to variability in parental reactions. If the cause is known and could not be controlled by the parents (for example, brain injury at birth, nonhereditary chromosome problem), the parents generally have less guilt to contend with than if the known cause is perceived by the parents as having been preventable (for example, prenatal infections of the mother, seizures resulting from the child falling or being dropped). However, probably the most difficult situation occurs when the cause of the handicap is unknown, as happens in approximately 75 percent of cases of mental retardation. The parents then may torture themselves about what the cause may be, and this process may interfere with progressively accepting the child and the handicap. Parents' fantasies of what may have caused the handicap range from concern over smoking during pregnancy to guilt over ambivalent thoughts about having the child. It is helpful for parents to share, discuss, evaluate, and come to understand these fantasies.

Finally, the manner in which parents are informed about the handicap affects their ability to cope. Although how parents are told about a disability is not a major determinant of long-term parental adjustment to a child's handicap, the way that parents are told can have a major effect on the beginning processes of adaptation to such news. When parents of handicapped children are surveyed, they almost uniformly have expressed appreciation for having been told early about the problem, rather than being first told that a child would "grow out of it" or being falsely reassured about their concerns (Valente, 1972; Carr, 1970).

Sensitivity to the needs and concerns of the particular family, along with a sound understanding of the specific problems of the child, is crucial (Drayer and Schlesinger, 1960; Valente, 1972; Gabel, 1980). While many clinicians urge exploration of possible emotional disorders and stress when dealing with the parents' feelings, others place emphasis on helping essentially mature and rational people to learn more about their child (Matheny and Vernick, 1969). Probably a mixture of the two approaches is most helpful to the majority of parents. Realistic and complete information about the child's functioning should be given in an empathic and caring manner, and the parents' feelings and re-actions should be acknowledged and dealt with on a level comfortable for them. The clinician should stress the child's strengths as well as his or her limitations.

THE STAGES OF PARENTAL ACCEPTANCE

While parents' reactions to recognition of a handicapped child vary owing to the factors discussed above, parents tend to go through observable phases in coping with having a handicapped child in the family. To accept a handicapped child, the parents must mourn the loss of the healthy, perfect child that they had hoped and longed for (Solnit and Stark, 1961). Each parent, in-dividually, goes through the process of mourning at his or her own pace.

The steps in reacting to a child's hand-icap are believed to be analogous to those that occur when a loved one dies (Kübler-Ross, 1969). These stages include:

1. denial, including shock, numbness, disbelief, and "shopping around" for more hopeful opinions;

2. anger and guilt (including "Why us?" and accusations directed toward the spouse), shame, sense of failure, fantasies about the cause of a handicap, and wishes that child had not been born or would die;

3. despair, including hopelessness, physical symptoms of depression, with-drawal, and loss of warmth in other rela-tionships; and

4. acceptance, which involves viewing the child realistically, and withdrawal of emotional investment from the lost, healthy child and attachment to the real, handicapped child.

Acceptance is a gradual and continu-ous process, which may occur as an ebb and flow over a period of several years. Some clinicians who work with families of handicapped children argue that mourning can never be completed when one lives with a handicapped child; this, these professionals say, is similar to what an individual experiences when a loved one dies. Instead, the family experiences "chronic sorrow," a nonpathologic state for families with handicapped children (Ol-shansky, 1962). The realities faced by par-ents of a severly handicapped child justify such chronic sorrow; however, this non-neurotic sadness does not interfere with the parents' deriving satisfaction from the child's growth and modest accomplish-ments.

The stages that parents of a handi-capped child experience have been elo-quently elucidated by the father of a se-verely retarded child (Robinson, 1951):

Years later, when we could face facts, we learned that we had followed a pattern so un-deviating from the usual one as to be tragic. Parents, when they learn of a child's affliction, pass through three well-defined stages. Each of the first two stages is punctuated by a short intermission marked by despair of ever curing the child's idiocy. But once rested, the couple invariably sets out again on the long journey.

We went through all three stages.

Stage I is a period of frantic searching for proof that the child is not subnormal. It consists of: (a) repudiation of the family physician, (b) correspondence with authorities in the field of abnormal child psychology, and (c) visits to psychiatrists and specialists all over the land. This period lasts as long as family finances allow.

Stage II is a crusade to prove the specialists wrong. During this time the husband senses a gradual change in his wife. She (a) loses all interest in sex, (b) refuses to mix in society, (c) neglects her ordinary work, and (d) devotes every waking hour to frenzied training of her child. She often convinces herself that the child is actually a misunderstood genius.

This is the most dangerous stage. If it persists too long, it leads to a broken home, and sometimes to the mother's complete insanity. Birth of an afflicted child leads to divorce in 50 percent of the cases.

Stage III takes place only when both par-ents accept their child as subnormal and ar-range their lives accordingly. If a separation has already taken place, the mother often devotes her days to the child's care. Sometimes a sem-blance of home life remains, but the parents, through fear, resolve never again to have chil-dren. The most stable people place their child in an environment specifically created to care for him. These parents have two alternatives. First, they can keep the child at home, have other children and build as nearly normal a homelife as possible. Second, they can put him in an institution, have other children, and build a happy life without him.

FAMILY ADAPTATIONS

Once parents have accepted the reality of having a handicapped child, they make adaptations to the handicap that may be either functional or dysfunctional for the child and the family. The most functional adjustments involve accommodating the family's routine and way of life to take into account changes required as a result of the handicapped child's needs, but keep the needs of other family members in mind also. The family must develop a concept of the child that includes both normalcy and deviance; otherwise, they either make their child into a "sick" person or spend immense energies trying to give him or her the feeling of being "like everyone else" (Minde and colleagues, 1972).

While most families adapt appropriately to the stress of having a handicapped child, there are several self-defeating styles that the clinician should be able to observe and help families understand. The first such style is overprotection of or overinvolvement with the child. Indeed, this may be the most common dysfunctional response to having a handicapped child. Generally, it is the mother who responds in this fashion; she may spend all her waking hours caring for the child or trying to stimulate development. One or both parents may feel that no babysitter or even any other family member can care for the child adequately, so that there is never any relief from the highly demanding job of parenting the handicapped child. Guilt is frequently the motivation of this dysfunctional style. A parent may feel that he or she must devote enormous time and effort to this child because of guilty fears of having caused the handicap, or a parent may feel shame about harboring negative feelings toward the handicapped child. This mode of adopting trends to enmesh one parent with the handicapped child, with the result that the other parent feels excluded and neglected. The marital relationship may be threatened because the parents spend little time or energy with each other. Another result is that other children in the family may also feel neglected; in fact, they may not receive adequate parenting in such a situation. Both

siblings and the neglected spouse often experience rage toward the handicapped child, whom they perceive a an impediment to the satisfaction of their needs.

A second dysfunctional style involves some degree of rejection of the affected child. Parents may withdraw emotionally from the handicapped child because being more involved is too painful. The occurrence of this reponse in both parents is probably most common when the handicap is evident at birth or within the first few months of life—before a strong attachment has developed between parents and child. The parents may, in fact, be unable to come to grips with the discrepancy between the wished-for healthy child and the actual handicapped child. Generally, however, only one of the two parents is out of touch with the child, he or she may be unaware or neglectful of the child's needs—especially the child's emotional needs. Such a rejection is usually accompanied by guilt, and avoidance of contact with the child is intensified by the parent's effort to manage these feelings. At the extreme, rejection of the child can lead to disruption of the family system through voluntary placement of the child in foster or insitutional care, or through child abuse or neglect.

Anger or blame directed toward the spouse represents a third dysfunctional coping style. This kind of strategy may threaten the marital relationship because one spouse harbors negative feelings toward the other. One parent may blame the other for their child's handicap. Blame may be expressed as, "If only you hadn't drunk wine during pregnancy," "I didn't want another baby, only *you* did," or "This wouldn't have happened if you hadn't made me so nervous by staying out until all hours of the night while I was pregnant," and so on. Conversely, the marital relationship may also be threatened if one spouse, feeling guilt about perhaps having casued the handicap, internalizes the blame and withdraws from the other. A common source of anger toward a spouse involves projection. One parent may feel very angry or resentful toward the handicapped child but feels too guilty to admit anger toward a helpless child; therefore, that parent may turn the anger against the other spouse. Changes in lifestyle necessitated by the demands of the handicapped child can be a further source of disruption in the pattern of relating that the parents had established. These stresses on the relationship can have serious consequences. Studies have consistently shown that marital difficulties and divorce are much more common among parents of children with handicaps than among parents of nonhandicapped children (Heatherington, 1979).

STAGES AT WHICH PARENTS REEXPERIENCE STRESS

After a period of adjustment, families with a handicapped child generally settle into a stable coping pattern that is acceptable to its members. However, acute stress is likely to be reexperienced at certain critical developmental stages, and conflicts and coping styles (adaptive or maladaptive) are then reactivated in the family. While there are certain stress points unique to each family, based on their own values and experiences, there tend to be four stages in the developmental sequence when many families with a handicapped child reexperience strong stress reactions. These are also points in the life of a handicapped child when the family's sorrow is acute and excruciating.

One stressful time tends to be when a delayed child develops locomotion. It is very difficult for parents to watch their child struggle to roll over to reach a toy when all the other 18-month-olds in the neighborhood are walking and running.

The time of school entry is another period when parents commonly reexperience stress. When all of the 5-year-olds walk to the neighborhood kindergarten, it is particularly painful to most parents to see their handicapped child board a bus to go to a special school.

When a handicapped child reaches puberty—typically later than average—parents frequently feel stressed. The contrast between their child's physical and mental maturity and that of nonhandicapped children can be very upsetting to parents.

Parents also experience the reemerg-ence of stress when the disabled individual reaches adulthood. If the handicapped person cannot live independently, the family is faced with continued dependency; the parents must face the task of planning for future care, even past the point of their own death.

STRESS COMMON TO SIBLINGS OF A HANDICAPPED CHILD

Other children in a family also experience a particular set of stresses when they live with a handicapped brother or sister. The afflicted child often requires special care that takes a great deal of the parents' time, so that natural sibling rivalry is exacerbated. Other children may feel unloved or neglected and may resent the attention given to the special child. Guilt is a further complicating factor. For example, the nonaffected sibling may feel guilty because of having resentment for the handicapped child; or the sibling may feel guilty for being glad the handicap did not happen to him or her. In addition, the handicapped child often does not easily fit into the sibling group, and other children in the family have to contend with the consequences.

Some of the difficulties siblings experience include having to defend the handicapped child against the teasing and curiosity of neighborhood or school acquaintances. In addition, whether the handicapped child is older or younger, the siblings may perform parental functions for that child, such as babysitting or helping the child to dress. Finally, the siblings may wonder whether this child will ultimately be their responsibility; even at a relatively young age, they may experience concern about the disruptive effect the handicapped child will have on their lives in the future.

THE EFFECT ON AND OF THE EXTENDED FAMILY

Members of the extended family—the grandparents, aunts, uncles, and cousins—also have reactions to a handicapped child. Their responses may be adaptive or maladaptive, and may either help or hinder the functioning of the nuclear family unit. The most common maladaptive response from members of the extended family is denial of either the existence of the handicap or of its extent. Comments to parents may include, "She'll catch up very soon," "There's never been anything like that in *our* family," or "He'll grow out of it by the time he's ready to go to school." Often, denial by the extended family strengthens the parents' own denial. Less frequently, members of the extended family may comment that the child has an apparent difficulty even when the parents are denying it. In such cases, the extended family may push the parents to have the child evaluated. The support and sensitive response of the extended family is invaluable to families with a handicapped child and can be an important resource if the nuclear family is coping in a maladaptive manner.

Participation in parent groups that are affiliated with school programs is often invaluable for parents with handicapped children. Most families manage to cope in a healthy and acceptable manner, although additional support from parent groups is often uniquely helpful to facilitate the adaptation. It is indeed difficult for professionals who have not experienced having a handicapped child in their own family to appreciate the depths of sorrow and joy that each family experiences with their handicapped child. The ultimate acceptance and adaptation of the handicapped child is a complex sociologic process that involves not only parental attitudes and expectations but also factors outside the family. The societal and cultural views of handicaps, religious affiliations and beliefs, community resources and responses to handicapped citizens, all influence the way the child becomes a part of society.

FAMILY SYSTEMS

The concept of the family as a system is useful for understanding the impact of having a handicapped child on members of the family and the child. Several authors have described family systems in depth (Minuchin, 1974; French, 1977) as they relate to children with handicaps. The model of a family system views the family as an organization that maintains a balance as each member functions within it. The family is seen as a system because it maintains a certain homeostasis as each person in the organization goes through various changes and growth. French (1977) conceptualizes the changes as evolving by way of assimilation, accommodations, and adaptations in a manner analogous to Piaget's model of cognitive development. As the family is confronted with various new or different stresses, the system responds to maintain order and find ways to encourage adaptation.

The health or dysfunction of a family system depends on the system's flexibility or adaptability in times of stress. Adding a member, losing a member, or recognizing a child's major handicap causes stress on the system, upsets the system's equilibrium, and forces a realignment of family roles.

It is also important that the clinician consider subsystems when looking at the functioning of a family system (Minuchin, 1974). A spouse subsystem is formed when a man and woman marry. When a child is born to the couple, the husband and wife need to maintain their spouse subsystem and create a separate but obviously overlapping parental subsystem. As other children are born, a sibling subsystem is developed. In well-functioning families, there are clear boundaries between the parents and the children (Minuchin, 1974). The boundaries should not be so diffuse that children are part of the spouse or parenting subsystems, nor should they be so rigid that children are denied access to their parents. For further understanding of family systems theory, the reader is referred to Guerin (1976), Munichin (1974), and Golddenberg and Goldenberg (1980).

The usefulness of family systems concepts in understanding families with a handicapped child can be illustrated by reexamining one of the maladaptive responses discussed earlier: overprotection of the child. In such a case, the boundary between the parental subsystem and the child is diffuse, and the child and one parent have formed an alliance that excludes the other parent. Overprotection thereby threatens the spouse subsystem. In working with such a family, the goal of the professional would be to include both parents in parenting functions, to nurture the spouse subsystem by encouraging the parents to spend time together without the children, and to allow the child more space to grow and develop a separate, independent identity. When attempting to understand the dynamics of a family system when there is a handicapped child, it is important for the clinician to examine how subsystems are functioning and interrelating, and to evaluate the clarity of boundaries between subsystems.

The following questions may be useful as a guide when trying to understand a family with a handicapped child:

1. Do both parents participate with the children and share in discussing the children?

2. Is one parent—or both parents—unusually overprotective or rejecting toward the handicapped child?

3. Is either parent blaming the other (or himself or herself) for the handicapping condition?

4. Does the handicapped child seem to have access to the parents similar to that of the other children in the family? Is he or she heard by them but not stifled or prevented from growing?

5. Do siblings receive appropriate time and attention from the parents?

6. Do siblings seem secure, or do they need to seek attention from their parents or others in negative ways?

7. Are family members allowed to express negative feelings toward the handicapped child? Is this done in a nondestructive way?

8. Do the parents support and nurture each other?

9. Do the parents spend some time together away from all the children?

10. Do family members have some sources of support to fall back on outside of the nuclear family (extended family, friends, and so on)?

SUMMARY

A child's handicap has a profound effect on the entire family, causing changes in roles, values, and attitudes. The family's reactions can be maladaptive or can facilitate the child's development, as well as for future family and marital functioning. Facing a child's severe handicap may be more difficult for the family than even the death of a child. This is because grieving and sorrow never completely end as the family faces crises at various stages in a child's development. Understanding the family's reactions to a child's handicap is vital in facilitating both the child's development and the family's adjustment.

REFERENCES

Carr J: Mongolism: Telling the parents. Develop Med Child Neurol 12: 213–221, 1970

Dalton J, Epstein H: Counseling parents of mildly retarded children. Soc Casework 20: 523–530, 1963

Drayer C, Schlesinger EG: The informing interview. Am J Ment Defic 65: 363–370, 1960

French AP: Disturbed Children and Their Families: Innovations in Evaluation and Treatment. New York: Human Sciences Press, 1977

Gabel S: The informing interview. In Gabel S, Erickson M (eds): Child Development and Developmental Disabilities. Boston: Little, Brown & Co, 1980

Goldenberg I, Goldenberg H: Family Therapy: An Overview. Monterey, CA: Brooks & Cole, 1980

Guerin PJ: Family Therapy: Theory and Practice. New York: Gardner Press, 1976

Heatherington EM: Divorce: A child's perspective. Am Psychol 34: 851–858, 1979

Kübler-Ross E: On Death and Dying. New York: Macmillan Publishing Co, Inc., 1969

Martin HP: Parental response to handicapped children. Develop Med Child Neurol 17: 251–252, 1975

Matheny AP, Vernick J: Parents of the mentally retarded child: Emotionally overwhelmed or informationally deprived? J Ped 74: 953–959, 1969

Minde KK, Hackett JD, Killou D, Silver S: How they grow up: Forty-one physically handicapped children and their families. Am J Psychiat 128: 1554–1559, 1972

Minuchin S: Families and Family Therapy. Cambridge, MA: Harvard University Press, 1974

Olshansky S: Chronic sorrow: A reponse to having a mentally defective child. Soc Casework 43: 190–193, 1962

Robinson R: Don't speak to us of living death. Today's Health June, 1951, 108-115

Solnit AJ, Stark MH: Mourning and the birth of a defective child. Psychoanalyt Study Child 16: 523–537, 1961

Valente M: Counseling parents of retarded children. Calif Med 116: 21–26, 1972

Chapter 18

THE PSYCHOLOGIST'S ROLE IN THE PARENT CONFERENCE

By

RICHARD R. SCHNELL

The efforts that have gone into the evaluation of a child can be seriously diluted if the evaluation results cannot be effectively communicated to the child's parents. However, informing parents that their child has a significant disability can be a very difficult task, one for which many professionals may not have been adequately prepared. There is no one right way of communicating with parents, for each situation demands an individual approach. The clinician must take into account the parents' expectations and characteristics, as well as his or her own professional skills and style. The parent conference is not merely an information-giving session, but one of counseling as well, with many therapeutic issues coming to the fore.

THE PROCESSES OF GRIEF AND COPING

A potentially helpful way of looking at the parent conference (or feedback session) is to realize that for the parents it is a "crisis." Indeed, it is a situation in which the parents are often confronted with new information that calls for the mobilization of psychological resources. Lindemann (1944) has discussed grief and mourning behavior as the result of stressful situations, and Caplan (1964) and Lindemann (1965) have elaborated further on the "situational crisis." The grief process can be used as a model in helping to understand the dynamics of responding to a crisis. It should be understood, however, that this is at best an artificial way of viewing this phenomenon. The grief process can be represented as having three consecutive stages. This process is summarized below in terms of what parents typically experience (Lindemann, 1944).

1. *Shock and disbelief.* In the initial phase of grief, the individual feels physical as well as emotional trauma. Somatic stress, such as a feeling of tightness in the throat or shortness of breath, occurs in waves lasting 20 minutes to an hour. Some individuals report an empty feeling in the abdomen and lack of muscular power as well. Many remain distant from other people emotionally and express an overwhelming feeling of guilt and a need to sigh continually.

2. *Developing awareness.* In the middle—and crucial—phase of bereavement, there is a persistent longing felt for what has been lost. This is accompanied by weeping, pain, and despair. The potential for personality disorganization is strong during this phase.

3. *Resolving the loss.* Resolution completes the work of mourning, or "grief work" as Lindemann put it (1944). At this stage, reorganization of the personality can occur, and appropriate coping mechanisms can emerge to allow the individual access to new relationships and resumption of social functioning.

When parents are presented with information about the significance of a handicap their child may have, mourning reactions for the loss of expectation for a "normal child" are frequently seen. Parents may be at any of these stages before the formal feedback session, or they may move from one stage to another during the conference: this often depends upon their prior awareness of their child's problems. A mother and father may also each be at different stages of grief. Having discussed the stages of grief, it should be recognized that while bereavement is a useful way of thinking about what some parents may undergo, it is neither necessary nor realistic to expect that all parents must experience these (or any) stages of mourning.

Hamburg and Adams (1967) have discussed the long-term consequences of crisis:

> The concept of crisis may be used to view the need for adaption both in terms of the situational requirements and the various phases over time of the mobilization of resources. The perception and definition of the tasks facing the individual, as well as the strategy selected for attempted management of these tasks become important parts of the process of resolving the crisis. The critical issues arise over the choice of these patterns of adaptation. These patterns may be predominantly regressive and defensive, functioning primarily for the protection of the self from disintegration, or may represent efforts to master the environment, restructuring the task ahead, and solve the problem of dealing with a novel situation. In most crisis situations the adaptive process is a complex and changing mixture of these regressive and progressive components, and it is to this dynamic process of search for individual styles and strategies of mastery that the term *coping* had been applied. (Hamburg and Adams, 1967, p. 128.)

Coping has come to mean adapting under relatively difficult conditions. White (1974) has posited three conditions for successful adaption which are clearly necessary for coping to occur: (1) securing adequate information about the environment, (2) maintaining satisfactory internal conditions both for action and for the processing of information, and (3) maintaining autonomy with freedom of movement. In other words, to adapt successfully, a person must continue to be open to what is happening around him or her, must accurately interpret and integrate that information, must be able to choose between courses of action, and must follow through on them. Clearly, everyone faced with a personal crisis needs a strategy of adaption. To cope

effectively requires that all three of White's processes be present and that a balance is held among them.

The clinician who would counsel parents effectively should also consider the presence and effect of stress, for high levels of stress may be engendered by communicating distressing news to parents. It should be remembered that while stress is a normal concomitant of everyday life, high levels of stress can be debilitating. Kahn and Antonucci (1980) have developed a theory of stress reduction which invokes the concept of social support to reduce stress. They define social support as interactions between people which include one or more of the elements of affect (expressions of liking, admiration, and respect), affirmation (expressions of agreement or acknowledgment that another person was right in what they did or said), and aid (giving assistance such as time, labor, or information). These elements of social support would seem to be necessary ingredients of a parent conference.

OTHER PARENTAL REACTIONS

The literature describes many different parental reactions to having a child with significant problems; it also delineates many different characteristics of parents thought to be important in determining these responses. For example, Wolfensberger (1967) has listed more than forty different parental reactions to mental retardation.

One of the parental reactions that has received a good deal of research attention has been the tendency of some parents to be unrealistic about their child's developmental status and potential (Sarason, 1959; Ross, 1963; Ross, 1964; Schlesinger and Meadow, 1972). Some research suggests that:

> About half of the parents of retarded children may be able to assign a developmental level to their child's present behavior which when transformed into a developmental quotient will fall with plus or minus 15 points of a professional judgment based on standardized measurement techniques. There seems to be a moderate correlation between parents' estimates of their children's developmental level

and professionals' assessment of this. (Pedulla, 1975, p. 102.)

With regard to prediction of their children's future functioning, the majority of parents tend to overestimate their children's adult potential (Meyerowitz, 1967; Barclay and Vaught, 1964; Wolfensberger and Kurtz, 1971).

Several factors appear to affect parents' reactions. One is that their emotional reactions to having a retarded child make it difficult for parents to be realistic. Another major factor, however, is the parents' lack of information about retardation. In 1970, Gottswald made a national survey and found that more than one-third of those interviewed had quite erroneous ideas about mental retardation. Unfortunately, these misconceptions persist today; laypersons in general appear to have little opportunity to learn the facts about mental retardation, emotional disturbances, and other handicaps. It is no wonder then, that parents may be confused and not completely realistic about handicapping conditions. During a parent conference, the clinician can take an important step in remedying this lack of accurate information.

Personality differences will also make a difference in how parents handle information. Janis (1974) has hypothesized that "the chronically anxious type of personality will generally have a lower threshold than the unanxious type with respect to feeling vulnerable and becoming emotionally aroused when subjected to either mild or strong threat stimulation" (p. 170). Pedulla (1975) found that well-adjusted mothers who were presented with diagnostic information about their children's mental retardation tended to be able to assimilate the information and to become more realistic. In contrast, less well adjusted mothers tended to deny their children's limitations and to become less realistic.

AN OVERVIEW OF THE PSYCHOLOGIST'S ROLE IN THE PARENT CONFERENCE

When presenting the results of an evaluation to parents, the clinician must use both tact and skill. If information about disabilities is not conveyed with sensitivity, parents may reject either the professional or their own child. In fact, "shattered hopes and feelings of humiliation make the parents extremely vulnerable to the professional manner" (National Society for Handicapped Children, 1967). Another common result of a poorly conducted conference is that the parent leaves feeling guilty. This guilt may be projected as blame to the other parent, or it may take the form of self-blame. In addition, guilt often leads to overprotection of the handicapped child by the parents.

One way sensitivity can be increased is by the psychologist making a real effort to be empathetic. Rogers (1975) defines empathy as the ability "to perceive the internal frame of reference of another with accuracy and with emotional components and meaning which pertain thereto as if we were that person but without losing the 'as if' condition" (p. 3). The psychologist also must achieve balance between the desire to be sensitive to the parents' feelings in conveying "bad news" without resorting to whitewashing the finds so that the parents will not feel badly. An argument can be made that it is difficult to accomplish both the reporting of findings and being sensitive to the parents in one session. However, as Taft (1973) has stated, "If there is no therapeutic understanding and use of one interview, many interviews equally barren will not help" (p. 10).

To be therapeutic, the clinician must come to grips with his or her own attitudes and feelings about handicapped children. If the clinician either consciously or unconsciously has ambivalent feelings about children whose development is compromised, or if there are doubts about the value of a child because of a handicap, that will be part of the unspoken message of the conference. The nuances of voice, posture, facial expression, time spent on specific issues, and so on, will carry the real message to the parents. Through personal experience with exceptional children, the psychologist should become aware that every child—no matter what the disability or IQ—has significant value and is important (Crocker, 1976).

In presenting data to parents of a

handicapped child, the psychologist would be wise to remember Gordon Allport's (1955) admonition: "The surest way to lose the truth is to pretend that one already wholly possesses it." (p. 34). Perfect predictions cannot be made about a delayed child's future development. This is particularly true as projections are made further into the future. Yet at the same time, parents need to have hope. Without hope, they can become depressed and resigned to a bleak future for their child. This is especially true for parents involved in the initial struggle to deal with the special pressures of a child's permanent handicapping condition. Thus, where there is the smallest possibility that a child will achieve certain goals, the parents should not be discouraged from aspiration to these goals. The psychologist can tell the parents that it is too soon to know precisely what the child may eventually be able to do. He or she can explain that follow-up visits will allow the staff to learn more about a child and perceive a more accurate developmental rate on a theoretical curve (Zadig and Crocker, 1975). Indeed, parents can be told that health professionals still have very much to learn about how far handicapped children can progress if given appropriate opportunity (Wolfensberger, 1972).

Giving parents direct and accurate feedback while not depriving them of hope is a difficult task. Obviously, parents need to be reassured and supported for what they have already done. In addition, when suggesting new things that the parents ought to do the clinician should not assume that new tasks will be easy for the parents. In fact, following professional recommendations may be very difficult and may require a great deal of parental energy. Depriving parents of hope can certainly drain their energy and is not conducive for helping them follow through. It must be noted, however, that while parents need to have things they can do to help their child, giving them unrealistic fantasies that their child can be "cured" of the handicap must be avoided. The best attitude for the clinician to adopt—and one that professionals working with handicapped children experience—is an abiding respect for parents who have a long, hard road ahead with a troubled child. Featherstone (1980) has written very sensitively about what it is like to be a parent of a handicapped child. "The pain of one's child's disability reshapes in unexpected ways, nonetheless, individuals endure." (p 12.)

PLANNING FOR A FEEDBACK CONFERENCE

The following is a brief outline of the logistic steps that can be taken in giving feedback to parents.

The first step is preparing feedback for parents. This process starts when a child is referred to the psychologist and the referral question is defined. Parental consent should be secured for the original referral to be made, and the parents should be made an integral part of the process all the way through so that they feel involved and do not assume the role of spectators. The reasons for the evaluation of their child should be thoroughly discussed with them initially so that during the feedback session the clinician can focus directly on the findings rather than on having to defend the necessity for the evaluation. Making parents partners in the evaluation process by asking their perspectives on a child's problems and valuing what they say goes a long way toward making them ready for what they will hear at the end of the evaluation.

Parents will often ask for feedback as various aspects of an evaluation are completed, and they are entitled to partial feedback on general issues to keep them invested in the process. However, it is often better to wait until all the data are in from the evaluation to present the most meaningful feedback. Delaying feedback until all evaluation results are available requires the psychologist to diplomatically balance the parents' need to know immediate results against the professional problem of not being prepared and organized to give them full results. The clinician must also strongly encourage both parents to be present for the feedback session, rather than expecting one parent to relay the information to the other.

When sufficient data have been gathered about the child so that reliable conclusions can be drawn, formal parental feedback can be planned. At that point, the professionals involved must decide who is appropriate to give the feedback. When a team has been involved in an evaluation, those people from the team who are most central to the child's problems or who have the best relationship with the parents are the ones who should be involved. However, the number of professional participants should be kept small so that real dialogue can take place and so that the session will not just evolve into the presentation of reports. The roles each professional will take in the parent conference and who will present what information should be decided ahead of time so that the information can be given to parents in an organized and integrated manner. To ensure that the information presented to the parents is as clear as possible, there must be agreement among the team members about the assessment results and recommendations. In addition, when deciding how to present the information, the team ought to take into consideration the family's background, culture, and comfort in the situation.

The feedback should take place in a comfortable room, free of interruption and disturbances. The child should not be present for the parent feedback session, but he or she can receive feedback from a staff member outside of the parent conference if this is thought to be appropriate.

One member of the team—the person who chairs the parent conferences—should be designated as the contact and follow-up person for the parents. If the information to be given to the parents is complex, or if it is thought that the parents might have difficulty really hearing the information, several feedback sessions might be planned. In fact, most parent conferences should be scheduled for a longer period of time than is usual (1 hour) so that the parents will not have to leave the conference before major issues are fully resolved.

The major objective in the feedback session is to provide the parents with information about their child in order for them to understand the nature of the child's disability. During such sessions, the parents must be given support and should be encouraged to ask questions so that their initial feelings about the findings can be dealt with. When this objective has been achieved, the parents can then be enlisted to help the child (directly through their own day-to-day behavior, and indirectly through supporting and advocating appropriate programming).

CONDUCTING THE FEEDBACK CONFERENCE

The professional who is selected to conduct the parent conference can begin by introducing the staff members and explaining their role. This should be done even though the parents may have briefly met the staff members previously and is important because it can be difficult for some parents to admit that a professional's role has been forgotten in the press of the evaluation. Next, the parents can be asked how they feel the evaluation has gone and whether they have major concerns about the process. The time to deal with complaints is before giving the data. When this is done, the parents are less likely to be preoccupied with issues they feel may have contaminated the evaluation process.

The reasons for the referral and the feedback conference may then be reiterated. If possible, descriptions of the child's behavior as given by the parents during the evaluation process should be introduced as explanatory examples of the child's problems. These concrete examples, which should be used to support each explanation, are much more meaningful to parents than hypothetical examples. The terms used in explaining the issues and and findings should be in lay language; professional jargon should definitely be avoided. Even though parents sometimes choose to use technical language, they may not understand the precise meanings of such language.

A stereotypic label for the child and his or her behavior should always be avoided. When using labeling terms to help the parents know how their child will be grouped for program purposes or treatment, great care should be taken in describing how the child's behavior fits and does not fit that designation. For example, no two children with autism are exactly alike and neither are children with Down

Syndrome, and so on. Indeed, the child's strengths and individuality should never be forgotten. The emphasis should not be exclusively on the child's dysfunction, but should also be on ameliorating or overcoming its effects in the child's adjustment and adult potential. At the end of the feedback session, the parents should be left with a picture of their child not as a syndrome—but as a child.

There are a number of issues that commonly arise during a parent conference which can trigger strong feelings on the part of the parents. To deal with these issues effectively, the psychologist or other staff member must be in touch with his or her own feelings about the child, about the handicap, and about his or her own professional responsibilities. There is no easy way to tell parents about a handicap, but the best procedure is to try to deal with the issues honestly and directly and to leave the parents with a sense that there are things that can be done that will help. Two of the most common problematic issues that often have to be discussed are presented next.

The first is the issue of mental retardation. Explaining to the parents that their child is retarded requires skill. This is because the label "mentally retarded" conjures up all sorts of disparate images to parents. They may envision a child who is behind but who will catch up given enough time, or they may visualize a child who will never learn anything and will never grow up. To combat this problem, the parents who are being told that their child is "retarded" should be asked what that term means to them. Their response can be used as a basis for discussing how the child does and does not fit this description. The distribution of achievement within the retarded range as it relates to the normal curve can be graphically shown to the parents. As has already been noted, the professional should present problems of predicted future development fairly. Parents need to understand that no one can say with great certainty what will happen to the child in adolescence or adulthood.

A second "loaded" issue involves emotional disturbance. A description of the problematic behavior and a comparison of it with the normal behavior of other chil-

dren can be useful in helping the parents to see there is reason for concern. It will also help them to see what is needed to bring the child's behavior closer to normal. Often, the mention of "emotional disturbance" engenders guilt in the parents who think that when a child has an emotional problem it is the parents' fault. Even when it is clear that the parents have significantly contributed to the problem, it is better to focus on what can be done to help the child. Acknowledging that changes in parents' behavior may be helpful but assigning specific blame is counterproductive.

DEALING EFFECTIVELY WITH PARENTS' FEELINGS DURING THE CONFERENCE

The parents of a handicapped child, like all of us, have conflicting feelings about what is being discussed. The psychologist must be sensitive to the fact that parents may defend themselves against the implications of the findings. The clinician should allow the parents to express their negative feelings and question what has been said without getting defensive, and without repeating the same information again and again to help it "sink in." While the psychologist must assist the parents in confronting the issues, such help should be given in a gentle and supportive manner. Even if the parents do not really incorporate what was said during the session, a positive relationship can be built with them so that they will be willing to come back when they are more ready to really hear what is being said. This process may take a few weeks, or in some cases it may take a few years; nevertheless, it is vitally important for the future functioning of the child.

Earlier in this chapter, parental reactions of grief and coping were discussed. Next we will discuss how the psychologist can specifically deal with five common parental reactions.

The wish not to admit to the problem is often a first response of parents in a feedback session. As has been previously noted, the parents should be allowed to express these feelings of disbelief. But how can the clinician respond? In some instances, referral to others for a second opinion should be suggested. This would no doubt be preferable to trying to strip the parents of their defensive response. Often, the clinician who listens patiently to parents' reasons for not believing what is said and who supports their feelings will make it easier for parents to move past this response.

A second common parental response is passivity. While the lack of response from parents can be interpreted as a sign that they understand what is being said to them and have no need to comment or ask questions, this can be nothing more than wishful thinking on the psychologist's part. Most often, a passive response is a sign of resistance to what is being said. Parents who do not participate or who even ignore what is said can be indicating their shock, surprise, or denial. The temptation for the professional is to go quickly over the findings and terminate the conference; this should definitely be avoided. Instead, patient attempts should be made to draw the parents into a discussion by asking for comments or acknowledgment of various points, as well as by requesting them to recapitulate what has been said.

Verbal evasion is another common response of parents during a conference. Nothing can be more frustrating to a professional than a parent who engages in a number of evasive maneuvers by asking irrelevant questions, or who goes off on verbal tangents. In fact, some parents can be rather skillful in blocking attempts to give them information. This situation can frequently be handled not by an interpretation of their resistance; instead, the clinician can take a direct and firm approach that makes it clear that there is a need for the clinicians and parents to take turns in offering information in order for the conference to stay within reasonable time limits. Additional sessions to help parents discuss issues that are important to them should also be offered.

If parents become angry during a conference, it is easy for the psychologist to become angry in return or to withdraw from the situation. A more effective strategy involves trying to determine why the parents are angry. With this information,

the clinician can work to eventually restore a more appropriate forum for discussion. It is important that the psychologist not become defensive; instead, he or she must acknowledge the parents' feelings without being judgmental.

One final response that can be frequently expected from parents is crying. When parents cry, psychologists often become distressed themselves and have difficulty knowing what to do. Professionals who are not experienced with feedback sessions frequently feel guilty for making the parents cry; this guilty feeling is a normal response. One danger, however, is that the inexperienced clinician feels helpless to change the situation unless he or she takes back what has just been said to the parents; obviously, this is unproductive. Another frequent response is to ignore the crying parent—a response which can make that parent feel even worse. The clinician should remember that the crying can be as a result of the shock, or it may be part of the process of working through grief. A better way to handle the situation is for the psychologist to acknowledge that the crying is appropriate because sad circumstances are being discussed. Allowing parents to feel badly openly helps them come to grips with the problem.

Having conducted a feedback session with sensitivity to parents' needs and feelings, the professional must bring the session to a conclusion. At the end of the conference, a brief review of the major points and recommendations can help to assure that there has been effective communication. The parents must leave the session knowing what their responsibilities are for carrying out the recommendations, and the psychologist and other staff members must know what they will do. The assignment of responsibilities to the parents will, of course, vary, depending on what each can be expected to do given their own circumstances; then staff responsibilities can be assigned.

One of the most awkward situations in the conference can involve asking the parents to obtain individual or group counseling for themselves. Because the parents were not the focus of the evaluation, the recommendation for parents to seek help usually has to be tied to the recommendations for the child. This must be done in a manner that will not make the parents feel unduly guilty. Finally, the staff members should establish an appropriate time schedule to monitor the implementation of the recommendations, including the response of the parents and other involved agencies.

SUMMARY

In summary, the psychologist should remember that the feedback session is a time of crisis for parents who may be learning that their child has a developmental handicap. Parents may exhibit signs of grief, including shock, disbelief, and a longing for what has been lost; in addition, they may show signs of resolving the loss through development of coping mechanisms. Parents may also exhibit symptoms of stress and may be unrealistic about their child's current status and developmental future.

The clinician who conducts parent conferences must be sensitive to the parents' feelings and needs; to do this, he or she must examine personal feelings about handicapping conditions. Parents must be given hope during the conference, but care must be taken to ensure that the hope is not unrealistic. Parents must be involved in the evaluation process from the start so that they feel involved in the feedback session.

The team who will participate in the conference must decide in advance who the leader will be and should ensure that information presented to the parents is not contradictory.

When conducting a feedback session, the psychologist should review the child's problems, using examples of everyday behavior, and should present findings in layperson's terms. Topics likely to evoke strong emotional responses in parents include mental retardation and emotional disturbance. Psychologists should be prepared to deal with such typical parental responses as denial, passivity, verbal evasion, anger, and crying. We should, however, not forget that it is the parents who have a long, hard road ahead of them.

REFERENCES

Adams JE, Lindemann E: Coping with long-term disability. In Cuelho G, Hamburg DA, Adams JE (eds): *Coping and Adaption.* New York: Basic Books, 1974

Allport G: *Becoming.* New Haven, CT: Yale University Press, 1955

Barclay A, Vaught G: Maternal estimates of future achievement in cerebral palsied children. Am J Ment Defic 69:62–65, 1964

Caplan G: *Principles of Preventive Psychiatry.* New York: Basic Books, 1964

Crocker AC, Cushna B: Ethical considerations and attitudes in the field of developmental disorders. In Johnson RB, Magrab PR (eds): *Developmental Disorders.* Baltimore, MD: University Park Press, 1976

Featherstone H: *A Difference in the Family: Life with a Disabled Child.* New York: Basic Books, 1980, p 12

Gottswald H: *Public Awareness about Mental Retardation.* Arlington, VA: The Council for Exceptional Children, 1970

Hamburg D, Adams JE: A perspective in coping behavior. Arch Gen Psychiat 17:277–284, 1967

Janis AS: Vigilance and decision-making in personal crisis. In Cuelho, GV, Hamburg DA, Adams JE (eds): *Coping and Adaptation.* New York: Basic Books, 1974

Kahn R, Antonucci T: Faltering economy takes its toll on America's mental health, social psychologists say. Inst Soc Res News 8(4):3,4,8, 1980

Lindemann E: Symptomatology and management of acute grief. Am J Psychiat 101:141–148, 1944

Lindemann E: The timing of psychotherapy. *6th International Congress of Psychotherapy: Selected Lectures.* New York: S. Krager-Basel, 1965, pp 75–90

Meyerowitz JH: Parental awareness of retardation. Am J Ment Defici 71:637–643, 1967

Pedulla B: *Mothers' Perceptions of their Retarded Children's Development: The Relationship of Selected Mother and Child Variables to Realism.* Unpublished doctoral dissertation, Boston College, 1975

Rogers C: Empathic: An unappreciated way of being. Counsel Psychol 5:2–10, 1975

Roos P: Psychological counseling with parents of retarded children. Ment Retard 1:345–350, 1963

Ross AO: *The Exceptional Child in the Family.* New York: Grune & Stratton, 1964

Sarason SB: *Psychological Problems in Mental Deficiency.* New York: Harper & Row, 1959

Schlesinger HS, Meadow KP: Emotional support to parents: How, when, and by whom? In Lillie L (ed): *Parent Programs in Child Development Centers,* 1972

Stress in Families with a Mentally Handicapped Child. London: National Society for Mentally Handicapped Children, 1967

Taft J: Dynamics of Therapy in a Controlled Relationship, rev ed. Gloucester, MA: Dover Publications, 1973

White RW: Strategies in adaption: An attempt at systematic description. In Cuelho GV, Hamburg DA, Adams JE (eds): *Coping and Adaption.* New York: Basic Books, 1974

Wolfensberger W: Counseling parents of the retarded. In Baumeister AA (ed): *Mental Retardation: Appraisal, Education, and Rehabilitation.* Chicago, IL: Aldine, 1967

Wolfensberger W: *The Principle of Normalization in Human Services.* Toronto: National Institute on Mental Retardation, 1972

Wofensberger W, Kurtz RA: Measurement of parents' perceptions of their children's development. Genet Psychol Monogr 83:3–92, 1971

Zadig JM, Crocker AC: A center for study of the young child with developmental delay. In Friedlander BZ, Sterrit G, Kirk G (eds): *Exceptional Infant,* vol 3. New York: Brunner/Mazel, 1975

APPENDICES

part four

Appendix A

OVERVIEW OF ASSESSMENT TECHNIQUES

By

KAREN E. HOSKING AND GORDON ULREY

The purpose of this chapter is to discuss factors relevant to the cognitive assessment of infants and preschool children. Some general guidelines for test selection are presented, as well as specific information about the most widely used and useful procedures. What can be learned from the results of the assessment in terms of current functioning and cognitive potential is also discussed.

FACTORS IN TEST SELECTION

Purpose of the Evaluation

The purpose of the psychological evaluation is a major factor in deciding which tests and procedures are appropriate. What questions have been asked about the child by the referring person or agency? The selection of tests should initially be based on the specific questions being asked. These questions usually concern the cognitive level of the child and/or the child's emotional development. Some questions psychologists can be helpful in sorting out are: What is the child's intellectual level? What are the child's strengths and weaknesses? What are the child's specific learning styles? Is the child developmentally delayed, and if so, to what extent? Does the child have a specific learning disability? Is the child's potential different from his or her current level of functioning?

Another important factor influencing

test selection is whether or not the evaluation calls for screening, or whether it requires a comprehensive evaluation. Screening is quicker and less comprehensive than a full evaluation and usually involves a single test, which may be given by different kinds of professionals. Screening tests are designed primarily to select from larger numbers of children those who need more comprehensive assessment. These tests are useful in determining if further information is needed; however, a child should never be placed in a special program based solely on data from a screening test. For an in-depth review of screening tests and procedures see Frankenburg and Camp (1975).

A more comprehensive evaluation is indicated if (1) a child fails a developmental screening test, (2) parents or teachers report concerns about a child's level of development or specific learning difficulties, or (3) a special intervention or educational program is being planned. This appendix focuses primarily on the selection of test procedures for a comprehensive evaluation of cognitive functioning.

Behavior of the Child

The behavior of the child must be taken into account in selecting appropriate assessment procedures. Important sources of information about the child's behavior include not only the psychologist's observations, but must also include reports from parents, teachers, and other significant persons in the child's life. The psychologist needs to know if there are behaviors that might interfere with testing, such as an attentional deficit, extreme interpersonal anxiety, or overactivity.

These interfering behaviors will have an effect on the selection of appropriate test procedures. For example, if a child experiences extreme interpersonal anxiety, it can be helpful to use a test with many nonverbal items, since some children can be made more comfortable by doing nonverbal, noninteractional tasks before going on to verbal items. On the other hand, some children—especially those with a perceptual motor problem—may be made more comfortable by beginning with verbal items or more verbally oriented tests.

While it is important to the psychologist to select tests based upon a full picture of the child's abilities in verbal, nonverbal, and perceptual-motor areas, the order in which items and tests are presented can also have an important impact on the child's performance. Some behavioral considerations relevant to the use of specific tests are discussed below.

Does the Child Have Any Known Deficits?

An important consideration in test selection is whether or not the child has any known deficits. Deficits may be generally categorized as cognitive (for example, retardation or a specific learning or behavioral/emotional disability), language, and/or physical (for example, a sensory or motor deficit, or a medical or neurologic condition). While there are some ways to adapt standard cognitive tests for these difficulties (some of which are discussed below), it is also important to note that specialized tests for handicapped or multihandicapped children may be necessary. The more standard assessment techniques may be used to supplement these specialized tests or adapted test procedures.

AVAILABLE TESTS

The discussion that follows is intended to be an introduction to some of the available tests and procedures used for cognitive assessment. It is not an exhaustive survey but rather reviews tests that are historically significant, widely used clinically, or useful supplements to widely used tests. Information about each test and potential uses are described, as are some of their limitations. See Table 1 for addresses of distributors for tests described in this appendix. See Table 2 for additional tests for young handicapped children and names and addresses of the distributors.

Infant Scales

Infant scales of behavior have been developed to study the course of normal mental development in the first few years of life, as well as to help in diagnosing developmental delays, brain damage, and physical and sensory disabilities. Infant scales typically consist of a number of sensorimotor behaviors or responses to objects and people as they emerge developmentally. The average age of emergence of each behavior is determined in the test's standardization.

Infant tests usually have several objects, such as blocks or a bell, which are used at a number of age levels. This makes it possible for the examiner to present the object to the infant, observe what the infant does spontaneously, and then score the behavior on a number of different items at once. For example, on the Bayley Scales of Infant Development, the age range of items that use 1-inch blocks alone is from 4 to 30 months. By presenting several of these objects that span a relatively large age range, the examiner gets an idea of the infant's approximate developmental level. He or she can then begin to administer other items around this level in both directions until the infant passes a number of consecutive items (the *basal*) and fails a number of consecutive items (the *ceiling*). It is interesting to note that the sequence of the child's spontaneous behavior with an object frequently follows the expected developmental pattern; for example, the child frequently responds to the sound of a bell, localizes the sound, picks up the bell, examines the bell's details, and rings the bell.

Table 1   Distribution of Tests for Assessing Young Children

Arthur Adaptation of the Leiter International Performance Scale by Grace Arthur

Stoelting Co.
1350 South Kostner Avenue
Chicago, Illinois 60624

Assessment in Infancy: Ordinal Scales of Psychological Development by Ina C. Uzgiris and J. McVicker Hunt

University of Illinois Press
Urbana, Illinois 61801

Bayley Scales of Infant Development by Nancy Bayley

Psychological Corp.
757 Third Avenue
New York, New York 10017

Cattell Infant Intelligence Scale by Psyche Cattell

Psychological Corp.
757 Third Avenue
New York, New York 10017

Denver Developmental Screening Test (DDST) by William K. Frankenburg and Josiah B. Dodds

Ladoca Project and Publishing Foundation, Inc.
East 51st Avenue and Lincoln Street
Denver, Colorado 80216

Developmental Test of Visual-Motor Integration (VMI) by Keith E. Beery and Norman A. Buktenica

Follett Publishing Co.
18216 Bayberry Way
Irvine, California 92715

Gesell Developmental Schedules by Arthur Gesell, H. Knobloch, and B. Passamanick

Nigel Cox
69 Fawn Drive
Cheshire, Connecticut 06410

McCarthy Scales of Children's Abilities (MSCA) by Dorothy McCarthy

Psychological Corp.
757 Third Avenue
New York, New York 10017

Merrill-Palmer Preschool Performance Tests by Rachel Stutsman

Stoelting Co.
1350 South Kostner Avenue
Chicago, Illinois 60624

Wechsler Preschool and Primary Scale of Intelligence (WPPSI) by David Wechsler

Psychological Corp.
757 Third Avenue
New York, New York 10017

Table 2   Distribution of Additional Tests for Assessing Young Children

Assessment of Deaf Blind Children: The Callier-Azusa Scale by Robert D. Stillman

Evaluates motor development, perceptual development, language development, daily living, and socialization skills in deaf-blind children. May be used with low functioning deaf-blind children for whom other assessments are inappropriate.

Council for Exceptional Children
1920 Association Drive
Reston, Virginia 22901

Assessment Program of Early Learning Levels (APELL) by Eleanor V. Cochran and James L. Shannon

A screening and diagnostic test designed to isolate the strengths and weaknesses in the language, reading,

and math skills of children from 4½ to 7 years old. Machine scored. Takes about 20 minutes over the course of two sessions.

Edcodyne Corp.
1 City Boulevard West
Suite 935
Orange, California 92668

Assessment-Programming Guide for Infants and Preschoolers by W. Umansky

A guide to the systematic observation of infants and preschool children, designed to aid in determining the needs of a child and in educational program planning. Covers six developmental areas: motor, perceptual-motor, language, self-help, social-personal, and academic. Groups skills within each area by the age at which they appear in a majority of the population. Items are planned for spontaneous exhibition rather than for a structured test situation.

Table 2 Continued

Requires familiarity with the developmental scales and evaluation procedures outlined.

Developmental Services, Inc.
1541 Hutchins Avenue
Columbus, Indiana 47201

Balthazar Scales of Adaptive Behavior, I: Scales of Functional Independence by Earl E. Balthazar

Uses direct observation to assess self-help skills including eating, dressing, and toileting. Scoring procedures vary according to the skill being assessed. Results can be plotted on individual profiles. Envisions the use of ward staff as rater.

Consulting Psychologists Press
577 College Avenue
Palo Alto, California 94306

Balthazar Scales of Adaptive Behavior, II: Scales of Social Adaptation by Earl E. Balthazar

Uses direct observation to assess social coping behaviors in six categories: unadaptive self-directed behaviors, adaptive interpersonal behaviors, verbal communication, play activities, response to instructions, and nine checklist items of personal care and other behaviors. Scores are recorded as a frequency count per unit of time.

Envisions the use of ward staff as raters.

Consulting Psychologists Press
577 College Avenue
Palo Alto, California 94306

Bayley Scales of Infant Development: Modifications for Youngsters with Handicapped Conditions by H. Hoffman

A measure designed to assess cognitive development in handicapped babies, ages 2 to 30 months. Accomplishes this by circumventing the effects of their physical limitations. Derives an initial score using the standard Bayley Scales of Infant Development. Achieves a second score by modifying standard testing procedures through changes in positioning the child, and/or additional team members or parents participating in the testing, and/or the use of alternative equipment that has physical qualities that allow the handicapped child to demonstrate understanding of the task required.

TMA Outreach Program
Suffolk Rehabilitation Center
159 Indian Head Road
Commack, New York 11725

Birth to Three Developmental Scale by Tina E. Bangs and Susan Dodson

A scale designed for the early detection and assessment of developmental delay in four behavioral areas: oral language, problem solving, social/personal, and motor. Directed to children from newborn to age 3. Includes a manual, five different scoring forms, and a pad of fifty scoring forms.

Teaching Resources Corp.
100 Boylston Street
Boston, Massachusetts 02116

Columbia Mental Maturity Scale, 3rd ed. by Bessie B. Burgermeister, L. Blum, and I. Lorge

An individual test of mental ability for mental ages 3.5 to 10 years. Consists of drawings on cards from which the subject selects the drawing that does not belong. Requires no verbal and a minimum of motor response. Takes about 15 minutes. Includes twenty-five record forms, a manual, and a set of record forms.

Western Psychological Services
12031 Wilshire Boulevard
Los Angeles, California 90025

Developmental Assessment for Severely Handicapped (DASH) by Mary Kay Dykes

A test designed to assess the motor, language, self-help, social/emotional, and academic skills of severely handicapped individuals with mental ages between newborn and 6 years of age. Covers the student's level of independence, level of task approximation, time, rate, distance, and other mastery dimensions.

Exceptional Resources, Inc.
7701 Cameron Road
Suite 105
Austin, Texas 78752

Hiskey-Nebraska Test of Learning Aptitude by Marshall S. Hiskey

Consists of 124 test items arranged according to difficulty under 11 types of measurement for learners ages 3 to 16 years. Requires administrator to pantomime instructions for each item. Takes about 45 to 60 minutes. Skills tested include memory for colored objects, bead stringing, block building, paper folding, visual attention span, puzzle blocks, and pictorial analogies.

Marshall S. Hiskey
5640 Baldwin
Lincoln, Nebraska 68508

Table 2 Continued

System of Multicultural Pluralistic Assessment (SOMPA) by Jane R. Mercer and June F. Lewis

An integrated system for individual assessment of the cognitive abilities, sensorimotor abilities, and adaptive behavior of culturally different children 5 to 11 years old. Gathers information about a child through a three-part parent interview and a six-part direct examination of the student. Incorporates use of the Wechsler Intelligence Scale for Children (Revised) (WISC-R) and the Bender Visual Motor Gestalt Test. Yields an assessment profile. Requires approximately 60 minutes for the parent interview, 20 minutes for the individual

examination of the child, and the time to administer the Wechsler and Bender-Gestalt. Includes materials for twenty-five students, excluding the WISC-R and Bender-Gestalt, which are sold separately.

Test purchase restricted according to principles stated in *Ethical Standards for Psychologists.* Eligibility is determined by training and experience.

Norming data is available from the publisher.

Psychological Corp.
757 Third Avenue
New York, New York 10017

GESELL DEVELOPMENTAL SCHEDULES

Age Range.   One month to 7 years.

Date of Standardization.   1920s and 1930s.

Description of Standardization Sample. A homogeneous group of 107 boys and girls from carefully selected, white, middle class homes were seen longitudinally; that is, each child was tested periodically over a period of years.

Description of Test. The Gesell Schedules present procedures for evaluating observed behavior. Most items are purely observational, while others use a set of standard toys and objects. The items are grouped into four subtests:

1. Motor—includes gross and fine motor development, reaching, and grasping.

2. Adaptive behavior—includes visual motor coordination, solution of practical problems, and exploration of objects.

3. Language behavior—includes preverbal behaviors and gestural communication.

4. Personal-social—includes responses to other people, play behavior, and training in socially imposed situations.

Uses. This scale, which is used primarily by physicians, is rarely used by psychologists. It can be helpful in assessing children who are similar to the standardization sample, but the small and homogeneous nature of the sample limits the usefulness of its norms. The directions for giving and scoring the Gesell tests are short and somewhat objective. Thus, the Gesell

is more useful for obtaining a description of a child's abilities rather than for comparing the child with other children.

Psychometric Properties. The reliability and validity of these schedules have not been adequately studied. The scale and clinical applications are described in depth by Knobloch and Passmanick (1974).

CATTELL INFANT INTELLIGENCE SCALE

Age Range. Two months to 36 months.

Date of Standardization. 1930s.

Description of Standardization Sample. A total of 1346 examinations were made on 274 children who were from white, middle class families residing in the Boston, Massachusetts, area. Like Gesell's sample, the children were selected prenatally if all evidence pointed to the delivery of a normal child.

Description of Test. The Cattell (1940) contains a number of varied and interesting tasks arranged into an age scale. This means that test items that are passed by the average child of a given age are grouped together. For example, the six test items that occur at the 17-to 18-month level are items the average 17-to 18-month-old child passed. The test has many motor, perceptual-motor, and imitation items at the earlier age levels, but at the later ages it contains more cognitive and language items.

Uses. The age-scale format of the Cattell facilitates translating a child's behavior into an age equivalent. This also helps the examiner to know when to stop testing. Many of the early items are identical to items from the Bayley Scales of Infant Development, but there are fewer items at each age level. The Cattell therefore can be given more quickly than the Bayley, but it is not as sensitive an instrument. The Cattell is useful when testing an older infant or a young preschool-age child. The items at the upper end of the Cattell (28 months and above) are from the Stanford-Binet Intelligence Test, a widely used test for preschoolers. When testing a child who is functioning around this age level, a smooth transition can be made from the Cattell to the Stanford-Binet. One limitation of the Cattell is the small size and narrow range of its standardization sample.

Psychometric Properties. This test's validity and split-half reliability is very low for infants 3 months of age and below. Reported levels of reliability and validity are acceptable for clinical use by 6 to 24 months of age. A comparison of the scores on the Bayley and Cattell by Erikson, Johnson, and Campbell (1970) reported sufficient correlations between the scales to use them interchangeably.

BAYLEY SCALES OF INFANT DEVELOPMENT

Age Range. Birth to 30 months.
Date of Standardization. 1958 to 1960.
Description of Standardization Sample. This is a sample of 1262 American children stratified for sex, white-non-white, urban-rural residence, and educational level of head of household.
Description of Test. The Bayley (1969) has three parts, including a mental scale, a motor scale, and an infant behavior record. The mental scale is designed to assess perceptual abilities, object permanence, memory, problem-solving skills, the beginning of language, and the beginning of abstract and symbolic thinking. The motor scale consists of items designed to assess motor development and coordina-

tion. The behavior record helps the examiner to assess the child's social, behavioral, and emotional functioning. There are many colorful materials and varied tasks. A useful feature of the Bayley is that the average age at which children pass each item is given, as is the normal range. For example, the median age at which a child can build a tower of three cubes is 16 months, but the age range that is still considered average (±2 standard deviations) for this skill is 13 to 21 months. This format therefore helps the examiner to assess deviations from the mean.

Uses. The Bayley is the most widely used infant test. It is preferred because it has the newest and most representative norms; it is also popular because it is constructed so that the clinician can compare a child's function in three broad areas (mental, motor, and behavior) to the *same* sample. This way, differences in a child's *relative* placement in the three areas are not attributable to comparison with three different samples. Because many of the tasks are imitative motor tasks, the Bayley is less useful for children with impaired motor function; however, at the upper level the tasks are more abstract, and language items are more frequent.

Psychometric Properties. The Bayley has been shown to be a reliable instrument for use with infants—although as with all infant tests, it is not predictive of later intellectual levels of nonhandicapped children. Its concurrent validity is demonstrated by high positive correlations with other infant tests, such as the Cattell and Gesell (Bayley, 1969).

INFANT PSYCHOLOGICAL DEVELOPMENT SCALE (IPDS)

Description of Test. The infant tests mentioned above (the Gesell, the Cattell, and the Bayley) are norm-referenced. That is, they are based on what the average infant does at different ages on a variety of tasks that may appear to be totally unrelated. In contrast to norm-referenced tests is the Infant Psychological Development Scale (IPDS). This scale is based on Piaget's model of development in the first 2 years of life, which was generally called the sensorimotor period. The IPDS is a criterion-referenced test. This means that a child is evaluated not according to any group norms, but only with respect to whether or not he or she can do certain tasks, or whether or not his or her behavior meets certain criteria. The tasks reflect the developmental sequence of a number of sensorimotor skills, such as imitation, object permanence, and understanding means-ends relationships. This test is useful in determining the child's current sensorimotor skills but does not yield age-ralated scores or a measure of general cognitive ability. Because the skills represented on this scale are arranged in a developmental sequence within areas of sensorimotor competence, it is an assessment tool that is also useful in planning interventions. Some clinical use of this scale and general principles of sensorimotor assessment are discussed in Chapter 4.

Tests for Preschool-age Children

In contrast to infant tests, cognitive tests for preschool-age children contain a wider variety of tasks. Relatively more abstract and language items are presented (both expressive and receptive). Perceptual-motor and imitation tasks are typically less frequent on preschool tests, and their nature is somewhat different. For example, the preschooler is required to do more visual- constructive tasks, some of which require abstract thinking. In general, tests for preschoolers are more predictive than infant tests of later cognitive ability and school achievement.

STANFORD-BINET INTELLIGENCE SCALE

Age Range. Two years to adult.

Date of Standardization. The latest standardization of the Stanford-Binet was carried out during 1971 and 1972 to update the norms to reflect performance of children in the 1970s. (The earlier normative data were from 1937.)

Description of Standardization Sample. A total of 2100 subjects were used, 100 at each Stanford-Binet age level (2 through 18 years). The children were drawn from seven mostly Western com-

munities. Some nonwhite and non-middle class subject participated, but the stratification was mainly to ensure proportionate representation of all ability levels within each age group.

Description of Test. The Stanford-Binet follows an age scale format. Six items are grouped into 6-month intervals for the levels between 2 and 5 years, at yearly intervals between 5 and 14 years, and at each of the four adult levels (average and superior I, II, and III). Each level has an alternate test for use when the administration of an item is spoiled. The Stanford-Binet consists primarily of verbal items, although the first four year levels contain both verbal and nonverbal tasks. The test yields a deviation IQ, although in the past a mental age was also determined. Since the 1972 norms do not fit the mental ages (developed from the 1937 norms) at many of the age levels, the mental ages should not be used.

Uses. The Stanford-Binet requires a verbal response at the 3-year level. It is not useful for children with significantly impaired sensory, motor, or language skills. However, one advantage of the Stanford-Binet is the large age range it covers. It is the most widely used test for preschool children because of its extremely good reliability and validity.

Psychometric Properties. Reported levels of reliability and concurrent validity are high (Terman and Merrill, 1972). Its predictive validity (correlation with later academic achievement) is the highest of any preschool measure of general intelligence (Anastasi, 1968).

MERRILL-PALMER SCALE OF MENTAL TESTS

Age Range. One-and-one-half years to 6 years.

Date of Standardization. 1960s.

Description of Standardization Sample. Six hundred thirty-one children, half boys and half girls, were obtained from a variety of sources in the Detroit, Michigan, area.

Description of Test. This test consists of verbal, perceptual-motor, and nonverbal cognitive test items grouped into 6-month age ranges. It contains numerous brightly colored objects and puzzles that have high intrinsic interest level to preschoolers. It can be administered and scored as a nonverbal test or as a combined verbal and nonverbal test. A mental age equivalent and an IQ can be obtained.

Uses. Because it can be administered as either a verbal or a nonverbal test, the Merrill-Palmer is extremely useful for evaluating the cognitive abilities of children with language delays. It provides measurement of strengths and weaknesses in motor skills and can also help in assessing a child's perceptual-motor skills relative to his or her more cognitive nonverbal problem-solving skills. Many of the items are timed, and this can be a problem, since speed may not yet be a goal for many preschool children. The high interest level of items makes this test very useful for assessing overactive or impulsive children. It can also be used as a supplementary test for children who are of normal intellectual ability but who are shy or anxious. The Merrill-Palmer norms are considered out of date and representative of a narrow sample of the population. Because it is poorly standardized, it is most useful when used to supplement better standardized tests, such as the Stanford-Binet or Bayley Scales. The examiner using the Merrill-Palmer Scale must be highly trained in assessing young children.

Psychometric Properties. Acceptable levels of reliability have been reported, but it has never been adequately validated. Correlations between the Merrill-Palmer and the Stanford-Binet vary widely (Anastasi, 1968).

THE EXTENDED MERRILL-PALMER SCALE

Age Range. Three years to 5 years.

Date of Standardization. 1969 and 1970.

Description of Standardization Sample. A sample of 1,242 white American children was roughly divided into equal numbers of boys and girls, and 3-, 4-, and 5-year-olds. One-half of the mothers were college graduates and another one-fourth were ninth-grade graduates.

Description of Test. This test was introduced 47 years after the original Merrill-Palmer. It has sixteen tasks that are designed to assess four abilities: semantic production and evaluation (roughly corresponding to verbal expression and understanding), and figural production and evaluation (roughly corresponding to perceptual-motor and cognitive nonverbal skills). Each of the four abilities is assessed individually; a single index of cognitive ability is not obtained. The extended scale uses some of the same materials as the original scale, but most are new. Unfortunately, the materials are less colorful and less intrinsically interesting than those of the original scale.

Uses. Unlike the original Merrill-Palmer, the extended scale requires a great deal of verbal mediation. This makes it less useful with children who are language impaired. The administration of the extended scale is also quite highly structured; therefore it is less flexible for use with children who are difficult to engage in the testing.

Psychometric Properties. This test is new, and its reliability and validity have not been adequately assessed.

LEITER INTERNATIONAL PERFORMANCE SCALE—ARTHUR ADAPTATION

Age Range. The age range of the original Leiter is from 2 years to adult. The Arthur Adaptation of the Leiter, the recommended manual for administration, covers ages 2 through 12 years. Arthur's standardization however, was on children 2 to 8 years of age.

Date of Standardization. 1940s.

Description of Standardization Sample. A total of 289 middle class children, ages 3 through 7, made up the original standardization group. Three years later, 48 children were reexamined to evaluate test-retest performance.

Description of Test. The Arthur Adaptation of the Leiter (Arthur, 1947) consists of forty tasks arranged on an age scale. Each item uses 1-inch blocks, a formboard into which the blocks fit, and a stimulus card placed along the top of the formboard. The subject is required to sequence the blocks by placing them into the appropriate recess in a way suggested by the stimulus card. This can be done by simple matching or by conceptual matching. No verbal instructions are needed, and there is no time limit.

Uses. The Leiter was developed for use with hearing impaired or language disabled subjects. It is also sometimes useful with motor handicapped persons. The flexible administration of the early items is helpful in determining if the subject can learn a new task. One limitation of the Leiter is the small number of tasks at each age level. Because of its psychometric properties, its small and narrow standardization group, and the limited range of behavior sampled, the Leiter is a useful aid in clinical diagnosis rather than as a measure of general ability.

Psychometric Properties. Acceptable levels of reliability have been reported, but the standard deviation of the IQs at different age levels fluctuates considerably. The concurrent validity is variable, and the test correlates more highly with other nonverbal measures than with verbal measures.

McCARTHY SCALES OF CHILDREN'S ABILITIES

Age Range. Two-and-one-half years to 8½ years.

Date of Standardization. 1970 to 1971.

Description of Standardization Sample. A sample of 1,032 American children was stratified for sex, ethnic background (white-nonwhite), geographic region, and father's occupation.

Description of Test. The McCarthy is divided into six subscales that include eighteen subtests. One of the scales, the General Cognitive Index, is derived by combining the Verbal, Perceptual Performance, and Quantitative Scales, and is roughly equivalent to the Stanford-Binet IQ. In addition, there is a memory scale and a motor scale.

Uses. This test is most useful with young children who are not retarded but who have mild learning deficits. Its construction represents a more systematic attempt than the Stanford-Binet to analyze strengths and weaknesses within specific developmental cognitive areas. Because it

has many different tasks and colorful, high-interest materials, it can be good for children who are inattentive or hard to motivate; however, its length may require that it be administered in two or more sessions. The results are difficult to interpret unless the entire test is given.

Psychometric Properties. The reported reliability is appropriate for clinical use, but validity data (especially concurrent validity) are incomplete. The reliability coefficients are high for general cognitive ability but are lower for the subscales. The clinical uses of the McCarthy Scales have been reviewed in depth by Kauffman and Kauffman (1977).

WECHSLER PRESCHOOL AND PRIMARY SCALE OF INTELLIGENCE (WPPSI)

Age Range. Four years to 6½ years.

Date of Standardization. 1953 to 1966.

Description of Standardization Sample. A sample of 1,200 American children was stratified for sex, geographic region, place of residence (urban-rural), ethnic background (white-nonwhite), and father's occupation.

Description of Test. This test was modeled on Wechsler's widely used tests for older children and adults. It has eleven subtests divided into two scales, one with verbal tasks and one with nonverbal tasks. A child's performance can be evaluated individually on each of the subtests and can then be grouped to produce a verbal IQ, a performance IQ, and a full scale IQ.

Uses. A child must have verbal and performance skills at about the 3-year level to obtain a reliable measure of skills on this test. The norms, however, cannot be used unless the child is between 5 and 6½ years of age; this relatively restricted range limits the test's usefulness. The performance items can be used with language and/ or hearing impaired subjects, while several verbal subtests can be used with visually impaired children. The structure of the test allows for comparisons of individual subtest results, as well as of verbal and nonverbal skills.

Psychometric Properties. The reliability levels reported for the verbal, performance, and full scale scores are satisfactory; however, the reliability of the subtests is too low for individual use. The concurrent validity of the WPPSI, using the Stanford-Binet as the criterion, is satisfactory; however, the Stanford-Binet yields higher correlations with later academic achievement (Wechsler, 1967).

Structured Interview with an Informed Person

A structured interview with an informed person is an important way to obtain information and is the procedure most often used to supplement cognitive testing. This procedure consists of interviewing an adult (usually a parent) who is knowledgeable about the child's adaptive behavior in his or her natural environment. In a structured interview format, the parent is asked to describe the child's behavior on specific tasks that cannot be measured in formal testing. For example, a parent may be asked about the child's self-care skills and use of leisure time. An important side benefit of this kind of assessment procedure is the parent's response to it. Parents realize that the child's ability is not being diagnosed solely on the basis of what they may see as purely academic skills or in a situation in which they feel the child is anxious and not performing up to par. However, there are several general limitations of this procedure.

One limitation has to do with the reliability and accuracy of parental reports. Reports about a child from involved persons must be evaluated carefully. While these reports are sometimes very accurate and insightful, the psychologist must remember that these people—because of their involvement with and responsibility and concern for the child—are not always reliable, objective reporters. Parents, for example, may attempt to report accurately; however, they may tend to report what they wish was true rather than what is true. (The use of data from parents data and paraprofessionals is discussed further in Chapter 3.)

A second limitation concerns the factors that determine a person's level of adaptive behavior. Because a child's level of adaptive behavior and social maturity is strongly influenced by the environment, this procedure is more useful in determining actual levels of functioning rather than cognitive ability per se. For example, two children of the same intellectual ability would be expected to show a difference in their adaptive behavior if one lived in a deprived environment (for example, an institution), and the other lived in an enriched environment (for example, an intact, emotionally stable, upper middle class family). The ways in which interview procedures are used in conjunction with cognitive tests is discussed below.

Adaptive Behavior Scales

VINELAND SOCIAL MATURITY SCALE

Age Range.   Birth to adult.

Date of Standardization.   1930 to 1935.

Description of Standardization Sample.   Subjects were obtained through door-to-door interviewing by one person in Vineland, New Jersey, an area considered as "progressive semi-rural." Ten males and ten females at each age from birth to age 30 years were studied, yielding a total sample of 620. The informant was usually the subject's mother.

Description of Test.   This scale provides age norms for behaviors which fall into eight categories: general self-help, eating skills, dressing skills, locomotion, communication, occupation, self-direction, and socialization. The scale consists of a brief manual that describes the behaviors to be assessed. In general, each behavior is scored according to whether or not it occurs or is beginning to emerge. The accompanying record form lists the 117 items in ascending order of difficulty. The items are divided into age periods of 1 year up to the 12th year, and longer periods up to 25 and more years. The average age of emergence of each behavior is also given. A social age and a social quotient can be obtained.

Uses.   The Vineland is useful as a supplement to cognitive test procedures to help determine a child's level of adaptive skills. It is frequently a critical part of the assessment of a severely or profoundly retarded person because it does not require test performance. Since each category of behavior does not occur at each age level, a refined analysis of skills is not always possible. The scale's usefulness is also limited by its relatively out-of-date norms and restricted sample. Another difficulty with the Vineland is that the descriptions of the behaviors are sometimes vague and ambiguous.

Psychometric Properties. Reliability is acceptable for clinical use. Correlations between the Vineland and the Stanford-Binet are sufficiently low to indicate that the two scales measure different aspects of functioning (Doll, 1965).

Other Adaptive Behavior Scales

Since this is a fairly new area of psychologic assessment, test development is in its early stages. Several scales of adaptive behavior are in use nationally, including the following.

1. The *Progress Assessment Chart of Social and Personal Development* was developed by H. C. Gunzburg in England as a way of systematically observing the social behavior of mentally retarded children and adults. Five levels of tasks are broken down into four areas: self-help, communication, socialization, and occupation. Each area is measured separately, allowing a profile of strengths and weaknesses to be determined. This scale has been found to be quite useful for educational programming, as well as description.

2. The *Adaptive Behavior Scale* is recommended by the American Association on Mental Deficiency for use with mentally retarded children and adults. Norms are available on performance of institutionalized and noninstitutionalized mentally retarded persons ranging from infancy to old age and representing all levels of retardation. Two major sections of the scale—adaptive behaviors and maladaptive behaviors—are broken down into a total of twenty-three subscales, which allows for detailed profiling and comparisons of skills across areas for an individual. This is probably the most widely used adaptive behavior measure in use today.

INTERPRETATION OF TEST RESULTS AND REPORTING DATA

A child's overall ability, as well as more specific skills, can be expressed in age levels. For example, an 18-month-old boy may be currently functioning at the 15-month level in gross motor development, but at the 20-month level in language skills. A 5-year-old child may be functioning at 5½-year level in general cognitive ability but may show perceptual-motor development at a 4½ year level. In addition to perceptual-motor functioning, age levels can frequently be obtained for the child's level of expressive and receptive language, fine motor development, and memory. Age levels in these more specific functions which are significantly below the child's overall level may indicate the presence of a learning disorder (see Chapter 13).

An examination of the child's behavior during test performance can provide the psychologist with more knowledge about the child's specific deficits. For example, a child who shows a perceptual-motor lag may have difficulty with pencil grasp, fine motor control, or visual-motor integration. A child who shows a language delay may exhibit difficulty processing two-step commands, difficulty with abstract thinking, or difficulty in discriminating between similar sounds.

Carefully observing the child and analyzing the test results also give valuable information about the child's "cognitive style." That is, what style does the child use in solving problems? Is his or her style systematic, or does it reflect random trial-and-error behavior? Has the child learned strategies to help compensate for deficits? Does the child have strengths that may be expanded to help him or her compensate for deficits?

Interviewing procedures (such as talking to the child, observing a play situation, and talking to the parents) are also used to help assess the child's level of cognitive functioning. Does the child relate to the interviewer in an age-appropriate manner? Is the complexity and content of the child's language appropriate? What level of cognitive functioning is suggested by the child's drawings and doll play? In a free play situation, does the child structure the environment in a way that is consistent with his or her chronologic age? (Chapter 7 presents a description of the play interview.) Scales of adaptive behavior give the psychologist important information about the child's level of functioning which cannot easily be obtained by direct observation. The child's self-care skills, independence, social maturity, and so on, can be compared with skills of other children of the same age, and delays can thus be detected. The child's abilities can also be expressed in age levels. For example, a 5-year-old child may have the eating and dressing skills of a 2-year-old.

Informal assessment procedures also serve as a reliability check on the formal cognitive measures. A discrepancy between formal test results and adaptive skills is usually diagnostically significant; this comparison is especially important if the child's test results suggest a significant developmental delay (two standard deviations below the mean). There may be several reasons that a child performs below age level on cognitive tests, only one of which is the presence of a genuine cognitive deficit. For example, the child may come from a deprived environment, may have serious emotional problems, or may have an inadequate school environment. If a child's performance is higher in general functioning than on formal tests, then a higher intellectual potential may be inferred. If the child functions at or above age level in adaptive skills, then a diagnosis of mental retardation based on intellectual testing cannot be made. If a child performs better on cognitive tests than on measures of adaptive behavior, then the child's environment should be looked at in more detail. Is the child being overprotected at home? Is the school setting unchallenging or otherwise ineffective in maintaining the child's interest?

Behavioral/Emotional

In addition to information about a child's level of cognitive functioning, formal cognitive tests (as well as the other assessment procedures) are rich sources of information about a child's behavioral and emotional development. Some important behaviors for the psychologist to note are how the child relates to the examiner, to other children, and to parents and adults. Other important behaviors include cooperation, self-confidence, attention span and level of activity, and anxiety level and response to such stress as failure. Does the child show bizarre behaviors or present a behavior management problem? (See Chapter 14 for more information.)

SUMMARY

When a child is referred for a comprehensive cognitive evaluation, there are several factors that have an important bearing on which test or procedures are selected. The child's behavior is very important, particularly if there are behaviors that will interfere with reliable test administration. The presence of known deficits, such as sensory or motor handicaps, is also an important consideration.

A large number of tests exist for evaluating both infants and preschoolers, and some of these have been reviewed along with their particular strengths or limitations in evaluating handicapped children. Additional procedures, such as parent interviews and scales used to assess functional living skills, are an important component of a comprehensive evaluation.

The comprehensive evaluation will typically yield information about a child's overall level of functioning, as well as about his or her ability in specific skill areas. Observing the child also provides valuable information about the child's methods of solving problems and emotional and behavioral development.

REFERENCES

Anastasi A: Psychological Testing, 3rd ed. New York: Macmillan Publishing Co, Inc, 1968

Arthur G: A Point Scale of Performance. (Revised form II): Manual for Administering and Scoring the Tests. New York: Psychological Corp, 1947

Bayley N: Infant Scales of Psychomotor and Mental Development. New York: Psychological Corp, 1969

Cattell P: The Measurement of Intelligence of Infants and Young Children. New York: Psychological Corp, 1940

Doll E: Vineland Social Maturity Scale: Condensed Manual of Directions, Rev ed. Circle Pines, MN: American Guidance Service, 1965

Erikson M, Johnson M, Campbell F: Relationships among scores on infant tests for children with developmental problems. Am J Ment Defic 75: 102–104, 1970

Frankenburg W, Camp B: Pediatric Screening Tests. Springfield, IL: Charles C Thomas, 1975

Kauffman A, Kauffman N: Clinical Evaluation of Young Children with the McCarthy Scales. New York: Grune & Stratton, 1977

Knobloch H, Passamanick B (eds): Gesell and Amatruda's Developmental Diagnosis: The Evaluation and Management of Normal and Abnormal Neuropsychologic Development in Infancy and Early Childhood. New York: Harper & Row, 1974

Terman E, Merrill M: Stanford-Binet Intelligence Scale Manual, 4th ed. Boston: Houghton-Mifflin, 1972

Wechsler D: Wechsler Preschool and Primary Scale of Intelligence: Manual. New York: Psychological Corp, 1967

Appendix B

COGNITION*

By

SALLY J. ROGERS AND ELEANOR W. LYNCH

The cognition section of the *Preschool Developmental Profile* is based on the preoperational stage of thought theorized by Jean Piaget. We chose to focus on preoperational thought because it is an area that has been long neglected by cognitive theorists who tend to describe preoperational thought in terms of its deficits—the child can't conserve, can't reverse, can't de-center, etc. Yet preschoolers develop many cognitive skills long before they become operational thinkers, and these preoperational cognitive skills are the foundation for the child's construction of concrete operations.

The items on the cognition section, because they describe the child's developing understanding of the physical world, do not assess the typical school readiness skills found in most preschool scales. Rather, they examine the cognitive constructs which are prerequisites to academic learning. The cognitive skills examined here include classification, number, space (spatial relations), seriation, and time (temporal relations).

The classification items assess the child's ability to group objects into classes and subclasses based on various characteristics of the objects, a skill necessary for understanding mathematics and science. The number items assess the child's understanding of quantity and of the characteristics of cardinal numbers. The spatial relations items assess the child's understanding of the positional relationships

among objects. The seriation items assess the child's ability to compare and order objects according to various properties of objects, a concept fundamental to understanding mathematics. The time items assess the child's understanding of such temporal relationships as age, relative speed of objects, and using time to order events.

The cognition section was constructed quite differently from the other sections in the profile. The other sections are a compilation of developmental tasks which have for the most part been used by many people for many years to assess development, and have thus been standardized in various studies. The cognition section, however, examines preschoolers' cognitive abilities in a fairly novel way. Few other authors have looked at preschoolers' thought from a Piagetian perspective, and there is not a group of standardized test items in the developmental literature which could be integrated into a cognition section for the purpose of this profile.

Thus most of the items in the cognition section are original. Some were developed by the authors from Piaget's descriptions of his observations and experiments as he compared preoperational and operational abilities of children in the 4- to 9-year age range. Other items came from the authors' many experiences with preoperational children, both handicapped and nonhandicapped. The authors compiled a group of sixty items and then set about to see how well these items reflected cognitive growth in preschoolers by testing the items on a group of ninety-two children.

The children were drawn from three preschool/day care settings in southern Missouri. All the children were white and

*Developmental Programming for Infants and Young Children, Volume 4: Preschool Assessment & Application. University of Michigan Press, 1981, Ann Arbor, Michigan. Reproduced with permission.

the group included both lower and middle socioeconomic levels. According to psychometric results from this group, the children seemed to be a typical group of young children in preschool programs, a little above average on intelligence tests but generally within one standard deviation of the mean. The group had several members who were functioning quite a bit below the mean, as well as several who were much higher than the mean.

Scalogram analyses were performed on each of the five cognitive subscales (classification, number, space, seriation, time) to determine whether there was any inherent developmental order to the skills, whether there was a set sequence to the way these various skills emerged. All five sets of items revealed such a sequence on the way the sample group of children performed on the items. In three of the five subscales (number, space, seriation) all the items are arranged in an order which represents statistical significance. Thus, the order of items on these three subscales represents the order in which the sample children consistently performed. On the other two subscales, classification and time, some, but not all, of the items formed such a statistically significant scale. However, items which did not reach statistical significance were also included, and marked with double asterisks (**), because these items reflect important cognitive skills which should be part of developmental programming in the cognitive area. The order for these items was determined by the mean age of children passing the items.

The age levels for each item were arrived at in the following way. First, all children in the sample were grouped into six age ranges (year and month): 3.0 to 3.6; 3.7 to 3.12; 4.1 to 4.6; 4.7 to 4.12; 5.1 to 5.6; 5.7 to 5.12. The criterion for including any item at a specific age range was 50 percent passing. Thus, for example, if 50 percent or more of the children in the 4.1 to 4.6 age range passed an item, then that item was assigned a 4 to 4½ age range. Of course, 50 percent or more of children in older ranges would also pass that item. Thus each item is placed at the lowest level at which 50 percent of the sample children passed. Not all age ranges are represented in all subscales. These age ranges should be considered *very* approximate, since ninety-two children divided into six groups makes only fifteen per group on the average. Thus the age ranges are based on a very small sample of children.

For more detailed information on the statistical analyses of the sample's performance on the cognition section, contact Sally J. Rogers.

EQUIPMENT NEEDED

Sample sheet pictures and cards
Twelve 1-inch red cubes and three 1-inch blue cubes
Ten cards each 3-by-3 inches, with one number from 1 to 10 printed on each
Tennis ball
Pencil
Comb
Key
Spoon

CLASSIFICATION

3–3½ YEARS

36. **Tells whether pictures are the same or different (see sample sheet)**
Place the picture of a banana and the picture of a car in front of the child. Ask if they are the same or different. Place two of the pictures of cars in front of the child. Ask if they are the same or different. Place the pictures of the triangle and the square in front of the child. Ask if they are the same or different. Pass if the child answers correctly on two out of three questions.

37. **Points to picture that doesn't belong (see sample sheet)**
Show the child the three-picture strip (fish, apple, apple). Ask the child, Which picture doesn't belong? Pass if the child points to the fish or says *fish*.

3½–4 YEARS

38. **Names things asked for by use**
Ask the child to tell you two things that s/he eats, wears, builds with, and rides in. If the child names only one,

prompt by saying, *What else? Name one more.* Pass if the child is able to name two things in at least three categories. This item can be modified to score a nonverbal response.

39. **Groups identical pictures (see sample sheet)**
Randomly place the four pictures of bananas and the four pictures of cars on the table in front of the child. Ask the child to put the ones that are the same together. Pass if the child groups all the pictures of bananas together and all the pictures of cars together.

40. **Names two things that are round**
Say to the child, *Tell me three things that are round.* If the child names only one or two, prompt by saying, *What else? Can you think of anything else?* Pass if the child names at least two objects. This item can be modified for a nonverbal child by asking the child to show you three things in the room that are round.

5–5½ YEARS

41. **Groups like pictures** (see sample sheet)**
Randomly place three pictures of plants, three pictures of animals, and three pictures of foods in front of the child in a matrix. Say to the child, *Put the pictures of foods that go together in the same pile.* Pass if the child correctly groups eight of the nine pictures.

42. **Groups pictures by use (see sample sheet)**
Randomly place the pictures of tools, clothes, and transportation in front of the child. Say, *Put the things that go together in the same pile.* Pass if the child places all but two pictures in the correct group.

5½–6 YEARS

43. **Describes similarities and differences**
Ask the child, *How are a man and a dog alike?* (Sample answers: they both eat, walk, are alive.) Then ask the child, *How are they different?* (Sample answers: a dog barks, a man doesn't; a dog walks on four legs, a man on two.) Pass if the child correctly answers both questions.

44. **Uses multiple classification**
Randomly place five red cubes and three blue cubes in front of the child. Ask the child, *Are there more red cubes (blocks) or more wooden cubes (blocks)?* Pass if the child answers *more wooden cubes (blocks).*

NUMBER

3–3½ YEARS

45. **Answers, *How many?* through two**
Place one 1-inch cube in front of the child. Say, *How many cubes (blocks) are there?* Add the second cube and say, *How many are there?* Pass if the child answers both correctly.

3½–4 YEARS

46. **Counts five objects using one-to-one correspondence.**
Place five 1-inch cubes in front of the child. Say, *Count how many. Point as you count.* Pass if the child counts and touches one cube for each number.

47. **Indicates the number of halves in a whole**
Say to the child, *If I cut a cookie in half, how many pieces will I have?* Pass if the child answers two or nonverbally indicates two.

4–4½ YEARS

48. **Answers, *How many?* through five**
Place three 1-inch cubes in front of the child. Say, *How many cubes (blocks) are there?* Repeat with four and five cubes. Pass if the child is correct on all.

49. **Names numerals 1 through 10**
Present the numeral cards one at a time in random order and say, *Tell me the name of this number. What's this number?* Pass if the child answers correctly on seven out of ten.

4½–5 YEARS

50. **Gives up to ten objects to the examiner when requested**
Place twelve 1-inch cubes in front of the child. Say, *Give me seven cubes (blocks).* Repeat with ten. Pass if the child is correct on one.

51. **Performs simple addition****
Say to the child, *If you have two rabbits and I give you one more, how many will you have?* Pass if the child answers three or nonverbally indicates three.

52. **Conserves five objects**
Put twelve cubes on the table and place five of the cubes in a line, an inch or so apart. Ask the child to match your line, to put out as many cubes as you have. Once s/he has, ask *Do I have more cubes (blocks), or do you have more, or are they the same?* If the child does not say the same, tell him/her to make them the same. Then spread your line of blocks out much farther apart, and ask, *Now, do I have more, or do you have more, or are they the same?* Then mass your cubes into a heap, and ask the child the same question. Pass if the child answers all three questions correctly.

5–5½ YEARS

53. **Performs simple subtraction****
Place seven 1-inch cubes in front of the child. Say, *Give me all but three cubes (blocks).* Pass if the child gives you four cubes.

SPACE

3–3½ YEARS

54. **Names familiar objects through tactile recognition**
Seat the child at a table high enough so that s/he can reach well under the table and ask the child to place his/her hands under the table. Place the following objects, one at a time, in the child's hands so s/he cannot see the objects: tennis ball, pencil, comb, key, spoon. In each case, tell the child to

feel the object and tell you what it is. Pass if the child gets three or more correct. This item can be modified to score a nonverbal response.

55. **Tactually matches forms which differ topologically to a visual model (see sample sheet)**
With the child seated at the table as described in item 54, place the cardboard cutout of the circle and the doughnut on the table. Tell the child, *I'm going to give you a shape which is like one of these. Feel the shape, then give it back to me and show me which one you had.* Place the circle or doughnut shape in the child's hand. After she has felt it, ask for it back, and then ask the child to show you the shape it matches. Remove the shapes and present the shapes of the doughnut and arch, then the arch and jagged arch. Each time present one matching shape of the pair for the child to feel. Pass if the child chooses the correct shape two out of three times.

3½–4 YEARS

56. **Reproduces forms representing topological relations (see sample sheet)**
Put one topological relations card in front of the child and lay one large circle cutout below the card. Give the child a small circle cutout and ask the child to place the small circle so it matches the cutout picture above it. Repeat with the other two cards. Pass if the child places the small circle correctly for two of the three cards.

57. **Visually and tactually matches Euclidean forms (see sample sheet)**
Place the cardboard cutouts of a circle and a square in front of the child. Then tell the child that you will be handing him/her some shapes and you want him/her to show you whether each one is more like the circle or the square. Hand the child the diamond and ask the child to show you which it is more like. Do the same for the circle, rectangle, ellipse, and triangle. Pass if the child responds correctly for all the shapes.

4-4½ YEARS

58. **Arranges objects in a straight line by using table edge**
Place two cubes 12 to 15 inches apart and 3 to 4 inches from the table edge. Hand the child eight cubes and tell him/her, *These soldiers have to be put in a very, very straight line along the road. This soldier is at the beginning of the road, and this one is at the end. You arrange the rest of the soldiers in a straight, even line.* Pass if the child forms a relatively straight line with the cubes spread fairly evenly.

59. **Reproduces a straight sequence with model present (see sample sheet)**
Using both sets of animal cards, select six of one set and place them in a line and give the other set of nine to the child. Then tell the child, *The animals are all lined up for a parade. Can you line your animals up just like mine?* Pass if the child chooses the correct animals and places them in the same order as the model.

4½-5 YEARS

60. **Reproduces circumscribed figures (see sample sheet)**
Place the cutouts of one triangle, two identical circles, one small circle, and one large circle in front of the child. Present the cards of the circumscribed figures to the child one at a time and ask the child to make the same figure using the circles and triangles in front of him/her. Pass if the child reproduces the figures correctly.

5½-6 YEARS

61. **Draws simple geometric forms from tactile model (see sample sheet)**
Hand the child the circle, triangle, rectangle, and x cutouts under the table, one at a time. Tell him/her to feel it carefully and then to give it back to you and draw the shape s/he just felt. Do this for each shape. Pass if the child draws all four recognizably. (Note: if reproducing the shape by drawing is difficult for the child, modify the response required by asking the child to

reproduce the shape with clay or sticks.)

62. **Reproduces a circular sequence with model present (see sample sheet)**
Using the same basic format as item 59, place six animals in a circle and tell the child, *The animals are all in a circle, like in a circus. See if you can make a circle with animals that is just like mine.* Offer no more help and pass if the child finally ends up with the correct animals and the correct sequence in a circle.

SERIATION

3-3½ YEARS

63. **Points to bigger, smaller, longer, shorter, taller (see sample sheet)**
Use cards with small and large circles, long and short sticks (horizontal presentation), tall and short glasses. Present each card twice, removing it from the child's sight and presenting it again, half the time reversing it, half the time not. Ask the child the following questions:

> *Show me which circle is bigger—the bigger circle.*
> *Show me which circle is smaller—the smaller circle.*
> *Show me which stick is longer.*
> *Show me which stick is shorter.*
> *Show me which glass is taller.*
> *Show me which glass is shorter.*

Pass if the child answers five out of six correctly.

3½-4 YEARS

64. **Seriates five items by matching (see sample sheet)**
Use two sets of five circles. Instruct the child to watch, and place one set of circles on the table. Then slowly arrange them in a line, in ascending order, saying, *The smallest one goes here, then the next largest here,* etc., until all are placed. Then, leaving those circles there, place the other set of circles on the table and instruct the child to arrange his/hers just like yours.

Give no help. Pass if the child arranges them correctly in ascending order without help, even if s/he initially makes errors, or succeeds by matching his/hers to yours.

65. Seriates three items (see sample sheet)

Give directly after item 64. Use the smallest-(first), third-, and fifth-sized circles. Ask the child to arrange them with the smallest one here (point to the child's left), then the middle one, then the largest one (do not indicate placement of the last two cards). Pass if the child correctly arranges the circles in ascending order without further help.

4½–5 YEARS

66. Makes one or more small series when asked to seriate seven items (see sample sheet)

Give the child all seven circles. Ask the child to arrange them from the smallest to largest beginning with the smallest one *here* (point to the child's left). Pass if the child's final order contains or more more three-circle series (smallest to largest) in either ascending or descending order. Note that the child is *not* required to seriate all seven correctly.

Example:

correct

67. Seriates a double row of four items each (see sample sheet)

Give the child the first to fourth circles and ask him/her to arrange them from smallest to largest. Then give the child the first to fourth stick cards and say, *Each stick goes with one circle. Would you please put each stick right below the circle it goes with? When you put them together they will look like trees (lollipops).* Pass if the child arranges both series correctly and in parallel.

5–5½ YEARS

68. Seriates five items by length and area (see sample sheet)

Use the first to fifth circles and the first to fifth sticks. Give directions as in item 66 first with the circles, then the sticks. Pass if both series are arranged correctly.

TIME

3–3½ YEARS

69. Predicts which car will win when shown a slow- and a fast-moving car (see sample sheet)

Using two car cards, tell the child that the cars are going to race to the edge of the table. Then move one car with each hand, beginning their movements at the same time from the same place (other edge of table) and move them rather slowly, but with one moving obviously faster than the other. When the fast car is one-half to two-thirds of the way across, ask the child to touch the car which is going to win. Pass if the child indicates the faster car.

3½–4 YEARS

70. Answers, *Why do we have clocks?*

Pass if the child gives an answer which is related to knowing what time it is. Do not pass if the answer does not relate to time, as in, *it ticks, cuckoos, alarm rings,* etc.

71. Answers questions about day and night

Ask the child, *What happens at night? What happens in the daytime?* Pass if the child answers one of the two questions with an activity that is only performed at night (go to sleep, go to bed, put on pajamas) or in the day (play outdoors, eat breakfast, go to school). This item can be modified for a nonverbal child by having the child point to pictures or act out the response.

72. Answers which part of a trip took longer (see sample sheet)

Lay out a small map in the following

way: on a piece of paper draw a vertical line the full length of the sheet (11 to 14 inches long). Then place the house card at the end of the line nearest the child; place the store card up one-third of the line and beside the line; draw two parallel lines intersecting the line at two-thirds of its length to represent train tracks; and put the beach card at the far end of the line. Now take one car card and drive it slowly along the road as you narrate, *Jimmy and his family are going to the beach today. First they leave their house and go to the store to buy some hot dogs. Then they reach the train tracks, look to see if there is a train, and drive across. Then they reach the beach and go swimming.* Then ask the child, *Did it take more time to get to the store or to get to the beach?* Pass if the child answers correctly.

73. **Predicts which car will take more time when moving at different speeds (see sample sheet)**
After item 72, return the first car to the house, and add the second car. This time tell the child, *Jimmy's family is going to the beach, and his grandpa is going too. Let's watch them go.* Begin both cars at once and move them slowly toward the beach, with one moving noticeably faster than the other. When the faster car is almost to the train tracks, tell the child, *Show me which car will take more time to get to the beach.* Pass if the child indicates correctly.

4½–5 YEARS

74. **Answers what landmark was passed before or after another****
Review the narration of item 72 and then ask the child, *Where did they go before they crossed the train tracks? Where did they go after they crossed the train tracks?* Pass if both are answered correctly.

75. **Answers, *Was your father ever a baby? Was I ever a baby?*****
Pass if both questions are answered *yes.*

5–5½ YEARS

76. **Orders landmarks**
Present this item immediately after item 74. Ask the child, *Where did Jimmy's family stop last? Where did they stop first? Where did they stop next?* Pass if two of the three questions are answered correctly.

77. **Answers *Which is longer, a minute or an hour? A day or a year?***
Pass if the child answers both correctly.

5½–6 YEARS

78. **Arranges three cards in correct temporal order (see sample sheet)**
Present the three dressing cards to the child, saying, *Here are pictures of Susan getting dressed. Which of these pictures would she do first?* If the child does not answer correctly, show the child the correct card and explain why—*First she has to put on her underpants.* Then ask, *Which does she do next? Which one does she do last?* Pass if the child correctly shows two out of three.

79. **Answers who was born before or after one another** (see sample sheet)**
Show the child cards of three children, each one larger than the next. As you lay out the first card say, *This is Jimmy. He is six years old.* Then present the next card: *This is Sandy. She is four years old.* Then the third card: *And here is Robin. She is three years old.* Then ask the child, *Now, who was born before Sandy? Who was born after Sandy?* Pass if both are answered correctly.

Name _____

ITEM NUMBER	DEVELOPMENTAL LEVELS AND ITEMS	DATE	DATE	DATE	DATE

Classification   3–3½ years

36	Tells whether pictures are the same or different				
37	Points to picture that doesn't belong				

3½–4 years

38	Names things asked for by use				
39	Groups identical pictures				
40	Names two things that are round				

5–5½ years

41	Groups like pictures**				
42	Groups pictures by use				

5½–6 years

43	Describes similarities and differences				
44	Uses multiple classification				

Number   3–3½ years

45	Answers, "How many?" through two				

3½–4 years

46	Counts five objects using one-to-one correspondence				
47	Indicates the number of halves in a whole				

4–4½ years

48	Answers, "How many?" through five				
49	Names numerals 1 through 10				

4½–5 years

50	Gives up to ten objects to the examiner when requested				
51	Performs simple addition**				
52	Conserves five objects				

ITEM NUMBER	DEVELOPMENTAL LEVELS AND ITEMS	DATE	DATE	DATE	DATE
	5–5½ years				
53	Performs simple subtraction**				

Space   3–3½ years

54	Names familiar objects through tactile recognition				
55	Tactually matches forms which differ topologically to a visual model				

3½–4 years

56	Reproduces forms representing topological relations				
57	Visually and tactually matches Euclidean forms				

4–4½ years

58	Arranges objects in a straight line by using table edge				
59	Reproduces a straight sequence with model present				

4½–5 years

60	Reproduces circumscribed figures				

5½–6 years

61	Draws simple geometric forms from tactile model				
62	Reproduces a circular sequence with model present				

Seriation   3–3½ years

63	Points to bigger, smaller, longer, shorter, taller				

3½–4 years

64	Seriates five items by matching				
65	Seriates three items				

4½–5 years

66	Makes one or more small series when asked to seriate seven items				
67	Seriates a double row of four items each				

ITEM NUMBER	DEVELOPMENTAL LEVELS AND ITEMS	DATE	DATE	DATE	DATE
	5–5½ years				
68	Seriates items by length and area				
Time	3–3½ years				
69	Predicts which car will win when shown a slow- and a fast-moving car				
	3½–4 years				
70	Answers, "Why do we have clocks?"				
71	Answers questions about day and night				
72	Answers which part of a trip took longer				
73	Predicts which car will take more time when moving at different speeds				
	4½–5 years				
74	Answers what landmark was passed before or after another**				
75	Answers, "Was your father ever a baby? Was I ever a baby?"				
	5–5½ years				
76	Orders landmarks				
77	Answers, "Which is longer, a minute or an hour? A day or a year?"				
	5½–6 years				
78	Arranges three cards in correct temporal order				
79	Answers who was born before or after another**				

Chapter Appendix C

PARENT QUESTIONNAIRE FOR PSYCHOLOGICAL EVALUATION
John F. Kennedy Child Development Center
University of Colorado School of Medicine

GENERAL INFORMATION

DATE_____

Child's Name_____Birthdate_____Sex   M   F

Home Address_____Phone_____

_____
County   City   State   Zip Code

Natural Father_____Birthdate_____

   Occupation_____Religion_____

   Ethnic Background_____Years of Schooling_____

   Health_____

Natural Mother_____Birthdate_____

   Occupation_____Religion_____

   Ethnic Background_____Years of Schooling_____

   Health_____

Family Income   Are you receiving public assistance?

  Before taxes: _____Under $5,000   (e.g., ADC, Medicaid) _____Yes _____ No

               _____ 5,000 - 10,000   If yes, please specify_____

               _____ 10,000 - 15,000

               _____ 15,000 - 20,000   Do you have insurance coverage other

               _____ 20,000 - 25,000   than via public assistance ___Yes ___No

               _____ Over 25,000   If yes, please specify_____

Who referred you here for evaluation? _____

What is it about your child that concerns you? _____

_____

_____

_____

When was it first noticed? _____

What have you been told with regard to the problem? _____

_____

_____

_____

What things do you presently <u>not</u> understand about your child? _____

_____

How do you think that we might be able to help you? _____

_____

_____

How do you feel your child can best be helped? _____

_____

_____

Additional information that you think would be of value, including results of
previous testing, (the parent/caretaker not primarily completing the questionnaire
is also encouraged to use this space, referring to the above question).

_____

_____

_____

_____

_____

_____

_____

_____

PREGNANCY HISTORY

Past pregnacies in this marriage: Number of times pregnant _____

Live Births _____Stillborn_____Miscarriages_____

List dates of past pregnacies; indicate if there was a miscarriage; threatened
miscarriage (bleeding); premature birth; twins; deformity or other difficulty with
live-born children; or any other complication. Please list any birth defects,
however unimportant you consider them.

Name	Birthdate	Birth Weight	Grade in School	Any School or Health Problems

PREGNANCY

Questions in this and the following section refer to the pregnacy of the child whose problem has caused you to seek assistance.

During which month did you start prenatal care? _____ Where? _____

Weight before pregnancy _____ Weight gain _____

Any weight loss in any part of pregnancy? _____

Medicines taken and when (include all, such as vitamins, birth control pills, etc., including aspirin if taken frequently) _____

_____

Did you smoke during the pregnancy? _____ How many cigarettes a day? _____

How much alcohol did you consume during your pregnancy? _____ Number of drinks/wk___

Any narcotic drugs during or prior to this pregnacy?_____

Any illness? _____

Did you have hay fever during pregancy? 1st 3 mo.____ 2nd 3 mo.____ last 3 mo.____

Is so, how high was fever? _____and for how long did it persist? ___hours or __days

Vaginal bleeding? _____High blood pressure? _____

Much morning sickness? _____Much swelling? _____

Hospitalizations? _____

Operations? _____

Accidents? _____

Unusual worries? _____

Special diet? _____

BIRTH HISTORY

Was the baby born on time, early, or late? _____

Any stimulation of labor used? _____ Type _____

Length of labor in hours _____ Length of hard labor _____

Type of delivery:

    Natural (vaginal) _____   Breech _____

    Caesarean section _____   Forceps _____

Infant's condition:

Breathed immediately _____   Cried immediately _____

Required oxygen _____   Length of stay in nursery _____

Problems during the first week (e.g., incubator, yellow skin, feeding difficulties, etc.) _____

_____

Baby's birth weight _____Birth length _____Head circumference _____

Later hospitalization of child:

Hospital   Date   Reason

_____

_____

_____

_____

FAMILY HISTORY

Please indicate whether there are any relatives of the child, including parents, grandparents, aunts, uncles, and cousins, who have the same or a similar problem for which you are seeking evaluation. Also indicate for these persons whether there are serious, chronic, or recurrent illnesses or abnormalities, such as birth defects, miscarriages, diabetes, convulsions or epilepsy (fits), mental or emotional disorders, slow development, mental retardation, school problems, cerebral palsy, muscular disorders, cancers, leukemia, thyroid disease (goiter), deafness, or blindness. (Please be as specific as possible, giving relationship to child, age, and problem.)

Mother's family: _____

_____

_____

_____

Father's family: _____

_____

_____

_____

ENVIRONMENT

Who lives in home besides child, parents, brothers, and sisters? List age, relation, and health: _____

Has your child ever been separated from the family? (age, duration, and reason):

_____

Date of marriage of child's parents: _____

(If appropriate, date of separation _____ date of divorce _____)

Step- or adopted father _____ Birthdate _____

    Occupation _____ Religion _____

    Ethnic background _____ Years of Schooling _____

    Health _____

Step- or adopted mother _____ Birthdate _____

    Occupation _____ Religion _____

    Ethnic background _____ Years of Schooling _____

    Health _____

HEALTH

Breast or bottle fed? _____ Did child eat well? _____

If you child has had any of the following, please indicate and explain details:

Accidents _____

High fever, unknown cause _____

Vision problems _____

Crossed eyes _____

Speech problems _____

Difficulty eating or feeding self _____

Hearing problems _____

Frequent ear infections _____

Foot problems (any special shoes, braces, etc.) _____

Seizures or convulsions _____

Unusual fears _____

Sleeping difficulties and night terrors _____

Head banging _____

Breath holding _____

Temper tantrums _____

Discipline problems _____

Ingestion of drugs, cleaners, or non-food items _____

Other illnesses _____

_____

_____

DEVELOPMENT

We would like to have information about some of the developmental milestones of your child. Indicate the age in months when your child first did each of the following; indicate that the child has not yet done it by writing "no;" if you do not remember, "NR." Please be as specific as possible in pinpointing the age.

Held head erect _____   Stood alone _____

Smiled _____   Walked without holding _____

Rolled over front to back _____   Rode tricycle_____

Rolled over back to front _____   Ran with good control _____

Sat alone_____   Played pat-a-cake, peek-a-boo, or

Recognized parents _____   bye-bye _____

Showed fear with strangers _____   Toilet training started _____

Crawled _____   Toilet training finished _____

Said mama or dada _____   Masturbation _____

Said other single words _____   Used 2 to 3 word phrases _____

Drank from cup _____   Used sentences _____

Pulled to standing _____

SCHOOLS

Has child ever been in preschool? When and where? _____

_____

List schools that child has attended:

<u>School</u>   <u>Dates</u>

_____

_____

_____

_____

Has child ever been in Special Education? When, where, and what kind? _____

_____

Has child ever been in remedial classes? When, where, and what kind? _____

_____

Has child ever had special tutoring? When, where, and by whom? _____

_____

Has child ever received speech therapy? When, where, and by whom? _____

_____

Has child ever received any other type of therapy? _____

_____

Describe any school problems that you are presently aware of: _____

_____

_____

_____

_____

_____

ACTIVITIES

What things does your child like to do? _____

_____

_____

What things does your child do well? _____

_____

_____

What things present the greatest difficulty for your child? _____

_____

_____

Describe play indoors: _____

_____

_____

Describe play outdoors: _____

_____

How does your child play and/or get along with other children? _____

_____

_____

_____

Give a detailed description of an average day: _____

_____

_____

_____

_____

_____

_____

_____

_____

Completed by _____ Date _____

Appendix D

PRESCHOOL OR DAY CARE CENTER TEACHER QUESTIONNAIRE

John F. Kennedy Child Development Center
University of Colorado School of Medicine

Dear Colleague:

The attached form is being sent to you to help us learn more about _____

_____, who has been referred to the Kennedy Child Develop-

ment Center. Your responses will assist us in the evaluation of this youngster as

well as in educational programming recommendations. Your input is very important

because you see this child every day and have come to know him/her in a way that is

very different form the clinical setting. In addition to this report, one or two of

our team may be coming to observe the child in his/her classroom setting if this

meets with your and the parents' approval.

Completed by:

     Teacher _____
                              (Name)
     Position if other than teacher _____

Current Date: _____

Child's Name: _____

Birthdate: _____ Age: _____

School: _____ Grade or Placement: _____

Address: _____ School Phone: _____

City: _____ State: _____ County: _____

The information form begins on the back of this sheet. Please respond to as many

questions as you feel appropriate. Thank you very much for your cooperation and

assistance.

REFERRAL INFORMATION

1. Who initiated the referral to the JFK Child Development Center?

2. What is the referral source's position or relationship the the student?

3. Describe the child's current school placement (type of class, number of students, time per day in placement).

4. Is there anything in the present school environment that you believe contributes to the child's problem   (e.g., constitution of the group, facilities, curriculum, instruction, etc.)?

5. Which of these areas is of concern to you?
    motor development --
    cognitive development --
    social adjustment --
    emotional adjustment --
    behavior adjustment --
    self-care --
    other (specify) --

6. What is the most important question that JFK could attempt to answer for you?

FAMILY INFORMATION

1. How do you perceive the home-school relationship?

2. Have you had contact with the other siblings?

    Yes _____   No _____   If yes, please explain.

3. Have you made a home visit?   Yes _____   No _____
    Why? What were your impressions?

MEDICAL INFORMATION

1. Is the child on medication? Yes _____ No _____
   If yes, indicate type, dosage, and administration schedule.

2. If yes, do you see a difference in the child's behavior when off medication?
   Yes _____ No _____
   If yes, what differences?

3. Has the school nurse had contact with this child or family?
   Yes _____ No _____
   If so, please comment.

4. Please list and describe any other health concerns for this student you may have.

SELF-HELP SKILLS

1. Please check the appropriate box and elaborate below the chart if necessary.

Activity	Cannot Perform	Cannot perform without help	Performs independently	Performs well independently
Toileting				
Feeding or eating				
Dressing				

2. What other skills do you feel this student should be able to do independently?

GROSS MOTOR SKILLS

1. Please check the appropriate box.
   Indicate the child's performance level in the gross motor area. In the blank spaces in the Activity column, please list other gross motor activities (e.g., hopping, swimming, baseball, etc.). Elaborate below chart if necessary.

Activity	Cannot Perform	Cannot perform without help	Performs independently	Performs well independently
Walking				
Jumping				

FINE MOTOR SKILLS

1. Indicate the child's performance level in the fine motor area. In the blank spaces in the Activity column, please list other fine motor activities, (e.g., stringing beads, playing a musical instrument, etc.). Elaborate below the chart if necessary.

Activity	Cannot Perform	Cannot perform without help	Performs independently	Performs well independently
Picking up objects				
Cutting				
Puzzles				
Prints				
Writes				

PERSONAL–SOCIAL SKILLS

1. Do you consider that the student has problems in any of the following areas? Check the appropriate space.

	Yes	No
Socializing with peers	_____	_____
Socializing with adults	_____	_____
Showing caution in approaching	_____	_____
Striking out at others without reason	_____	_____
Exhibiting a sexual problem	_____	_____
Liking to go to school	_____	_____
Destroying property	_____	_____
Responding appropriately in hazardous situations	_____	_____
Finding way around school independently	_____	_____

ACADEMIC SKILLS

A. Readiness

Can this student	Yes	No
match colors	_____	_____
label colors	_____	_____
match shapes	_____	_____
label shapes	_____	_____
put things on	_____	_____
under	_____	_____
over	_____	_____
between	_____	_____

B.   Language

Does this student

        communicate with gestures   _____ _____

        use single words   _____ _____

        speak intelligibly   _____ _____

        use sentences   _____ _____

        follow directions   _____ _____

        relate an event intelligibly   _____ _____

C.   How does this child usually play?   Yes   No

        Independently   _____ _____

        In small groups   _____ _____

        Other   _____ _____

D.   Can this child attend in

        Small groups   _____ _____

        Total groups   _____ _____

        Only one-to-one   _____ _____

E.   Given free choice of doing anything, what three things would the child choose to do at school   (e.g., play in housekeeping corner, play with trucks, water, puzzles, tease others, daydream, "read" books)?

        1.

        2.

        3.

BEHAVIOR

Please comment on the following.

Response to classroom control:

Self-stimulates: Yes _____   No _____

        If yes, explain how

        In what situation

        How is this controlled

Self—mutilates: Yes _____   No _____

      If yes, explain how

      In what situations

      How is it controlled

Is easily distracted: Yes _____   No _____

      If yes, in what situations

      What is done to regain attention

Is hyperactive: Yes _____   No _____

      If yes, in what situation

      How is hyperactivity reduced

Is hypoactive: Yes _____   No _____

      If yes, in what situations

      What is done to discourage this

Accepts changes in routine: Yes _____   No _____

      If no, explain

      How can change be accomplished without fuss

Thank you for your time and cooperation in responding.

Appendix E

CLASSROOM OBSERVATION AND CONSULTATION FORM

John F. Kennedy Child Development Center
University of Colorado School of Medicine

A. Name of client _____ Pt. # _____ Sex _____

School _____ Age Group _____ D.O.B. _____

School Address _____

_____ Telephone #: _____

Funding Agency _____
        (Head Start, church, school; if public school, give district; private
        preschool, day care center)

Date of Visit _____ Pre-Eval. _____ Post-Eval. _____

Type of Classroom Visited _____
        (special, mainstream)

Duration of visit _____ hours

Name of JFK visitors _____

_____

_____

B. Personnel contacted   _____

Classroom teacher   _____

Aides   _____

Psychologist   _____

Speech therapist   _____

Occupational therapist   _____

Physical therapist   _____

Other school personnel (specify)   _____

C. This visit was concerned with the following aspects of this child's school situation:

1. Nature of academic setting (number of students per room; student-teacher ratio)

2. Special resources available

3. Special services to child-client

4. Parent-school relationship

5. Child's social relationships

6. Child's behavior in school

7. Program:

   a) Daily schedule (list)

   b) Learning centers (list)

   c) Availability of materials for child's use: Yes _____ No _____

   d) Activities planned daily for gross/fine motor, cognitive/language, social/self-help?

   e) Activities are geared toward:

      1. Whole class
      2. Groups
      3. Individual
      4. All of the above

8. If whole class or groups, are all the children in the group doing the same thing or are there different levels of instruction or expectations? If yes, explain or give an example.

9. Teacher's teaching style

   Does he or she give exact instructions?

   Does he or she use visual aids?

   Does he or she ask questions that are open-ended?

   Does he or she ask questions that are designed for one answer?

   Does teacher use contingency management? If no, describe approach to discipline.

10. Is there a disparity between child's behavior and reports or observations?

11. What is the teacher's understanding/attitude toward this child's needs?

12. Does this school system have necessary support services for teachers' teaching needs?

13. Other (please briefly describe) _____

_____

_____

_____

14. Recommendations and summary

Signatures of observers   _____

_____

Appendix F

THE PLAY INTERVIEW

By

LANI TASHIRO BENNETT

Because children construct play scenes out of important feelings, fantasies, and events in their lives, observing a young child's symbolic play provides a glimpse of the child's emotional life. When there are questions about a child's emotional health, the use of symbolism acted out in play facilitates diagnosis, for in the complexity of play, the child presents a collection of conscious and unconscious expressions. Play's separation from reality allows the child to freely express concerns in fantasy, while the close relationship between play and reality allows the interviewer to enter a child's fantasy and interpret it. While spontaneous play occurs frequently and can be used diagnostically as well, this appendix will focus on the use of play interviews as assessment tools.

Play interviews are typically used for children of latency age and younger, for nonverbal children, and for the exploration of a child's emotional status. Because play interviews are unstructured in nature, they provide unique opportunities to build rapport and to observe the child in settings less formal than testing situations.

Before discussing ways to set up a play interview, it is useful to address the mutual anxieties inherent in such a situation. Simmons (1974) captures the fears shared by all inexperienced in play interviews and those accustomed to relying on "tests." That fear includes the question, "What am I supposed to look for?" A second concern might be, "What will people think if the child refuses to talk?" This fear can be alleviated with experience; in addition, ways to facilitate information gathering and sharing are discussed in this appendix.

It is useful to remember that the child

and parents are also typically anxious about a play interview, and that there are things that can be done to alleviate their uncertainty. Since the parents and child are likely to be nervous about the unknown, they can be assured by information about what is to be done with the child and when they will be told of the findings. It is also helpful if the parents are given suggestions prior to the visit about how to prepare the child (for example, "We are going to see a doctor to talk about your worries and troubles about X.").

PHASES OF INTERVIEWING

In organizing the play interview, it is useful for the psychologist to conceptualize the interview as having three major parts. These include the beginning phase, or free play; the middle phase, or structured exploration period; and the end phase, or closing. Useful discussions of waiting room protocol and observations can be found in Simmons (1974) and Werkman (1965).

The beginning phase involves orienting the child. This includes introductions, playroom rules, and explanation of the length of interview and activities planned. Issues of confidentiality should be discussed with the child; if information will be shared with the child's parents, the child should be apprised of that. (The author usually tells the child that he or she will be informed before the parents are seen; the child is also told when the parents will be seen, and what they will be told.)

After the orientation, the child should be encouraged to "take a look at the toys in the room." In this free play period, the interviewer encourages the child to take the initiative, remaining as nondirective as possible. This and other aspects of the role of the interviewer are elaborated later in this appendix.

The goal of the beginning phase is to build rapport, to get the child to like and trust the interviewer (so that he or she is more likely to reveal feelings and conflicts), and to facilitate the expression of feelings. The importance of this phase must be emphasized, since most children do not leap into florid, dramatic play. Instead, most need some preparation and support before revealing their innermost thoughts and feelings. Indeed, some children will be reluctant to participate at all.

The middle period is characterized both by increased structure and increased activity on the part of the interviewer. The psychologist should not rely entirely on nondirective play, because by doing so one can miss an opportunity to gather more information. In addition, complete lack of structure makes children more anxious, for it may give the impression that the purpose of the visit should be avoided; this may only affirm the child's fear that his or her problems are too "bad" to talk about. The interviewer's more intrusive role in the play interview distinguishes it from play therapy, where the therapist is typically in a less active role. In the interview, the purpose is to gather information in a compressed period of time, and the interviewer does not have the luxury of waiting several sessions for the child to deal with certain issues.

During the middle phase, the interviewer has an opportunity to gather more information, to pursue areas needing clarification or elaboration, and to test hypotheses about the child's concerns. The three principal ways of achieving this are through fantasy play, through asking questions, and through involving the child in projective activities. The interviewer may want to elicit fantasies to test hypotheses about the child's relatedness, aggression, family situation, or fear of abandonment. For example, in a free play situation a child may comment that only cars live in his or her house. By using a doll family situation, the psychologist can pursue questions about the child's relationships with other family members, such as who would be included in the doll family, the characteristics ascribed to the dolls, and whether (and how) the dolls interact with each other. When faced with a child who is constricted and who demonstrates little affect, it might be fruitful for the clinician to discover whether the child can indeed cope with strong emotions. The introduction of frightening or angry animal puppets usually provokes a response from the child; he or she may become paralyzed, warm up slowly, unleash uncontrolled anger, or fight back in appropriate ways.

Questions help the child to elaborate on a situation. "I wonder, can you tell me what you are here for?" is a standard question (Simmons, 1974). Such an approach provides rich information on what the child has been told and thinks of his or her "problem." If a young girl says that her mother doesn't want her to grow up, the psychologist could ask her, "What would happen if you grew up?" or "What's good about staying a baby?" or "What's it like to be grown up?" The purpose of the questioning is to uncover the child's underlying affect. It is usually safe to assume that if a child introduces a topic, it can be pursued. Direct, leading questions can be used sparingly—but effectively—to explore issues and bring preconscious material to the surface (for example, "Mothers can be mean sometimes, can't they?").

The specific wording of questions is critical. "I wonder if . . ." conveys some uncertainty on the part of the interviewer and invites an active problem-solving approach by the child. Avoid "Why?" questions whenever possible. They are difficult for children to respond to; children questioned with "whys" may become defensive and feel that they are being challenged. Often the question can be asked another way to get at the same material. Displacement is often also effective in helping children express themselves more comfortably; this includes comments like, "A lot of children worry about going to sleep at night." In addition, questions are more likely to be productive if they are open-ended, if they cannot be answered "yes" or "no," and if the interviewer is able to say everything four or five different ways. In the structured, probing part of the interview it may also be useful for the psychologist to confront the child if that child is unclear or contradictory.

Projective techniques are a third way to elicit information. Human Figure Drawings (Koppitz, 1968), Kinetic Family Drawings (Burn and Kaufman, 1970; Koppitz, 1968), Duss-Despert Fables (Würsten, 1970), or a Sentence Completion Test are fruitful ways of gathering further information from the child. In addition, there are a variety of "magic" questions that can be used. These include the "Three Wishes," which can be expressed as follows: "If you had three wishes, what would you wish for?" Then, "What would you do if your wish came true?" The second "magic" question involves the "Invisible Person:" "If you were invisible and no one could see you, where would you go? What would you do?" The third question involves "Desert Island" and includes such questions as: "If you could take only one person with you to a desert island, whom would you take?;" and "Animals:" "If you could be any animal, what would you be? What would each of your family members be?"

The middle phase requires more direct participation on the part of the interviewer. In addition, this phase provides an opportunity for gathering more information and elaborating and clarifying issues presented by the child. A number of techniques facilitate the development of the middle phase.

The end phase of the interview is important, because children appreciate having some warning that their time is about up and having some closure on the session. If the child has expressed strong feelings or is agitated, he or she should be helped to regain composure; often moving to a neutral activity suffices. The child should have a chance to ask questions about what has been done, to reiterate the confidentiality of the material and/or the limits of the confidentiality, and to share what the future plans are for the child.

ECOLOGIC ASPECTS OF THE INTERVIEW

Although the play interview is often considered to unfold naturally, and the child's play is often seen as pure, raw material, one needs to acknowledge that the interview situation is influenced by the emotional environment in the playroom. This includes the type and number of toys and the behavior of the interviewer.

The emotional environment in the playroom can determine what evolves in play. What is the atmosphere? Is it accepting, critical, permissive, or relaxed? What are the child's expectations and assumptions about the meeting with the psychologist? What was the child told about this visit? Sometimes a child's expression of anger is mistakenly attributed to hostilities about a family situation rather than as a sign of unhappiness and anger about coming to the clinic.

The kinds of toys available influence a child's play. With infants, stimulus complexity and novelty make toys more effective in recruiting and sustaining interest (Hutt, 1971; McCall, 1974). Some toys facilitate social interactions, while others lead to isolate play (Parten, 1933; Quilitch and Risley, 1973). To state an obvious fact, different toys lend themselves to different kinds of activities (Murphy and Krall, 1960). Puppets and doll houses frequently result in fantasy play; clay and paper and pencil result in solitary activities; toy telephones result in communicative activity; and bats and balls result in motor play. In addition, wild animals, soldiers, and guns are aggressive toys. A wide range of toys is likely to provide the child with an opportunity to express him- or herself fully.

The number and arrangement of toys also affect the child's play. The toys should be arranged neatly and placed in cabinets and shelves so that they are readily available to the child. When there are many toys to distract the child, he or she is less likely to play with toys that elicit fantasy play; instead, the child may avoid dealing with difficult issues that fantasy play often arouses.

A critical influence in the course of the play interview is the behavior of the clinician. The interviewer's role is to provide support and approval; a passive, accepting, permissive stance is best, for it aids spontaneity. Whatever the child is expressing must be accepted as an honest statement of feeling, even though the feelings and words may be difficult to accept. Support and acceptance can be conveyed by the interviewer in many ways. First, the psychologist should stay in contact with the child and verbalize what the child is doing (for example, "The Hulk just threw the man out of the house."). The psychologist should not react harshly or with surprise to the theme or affect of a child's play, for that would demonstrate disapproval. Second, the clinician should reflect the child's feelings and the tone of those feelings so that the child will know that he or she is understood. Third, the interviewer must be patient and give the child time to tell his or her own story. Often interviewers are in too much of a hurry to get to what they consider to be the "heart of the matter," and miss an important message that the child is struggling to convey.

There are several approaches an interviewer can use which facilitate information gathering. Most important is the interviewer's use of the symbolic level of play. The literal aspects of the toy should be avoided; instead, the clinician should focus on the child's message and affect. In the example where the child pretended that the Hulk was throwing a man out of a building, the psychologist might comment that the Hulk "must be pretty angry," or might ask how the Hulk is feeling. This would be preferable to asking, "From how many feet did the man fall?" or stating, "The Hulk is green."

If a child were to pretend that a car was careening down a hill out of control, the clinician should focus on the fact that something is being pictured out of control and disaster might result—rather than that the brakes are failing. This technique allows for exploration of the child's theme, and facilitates the expression of feelings. It is also helpful if the interviewer remembers to keep the play at the symbolic level and stay away from dynamic interpretations (see Hammer, 1968, for a discussion of different levels of interpretation.) Finally, the psychologist should refrain from cutting the child off or rushing in to solve the child's problem. If a toy breaks, it is best to observe the child's problem-solving ability and frustration tolerance rather than fixing it too quickly.

ASSESSING A CHILD'S EMOTIONAL HEALTH VIA THE PLAY INTERVIEW

The themes of play themselves do not allow one to make decisions about pathology. For the most part, themes of fear, jealousy, and anger are normal (see Table 1 for age-related fears); it is the ways in which these themes are expressed that are the significant elements. In assessing a child's play, it is useful to make a distinction between the structure (or the process) of play and its content. Typically, the *structural* aspects of play are most useful in understanding the level of a child's disturbance. Structural aspects focus on *how* the child tells his or her story (for example, is it disorganized or orderly?). The *content* elements (or *what* the child says) help to flesh out one's understanding of the child and give clues about what it is that may be troubling the child.

In evaluating the structure of the play, it is useful for the psychologist to focus on three related aspects: how the child handles intense feelings in play, how the child organizes the play, and how the child copes with stress. These three points will be examined next.

How Does the Child Handle Intense Feelings in Play?

Expression of feelings is normal. As noted in Table 1, it is normal for children to be fearful, and there are developmental changes in the sources of fear (Bauer, 1976). It is the child's ability to deal with these feelings that is diagnostic. Is the child able to express these feelings at all, or is he or she so overwhelmed or withdrawn that he or she is noncommunicative? When the child is able to express feelings, what happens? Play disruption, immobilization, general disorganization, and lack of control are indicators that a child may need help in dealing more effectively with these intense issues. Sometimes discharge of emotions leads to greater relaxation and relief from anxiety. In those situations, the child has used play to gain some distance from a conflictual situation and as Erikson (1950) describes it, to "master reality."

Table 1   Age-Related Fears

Birth to 2 years
  Loud noises
  Animals
  Dark rooms
  High places
  Sudden displacement
  Being alone or being left
  Strange places

2 to 6 years
  Peak period of the specific fears listed above
  More fears in this age group than in other two

6 years and older
  Supernatural dangers
  Death
  Injury
  Thunder and lightning
  Self/status (failing, being different)

How Organized Is the Child's Play?

The psychologist's subjective response to the play as it unfolds is often a useful tool in assessing the level of organization. Does the child's play leave you, as the observer, with confusion or clarity? Is it clear who people in the child's play are and how they are feeling, or are their identities temporary and changing? Does the child show confusion around feelings (for example, that "happy dogs kill" and "sad cows laugh")? It is useful for the psychologist to ask him- or herself: How is the child relating to me and people in general? Is he or she relating to people as though they were objects to use, like tables and chairs? Or is the child relating to people in a way that shows an appreciation that people have feelings, people can interact, and people have stable identities? When a child's play is disorderly, a useful distinction to make is whether the play suggests chaotic thinking or a realistic portrayal of a chaotic environment.

How Does the Child Cope with Stress?

All children experience stress, and there are adaptive and maladaptive ways of dealing with stressful events. How does

the child protect or defend him- or herself? Is the child able to enlist adult support or respond to opportunities for gratification? Is the child's response active or passive? A typical response of an abused child to stress would be to remain frozen and helpless, rather than to reach out for or respond to adult support. The abused child's passive response is maladaptive because it does not help lessen the child's stress. A child who has the capacity to be redirected, who can change with support, and who is free from obsessive tendencies will probably not require professional help.

Play Content

The themes of the child's play give clues about what may be important to the child (Amster, 1964). Are there particular areas of conflict that lead to inhibition or preoccupation? What toy does the child choose and what affective value does it have? Who is the object of anger? Themes of anger and destruction are frequently observed in the dramatic play of children and should not be considered abnormal per se. It is more important for the psychologist to focus on the structure and process of play as it unfolds. For example, the clinician might consider whether the play is controlled. By 5 to 6 years of age children should be able to control their play enough that aggression is kept within the limits of the play and does not control the child.

Fantasy that deals with real life problems is healthy. But when the fantasy is not relevant to the real situation and is replete with sadism and destruction, the child is likely to be disturbed. To make a firm judgment about the child's ability to distinguish fantasy from reality, it is crucial that the clinician know something about the child's family situation.

A child who portrays themes suggesting confusion (in which sad people laugh and happy people cry, for example) may be expressing disturbance in affect or thought. Alternatively, the child may be accurately reflecting the level of disturbance in the family.

SUMMARY

In summary, play is a unique modality for assessing a child's development. Through play, the child is able to present conscious and unconscious fantasies in a way that allows the interviewer to interpret the child's concerns. The interview begins with the child's initiative; with the interviewer's support, it moves into a more structured period of exploration in which the interviewer is more active. It closes with a short period of sharing. The emotional atmosphere of the interview and selection of toys should be considered. A critical factor in the effectiveness of the play interview as an assessment tool is the behavior of the therapist. Interviewers frequently lose sight of the fact that the child is here to tell his or her story; instead, the interviewer must be patient, must stay away from interpretations of the play, must resist temptations to take over the play, and must be open to what the child is saying. Often, the interviewer's impatience precludes being able to understand what the child is saying.

REFERENCES

Amster F: The differential use of play in the treatment of young children. In Haworth M (ed): *Child Psychotherapy.* New York: Basic Books, 1964

Bauer D: An exploratory study of developmental changes in children's fears. Child Psychol Psychiat 17: 69–74, 1976

Burn RC, Kaufman SH: *Kinetic Family Drawings (K-F-D).* New York: Brunner/Mazel, 1970

Erickson EH: *Childhood and Society.* New York: W. W. Norton, 1950

Hammer E: Interpretive technique: A primer. In Hammer E (ed): *Use of Interpretation in Treatment.* New York: Grune & Stratton, 1968

Hutt C: Exploration and play in children. In Herron R, Sutton-Smith B (eds): *Child's Play.* New York: John Wiley & Sons, 1971

Koppitz E: *Psychological evaluation of children's human figure drawings.* New York: Grune & Stratton, 1968

McCall R: Exploratory manipulation and play in the human infant. Monographs Soc Res Child Develop 39(2): 1–88. 1974

Murphy LB, Krall V: Free play as a projective tool. In Rabin A, Haworth H (eds): *Projective Techniques with Children.* New York: Grune & Stratton, 1960

Parten M: Social play among preschool children. J Abnorm Soc Psychol 28: 136–147, 1933

Quilitch H, Risley T: The effects of play materials on social play. J Appl Behav Anal 6(4): 573–578, 1973

Simmons JE: *Psychiatric Examination of Children.* Philadelphia: Lea & Febiger, 1974

Werkman SL: The psychiatric diagnostic interview with children. Am J Orthopsychiat 35(4): 764–771, 1965

Würsten H: Story completion: Madeleine Thomas stories and similar methods. In Rabin A, Haworth R (eds): *Projective Techniques with Children.* New York: Grune & Stratton, 1970

INDEX

DATE DUE